AGE OF THE
NANDAS AND MAURYAS

AGE OF THE NANDAS AND MAURYAS

Edited by

K. A. NILAKANTA SASTRI

MOTILAL BANARSIDASS

Delhi Varanasi Patna

Bangalore Madras

Second Edition: 1967
Reprint: Delhi, 2023

MOTILAL BANARSIDASS
Bungalow Road, Jawahar Nagar, Delhi 110 007

Branches
Chowk, Varanasi 221 001
Ashok Rajpath, Patna 800 004
24 Race Course Road, Bangalore 560 001
120 Royapettah High Road, Mylapore, Madras 600 004

ISBN: 81-208-0465-1 (Cloth)
ISBN: 81-208-0466-x (Paper)

PRINTED IN INDIA

BY JAINENDRA PRAKASH JAIN AT SHRI JAINENDRA PRESS, A-45 NARAINA INDUSTRIAL AREA, PHASE I, NEW DELHI 110 028 AND PUBLISHED BY NARENDRA PRAKASH JAIN FOR MOTILAL BANARSIDASS, DELHI 110 007.

PREFACE

The Bhāratīya Itihās Parishad was founded in 1937 with the specific object, among others, of preparing a New History of the Indian People in twenty volumes. The scheme was initiated by Dr. Rajendra Prasad, Rector of the Parishad, and Sir Jadunath Sarkar, Editor-in-chief. Volume VI, THE VĀKĀṬAKA-GUPTA AGE (C. 200-550 A. D.) edited by Dr. R. C. Majumdar and Dr. A. S. Altekar was published for the Parishad in 1946 by Messrs Motilal Banarsidass of Lahore.

The plan for the present volume, IV in the series, was finalised in 1941, and thanks to the cooperation of the scholars who were invited to contribute the different chapters to it, the manuscript became ready for the press in 1945, and it was despatched to Sir Jadunath Sarkar in April of that year. The printing of the book was commenced, but before much progress was made, the Publishers met with a serious disaster in the Lahore riots. For this reason and others of a similar nature, the printing had to be stopped and could only be resumed in 1950 after the publishers had successfully rehabilitated themselves and found a new home in Banaras and Patna.

Meanwhile at the suggestion of the Government of India the scheme for the New History of the Indian People came to be amalgamated in 1948 with another started by the Indian History Congress, one of the terms of the amalgamation being that the Bhāratīya Itihās Parishad will not continue their series of the New History but may print or re-print the volumes already prepared. Accordingly the present volume is issued as an independent book styled AGE OF THE NANDAS AND MAURYAS.

The names of the contributors of the different chapters are mentioned in the table of contents. I must thank them all for their valued cooperation and more for their patient waiting as the publication has been delayed so long for reasons beyond control. I must also express my gratitude to Dr. Rajendra Prasad, now President of the Indian Union, who has throughout taken a personal interest in the production and publication of the volume. Sir Jadunath Sarkar, although he felt constrained to give up his place as Editor-in-chief in 1946, continued to make kind enquiries about the progress of the work and my thanks are also due to him. They are also due to Dr. N. P. Chakravarti, formerly Director-General of Archaeology, for permission to reproduce the map of Aśoka's Empire published by him in *Ancient India*, No. 4. I must also thank the Director-General of Archaeology and the other authorities mentioned against particular illustrations for their permission to reproduce them in the volume. The authorities of the British Museum kindly supplied the casts of the coins illustrated in Plate I. Sri Jayachandra Vidyalankar, Secretary of the Bhāratīya Itihās Parishad, did me the favour of reading my chapter on Alexander's campaigns in India and offering suggestions of value. The publishers, it will be seen, have spared no effort to make the volume worthy of their great standing among Indian publishers. The reader will notice that the transliteration is not uniform, but combines two systems using ṣ-sh, and c-ch indiscriminately; this has been due in part to my ill health at the time I prepared the book for the press, and I crave the indulgence of the reader for any inconvenience he may feel on this account.

Nileśvar, Madras. K. A. N.

26. 12. 1951.

TABLE OF CONTENTS

CHAPTER III

India in early Greek and Latin Literature

By Prof. K. A. Nilakanta Sastri

APPENDIX TO CHAPTER III

CHAPTER IV

Chandragupta and Bindusara

By Prof. H. C. Raychaudhuri

CHAPTER V

Mauryan Polity

By Prof. K. A. Nilakanta Sastri

CHAPTER VI

Asoka and his Successors

By Prof. K. A. Nilakanta Sastri

CHAPTER VII

South India and Ceylon

By Prof. K. A. Nilakanta Sastri

CHAPTER VIII

Industry, Trade and Currency

By Dr. U. N. Ghoshal

CHAPTER IX

Religion

By Dr. P. C. Bagchi

CHAPTER X

Language and Literature

By Dr. S. K. Chatterji and Dr. V. Raghavan

CHAPTER XI

Mauryan Art

By Dr. Niharranjan Ray

List of plates

Map

List of Abbreviations

ABORI. Annals of the Bhandarkar Oriental Research Institute

Ait. B. Aitareya Brāhmaṇa

ASI. / ASR. } Archaeological survey of India, Annual Reports

BMC. British Museum Catalogue

BSOS. Bulletin of the School of Oriental Studies, London

BS. Brahma Sūtras

Bom. Gaz. / BG. } Bombay Gazetteer

CAI. Catalogue of the Coins of Ancient India (in the British Museum) by John Allan, London, 1936

CHI. Cambridge History of India Vol. I.

CII. Corpus Inscriptionum Indicarum. Vol. I. Inscriptions of Ascka Ed. E. Hultzsch.

CL. Carmichael Lectures

DKA Dynasties of the Kali Age (Pargiter, London, 1913)

DV. Dīpavaṁsa.

DPPN Dictionary of Pali Proper names

EHI. Early History of India by V. A. Smith, (4th Edition Oxford, 1924.)

EI or EpInd. Epigraphia Indica

HC. Harsha Charita

Ind. Alt. Indische Alterthumskunde (Lassen)

IC. Indian Culture

JRAS. Journal of the Royal Asiatic Society of Great Britain and Ireland, London

JHS. Journal of Hellenic Studies

JNSI. Journal of Numismatic Society of India, Bombay

JBORS. Journal of the Bihar and Orissa Research Society, Patna

JASB.	Journal of the Asiatic Society of Bengal, Calcutta.
Jat.	Jatakas
JISOA.	Journal of the Indian Society of Oriental Art, Calcutta.
KA.	Kauṭilya's *Arthaśāstra*
KS	Breloer, Kautilya Studien
Mbh.	Mahābhārata
NIA.	New Indian Antiquary
MV.	Mahāvamsa
PE.	Pillar Edict
PTS.	Pali Text Society
RE.	Rock Edict
SBE.	Sacred Books of the East
WZKM.	Weiner Zeitschrift für die Kunde des Morgenlandes.
ZDMG.	Zeitschrift der Deutschen Morgenlandischen Gesellschaft, Leipzig
ZII.	Zeitschrift für Indologie und Iranistik

INTRODUCTION

THE natural frontiers of India, the mountains and the seas that serve to emphasise her inherent unity, have seldom acted as barriers to her intercourse with foreign lands. The progress of Indian historical studies has shown that the isolation of India is a relatively recent feature, and that in the earlier epochs of her long and by no means uneventful history, she maintained live contacts with many lands, far and near, to the mutual advantage of both sides. The age of the Nandas and Mauryas (*c.* 400-185 B. C.) witnessed great changes sweeping over the face of Western Asia, over lands with which India had much to do from the dawn of history, and account must be taken of their effects, direct and indirect, on the political, economic and artistic life of India. In this seminal period when Indo-Aryan civilization may be said to have attained its maturity, India did not hesitate to borrow political and economic plans and artistic motifs from abroad, and put them to the most appropriate uses in her own institutions and monuments. Thus to view the history of India on a wider background and point to her contacts with her neighbours is by no means to detract from the independence and originality of her culture; but only to lay stress on the catholicity of its outlook and taste, and its genius for drawing sustenance and strength from diverse sources. For in no single instance did borrowing result in mere imitation, but led to a thoughtful and harmonious integration of the borrowed feature with the indigenous setting in which it was placed.

Alexander, Chandragupta, Chāṇakya, and Aśoka dominate the period. The overthrow of the Achaemenid empire of Persia by Alexander, his campaigns in the north-west of India, intended perhaps more to complete and round off his conquest of Persia than to further a scheme of world conquest, and his early death (323 B. C.) followed by the partition of his extensive empire into large territorial monarchies formed a chain of events that in one way and another prepared the ground for the extension of the Mauryan empire in the North-West, and fixed the political map of the regions with which that empire was to maintain a fairly lively intercourse for well over a century. The revolt of Bactria and Parthia from Syria (*c.* 250 B. C.)was the only notable change; but during our period their independence was far from assured, and the revolts had little historical significance as yet to India except perhaps by inducing the distracted Seleucid rulers of Syria to maintain friendly relations with their powerful neighbours on the east, the Maurya emperors. The importance of Alexander's Indian campaign has been both exaggerated and under-estimated. There was no Macedonian occupation of Indian territory worth the name, and what there was of it lasted only a few years. Yet there ensued two abiding results. The monarchies and tribal republics of the North-West were much exhausted by their sanguinary conflicts with the invader; this paved the way for the easy establishment of the Mauryan empire in these lands by weakening their power of military resistance to the advance of the empire, and possibly also by teaching them that submission to a strong state within the country was the best protection against the recurrence of danger from outside. Secondly, the Macedonian episode opened an era of some centuries during which Hellenism was to be the dominant factor of government and civilization on the western confines of the Indian world. The contact between India and the Mediterranean world became more direct and constant. And this is a fact of immense significance not only to the history of India, but to that of the world.

In marked contrast to the precise and detailed notices of Greek and Latin authors on Alexander and India, are the vague and contradictory legends which issue from various sources and constitute the only aid to our knowledge of Chandragupta and Chāṇakya. There is little reason to doubt the truth of the main story in its outline : an unusually valiant Kshatriya warrior and a Brahmin statesman of great learning and resourcefulness joined to bring about the downfall of an avaricious dynasty of hated rulers, and establish a new empire which made the good of the people the object of its chief concern; they freed the land from the foreign invader, and from internal tyranny, and established a state which in due course embraced practically the whole of India;

together they organised one of the most powerful and efficient bureaucracies known to the history of the world. Kshatra (Imperium) and Brahma (Sacerdotium) came together and engaged in the most fruitful cooperation for the great good of the land and the people. The *Arthaśāstra* of Kauṭilya (Chāṇakya) holds a place in the literature of Indian polity corresponding to that of the Mauryan empire in Indian history; there are two sides to both. The Mauryan empire was the culmination of a long centripetal development of which Magadha had become the nucleus for centuries; but its administrative system made new and bold departures from ancient practices and started innovations inspired by alien models, perhaps immediately Hellenistic, but traceable ultimately to Achaemenid Persia. Likewise, the *Arthaśāstra* is the culmination of the Indian political thought of several generations on the one side, while on the other, large sections of it were consciously based on the study of political practice, a good part of it doubtless contemporary and foreign.

The forty years of Aśoka's rule form a great epoch not only in the history of India, but in the annals of mankind. In the remarkable series of his inscriptions found over the entire length and breadth of India, we hear the authentic voice of the great emperor explaining the purpose behind many of his actions. This enables us to check and control the numerous legends that have gathered round his name, as around the names of all great leaders of humanity. One war of conquest was enough to turn the mind of this monarch for ever from all thought of war and military conquest, so sensitive was he to the sufferings of men, and indeed of animals as well. He found instruction in the company of the Sangha and solace in the religion of the Buddha. His abstention from war and conquest was by no means a mere negation of a part of the king's duty as it was generally understood; the true emperor was a conqueror (*vijigīshu*) according to the political theory of Ancient India, and Aśoka accepted this ideal, and practised it vigorously for the rest of his life; only the conquest he pursued was of a higher order than that dictated by lust of power or territory ; he became a *vijigīshu* in the cause of Dhammavijaya. But he was no visionary who sacrificed temporal well-being in the pursuit of spiritual objects. He combined energy and benevolence, justice and charity, as no one else did. He bent all the material resources of his great empire to the ethical education of his subjects and to the organisation of peace within his realm, and universal amity and order throughout the world. Aśoka strikes us as the most modern of all the great rulers of India.

The work of the historian, unlike that of the novelist, is limited by the nature of his sources. Little or no evidence worth the name is forthcoming on many matters of interest in our period, and several questions that naturally rise in the mind as we recall its main events have to remain unanswered. Did Chandragupta deliver his attack on the Nanda empire at its heart and effect a revolution in the capital to start with, or did he begin by building up his power in the North-West at the expense of the Greeks and then proceed against the Nandas ? What exactly was the role of Kauṭilya in the events that led up to the *abhisheka* of Chandragupta ? How long did Chandragupta take to build up his empire, and who were the enemies, if any, who gave him fight ? Did he turn Jain and abdicate towards the close of his reign as Jaina legends allege ? What happened in the Mauryan empire during close upon three decades of Bindusāra's rule ? We hear little of that monarch besides his love of Greek wine and figs, and his futile effort to buy a Greek philosopher. Yet this king could not have lacked ability as soldier and statesman, for he successfully guarded the vast empire, perhaps even extended it into the Deccan, and handed it over intact to his successor. Was Aśoka's succession to the throne disputed ? Did he rule as emperor to the end of his life, or did he abdicate and live as a monk in his last years ? And why did not the empire, reared by three generations of exceptionally talented rulers, hold together for many years after Aśoka's time ?

Historical truth is many-sided, and there is always scope for differences of interpretation of the evidence at hand; the scope for such differences is particularly wide in our period in which almost all the sources bear a certain bias—Brahmanical, Buddhist, Jaina—and offer divergent accounts of the same set of events. As nothing is gained and something may be lost by an artificial smoothening of these differences, it has appeared best to leave untouched the slightly differing views of the contributors of the different chapters and give the reader the opportunity of realizing the difficulty of reaching categorical conclusions on complex issues.

The account of the period opens with a chapter (I) on India in the Age of the Nandas from the pen of Prof. H. C. Raychaudhuri who reconstructs, with great ingenuity, from very meagre sources a vivid picture of the establishment of the empire of the Nandas and its polity; in his survey of the outlying parts of India, he offers a succinct treatment of the political geography of North-Western India and of the advance of Persia and its rule on the banks of the Indus, and prepares the ground for the detailed study of the Indian campaigns of Alexander by the present writer (Chap. II). The hardest fights in which that great Macedonian warrior engaged were all fought on Indian soil, and his Indian opponents, though they did not win victories against him, generally won his approbation of their fighting qualities. These campaigns have been treated at some length, and their place in the history of India and of the world has been adverted to above. Alexander was accompanied by several scientists and literateurs whose writings communicated to Europe a vast amount of knowledge about India; they also formed the basis of many of the observations made by the ambassadors of the Hellenistic monarchs to the Mauryan empire, of whom Megasthenes is, of course, the most celebrated; in one chapter (III) all the notices of India by Greek and Latin authors bearing on our period have been brought together and reviewed also at full length with a view to put the reader in possession of most of the primary data now available; the chapter is followed appropriately by a comprehensive note, by Dr. J. N. Banerjea, on the foreign coins of the period found in India.

The thread of the main story is taken up again by Prof. Raychaudhuri in the chapter (IV) on Chandragupta and Bindusāra. A brief criticism of the sources is followed by a discussion of chronology which may with advantage be read together with a further discussion of the same topic that follows in the chapter on Aśoka (VI). Prof. Raychaudhuri holds that the classical sources were well aware of the overthrow of the Nandas by Chandragupta though it might appear to some that in speaking of his overthrow of the existing government and liberation of India they meant only the destruction of the Macedonian domination in the Indus valley. He discounts heavily the part attributed to Chāṇakya in the internal revolution that resulted in the fall of the Nandas and the establishment of the Mauryan empire, and is inclined to consider Chandragupta as the hero of the drama. He has also grave doubts about the age and authenticity of the *Arthaśāstra*. But the whole of his narrative shows that he is quite fully aware of the possibility of other views being taken on these subjects and of the need for putting before his readers all the available evidence to enable them to form their own opinions.

A brief study of the Mauryan polity, based mainly on the *Arthaśāstra*, follows (Chap. V); this sums up the state of government and administrative organisation as it was in the reigns of the first two emperors and provides the background necessary for the proper appraisal of the innovations of Aśoka in the administrative system, to which references occur in the inscriptions of that ruler. The present writer is inclined to accept the *Arthaśāstra* as a valid picture of conditions that prevailed in the Mauryan empire and has attempted to explain the basis for this view in an excursus on the *Arthaśāstra* at the end of the chapter.

The chapter (VI) on Aśoka and his successors, also by the present writer, aims at presenting the primary evidence arranged under convenient heads with the necessary minimum of comment and criticism. The object has been to let the inscriptions tell the story as far as possible and to accept legendary evidence only to the extent to which it works in with and is not contradicted by the inscriptions. Aśoka's relations with the Sangha, the nature and content of the Dhamma he propagated, the extent of success that attended his missionary efforts, and the question whether he was both monk and monarch at one and the same time have been considered in some detail; the legends connecting Aśoka with Kashmir, Khotan and Nepal have also been considered with some care. All is darkness after Aśoka; the faint gleams from late and diverse sources, the earliest being the *Divyāvadāna* and Purāṇas, just render the darkness visible; no connected history is possible here; the available evidence has been summed up and the process of the dissolution of the Mauryan empire has been left largely to the imagination of the reader aided by the few scraps of evidence set forth at the end of the chapter. A brief account (Chap. VII) of South India and Ceylon rounds off the political history of the period; the vexed question of the identity and location of Satiyaputa has been discussed; and all the references to Nandas and Mauryas in early Tamil literature have been described in their proper setting and their historical value determined ; and the evidence of the early Brāhmī inscriptions of the Tamil districts and of Ceylon, as also that of the Ceylonese tradition in the *Mahāvamsa* assessed.

The remaining four chapters in the volume are devoted to studies of different aspects of the culture of the period. Dr. U. N. Ghoshal describes the Industry, Trade and Currency of the times in a chapter (VIII) which is as well documented, as it is replete with significant facts culled from various sources and set forth with remarkable lucidity and cogency. A perusal of this chapter and portions of the chapter on Art which form an excellent supplement to it, may well set at rest the doubts, sometimes expressed by scholars, that the state of technical arts depicted in the pages of the *Arthaśāstra* appears to be too advanced for the age of the Mauryas; for relying only to a very little extent on the evidence of the *Arthaśāstra*, the writers of these chapters have sought to trace the trend of development from earlier epochs up to and beyond the Mauryan epoch, and to indicate clearly the place of that epoch in the course of this development.

In the chapter (IX) on Religion Dr. P. C. Bagchi makes a penetrating study of the ascetic movements in general, of Brahmanism, Ājīvikas and Nirgranthas, as well as of Buddhism and of the beginnings of theistic movements; he may appear to rely rather more on Buddhist texts than on other lines of evidence, but that has seldom stood in the way of the justice and truth of the interpretations offered by him. He has not included in the scope of his chapter forms of popular worship centring round flag-staffs, yakshas and so on, which have been noticed incidentally in the two succeeding chapters. The chapter (X) on Language and Literature and the life of the people is contributed by two scholars. Prof. Suniti Kumar Chatterji, the most competent linguist of India, offers a comprehensive and critical survey of the distribution and development of language and script in the various parts of Mauryan India. Dr. V. Raghavan's contribution in this chapter on Learning and Literature and popular life is the necessary complement to that of Dr. Bagchi on Religion. Depending more or less on exclusively Sanskrit and Brahmanical sources, Dr. Raghavan has produced a compact and illuminating account of the learning and literature of the age in their various branches, of the rites and forms of worship prevalent among the different strata of society, and of the habits, beliefs and modes of thought prevalent among the common people.

The final chapter (XI) on Art from the pen of Dr. Niharranjan Ray is a comprehensive and up-to-date survey of a difficult and interesting subject. The great acumen with which the author traces the development of the artistic tradition within the Mauryan period, even within a single reign, and adopts tests for the separation of the play of indigenous from that of foreign inspiration will not escape the attention of the discerning reader. Dr. Ray does not hesitate to declare as post-Mauryan several pieces that are generally held to be Mauryan on grounds of the material and technique which are hardly adequate in his eyes. His main thesis is that all the Mauryan art accessible to us is court art strongly marked by extraneous influences, Hellenistic and Achaemenian.

Viewed from any angle, the age of the Mauryan empire was an age of great endeavour and noble achievement. Politically India became one, and the cultural unity in the midst of diversity that has always characterised her civilization became more marked than ever in this period. India was in the van of human progress, and one of her greatest emperors sent forth into the world the message of universal peace and love. It is to be hoped that the different chapters in this volume may help its readers in some measure to recall the life and happenings of that great epoch.

CHAPTER I

INDIA IN THE AGE OF THE NANDAS

I. Empire of Magadha

The dominant characteristic of the period with which we propose to deal is the rise and growth of a New Monarchy in Eastern India of which we have a presage in the *Aitareya Brāhmaṇa* :

"In this eastern quarter (*prāchyām diśi*) whatever kings there are of the eastern peoples, they are anointed for imperial rule (*sāmrājya*); 'Oh emperor' (*samrāṭ*) they style him when anointed."[1]

The eastern peoples (*prāchyas*) are not specified by the Brāhmaṇa in the same way as those of the South, the North and the Middle Country. But there can hardly be any doubt that they lived to the east of the *dhruvā madhyamā diś* and thus answer to the *Prasii* of the Greek writers and the confederate nations who dominated the valleys of the lower Ganges and the Son. The most eminent among these nations was Magadha which embraced the modern districts of Patna and Gaya.

Several factors contributed to the greatness of the new star in the firmament of Indian politics. It occupied a strategic position between the upper and the lower parts of the Gangetic plain. It possessed an impregnable fort in a mountain fastness and built another at the confluence of two mighty streams, the highways of trade and commerce in those days. It had a fertile soil and its resources included an elephant corps which was truly formidable.

But advantages of position and material resources alone cannot raise a nation to eminence. It is the character and the spirit of the people "that give all their life and efficacy to them". As in Western Europe, so in Magadha, we have a commingling of races and cultures. Kīkatas and other *Anāryas* blended here with priestly and fighting clans of Aryan

1. Keith *Rigveda Br.*, p 330.

India as Celts did with Latins and Teutons in Gaul and some neighbouring lands of Western Europe. It is possible to detect two strands in the cultural as well as the ethnic texture of the Magadhan people. The same race that produced fierce warriors and exterminators of princes and peoples listened to the quiet teachings of Mahāvīra the Jina and Gautama the Buddha. It played a part in the evolution of a universal religion as it did in the foundation of a pan-Indian empire. The wide outlook of the Magadhans was not a little due to the absence of the rigidity that marked the social polity that evolved on the banks of the Sarasvatī and the upper Ganges. In their realm Brāhmaṇas could fraternize with *Vrātyas*. Kshatriyas could admit plebeian (Śūdra) girls to their harem, blue-blooded aristocrats could be done to death or otherwise deprived of the throne to make room for the child of a *nagara-śobhinī*, and a barber could aspire to imperial dignity.

Magadhan kings and statesmen were sometimes ruthless in their methods. But they had the wisdom to establish an efficient system of government in which high bureaucratic functionaries (*mahāmātras*) as well as village headmen (*grāmikas*) had their share. Foreign observers speak with evident approbation of their judiciary, roads, irrigation works and care of alien residents. While not fighting shy of metaphysics, they laid great stress on exertion (*parākrama*) in this mundane life with the object of welding the diverse elements of greater India (Jambuvdīpa) into a unit bound by political as well as cultural ties. This was facilitated by the ancient idea of the all-encompassing *Purusha*—later called *Mahā purusha* (The Great Being)—and his political counterpart the Sole Sovereign (*Ekarāṭ* or *Chakravartin*). In the Magadha minstrelsy the rulers of the Prasii had an instrument which they could use for popular education and inspiration in times of trouble and despondency. We owe much of our knowledge of ancient times to these bards.

The early dynastic history of Magadha is shrouded in darkness. We have occasional glimpses of war-lords and statesmen, some probably entirely mythical, others having more appearance of reality. True history commences with the famous Bimbisāra of the Haryaṅka *kula* who launched his people in that career of conquest and aggrandisement which only ended when Aśoka sheathed his sword after the conquest of Kaliṅga.

The family of Bimbisāra was responsible for the fortification of a village at the confluence of the Son and the Ganges which grew into the city of Pāṭaliputra and soon replaced the old capital, Girivraja-Rājagṛiha. It also saw, and actively supported, the growth of the religious movements associated with Vardhamāna Mahāvīra and Gautama Buddha.

According to Buddhist tradition the Bimbisārids made room for a new line styled Śaiśunāga. The Purāṇic chronicles, however, do not distinguish between the two families and make Śaiśunāga the common ancestor of the kings belonging to both the groups.

Śaiśunāga rule seems to have ended in a tragedy. The last notable ruler of the line fell a victim to a plot engineered by an all powerful official who had "advanced to too near a place in the confidence of the monarch".

The Nandas

With the passing of the Śaiśunāgas from the stage and the assumption of supreme authority by the regicide, who is no other than the famous founder of the Nanda line, we enter upon a new epoch in the history of this country. For the first time we have an empire which transcends the boundaries of the Gangetic basin. It is not a loose assemblage of virtually independent states or feudal baronies which have a wholesome respect for the power and might of a *roi soleil*, but an integrated monarchy under an *Ekarāṭ* (single ruler) possessed of vast resources in men and money. The old, almost uninterrupted, ascendancy of clans claiming the blue blood of Kshatriyas is at an end. The new ruler is a *novus homo* who wages a war to the knife on the Kshatriyas and rouses the relentless hostility of the most astute of the politically minded Brāhmaṇas of the age. He incarnates, according to the Purāṇic chroniclers, the spirit of the Iron Age (Kali) and his accession is taken to mark a chronological epoch like the birth of Parikshit several centuries earlier.

Unfortunately the chroniclers disagree among themselves as to the exact period of the rule of the first Nanda and show divergence from Jain and Buddhist traditions in regard to the duration of the dynasty as a whole. In the absence of a clear and unanimous tradition speculation is unprofitable. The family was still on the throne of Pāṭaliputra when Chandragupta, who was then but a youth,[1] met Alexander in the Punjab in 326 B. C. It had possibly come to power before the death of Xenophon sometime after 355 B. C. That famous historian refers in his *Cyropædia* to a powerful king of India who aspired to be an umpire in disputes between the great nations of Western Asia and was 'a very wealthy man', a description that has a special application to the Nandas. The enormous wealth of the kings of the line is vouched for by all our authorities. It is hinted at by the most famous of the Chinese pilgrims and was known to the Tamil poets of the Śaṅgam. Xenophon was referring to the sixth century B. C. But his description of the Indian monarch may have been reminiscent of his own days.

Some scholars read a reference to a Nanda era in the Hāthīgumphā inscription of Khāravela. No such era was however known to Alberuni who gives a concise account of the reckonings prevalent in his days in Chapter XLIX of his work on India. The interpretation of the expression *ti-vasa-sata*, which measures the interval between Nandarāja and Khāravela, is also a matter of controversy. In any case, the uncertainty of the precise date of the Hāthīgumphā record and the doubtful character of the readings of several of its passages, make the chronological references of little value in determining with accuracy the exact epoch of the first Nanda.

Curiously enough the dynastic name Nanda is not known to any contemporary authority. It is no doubt mentioned in the *Kauṭilīya Arthaśāstra*, which is traditionally assigned to the age of Chandragupta Maurya. But the work contains references which point to a much later date. The reading 'Nandrum' in the place of 'Alexandrum' suggested by some

1. M'Crindle, *Invasion of Alexender*, p. 311.

modern writers in the narrative of Justin, who epitomises the account of Pompeius Trogus and may have had access to earlier sources, is absolutely unjustified. Among extant works, which may, with some degree of plausibility, be assigned to a period anterior to the Ceylonese chronicles and the Purāṇas, it is the *Milinda-pañho* which refers to 'the royal family of Nanda'. But an earlier notice of Nandarāja is contained in two passages of the famous Hāthīgumphā record of Khāravela ;

Paṁchame cha dāni vase Naṁdarāja ti-vasa-sata oghāṭitaṁ Tanasuliya-vāṭā-pañādiṁ nagaraṁ pavesayati.

'And then, in the fifth year, (Khāravela) caused the canal, opened out by king Nanda three hundred (or one hundred and three) years back, to be brought into the capital from the Tanasuliya road".

Again, in connection with the twelfth year of Khāravela's reign we have a reference to *Naṁdarājajitaṁ Kaliṁga-jana saṁnivesaṁ* (or, according to another reading, *Naṁda-rāja-nitaṁ Kaliṁga Jina-saṁnivesa*), that is, a place for assemblage of people or a Jaina shrine in Kaliṅga acquired by king Nanda.

For a fairly connected history of the dynasty we have to make use of Indian tradition. Indian writers were concerned with the period of Nanda rule partly as marking a stage in a socio-political movement, and as an episode in the story of Jaina pontiffs, and partly as an important element in the *Chandragupta-kathā* of which we have Buddhist fragments in the *Milinda-Pañho* and the Ceylonese chronicles and commentaries, and Brahmanical versions in the Purāṇas, folk-tales, one famous drama, and certain works on polity.

Mahāpadma

The first Nanda bore the name Mahāpadma or Mahāpadmapati, "sovereign of an infinite host" or "of immense wealth", according to the Purāṇas, and Ugrasena according to the *Mahābodhivaṁsa*. The Purāṇas describe him as a son of the last king of the preceding line by a Śūdra woman. Jaina works, on the other hand, represent Nanda as the son of a courtezan by a barber. This tradition finds support in the classical account of the pedigree of Alexander's Magadhan contemporary who was the predecessor of Chandragupta Maurya. Referring to this prince who occupied the throne of Pāṭaliputra when, according to Plutarch, Chandragupta met Alexander in the Punjab, Curtius[1] informs us that "his father was in fact a barber, scarcely staving off hunger by his daily earnings, but who, from his being not uncomely in person, had gained the affections of the queen, and was by her influence advanced to too near a place in the confidence of the reigning monarch. Afterwards, however, he treacherously murdered his sovereign, and then, under the pretence of acting as guardian to the royal children, usurped the supreme authority, and having put the young princes to death begot the present king".

There has been some difference of opinion as to whether "the present king" (Agrammes) of Curtius ruling in 326 B. C. refers to the first Nanda himself or to one of his sons. The classical testimony leaves no room for doubt on the point. Agrammes was born to the purple. His father had already usurped supreme authority and put the legitimate heirs to the throne to death. The description of "the present king" can hardly be applied to the first Nanda who was *gaṇikākushi-janma* (born of a courtesan) and whose father did not exercise sovereign power. We have therefore to conclude that Agrammes, or Xandrames as he is called by Diodorus, belonged to the second generation of the usurping family and his father was the first Nanda, the Mahāpadma-Ugrasena of Indian tradition.

The murdered sovereign must have belonged to the line that preceded the Nandas on the throne of Pāṭaliputra. The ruler who answers best to the description given by Curtius and Diodorus is Kākavarṇa-Kālāśoka whose tragic end is alluded to in the *Harshacharita*, and whose sons—nine or ten in number—were, according to Buddhist tradition, ousted by Ugrasena Nanda. The name Agrammes is possibly a distorted form of the Sanskrit Augrasainya, "son or descendant of Ugrasena". It may be noted in this connection that Augrasainya as a royal epithet may be traced back to the

1. M'Crindle, *Invasion of Alexander*, p. 220.

Aitareya Brāhmaṇa where it occurs as a patronymic of Yuddhāṁśraushṭi.[1]

The rise of an all powerful official in the time of the later Śaiśunāgas probably indicates that the system of administration had undergone remarkable changes since the days of Bimbisāra. That monarch had exercised a rigid control over his *mahāmātras*, dismissing those who advised him badly and rewarding those whose counsel he approved. The result of the "purge" was the emergence of the type of official represented by Varshakāra and Sunītha whose rigour and efficiency are well illustrated in the Buddhist Texts. The situation must have changed considerably towards the end of the Śaiśunāga epoch. The career of Ugrasena reminds one of that of Bijjala in a later age, and his early relations with the preceding royal family had important points of resemblance with that between Cardinal Mazarin and the family of Louis XIII. If tradition is to be believed the office of a chief minister was maintained throughout the Nanda period, though the functionary in question never reached the preeminent position that Ugrasena occupied in the days of his royal master. Jaina and Hindu writers refer to a distinguished line of imperial chancellors from Kalpaka to Śakaṭāla and Rākshasa. It is difficult to say if these traditional figures had any historical reality. They are not mentioned in contemporary or semi-contemporary documents. But "advisers of the king", very small in number, but most respected on account of their high character and wisdom, are mentioned by Greek observers who wrote about conditions in the fourth century B. C.

Next to the "advisers of the king" probably stood the "generals of the army". One official of this class, Bhadrasāla, finds prominent mention in the *Milinda-Pañho*. The Nanda army was a powerful fighting machine and we are told by the classical writers that the last king of the line "kept in the field for guarding the approaches of his country, twenty

1. The use of patronymics, or metronymics, instead of the personal name, is by no means rare in Indian history. The cases of Assakenus, Porus, Pandion show that in several cases classical writers did not take the trouble of acquainting themselves with the personal designations of princes.

thousand cavalry, and two hundred thousand infantry, besides two thousand four-horsed chariots, and, what was the most formidable force of all, a troop of elephants which ran up to the number of three thousand".[1] Diodorus and Plutarch raise the number of elephants to four thousand and six thousand respectively. The latter puts the strength of the army of the Gangetic nations at eighty thousand horse, two hundred thousand foot, eight thousand war chariots, besides six thousand fighting elephants.

It is no wonder that the lord of such an immense host should aspire to be a sole monarch, an *Ekarāṭ*, of the vast regions stretching from the Himalayas to the Godāvari or its neighbourhood. The historians of Alexander speak of the most powerful peoples who dwelt beyond the Beas as being under one sovereign. Q. Curtius Rufus, for instance, gives the following particulars : "Beyond the river (Hyphasis or Beas) lay extensive deserts. . Next came the Ganges, the largest river in all India, the farther bank of which was inhabited by two nations, the Gangaridae and the Prasii, whose king was Agrammes"[2]. The account of Diodorus is similar. But he calls the king Xandrames instead of Agrammes. The account of Plutarch, or the English translation, seems to suggest that the "Gandaritai" (Gangaridae) and the "Prasiai" had separate kings, and this is said to find support in the number of horses, war-chariots and fighting elephants assigned to the "kings" of the two nations, which is larger than those assigned to Agrammes-Xandrames by Curtius and Diodorus. But the number of foot soldiers remains the same in all the accounts. The discrepancies regarding the number of elephants etc. may be due to divergence of tradition rather than reinforcement by contingents supplied by an allied king. Pliny informs us that the Prasii surpass in power and glory every other people in all India, their capital being Palibothra (Pāṭaliputra), after which some call the people itself the Palibothri, nay, even the whole tract of the Ganges.

1. M'Crindle, *Invasion*, pp. 221-22.
2. *Ibid.*

Jaina writers refer to the subjugation by Nanda's minister of the whole country down to the seas :—

Samudravasan śebhya āsamudramapi śriyaḥ!
upāyahastairākṛishya tataḥ so'kṛita Nandasāt' ।।

Purāṇic chroniclers speak of the extermination by Mahāpadma of all *kshatriyas*. This is taken to imply that he uprooted all the *kshatriya* families which ruled contemporaneously with the Śaiśunāgas (*tulya-kālam bhavishyanti sarv: hy ete mahīkshitah*)[1], viz., the Ikshvākus, Pañchālas, Kāśeyas, Haihayas, Kaliṅgas, Aśmakas, Kurus, Maithilas, Śūrasenas, and the Vītihotras.

The Ikshvākus were the ruling clan of Kośala, roughly corresponding to modern Oudh. They had been humbled by Ajātaśatru, the son of Bimbisāra. The history of the clan after the famous rulers Prasenajit and his son Viduratha is obscure. A passage of the *Kathāsaritsāgara* refers to the camp (*kaṭaka*) of Nanda in Ayodhyā. Apparently the king had undertaken an expedition to Kośala. An important section of the Ikshvākus seems to have been driven southwards as they are found in the third or fourth century A. D. in occupation of the lower valley of the Kṛishṇā.

The Pañchālas occupied the tract of country between the upper Ganges and the Gumti together with a part of the Central Doab. They do not appear to have come into hostile contact with the Magadhan monarchy before the rise of the Nandas, and must have been brought under control by that dynasty, as the evidence of the classical writers seems to suggest.

The Kāśeyas, or the people inhabiting the district round Benares, had come under the Magadhan sway as early as the days of Bimbisāra and Ajātaśatru. It is recorded in the Purāṇas that a Śaiśunāga prince was "placed in Benares" when the founder of the line took up his residence in Girivraja, the Magadhan capital in early times. It was apparently from a descendant or successor of this prince that Nanda wrested control over the people of Kāśī.

The Haihayas are found in possession of a part of the Narmadā valley down to mediaeval times. Their earlier

1. Pargiter, *DKA*., p. 23.

capital was at Māhishmatī, which has been identified by Pargiter with the rocky island of Māndhātā and by others with a town named Maheśvara on the northern bank of the Narmadā within the boundaries of the Indore state. The subjugation of this region by the Nandas does not seem to be improbable in view of the Purāṇic statement about the humiliation of the rulers of the neighbouring realm of Avanti by their Śaiśunāga predecessors. But there is lack of confirmation by independent witnesses. It has however to be remembered that both Malwa and Gujarat formed integral parts of the Magadhan empire in the days of Chandragupta towards the close of the fourth century B.C., and the way may have been prepared by the Nandas.

The Kaliṅgas occupied the extensive territory stretching from the river Vaitaraṇī in Orissa to the Varāhanadī in the Vizagapatam District. Its capital in ancient times was the famous city of Dantakura or Dantapura which has been identified with the fort of Dantavaktra near Chicacole in the Ganjam district, washed by the river Languliya (Lāṅgulinī). The conquest of a part of Kaliṅga by Nanda is suggested by the Hāthīgumphā record. The phraseology of the inscription hardly supports the view held by some scholars that the Nandarāja mentioned therein is a local chief. The reference is doubtless to a conqueror who established his authority over a *sanniveśa* (place) of Kaliṅga and constructed some irrigation works in the province.

The Aśmakas occupied a part of the Godāvarī valley with their capital at Potali, Potana, or Podana. The last form of the name reminds one of Bodhan to the south of the confluence of the Mañjīrā and the Godāvarī not very far from Nizamabad in the Hyderabad state. The existence on the Godāvarī of a city called "Nau Nand Dehra" (Nander), a little to the west of the Nizamabad District, renders it probable that the dominions of the "Nine Nandas" may have embraced the classic land of the Aśmakas, though independent confirmation by contemporary or semi-contemporary writers is not available.

The Kurus, as is well known, occupied the country to the west of the Pañchālas stretching from the Ganges to the river Sarasvatī (modern Sarsuti) which flows past the sacred site of Kurukshetra near Thanesar. The subjugation of this territory by the Nandas is not expressly mentioned by any contemporary authority, but is rendered probable by the Greek evidence in regard to "the dominions of the nation of the Praisioi and the Gandaridai" which seem to have embraced the whole tract of the Ganges.

The Maithilas were the people of Mithilā, a city famed in the epics owing to its connection with the heroine of the *Rāmāyaṇa* and her father Janaka. It has been identified with the small town of Janakpur within the Nepal border, north of where the Darbhanga and Muzaffarpur Districts meet. The greater part of Northern Bihar, over which the powerful confederation of the Vṛijis (including the Lichchhavis) had exercised sway, had been annexed by Ajātaśatru, and his successors are known to have graced Vaiśālī, the capital, with their presence on occasions. If the Purāṇic tradition has any value the chieftains of Mithilā must have retained a certain amount of independence in the fastnesses of the Nepalese Tarai. The periodical floods from the Gaṇḍak, the Bāgmatī and connected streams during the rainy season must have rendered this part of the country very difficult of access and it is not surprising that the forests of the Tarai should have sheltered an autonomous principality when the great city of Vaiśālī fell before the onslaught of Ajātaśatru. The Nandas attained greater success as they could operate from their base in Vaiśālī.

The Śūrasenas, the Sourasenoi of Megasthenes, had their capital at Mathurā on the banks of the Jumna. Their subjection to the Prasii appears very probable from the accounts of Alexander's historians.

The Vītihotras are closely associated with the Haihayas and the Avantis in Purāṇic tradition. Their sovereignty is said to have terminated before the rise of the famous line of Pradyota. If the Purāṇic statement, found in a later passage of the *Bhavishyānukīrtana*, about the contemporaneity of some of the Vītihotras with the Śaiśunāgas, has any value, the latter may have restored some scion of the old line when they took away the glory (*yaśaḥ kṛitsnam*) of the Pradyotas.

As already stated, the undoubted control that Chandragupta Maurya exercised over Western India including the Girnar region makes it highly probable that the way had been left clear by his Nanda predecessors. Jain writers expressly mention the Nandas among the successors of Pālaka, the son of Pradyota of Avanti.

Much of the information given above relating to the conquests of the first Nanda is derived from late works. But the evidence of Greek writers, taken together with the testimony of the Hāthīgumphā epigraph leaves no room for doubt that the dynasty that ruled over the eastern nations of India in the days of Alexander exercised sway over practically the whole of the Gangetic basin together with some portion, if not the whole, of Kaliṅga. Some ingenuity has been shown by certain writers in drawing a distinction between Pūrva Nandas (earlier Nandas) and Nava Nandas (new or later Nandas) and identifying a prince of the former group with the Nandarāja of Khāravela's inscription. But the theory rests on an unjustifiable interpretation of the expression *pūrva*. *Nanda* used by Kshemendra and other epitomisers and redactors of the *Bṛihatkathā*. The Purāṇic as well as the Ceylonese tradition knows of the existence of only one Nanda line and all writers including those belonging to Jaina persuasion take the word *Nava* in the expression *Nava Nanda* to mean *nine* and not *new*. Pūrva-Nanda is the designation of a single king and not of a dynasty and he is distinguished not from the Nava Nandas but from a pseudo-Nanda (Yogananda), the reanimated corpse of king Nanda.

Several Mysore inscriptions state that Kuntala, a territory which included the southern part of the Bombay Presidency and the contiguous portions of Hyderabad state and the state of Mysore, was ruled by the Nandas. But these are of comparatively modern date (*c.* A. D. 1200), and too much cannot be built upon their statement. It has however to be admitted that no satisfactory account is yet available of the expansion of the Magadhan empire beyond the Kṛishṇā and the Tuṅgabhadrā which must have taken place before the promulgation of the Aśokan inscriptions of the Kurnool and Chitaldroog districts dated in the third century B. C.

Administration

We have very little information as to the way in which the vast dominions of the Nandas were administered. If tradition is to be believed the founder of the line clearly aimed at the establishment of a unitary state. The reference to the extermination of all the Kshatriyas, coupled with the use of the terms *ekarāṭ* and *ekachchhatra* can have no other meaning. Greek writers, however, make separate mention of the Prasii and the Gangaridae, though hinting at their subjection to a common sovereign, and Arrian notices the existence beyond the Beas of "an excellent system of internal government under which the multitude was governed by the aristocracy, who exercised their authority with justice and moderation". The aristocratic government, to which the classical writer refers, cannot fail to remind one of the *sanghas* of the Kurus, the Pañchālas and others, mentioned by the *Kauṭlīya Arthaśāstra*, who bore the title of rājā (*rājaśabdopajīvinaḥ*). The flourishing condition of the areas in question where "the inhabitants were good agriculturists", the land exceedingly fertile and the internal government excellent, is in striking contrast with conditions prevailing in the home provinces of the Prasian (Magadhan) monarchy where "the king was detested and held cheap by his subjects". It appears from the evidence that is available to us that Nandas allowed a considerable amount of autonomy to the people in the outlying parts of their empire, e. g., the Gangetic delta and the territories lying beyond Oudh. But the home provinces embracing the ancient *janapadas* of Magadha (South Bihār), Vṛiji (North Bihār), Kāśi (Benares), Kośala (Oudh) etc. were treated in the same way as the sultans of Delhi dealt with the metropolitan province and the river country of the Doab. The presence of the king not only in Pāṭaliputra, the capital of Magadha, but also in Viśālā or Vaiśālī, the capital of the Vṛiji country in North Bihār, is vouched for by tradition, and we have also an interesting reference to an encampment at Ayodhyā. The strong position held by the Nandas in the heart of their dominions as contrasted with their comparative weakness in the frontier regions is the theme of certain interesting anecdotes that the Buddhist commentator on the Great Chronicle of Ceylon, and other late writers tell of Chandragupta's ambitious adventure on the threshold of his career. The stories no doubt belong to the domain of folklore and certain motifs have a surprising resemblance with the Alfred saga. But the central idea may have been based on genuine tradition.

Greek observers of the fourth century B. C. and the epitomisers of a later age allude to a system of provincial government under officials styled nomarchs and hyparchs. A nomarch is a local ruler or governor of a nome or district. The word hyparch is sometimes used to denote a satrap. But the functionary in question is at times spoken of as a subordinate of a satrap. Though the officials are mentioned chiefly in connection with the Punjab in the days of Alexander and the Magadhan empire in the Maurya period, it is permissible to conjecture that the provincial system under the Nandas, specially in the districts under their undisputed sway, was not very different. In the third century B. C. we hear of administrative charges called *āhāra*, *vishaya*, *janapada* etc. under functionaries styled *mahāmātras* *rājūkas*, *prādeśikas* and *rāshṭriyas* who seem to answer to the nomarchs and hyparchs mentioned by the Greeks.

The lowest administrative unit was the village. In the *Praśna Upanishad*, a later Vedic text, we hear of *adhikṛitas* appointed for *grāmas* or villages by the *samrāṭ* or emperor. *Grāmikas* or village headmen find mention in the early Pali Canon who possibly correspond to these *adhikṛitas*. In the early days of the Magadhan monarchy the king appears to have kept himself in close touch with these village functionaries. We hear of a big assembly of thousands of *grāmikas* held by Bimbisāra. There is no evidence that the Nandas followed this example and the detestation of the people, to which classical writers bear witness, ill accords with any close touch with life in the rural areas. Such a contact was only reestablished when Aśoka in the third century B. C. undertook pious tours even to villages in outlying areas in pursuance of his policy of *dharmānuśasti*.

According to certain manuscripts of the *Vāyu Purāṇa*, which is one of the oldest works of this class and is referred to by Bāṇa in the seventh century A.D., the first Nanda ruled for twenty-eight years, and was followed by his sons who ruled for twelve years. Tāranātha, too, assigns a period of twenty-nine years to Nanda. If this chronological scheme be accepted, the first Nanda could hardly have died before c. 338 B.C. as one of his sons was reigning in 326 B.C. and the dynasty must have come to power not earlier than *c.*367-66 B. C. But as stated above there is hardly any unanimity among our authorities, Purāṇic, Jain and Buddhist, regarding the reign period of Ugrasena Mahāpadma and the total duration of the rule of his family.

Later Nandas

Among the sons of the first Nanda referred to in the Purāṇas, Sahalya or Sahalin seems to have been the eldest. Most of the *Matsya* Mss. spell the name as Sukalpa. But a *Vāyu* Mss. gives the form Sahalya which, as pointed out by Barua, corresponds to Sahalin of the *Divyāvadāna*. The names of the sons of the first Nanda given in the *Mahābodhivaṁsa* are altogether different, and have not yet been confirmed from independent sources. The name of the last prince, Dhana Nanda is unknown to the classical writers who mention Agrammes or Xandrames as the name of the prince of the "barber" dynasty, who occupied the throne when Alexander was on the banks of the Beas.

Xandrames, the name mentioned by Diodorus, has been taken by some scholars to answer to the Sanskrit Chandramas, and identified with Chandragupta Maurya. But Plutarch clearly distinguishes between "Androkottos" and the king of the "Praisiai" in the days of Alexander, and his account receives confirmation from that of Justin. Xandrames or Agrammes was the son of a usurper born after his father had obtained the supreme authority among the Prasii, while Chandragupta was himself the founder of a new sovereignty, the first ruler of his dynasty. The father of Xandrames was a barber who could claim no royal ancestry. On the other hand, Indian writers are unanimous in representing Chandragupta as a scion of a race of rulers, though they differ in regard to the identity of the family and its claim to be regarded as of pure Kshatriya extraction. Jain evidence clearly suggests that the barber usurper is identical with the *nāpita kumāra* or *nāpitasū* who founded the Nanda line.

The figures of the eight princes who succeeded the first Nanda are rather shadowy and we do not know how far the tradition recorded by late writers can be accepted as sober history. The last of them is said to have been addicted to hoarding treasure. He amassed riches to the amount of eighty *koṭis*. In a rock in the bed of the river Ganges he caused a great excavation to be made for the purpose of burying the treasures he had acquired. Levying taxes, along with other articles, even on skins, gums, trees and stones, he amassed further riches which he disposed of similarly. This account taken from the commentary on the Great Chronicle of Ceylon can claim some antiquity. Professor Nilakanta Sastri points out that a Tamil poem contains an interesting reference to the "very famous" Nandas "victorious in war, who having accumulated treasure first in beautiful Pāṭaliputra hid it in the waters of the Ganges". Hiuen Tsang, the famous Chinese pilgrim of the seventh century A. D. refers to "the five treasures of king Nanda's seven precious substances"[1].

The accumulation of an enormous amount of wealth, to which all our authorities bear witness, probably implies a good deal of financial extortion and it is not surprising that the Nanda contemporary of Alexander "was detested and held cheap by his subjects as he rather took after his father than conducted himself as the occupant of a throne."

The oppressed people soon found a leader. Plutarch and Justin refer to a young lad named Androkottos or Sandrocottus, doubtless identical with the famous Chandragupta, who visited Alexander in the Punjab, and showed a keen interest in the affairs of the Prasii. "Not long afterwards" he mounted the throne and "shook off from the neck" of India "the yoke of servitude" by overthrowing the existing government in India and expelling the prefects of Alexander. Indian chronicles introduce by his side another figure, a *dvijarshabha* named

[1] Watters, ii p. 296.

Kauṭilya or Chāṇakya, whom tradition represents as an inhabitant of Taxila.

While some of the Indian writers. notably the author of the Sanskrit play entitled the *Mudrā-Rākshasa*, are chiefly concerned with the battle of intrigue conducted by Kauṭilya, the *Milinda Pañho* affords us a glimpse of the clash of arms between the contending forces of the Nandas and the Mauryas. "There was Bhaddasāla (Bhadraśāla), the soldier in the service of the royal family of the Nandas, and he waged war against king Chandagutta (Chandragupta). Now in that war, there were eighty corpse dances. For they say that when one great head holocaust has taken place by which is meant the slaughter of ten thousand elephants, and a lac of horses, and five thousand charioteers, and a hundred *koṭis* of soldiers on foot, then the headless corpses arise and dance in frenzy over the battle field". The passage contains a good deal of mythical embellishment. But we have here reminiscence of the blood bath through which Chandragupta had to wade to the throne.

The glamour of the Nandas has been dimmed by the greater splendour of the succeeding dynasty. But it is well to remember what the kings of the line bequeathed to their immediate successors and to posterity. They had, to use the words of Smith, "compelled the mutually repellent molecules of the body politic to check their gyrations and submit to the grasp of a superior controlling force". They developed a fighting machine that was used by the later rulers of Magadha with terrible effect in resisting the onslaught of foreign invaders and carrying on the policy of expansion within the borders of India that had been inaugurated by Bimbisāra and Ajātaśatru.

If tradition recorded by the epitomisers of the *Bṛihatkathā* is to be believed, Pāṭaliputra under Nanda rule became the abode (*kshetra*) of Sarasvatī as well as Lakshmī, the home of learning as well as of material prosperity. A galaxy of scholars—Varsha, Upavarsha, Pāṇini, Kātyāyana, Vararuchi, Vyāḍi—is said to have added lustre to the age. While much of the traditional account may be mere folklore unworthy of credence, we may well believe that the cultivation of grammer received an impetus in this age. The scholia on Pāṇini, presupposed by the great commentary of Patañjali, show acquaintance with the *Yavana lipi*, and it is by no means improbable that some of the predecessors of Patañjali are to be assigned to the Nanda Age. Kings of the line are credited by certain grammarians with the standardization of weights and measures. (*Nandopakramāṇi mānāni*).

In social matters the rise of Nandas may be regarded as symptomatic of a surging up of the lower classes. The Purāṇic chroniclers represent the dynasty as harbingers of Śūdra rule and as irreligious (*adhārmika*). The last statement is significant in view of the traditional connection of the family with Jain ministers and patriarchs. But the evidence on the point is of a character which makes it difficult to build too much on it.

II. Regions Beyond the Magadhan Empire

No account of India in the age of the Nandas is complete without a brief notice of the vast stretches of territory within the confines of this country that lay beyond the limits of their empire. Unfortunately, the exact boundary of the Nanda dominions cannot be determined with any amount of precision with the aid of available evidence. This is particularly true of the south. In the north the inclusion of the Ganges valley within the Nanda empire is, as already noted, suggested by Greek and Purāṇic evidence. We shall perhaps not be far wrong if we regard the upper reaches of the stream, that once flowed through the Ghaggar-Hakra bed, as forming roughly the boundary line between the Magadhan empire of those days and the autonomous tribes and kingships of the Uttarāpatha. In the south Greek evidence is not of much help. Purāṇic testimony, as we have seen, hints at the incorporation into their empire by the Nandas of the principalities of all the leading Kshatriya families of the day, including in all probability those of the south. Among the latter prominent mention is made of the Haihayas, Kaliṅgas and Aśmakas.

Following this evidence, which comes from sources assignable to the commencement of the Gupta Age, we may tentatively fix the southern boundary of the Nanda empire, or at least of the arena of its political and military activities, at the river Godāvarī. Barring some mediaeval Jaina treatises and inscriptions, of doubtful value for early times, there is hardly any evidence that the hegemony of the Nandas extended far beyond that famous river. Persian inscriptions, observations of Greek and Latin writers, supplemented by brief notices in Indian literature and epigraphs, enable us to say a few words about the two great regions of India—namely the Indus basin beyond the Ghaggar and South India beyond the Godāvarī—which, in the light of the evidence we have adduced, seem to have lain beyond the limits of the Nanda empire.

(i) *North-West India.*

A. PHYSICAL ASPECTS

Bounded on the north by the Outer Himalayas; on the west, by the eastern Hindukush, the Safed Koh, the Suleiman and the Kirthar ranges; on the south, by the surging waters of the Arabian Sea and the "immense salt-water waste of the Rann of Cutch"; and on the east by the sand-dunes of the Thar or the Great Indian Desert and the uplands and ridges of the Eastern Punjab, the extensive valley of the Indus and its feeders constituted a little world not much affected by the eddies and currents of Magadhan history before the rise of the Great Mauryas.

The country falls into three natural divisions :—(1) the mountainous regions extending from the upper reaches of the Sutlej to the basin of the Chitral and certain outlying rocky areas; (2) the flat rolling plains of the Punjab intersected by a network of rivers and brooks; and (3) the almost rainless tract of the lower Indus and its delta, an important part of which now forms the province of Sind.

The land described above presents great varieties of scenery. The eyes meet in the north the snow-clad speaks and glaciers of the Himalayas and the luxuriant vegetation that clothes the submontane region. A striking contrast to this is afforded by the plains of the Indus, which look like an "interminable waste", overgrown with tamarisk scrubs and ultimately merging in the great desert of Rajputana, the Registan of Sind and the sandy, surf-beaten shore of the Arabian Sea. The dreary and monotonous sight is only redeemed by the green verdure of the riverine fringes and "endless expanse of waving crops of different shades of colour" that covers the country at the approach of the harvest season.

The history of the region cannot be properly understood without a reference to its river-system. The central stream of the Indus, taking its rise in the heights of the Tibetan Plateau, meanders its course through the whole length of the land. It has not only given its name to our country but, according to some Greek writers, formed sometimes its north-western boundary. Near Attock in the north-western part of the Punjab it receives the combined waters of the Kabul and its confluents, including the Swat, the Panjkora, the Kunar and the Panjshir. The rivers which contribute most to the stream of the Indus, however, lie to the east and sweep through the plains of the Punjab proper, the "Land of the Five Rivers." The nearest among the "Five Streams" is the Jhelum or Vitastā, the Hydaspes of the Greeks. It adds to the wealth and beauty of the sunny vale of Kashmir and unites with the next stream, the Chenab, the ancient Chandrabhāgā or Asiknī, the Akesines of the Greek writers, near Jhang. The whirling of waters produced by the confluence threatened to spell disaster to a flotilla of Alexander in the fourth century B. C. The next of the sister torrents, the Rāvi, ancient Parushṇī or Irāvatī, the Hydraotis of the Greeks, rises in the Chamba State and falls into the united waters of the Jhelum and the Chenab. To the east of the Rāvi flows the Beas, ancient Vipāś or Vipāśā, the Hyphasis of the Greeks, which is now an affluent of the Sutlej, Śutudri, or Śatadru, the Hesidrus or Zaradros of the Greeks. The five streams mingle their waters into the Panjnad and join the Indus above Mithankot. The mighty river then sweeps on into the Arabian sea through a number of shifting channels. Traces of old river beds are found in several directions and remains of ancient cities stud the neighbourhood.

During winter the rivers of the Punjab look comparatively small but at the approach of the hot season, when the snow of the mountains begins to melt, and particularly when the monsoons burst, the streams are lashed to fury and rush through their wide beds "in uncontrolled vagary". Large tracts of the country assume an almost oceanic character. Greek writers, as we shall see, bear ample testimony to the vagaries of these rivers and their effect on the landscape.

Although drained by a large number of rivers the soil of the Punjab is comparatively poor. The scarcity of regular rainfall and the absence of sufficient facilities for irrigation in early times added to the difficulties of extensive cultivation. The forest-clad sub-montane region, including the country round Taxila, has, however, been noted for its fertility since times long gone by. Besides agricultural products, salt added to the wealth of the Indus basin, being found embedded in rocks particularly the Salt Range, and the delta of Sind. No trace of gold mines has been found in this region, but the metal was met with in the sands of the Indus, and the Kabul rivers and the upper reaches of several other streams.

The gold-washing industry is no longer remunerative. But Herodotus informs us that in the fifth century B. C. "India", *i. e.*, the Indus valley, paid a tribute of 360 talents of gold-dust. The existence of gold and silver "mines" in the countries of Sophytes and Mousikanos and certain other regions was reported to the companions of Alexander and the Chinese pilgrims of the seventh century A. D. The forests of Gandhāra supplied teak for a Persian palace, and the country in general ivory for its adornment. Alexander, too got timber for his flotilla from the hilly region flanking the north of the Punjab.

Geographical factors exercised a controlling influence upon the history of the Land of the Five Rivers as on the rest of the country. The mountains on the west and the north that frown on the riparian plains afforded shelter to fighting clans, who turned every rocky eminence into a citadel of defence and braved the wrath of the mightiest conqueror of antiquity. The numerous streams and rivulets that intersect the plains made each *doab* or strip of territory between two sheets of water nourish centres of autonomous political life. The mighty Indus with its confluent streams at times promoted an opposite tendency. They served as highways for ambitious rulers who sought to compel the political molecules of the Punjab and Sind to submit to one controlling force. The story of the mineral and agricultural wealth of the country must have been carried by travellers and merchants beyond its border so as to reach the ears of the King of Kings who held his court at Susa and Ekbatana from the sixth to the fourth century B. C. The riches of India and the lack of political cohesion among the children of the soil invited invasion from outside. The existence of a centralised monarchy in Iran indicated the source from which it was to come.

B. THE ADVANCE OF PERSIA TO THE INDUS.

Some sort of military activity in India and its border-land and even conquest of a well defined territory in this direction are attributed to Cyrus (558-529 B. C.), the founder of the Persian empire, by Xenophon and other writers. But the evidence points to the inclusion within the dominions of the first Achaemenid of only the Kabul valley as far as the Indus. We learn from Pliny that Cyrus destroyed the famous city of Kāpiśī and Arrian tells us that "the district *west* of the Indus as far as the Kophen (Kabul). . submitted to the Persians and paid tribute to Cyrus". Kāpiśī, the Ka-pi-shih of Hiuen Tsang and Ki-pin (cf. Greek Kophen) of other Chinese texts stood at or near the junction of the Ghorband and the Panjshir. The eastern part of the realm of Ki-pin comprised, according to later writers, K'ien-t'o-lo or Gandhāra. Classical writers thus make it clear that the region between the Panjshir and the Indus, embracing ancient Kāpiśī or Ki-pin and Gandhāra proper (Peshawar district), was under the sway of Cyrus, a fact that accords with the appearance of Gadara or Gandhāra among the subject peoples in the earliest epigraphs of Darius (522-486 B. C.).

Another eastern people who owed allegiance to the Persians were the "Thatagus" or the Sattagydians. They together with the Gandarians, the Dadicae and the Aparytae constituted the seventh satrapy. Herzfeld is inclined to regard the Sattagydians as an Indian people located in the Punjab. Rawlinson, however, thinks that they lived near the Arachosians (of Kandahar) and occupied a part of south-eastern Afghanistan. According to Sarre they are to be located in the Ghazni and Ghilzai regions. Dames placed them in the Hazara country. The exact position of the Sattagydians still remains uncertain and the matter cannot be finally decided until the discovery of fresh evidence.

A more famous name that occurs in several inscriptions of Darius in the list of subject peoples is Hidu (Hindu), which corresponds to the "Indians" of Herodotus. The circumstances leading to their subjugation, as described by the famous Greek historian, are too well known to need recounting. We are told that "the Indians, who are more numerous than other nations with which we are acquainted, paid a tribute exceeding that of every other people, viz., 360 talents of gold-dust. This was the twentieth satrapy." Herzfeld takes Hidu to refer to Sind. The description of Herodotus that "the tribes of India are more numerous than any other nation and do not all speak the same language", taken together with the information that they paid an amount of tribute exceeding that of every other people, suggests that the twentieth province of the Achaemenid Empire could not have been confined within the narrow limits of modern Sind. If the sandy tract, which is said to have lain 'eastward of India' refers to the desert of Rajputana, then we have probably to include a considerable portion of the southern Punjab, if not the whole of the *central* as well as the lower Indus valley within the borders of the twentieth satrapy. It may no doubt be argued in this connection that certain words of Megasthenes and Arrian suggest a more restricted dominion. The former says that "the Indians had never engaged in foreign warfare, nor had ever been invaded and conquered by a foreign power, except by Hercules and Dionysus and lately by the Macedonians". Arrian also makes the statement that "according to the Indians, no one before Alexander, with the exception of Dionysus and Hercules, had invaded their country." As both these writers often take the Indus to be the western boundary of India proper, their statements may be taken to imply that the Persian dominion in the east did not extend beyond the mighty Sindhu. But it has perhaps been rightly pointed out that "Alexander's historians may have been inclined to minimise the accomplishments" of the Persians "in order to bring into greater prominence the achievements of the famous Greek invader." In any case we should give more weight to the contemporary testimony of Herodotus than to the observations of Megasthenes and Arrian who wrote in much later ages.

The empire which Darius ruled with wisdom and vigour did not long survive his death. Xerxes, who succeeded his father in 486 B. C. and reigned till 465 B. C., had to face a sea of troubles. Rebellions broke out on all sides. We learn from a Persepolis inscription, usually assigned to the period between 486-480 B. C., that he destroyed the temple of the *daivas*. This, in all likelihood, has reference to India. It is, however, difficult to determine whether the Achaemenian ruler proclaimed a *jihad* in honour of Ahuramazda or was faced with a rebellion of the far-eastern province of his empire, the land of the Deva-worshippers. That the monarch succeeded in retaining some hold over the Indian provinces is amply attested by the fact that the people of Gandhāra as well as the Indians figured in the vast host that he led against Hellas in 480 B. C.

The discomfiture that the fleet and army of Persia suffered in the fight against the Greeks at Salamis and Plataea, Mycale and Eurymedon, clearly indicated that her days of conquest and ascendancy were over. The weak and incapable successors of Xerxes found more delight in the boudoirs of the harem than on fields of battle. The direction of state affairs gradually passed into the hands of ambitious women or all-powerful officials. Murder of princes, rebellions of satraps and popular outbreaks lined the path of national decline. But genius for intrigue and possession of gold enabled the agents of a corrupt and effete system to continue for sometime to wield an influence which the valour and enterprise of their antagonists failed effectively to eradicate.

The Achaemenians succeeded in retaining some control or influence over the tribes of the Indian borderland till 330

B. C. when their hegemony was finally extinguished by Alexander. Strabo informs us, on the authority of Eratosthenes, that "the Indus was the boundary between India and Ariana, which latter was situated next to India to the west and was in possession of the Persians at that time" (*i. e.* when Alexander invaded India).

Indian contingents fought side by side with the Persians against the Hellenic host at Guagamela. Arrian refers to *three* distinct groups of Indians who responded to the trumpet call of Darius III Codomanus (335-330 B. C.). The Indians who were neighbours of the Bactrians (of the Balkh region), possibly the inhabitants of Kāpiśī-Gandhāra, were arrayed with the Bactrians themselves and the Sogdianians (of the Samarkand territory) under the command of Bessus, the satrap of Bactria. A second group of Indians styled the "Indian hillmen" or "mountaineer Indians", possibly the Sattagydians or people of the principality of Sambos in Sind, were placed with the Arachosians (of the Kandahar area) under Bersaentes, Satrap of Arachosia. Besides these, we have pointed reference to a third group, viz. Indians on *this* side of the Indus, apparently those of the twentieth satrapy, who came to the help of the Persian king with a comparatively small force of fifteen elephants.

In the huge Persian army that Darius pitched against Alexander the Indians occupied the centre where the great king himself took up his position. They obviously enjoyed, in a special measure, the confidence of the sovereign and had the honour of protecting his person with his kinsmen, "the Persians whose spears were fitted with golden apples, the 'transplanted' Carians and the Mardian bowmen." Nor did they belie the trust reposed in them. When the attack began and the great king himself took to flight some of the Indians, together with the Persian cavalry, fell upon the enemy with great impetuosity and threatened one contingent (the army of Parmenio) with total annihilation. The timely help of Alexander saved the situation.

It is interesting to note that two important sections of Indians who joined the army of Darius III fought under the banner of the satraps of Bactria and Arachosia. This possibly implies that their territories were committed to the charge of those two satrapies. The amalgamation of two, or even three, provinces is a feature of the administrative history of the later Achaemenids. Like the *Daṇḍopanatasāmantas*, mentioned in Kauṭiliyan *Arthaśāstra*, Indian lieges furnished contingents to the paramount power in the hour of its need. The great provincial satraps had the assistance of district officials or local potentates of the rank of *nomarch* and *hyparch*. A number of these functionaries are mentioned as ruling in the Kabul and Indus valleys on the eve of the Macedonian invasion of 326 B. C. Alexander did not meet with any Persian satrap after he crossed the Indus. But *hyparchs* and *nomarchs* were to be found as far as the Salt range. Some of the chiefs assumed the full insignia of sovereignty and even styled themselves *Basileus* or king. The hold of the Persian king and satraps had by this time grown very weak. Each petty principality or chiefship cherished "with a passionate tenacity its individual life and.. political ambition, making wars and alliances as the interest of the moment might dictate."

C. SUCCESSORS OF THE ACHAEMENIDS

The little states in North-western India and the borderland that rose on the ruins of the Persian Empire may be grouped under three heads : (a) kingships, mainly of a tribal character, in the region between the Kunar and the Ravi, with a solitary hill-state apparently under oligarchical rule; (b) the autonomous tribes east of the Ravi and south of the junction of the Jhelum and the Chenab; and (c) monarchies and one state under 'diarchy' in the lower Indus valley below Mithankot, in parts of which Brāhmaṇas seem to have exercised considerable political influence.

The first group begins with the principalities in the hill country drained by the northern affluents of the Kabul river comprising the valleys of the Kunar, the Panjkora and the Swat, occupied by the Aspasians, the Gaureans and the Assakenians respectively. The name Aspasian is derived from the Iranian '*Aspa*', horse, corresponding to the Sanskrit '*Aśva*' or '*Aśvaka*'. They were thus identical with, or kindreds of, the Assakenians or Aśvakas. The ruler of the Aspasians is styled a *hyparch.* The chief wealth of the people seems to have consisted in cattle, 230,000 of which were captured by Alexander.

The territory occupied by the Assakenians lay in the Swat valley and was known in the Gupta Age as Suvāstu and Udyāna. The royal seat of the country was Massaga, a great city well fortified both by nature and art. It was surrounded by a wall of 35 stadia in circumference, built of sun-baked brick on a foundation of stone work. Towers and engines had to be employed by Alexander to bring about its fall. The Assakenian king had a powerful army of 20,000 cavalry, more than 30,000 infantry and 30 elephants. He was probably in alliance with the king of Abhisāra, as his brother, when attacked by Alexander, took shelter with the latter.

Somewhere in the rugged country to the west of the Indus stood the small hill-state Nysa "at the foot of Mt. Meros." Holdich locates it on the lower spurs and valleys of Kohi-Mor in the Swat country. The Nysaeans are alleged to have been Greek colonists, descendants of men who came to India with Dionysus. The presence of a Yona or Greek *janapada* on the Indian borderland in the days of the Buddha is vouched for by the *Majjhima-nikāya.* The people of Nysa lived under an aristocratic government and their laws received the approbation of Alexander. The members of the Governing Body numbered 300. Akuphis held the office of the President at the time of the Macedonian invasion.

The old territory of Gandhāra was in the latter part of the fourth century B. C. divided between two *hyparchs* viz., those of Pūshkalāvatī and Takshaśilā or Taxila. Pūshkalāvatī, or Peuc laotis of the Greeks, lay to the west of the Indus in the modern district of Peshawar. Taxila stood in the eastern part of ancient Gandhāra. The oldest city of that name is probably represented by the present Bhir mound near Saraikala, 20 miles north-west of Rawalpindi. It was a great and prosperous city in those days, "the largest of all which lay between the river Indus and Hydaspes (Jhelum)." Plutarch, giving an exaggerated estimate of the size of the realm of "Taxiles", says that it was "as large as Egypt, with good pasturage, too, and in the highest degree productive of beautiful fruits". Strabo refers to its "most excellent laws" and speaks of it as spacious and very fertile, adding that "some say that this is larger than Aegypt." The wealth of the country is testified to by the fact that one of its chiefs presented to Alexander 200 silver talents, 3,000 cattle for sacrificial offering, over 10,000 sheep and 30 elephants. The succeeding ruler gave Alexander and his friends golden crowns and 80 talents of coined silver. The attitude of Taxila towards its neighbours throws welcome light on interstate and inter-tribal relations in the later half of the fourth century B. C. It entertained no friendly feelings towards Pūshkalāvatī and was actually at war with "Abisares" (the Abhisāra chief) and "Porus" (the Paurava) both of whom held sway beyond the river Jhelum. It is difficult to determine the exact political status of the ruler of Taxila at the time of Alexander's invasion. Arrian styles him a *hyparch* but Strabo calls him a *basileus*. It is possible that he was one of the subordinate governors or vassal chiefs of the Persian empire and took advantage of the collapse of Achaemenian authority to declare his independence. The cases of several *nawabs* of the eighteenth century furnish us with close parallels.

"The hilly region above the Taxila country was occupied by Arsakes or the chief of Uraśā (Hazara district) and Abisares or Prince of Abhisāra (Punch and Nowshera districts)." It is interesting to note that like many of his brother chieftains on the borderland Arsakes is described as a *hyparch*.

The ruler of Abhisāra, on the other hand, is styled by Arrian as a *Basileus* or king. He was a very powerful prince and a man of shrewd political sense. He seems to have been a member of a powerful combination of chiefs consisting of Porus, Arsakes and possibly Assakenus. He was no friend of the king of Taxila and is known to have led an expedition against the Cathaeans and other self-governing tribes of the Punjab in alliance with Porus. He sensed the danger of the Macedonian invasion and tried to stop the invader at the gate of India. Thus he sent help to the frontier city of Ora and gave shelter to the brother of Assakenus. When Alexander actually arrived at Taxila he sent envoys offering his submission and yet before the battle of the Hydaspes (Jhelum) he made preparations for joining his forces with Porus.

To the south-east of Taxila between the Jhelum and the Ravi lay the twin territories of the Purus or Pauravas, a people already famous in the *Ṛig Veda.* The realm of the elder of the two chieftains roughly corresponded to parts of the modern districts of Gujarat and Shahpur. It was an extensive and fertile region containing three hundred cities. The second Paurava or Porus, styled a *hyparch* by Arrian, governed a principality between the Chenab and the Rāvi. A man of undaunted courage, brave as a lion, Porus the Elder towered like a triton among minnows. The king of Taxila on the west and his own nephew or cousin, styled the Younger Porus, on the east were both afraid of him. The Cathaeans and other self-governing tribes also had a wholesome respect for his prowess. Diodorus informs us that he was in alliance with Embisaros (Abisares or king of Abhisāra) and in the battle of the Hydaspes he received help from Spitaces, a *nomarch* who possibly owed him allegiance. The army he marshalled against Alexander numbered more than 50,000 foot, about 3,000 horses and above 1,000 chariots and 130 elephants.

Not far from the domains of the Pauravas stretched the principality of the *nomarch* Sophytes or Saubhuti. It included a mountain composed of fossil salt sufficient for the whole of India; Saubhuti is therefore sometimes represented as the "lord of the fastness of the Salt Range" stretching from the Indus to the Jhelum. Classical writers, however, agree in placing his territory to the *east* of the Jhelum. We have some coins of this potentate bearing on the obverse the royal head and on the reverse the figure of a cock. The issue of coins, like the assumption of the title of *Basileus* by the chief of Taxila, may point to the assumption of the rank of an independent king. Both Curtius and Diodorus agree that the people of the kingdom of Saubhuti lived under good laws and customs and beauty was held by them in the highest estimation. "Officers were appointed to discriminate between children with deformed or defective limbs and those with perfect and healthy constitutions and features. The former were put to death, and the latter were reared, not according to the will of the parents but according to the wishes of the state. In contracting marriages they did not seek an alliance with high birth nor did they care whether a bride had dowry or a handsome fortune, but made their choice by the looks and other advantages of the outward person. The inhabitants were therefore held in higher estimation than the rest of their countrymen and also excelled in wisdom."[1]

With the Pauravas and Saubhuti we take leave of the tribal chieftains, who held sway on the borderland and the western Punjab under the titles of *hyparch*, *nomarch* and, more rarely, *Basileus*. We now come to the territories of the autonomous clans. We have to mention first the Glauganikai or Glausians, whose country lay to the west of the Chenab close to the territory of the Pauravas. In their land were no less than thirty-seven cities; of these, the least populated had above five thousand inhabitants many of them had over ten thousand. There was also a large number of populous villages.[2] We have next to mention the Kathaioi or Cathaeans, who are placed by some on the far side of the Chenab and the Ravi. The name possibly stands for the Sanskrit Kaṭha. A brave and warlike race, the Cathaeans had their stronghold at Sangala, probably situated in the Gurudaspur district not far from Fathgarh, though some prefer the claims of Jandiala to the east of Amritsar, or that of Lahore itself. The people had a keen sense of beauty. Strabo, on the authority of Onesicritus, tells us that they chose the handsomest person as their king, and had customs that remind one of the realm of Saubhuti. Other observations of Onesicritus on the Cathaeans will be cited later.

Not far from the Cathaeans on the eastern side of the Ravi lived the Adraistai. Their main stronghold was Pimprama. Between the Ravi and the Beas we find mention of a chief named Phegeus or Phegelis. The name of the king probably answers to the Sanskrit Bhagala, known from the *Gaṇapāṭha* as a designation of a royal race of Kshatriyas.

Below the junction of the Jhelum and the Chenab, in the Shorkot region of the Jhang district lay the territory of a people, called the Siboi. They were probably identical with the

1. M'Crindle *Invasion* pp. 219, 279.
2. *Arrian* (Loeb) II 63, 65.

Siva people mentioned in the *Ṛig Veda* and the Śibis of the later literature. They were dressed with skins like Herakles and had clubs for their weapon, and further branded their cattle and mules with the mark of a club.[1] The nation mustered 40,000 soldiers to oppose Alexander. This people had the Agalassoi as their neighbours. Their army too numbered 40,000, besides 3,000 horse. Curtius tells us that "three largest rivers in India washed the line of the fortifications of their stronghold. The Indus flows close up to it, and on the south the Akesines unites with the Hydaspes."[2]

Below the confluence of these rivers, on the confines of a waterless tract and along the Ravi and the Chenab lived the people called Malloi. Their name, as is well known, represents the Sanskrit Mālava. Closely connected with them in Sanskrit and Greek literature were the Oxydrakai or Oxydracae (variously called Sydracae, Sudracae, Syrakousai) or the Kshudrakas. Strabo informs us that they were regarded as the descendants of Dionysus, judging from the vine of their country and their bacchanalian procession. Pāṇini refers to the Mālavas as living by the profession of arms. Arrian includes them among self-governing Indians ands ays that they were the most numerous and the most warlike of the Indians in these parts. The evidence of Strabo seems to suggest that the Kshudrakas were ruled by petty kings (*basileus*), comparable to the *Rājās* among the Lichchavis and the Mallas of Eastern India. Arrian in one passage refers to the mayors of the cities and rulers of districts (*nomarchai*) among them, who were entrusted with full power to negotiate with foreign potentates. Before the invasion of Alexander the Mālavas and the Kshudrakas were often at war with one another. But at the approach of the common enemy they decided to join forces. According to Curtius the combined army numbered 90,000 foot, 10,000 cavalry and 900 war chariots and they placed at their head a brave warrior of the nation of the Kshudrakas. A somewhat different account is given by Diodorus who says that the two nations at first mustered a force of 80,000

1 *Geography of Stabo* (Loeb) VII 11.

2. M'Crindle, *Invasion* p 233.

foot, 10,000 horse and 700 chariots and cemented their alliance by intermarriages, each nation taking and giving in exchange 10,000 of their young women for wives; but subsequently a dispute arose among them regarding leadership and they drew off into adjoining towns. Arrian's narrative seems to imply that Alexander reached the territory of the Mālavas before any help could come to them from their neighbours.

The territory on the lower Chenab, situated between the confluence of that river with the Ravi and the junction with the Indus respectively was occupied by several autonomous tribes, such as the Abastenœ, also called Sambastai, Sabaragae (Ambashṭhas), the Xathroi (Kshatri) and the Ossadioi (Vasāti). The Ambashṭhas find prominent mention in Sanskrit and Pāli literature, including the great epics, along with the Śibis, the Kshudrakas, the Mālavas and the Sindhavas. Curtius and Diodorus both agree that they were a powerful people with a *democratic* government. Their army consisted of 60.000 foot, 6,000 cavalry and 400 chariots in Alexander's time. The Xathroi and the Ossadioi possibly the Kshatris and Vasātis of Sanskrit texts, do not seem to, have shared the eminence of their famous neighbours.

Below the confluence of the five rivers lived the Sodrai and the Massanoi. The river Indus seems to have separated the territories of the two. The Sodrai are, in all probability, the Śūdras of the epic, a people closely associated with the Ābhiras dwelling on the Sarasvatī.

The major part of Sind from Sukkur to the delta was divided among a number of potentates of whom the most important was Mousikanos. The capital of this prince is usually placed at or near Alor. His country was reported to be the richest in India and Arrian tells us that Alexander much admired it and its capital. Strabo gives interesting information about the kingdom of Mousikanos on the authority of Onesicritus and this will be reproduced elsewhere.

From the account left by Arrian it appears that the "Brachmans" or Brāhamaṇas exercised considerable influence in the country. They instigated a revolt against the Macedonian invader. Nearchus informs us "that the Brachamanes engage in affairs of state and attend the kings as councillors".

Not far from the territory of Mousikanos lay the principality over which Oxykanos or Portikanos held sway. Arrian calls him a *nomarch.* The inhabitants of the region are styled by Curtius Praesti, possibly the Proshṭhas of the epic.

In the mountainous country adjoining the kingdom of Mousikanos ruled Sambos, called Sabus by Strabo and Sabbas by Plutarch. His capital was Sindimana or Sindomana, which has been identified, with little plausibility, with Sehwan, a city on the Indus. Arrian informs us that Sambos and Mousikanos were at enmity with one another. Sambos was appointed satrap of the Indian hillmen by Alexander; but if Plutarch is to be believed he rose in rebellion at the instance of the *gymnosophists.* This hints at the fact that "naked philosophers' who were either Brāhmaṇas or followers of the Jina had considerable political influence in the country of Sambos. Conditions therefore were not unlike those in the realm of Mousikanos. Diodorus makes explicit mention of a nation and country of the Brāhamaṇas in the neighbourhood of the Sindian chiefships. He also places at the extremity of the "country of the Brāhmaṇas" a city, called Harmatelia, which, as the evidence of Justin suggests, was ruled by a chief named Ambigerus.

In the delta of the Indus lay the territory of Patalene, referred as Pottala and identified with Tauala of Diodorus. The capital probably stood near the site of Bahmanabad. Diodorus tells us Tauala had a political constitution like that of Sparta. The army was commanded by two kings belonging to separate families, while a Council of Elders directed the affairs of the state with supreme authority. One of the kings in the time of Alexander is styled by Curtius Moeres, a name that sounds like Moriya or Maurya of Indian records.

To sum up, North-West India presented on the whole a picture of disunion when the Nandas held sway in the Ganges valley. Constant references to *hyparchs* and *nomarchs*, however, indicate that, as in the eighteenth century, agents of a defunct empire were, with few exceptions, still content with the subordinate titles they had in the palmy days of the rule of their former imperial masters. The time was ripe for interference from powers that dominated the tableland of Iran on the west and the valley of the Ganges in the east.

2. The Far South

In comparison with the North-West our information regarding the Far South of India beyond the river Godāvarī in the age of the Nandas is extremely meagre. The region falls into three well-marked natural divisions: (1) The high land enclosed between the Western and the Eastern Ghats, which has its 'orographical apex' at the Nilgiri where the great mountain systems of the south merge into one another; (2) a narrow strip of territory on its west extending as far as the shores of the sea, intersected by numerous coves and creeks, but "unbroken by the passage of any considerable river"; and (3) the broader eastern sea-board embracing the fertile deltas of the Godāvarī, the Kṛishṇā and the Kāverī as well as the "open treeless plains" of Madura and Tinnevelly.

The two low-lying strips of territory overlooking the Arabian Sea and the Bay of Bengal respectively are "filled with luxuriant vegetation, nourished by sea-borne mists and vapours", bedecked with groves of palm and cocoanut and adorned in places by a number of backwaters, lagoons or lakes. They afford a most picturesque sight to the traveller. The wide expanse of the table land of the interior, "in some parts mountainous and wooded, in others flat and undulating, with stretches of rich crop-growing fields as well as sterile soil", also presents a beautiful and diversified scenery. The south became justly famous for its natural wealth. The maritime belts are in many places exceedingly fertile and produced abundant crops of cereals. Ancient ports are found scattered all along the coastline through which a brisk trade was carried on with the countries of the west and the east from bygone times. Among the chief articles of commerce pepper, beryl and pearls were highly prized in Europe. The last-mentioned articles find prominent mention in the works of the Classical authors since the days of Megasthenes. Kauṭilya, too, refers to pearl called Tāmraparṇika, "that which is produced in Tāmraparṇī," besides articles produced in Pandya-kapāṭa and the cotton fabrics of Madura.

It is the wealth of the Far South, rather than the annals of its people, their manners and customs, religion and philosophy, that interested the earliest foreign observers. The contemporaries and immediate successors of Alexander seem to have had some vague knowledge of the south. A place called Keras is mentioned by Aristotle. But its identification with Kerala or Chera is not beyond doubt. Onesicritus, however, gives a description of the island of Taprobane (Tāmraparṇī or Ceylon). Eratosthenes in his description of India in the days of Alexander informs us that the most southerly part of India was occupied by the lands of Coniaci and Taprobane was seven days' sail from this place. He gathered the information that the most southerly capes of India rose opposite to the region of Meroe, from treatises written by men who had been to that region. Nearchus speaks of the setting of the Bears and if Megasthenes is to be believed this was a phenomenon observed in the southern parts of India. Aristobulus shows acquaintance with the products of "the southern land of India, (which) like Arabia and Aethiopia bears cinnamon, nard and other aromatic products." Strabo speaks of the people of the south as being like the Aethiopians in colour, but he does not specify his authority. Megasthenes speaks, in one of his doubtful fragments, of the Andrae (Andhras) who "possessed numerous villages, thirty towns defended by walls and towers, and supplied their king with an army of 100,000 infantry, 2,000 cavalry and 1,000 elephants." The tribe is referred to in certain *Brāhmaṇa* texts and is found in historical times in the region watered by the lower courses of the Godāvarī and the Kṛishṇā. Mention is also made of a tribe called the "Modubae" who are placed beyond the "Modogalingae". They are apparently identical with the Mutibas, a Dasyu tribe associated by the *Brāhmaṇa* texts, referred to above, with the Andhras.

The extreme south of India to which the designation Tamilakam or Draviḍa (Damirike of Greek writers of the earliest centuries A. D.) was applied in post-vedic times consisted of four independent principalities in the third century B. C. These were the Cholas, the Pāṇḍyas, Keralaputra and Satiyaputra. Of these Satiyaputra does not seem to have been mentioned by any author historically or traditionally assignable to the Nanda period. We shall therefore content ourselves with a brief notice of the three remaining regions.

The Chola country proper comprised the districts of Trichinpoly and Tanjore and was watered by the river Kāverī. The fame of the country in the age of the Nandas is vouched for by the celebrated grammarian Kātyāyana.

The Pāṇḍya country is represented by the modern districts of Madura, Ramnad and Tinnevelly together with the southern part of the Travancore state. It was drained by the rivers Kṛitamālā or the Vaigai and the Tāmraparṇī. Like the Cholas, the Pāṇḍyas too are mentioned by Kātyāyana. He derives the name of the country from the famous Pāṇḍu. Megasthenes also refers to the Pāṇḍaian (Pāṇḍya) country and repeats some confused traditions regarding the connection of the land with the North, with Śūrasena, Mathurā and Herakles. The Pāṇḍyan people were distributed in 365 villagee and on every day of the year a village brought the tribute to the treasury, "so that the queen (represented by the Classical writers as the daughter of Herakles) might always have the assistance of those men whose turn it was to pay the tribute in coercing those who for the time being were defaulters in their payments."[1] It is interesting to note that the chief ornaments of the Pāṇḍyas were made of sea-pearl. Arrian tells us that the Pāṇḍya queen received from her father 500 elephants, 4,000 horses and 130,000 cavalry. Pliny tells us that her descendants ruled over 3,000 cities and commanded an army of 150,000 foot and 500 elephants. According to the same authority Pāṇḍya 'is the only race in India ruled by women.' Later writers, however, refer to more than one such territory.

If the *Mahāvaṁsa* is to be believed the Pāṇḍya kingdom and its capital, were in existence even in the time of Vijayasiṁha, the traditional conquerer of Ceylon, who is represented as a contemporary of Buddha. In this region we should perhaps place the land of the Coniaci, whose name may represent Kumārikā of Indian writers. The identification with Dhanushkoṭi is less plausible.

1. M'Crindle, *Megasthenes and Arrian*, p. 159.

Kerala, the third among the classic realms of the Far South, corresponds roughly to south Malabar and seems to have extended down to central Travancore. As already stated, its identification with *Keras* of Aristotle is problematical.

Kerala may have embraced within its boundaries a district styled Mūshika. In a passage of Strabo, Onesicritus is said to have represented the "country of Mousikanos" as the *most southerly* part of India. The territory of the famous Mousikanos, the contemporary of Alexander, was, as is well known, located in the lower Indus valley. But it is not improbable that Onesicritus had heard also of the Mūshikas in the Far South and corrupted the name into Mousikanos. It may be pointed out in this connection that both Baharampur in the Murshidabad District of Bengal and Brahmapur in Ganjam have been corrupted into Berhampur by British officials.

CHAPTER II

ALEXANDER'S CAMPAIGNS IN INDIA

After Alexander's conquest of Bactria and Sogdiana, the Indian satrapy was the only province of the Persian empire into which he had not carried his arms. Of this province he must have gained some valuable knowledge from Sisikottos (Śaśigupta), the Indian mercenary leader who transferred his services from Bactria to her conqueror. Alexander also received an embassy in Sogdiana from Omphis (Āmbhi) of Takshaśilā (Taxila) which offered him the alliance of the Indian prince and sought the foreigner's aid against his powerful neighbour Porus, the first recorded instance of an Indian seeking foreign aid against fellow Indians.

At the end of the spring of 327 B. C., Alexander started on his Indian expedition leaving Amyntas behind with 3,500 horse and 10,000 foot to hold the land of the Bactrians. He crossed the Central Hindu Kush in ten days following the main road from Balkh to Kabul, and reached the rich and beautiful valley of Koh-i-Daman, where he had already founded an Alexandria, which he now strengthened with fresh recruits from the neighbourhood and from among his war-worn soldiers. He placed Nicanor in charge of the city, and appointed Tyriespes satrap of the area, dispositions intended, as was usual with Alexander, to secure his rear before advancing further.

Alexander then proceeded to Nikaia (Greek for 'city of victory'), a place that lay most likely on his route to the river Kābul. Here he offered a sacrifice to the goddess Athena, and met an Indian embassy headed by the king of Takshaśilā which 'brought him such presents as are most esteemed by the Indians' and gave him also all the elephants they had with them, twenty-five in number.

After leaving Nikaia and at some distance from the city on the way to the Kabul river, Alexander divided his army, and sent one part of it under Hephaestion and Perdiccas to the

Indus, along the course of the Kabul river, with instructions to take Peucelaotis (Pushkalāvatī, near Charsadda, N. E. of Peshawar) and other places on the way by force if they would not submit of their own accord. When they reached the Indus they were to make necessary preparations for the transport of the army across that river. We have the name of only one tribal chief, Astes, in the Peucelaotis region (the Yusufzai country) who ventured to offer resistance, and paid for it with his life. His city was captured after thirty days, and in his place was installed Sangaios (Sañjaya ?) who had quarrelled with him some time before and gone over to Taxiles. The boats built by the Greeks on reaching the Indus were such as could be taken to pieces and reassembled on reaching another river (Curtius).

Subjugation of the Swāt Valley

With the rest of the army Alexander set forth on a hard campaign in the mountains in order to secure the flank of his main line of communication. The people of these mountain tracts are called Aspasians, Gauraians and Assakenians by Arrian. The first and last of these terms are variants of the same tribal name, Aśmaka, a name known to Varāhamihira's list of tribes in North-Western India; the other rendering of the name into Aśvaka is supported by the fact that the Greeks translated it into Hippasioi (Hypasioi in Strabo). It is noteworthy that the Pushto name for the Yuzufzai still continues to be Asip or Isap. The Gauraians were doubtless closely connected with them and took their name from the river Gaurī (Panjkora), the Gouraios of the Greek texts. They were all obviously Indian tribes and are so described by the Greek writers.

The route taken by Alexander along the Khoes is not easy to follow in its details, but doubtless his operations led him for a considerable distance up the large and populous valley of the Kunar, where he fought many hard battles. In an encounter before the first important city taken by the invaders, Alexander was slightly wounded in the shoulder. The city was razed to the ground and all its inhabitants, excepting those who managed to escape to the hills, were put to the sword. Craterus and some other infantry officers were left behind to complete the subjugation of the district, while Alexander advanced to attack the Aspasians, who abandoned their capital on hearing of his approach, and were pursued with great slaughter to their mountain refuges.

Alexander then crossed the mountains to the east and entered the Bajaur valley. Here Craterus rejoined him after carrying out his orders, and was asked to find fresh inhabitants for the city of Arigaion which occupied an advantageous site, but had been burnt down and deserted by its original residents. Meanwhile Ptolemy, the son of Lagos, spotted the main Indian camp and brought news of its whereabouts to Alexander, who planned an attack against it in three divisions, one of which he led 'in person against the position occupied by the main body' of the Indian forces. Confident in the strength of their numbers, the Indians descended from the high ground they held to meet the invader on the plain below and sustained a defeat; the number of prisoners taken by the conqueror is said to have been no less than 40,000; then were captured also 230,000 oxen, from which Alexander chose the best to be sent over to Macedonia for use in agriculture. After the subjugation of the Aspasians, Alexander moved, according to Curtius, to the city of Nysa; Arrian records the visit in detail, but gives no indication of the position of Nysa, and is openly sceptical not only of the legendary details, but of the existence of the city itself. The inhabitants of Nysa offered no resistance, but sent an embassy with presents and claimed kinship with the Greeks on the score that their city had been founded by Dionysus and named after his nurse, Nysa, and that the Nysans were the descendants of his followers; the mountain near the city also bore the name Meros (thigh) because Dionysus grew, before his birth, in the thigh of Zeus. Nysa had remained a free city with its own laws ever since, and Alexander should permit them to continue as they were. 'It gratified Alexander to hear all this' from Akuphis, the leader of the Nysan deputation, and he was not inclined to be too critical of legends that were pleasing to the ears of his soldiers, and promised him the glory of excelling the achievements of Dionysus. So he offered a sacrifice to his divine predecessor and confirmed his colony in the enjoyment of its ancient laws and liberty as an aristocratic republic. When Alexander asked for three hundred horsemen from Nysa and one hundred of their best men to accompany him, Akuphis smiled and agreed readily to give the horsemen, but offered two hundred of the worst men of Nysa instead of the hundred best demanded by Alexander. The reply by no means displeased Alexander who took the cavalry and waived the other demand. He made a pilgrimage to Mount Meros (Koh-i-Mor ?) where his followers rejoiced at the sight of the ivy and laurel and wove chaplets of them for their heads while they joyfully chanted hymns to the divine forerunner of Alexander.

Marching across the land of the Gauraians and crossing the river Gaurī (Panjkora), a difficult task owing to the depth and swiftness of the stream, Alexander appeared before Massaga, 'the largest city in those parts'. Thus began the war in the upper Swat region against the Assakenoi. This powerful confederation commanded extensive territory including the whole of Swat, Buner and the valleys to the north of Buner, and extending right up to the Indus. It had an army of 20,000 cavalry'[1], and more than 30,000 infantry besides 30 elephants. Yet, it seems to have relied for defence against the invader not on fighting in open battle, but on the fortifications of its walled towns. The Greek accounts of the war contain details of several places besieged and taken by Alexander, but their position can seldom be fixed with confidence on modern maps. Stein, who knew the country very well, suggests that they 'were probably situated in the main Swat valley; for this at all times must, as now, have been the most fertile and populous portion of the territory'.

The siege of Massaga (Maśakavatī ?) the capital of the Assakenoi, lasted for four days; at the outset Alexander was wounded in the leg, 'though not severely', by an arrow from the besieged; but the Greek engines of war battered down the defences and inflicted great losses on the besieged, and their chief fell on the fourth day 'struck by a missile from an

1. Lassen and Stein give 2,000.

engine'. Among the besieged were 7,000 mercenary troops, who had no inclination to continue the arduous defence, especially after the death of the ruler of the city, and they started negotiations with Alexander; they were allowed to hill, leave the city, arms in hand, and encamp on a neighbouring on condition that they changed sides and accepted service under Alexander. But they had no wish to aid the foreigner against their countrymen and planned an escape by night to their homes; Alexander heard of this, surrounded their camp and cut them to pieces. Diodorus and Plutarch state that Alexander's conduct on this occasion was a 'foul blot on his martial fame'; he had made separate peace with the merceneries to escape the serious losses they inflicted on his forces, and then fell upon them treacherously. Massaga itself, deprived of its best defenders, was taken by storm, and according to Arrian, the mother and daughter of its ruler became prisoners of war. Curtius records a story that the queen of the city, who had an infant son whom she placed on Alexander's knees was treated indulgently by the conqueror, rather owing 'to the charms of her person than to pity for her misfortunes'. He adds that afterwards she gave birth to a child who received the name of Alexander. Justin mentions that the Indians called the queen 'the royal harlot'.

The final stages of the campaign in the Swat valley centred round Bazira (Bir-kot) and Ora (Udegram). Koinos was sent to Bazira, which was expected to surrender, and three other generals against Ora, with instructions to invest the place until the arrival of Alexander. Bazira, which stood on a lofty eminence and was strongly fortified, offered resistance to Koinos, and on hearing this, Alexander started to conduct the operations there himself. But then he learned of attempts to reinforce Ora, set on foot by Abhisares, the king of Abhisāra, territory east of the Indus. Alexander directed his march to that city first, and ordered Koinos to join him there after fortifying a position before Bazira and leaving there a garrison strong enough 'to keep the inhabitants from undisturbed access to their lands'. A sortie by the defenders of Bazira after the departure of Koinos was unsuccessful and they were confined more rigorously than before within the walls of their city. Ora was captured at the first assault with little loss to the invader, who took over all the elephants he found there. The news of the fall of Ora led the inhabitants of Bazira to abandon their city at dead of night and seek refuge in the more inaccessible heights of the neighbouring mountains. This was the end of the campaign in the Swat valley; Alexander turned Ora and Massaga into strongholds for guarding the country round about, and improved the defences of Bazira, before marching south towards the Peshawar valley to follow the line taken by Hephaestion and Perdiccas down the Kabūl river.

These generals had fortified a town called Orobatis (not identified) on their way to the Indus. Alexander now appointed Nicanor satrap of the country west of the Indus, and received the submission of Peucelaotis (Pushkalāvatī), the ancient capital of Gandhāra, stationing a garrison of Macedonian soldiers in the city under the command of Philip. Alexander then spent some days reducing minor strongholds, some on the way to the Indus, and some on its right bank, accompanied by two local chieftains Kophaios and Assagetes (Aśvajit ?).

Aornos

Before crossing the Indus, Alexander had still to deal with the last stronghold of the Assakenoi at Aornos to which they had all flocked for refuge. This place has been most satisfactorily located by Stein in the mountain ranges of Pīr-sār and Una-sār, which answer to all the topographical details contained in the Greek accounts of Alexander's operations against Aornos, accounts derived ultimately from Ptolemy, the son of Lagos, who took a prominent part in those operations.

A word may be said at this stage about political conditions in the North-West frontier of India at the time of Alexander's invasion; the Assakenoi and their neighbouring and allied tribes were supported by Abhisares, and probably also by Porus, in their resistance to the invader; Abhisāra proper is the name of the hill country between the upper Jhelūm and the Chenab; but the ruler of this territory at this time seems to have extended his sway in the west into Hazara (Urśa) up to the Indus, and on the east his territory might well have included parts of Kashmir. The ruler of Takshaśilā whose territory lay between the kingdoms of Abhisares and Porus, was on no friendly terms with them, and, as we have already seen, he welcomed the invader, hoping to have his support against his local enemies. It is not surprising then that the Assakenoi prepared themselves to defend their independence in a region impregnable because of its physical features and in close proximity to the territory of Abhisares, and that Alexander did not feel free to accept the welcome of Taxila until he had overthrown this last and most redoubtable stronghold of the tribes whose subjugation was the chief aim of the arduous campaigns he had fought in the Swat valley.

To get at this stronghold on the eastern frontier of the Assakenian country, Alexander had to move some way up the right bank of the Indus to Embolima (Amb), a city within two marches of Aornos. Here he 'left Craterus with a part of the army to gather into the city as much corn as possible and all other requisites for a prolonged stay, in order that the Macedonians, having that place as a base, might by protracted investment wear out those holding the rock, in case it should not be taken at the first assault. Alexander himself then advanced to the rock, taking with him the archers, the Agrianians, the brigade of Koinos, the lightest and best armed of the phalanx, two hundred of the companion cavalry and one hundred horse-archers'. He fixed his camp on the second day very near the rock.

Aornos is described by Arrian as a mighty mass of rock, 6,600 ft. in height with a circuit of about 22 miles; Diodorus halves the circuit, puts the height at 9,600 ft., and says that it was washed by the Indus on its southern side. 'It was ascended', says Arrian, 'by a single path cut by the hand of man, yet difficult. On the summit of the rock there was, it is also said, plenty of pure water which gushed out from a copious spring. There was timber besides, and as much good arable land as required for its cultivation the labour of a thousand men'. A report was current that this stronghold was once assaulted in vain by Hercules who had to abandon the attempt on the occurrence of a 'violent earthquake and signs from heaven', and this is said to have made Alexander the more eager for the capture of the stronghold. But it should be noted that Arrian discredits the story and says 'my own conviction is that Herakles was mentioned to make the story of its capture all the more wonderful'.

At first Alexander was at a loss how to proceed to the attack, when some people from the neighbourhood came to him, offered their submission and undertook to guide him to the most accessible portion of the rock, from which the assault on the main eminence would not be difficult. Alexander accepted their guidance and sent with them Ptolemy with a select body of light-armed troops, telling him that on securing the position he was to signal to him and to hold it with a strong force. Traversing a rough and difficult route which led most probably up the valley to the west of the Danda-Nurdai spur, Ptolemy succeeded in occupying the indicated position on the height known as Little Una, unobserved by the defending forces on the heights of Pir-Sar. He fortified his position with a palisade and a trench, and signified his success to Alexander by means of a beacon raised on a height from which it would be seen by Alexander. Alexander did see it, and he moved forward the next day with his army along the route that Ptolemy had taken; but the defenders soon saw what had happened and sent their men to the heights of Danda-Nurdai to obstruct the ascent of Alexander, which they did successfully, and then turned round and attacked the position held by Ptolemy higher up; after severe fighting in the latter part of the day, the Indians failed to carry Ptolemy's fortifications and retired at nightfall.

During the night, Alexander secured the aid of an Indian deserter and sent a letter to Ptolemy asking him not to be content on the following day with just holding his position but to attack the Indians in the rear when they sought to obstruct the passage of the main army up the hill. At daybreak he started again, and succeeded, after a hard fight in forcing a passage and effecting a junction with Ptolemy's men. But the assault on the main rock (Pir-Sar) could not be undertaken without much toil in filling up a ravine that lay between his position and the height held by the defenders. This task was begun the next day and Alexander himself supervised the operations of cutting stakes and piling up a mound towards the main rock. The mound was advanced to a length of 200 yards as a result of the first day's work, but progress became necessarily slower in the depths of the ravine. The Indians attempted to obstruct the progress of the work and, though by their sallies they inflicted some losses on the enemy, their main object was foiled by the missiles of the Greeks shot from engines which were being advanced along the mound as each section of it was completed. The work of piling up the mound went on for three days without intermission, and on the fourth a few Macedonians succeeded in forcing their way up a small hill and occupying its crest on a level with the rock. The work on the extension of the mound was continued until it was joined three days later to the small hill near the rock that had passed into Greek occupation. Seeing the extraordinary skill with which these daring operations were carried out and the success which attended them, the Indians began to feel that further resistance was hopeless and sent a messenger to Alexander offering to surrender the rock if he granted them terms of capitulation. While the negotiations were dragging on, the besieged formed plans of dispersing to their several homes under cover of night; Alexander saw this, allowed them to begin their retreat without any obstruction, and then with a picked body of seven hundred troops scaled the rock at the point abandoned by the defenders. The surprise was complete; many of the Indians were slaughtered, and many others fell over the precipices and were dashed to death; 'Alexander thus became master of the rock which had baffled Herakles himself'. He celebrated his success by offering sacrifice and worship to the gods and erected altars dedicated to Minerva and Victory. He also built a fort and gave command of it to Sisikottos before setting out to complete the conquest of the Assakenoi and rejoin his main forces on the banks of the Indus. The siege and capture of Aornos may be placed round about the month of April 326 B. C.

From Aornos, records Arrian, Alexander went in pursuit of the fleeing defenders of Aornos, who were led by a brother of the Assakenian chief killed in Massaga. The fugitives had taken refuge in the mountains with an army and some elephants. When Alexander reached Dyrta he found the city and its environs deserted, and thereupon he detached certain troops to reconnoitre the surrounding country and secure information about the enemy, particularly his elephants. Dyrta has not been identified, but the fact that a new road had to be made, without which the march across the country to the Indus would have been impracticable, seems to point to the central parts of Buner as the scene of the operations. From captives Alexander learned that the Indian prince had crossed the Indus and taken refuge with Abhisares, leaving his elephants at pasture near the Indus. These he succeeded in capturing with a loss of only two animals killed in the chase by their falling down a precipice. He also discovered a lot of serviceable timber, which he caused to be floated down the Indus to the bridge constructed long before this by the other section of the army.

When Alexander reached the bridge at Ohind, at the end of sixteen marches, he gave his army a rest of thirty days, entertaining them with games and contests. Here he was met by an embassy from Āmbhi of Takshaśilā who had recently succeeded to his father's throne, but was awaiting the arrival of Alexander to assume sovereignty. The embassy brought presents consisting of 200 talents of silver, 3,000 fat oxen, 10,000 sheep or more and 30 elephants; a force of 700 horsemen also came to the assistance of Alexander from the same prince and brought word that Āmbhi surrendered into Alexander's hands his capital Takshaśilā, 'the greatest of all the cities between the river Indus and Hydaspes'. Alexander then offered sacrifice to the gods on a magnificent scale and found the signs favourable for his crossing into India proper, the first European to set his foot on Indian soil.

Taxila

As the invader approached Takshaśilā a strange incident occurred. When he was at a distance of some four miles from the city, he was met by a whole army drawn in battle order and elephants ranged in a line; Alexander suspected treachery and instructed his troops to prepare for a battle; but Āmbhi seeing the mistake made by the Macedonians, left his army with a few friends and contrived to explain to Alexander, with the aid of an interpreter, that he meant not to fight, but to honour his foreign ally whose protection he had been soliciting for so long and with so much persistence. He surrendered himself, his army and kingdom into the hands of Alexander, and got them back as his favoured protege.

Alexander was entertained in Takshaśilā for three days with lavish hospitality, and on the fourth day he and his friends received presents of golden crowns and eighty talents of coined silver (Curtius). In his turn Alexander showed his gratification by sending to Āmbhi a thousand talents from his spoils of war 'along with many banqueting vessels of gold and silver, a vast quantity of Persian drapery, and thirty chargers from his own stalls, caparisoned as when ridden by himself'. Thus did a fraction of the loot from the store-houses of the old Persian kings find its lodgement in the palace of Takshaśilā. But Alexander's liberality on the occasion displeased some of the Macedonian generals, though it secured for him an additional force of five thousand men and the unfailing loyalty of a most useful ally. Embassies from Indian princes met Alexander here with presents and declared their submission to him; even Abhisares of the hill country sent his brother. Only Porus (Paurava), bearer of a great name coming down from the age of the *Ṛigveda*, sent a defiant reply to Alexander's message and said he would meet the invader at the frontier of his territory, but in arms. Porus was the ruler of a considerable kingdom, and its expansion was doubtless causing some stir among the neighbouring kings and tribes, and bringing about the political alliances and groupings among them at the time.

Preparing to leave Takshaśilā for the encounter with Porus, Alexander offered the customary sacrifices and celebrated a gymnastic and equestrian contest. He sent Koinos back to the Indus to dismantle the bridge of boats and bring it over to the Jhelum river, the ancient (Vitastā, the Hydaspes of the Greeks). He posted Philip, the son of Machatus, at the head of a garrison, as satrap of Takshaśilā and its neighbourhood, and began his march to the Jhelum with his own army and the

Taxilan contingent of 5,000 men commanded by their king in person. The route lay in a south-easterly direction over difficult country and was about a hundred miles in length. On his march Alexander found a defile on his road occupied by Spitaces, a nephew of Porus, with a body of troops; these he soon dispersed, and then completed his march without encountering any further opposition; Spitaces fought later on the side of his uncle and fell in the battle of the Jhelum.

Battle of the Jhelum

Alexander fixed his camp in the vicinity of the town of Jhelum on the right bank of the river; it was the spring of 326 B. C. Porus had ranged his entire forces on the opposite side, and stationed posts at various points up and down the river to watch the enemy's movements and give the alarm when he attempted to cross the river. The Paurava's army drawn from the populous villages of his principality was an imposing force. Arrian records that in the final encounter with Alexander, he employed all his cavalry, 4,000 strong, all his chariots, 300 in number, 200 of his elephants, and 30,000 efficient infantry. We should add to these numbers the 2,000 men and 120 chariots he detached earlier in the day under his son's charge to meet the enemy as he was crossing the river, as also the considerable section of the army he left behind in his original camp to oppose the crossing of the troops that Alexander left behind in *his* camp on the opposite bank. Alexander's army on the other side was made up of many elements. the heavy-armed Macedonian infantry carrying the long spear in phalanxes; and the highly disciplined cavalry; the 'Companions' of the king who were drawn from the aristocracy of Macedon and formed the core of the force. The original 2,000 Companions were much reduced in numbers and the four hipparchies into which they were now reorganised contained only one Macedonian squadron each. There were also mercenary soldiers in thousands from the Greek cities and half-civilized hill-men from the Balkan lands serving as light troops. 'But mingled with the Europeans were men of many nations. Here were troops of horsemen, representing the chivalry of Iran, which had followed Alexander from Bactria and beyond, Pashtus and men of the Hindu Kush with their highland-bred horses, Central Asiatics who could ride and shoot at the same time; and among the camp followers one could find groups representing the older civilizations of the world, Phoenicians inheriting an immemorial tradition of ship-craft and trade, bronzed Egyptians able to confront the Indians with an antiquity still longer than their own' (Bevan). The battle of Jhelum was indeed a battle of the nations. Alexander's army had already become 'a school for the fusion of races'. Of the numbers in Alexander's force we have no certain knowledge. Tradition counts 120,000 in his camp, and this number included camp followers, traders and scientific experts, besides the Asiatic wives of the Macedonian soldiers and their children. Tarn estimates the number of fighting men at some 35,000 and adds that the known formations of Alexander render any much greater number impossible. All our authorities agree that his cavalry decidedly outnumbered that of Porus.

Alexander soon saw that it was impracticable to cross the river in the face of so powerful and vigilant a foe, for the very sight of Porus' elephants would have thrown his cavalry into confusion. He had therefore to resort to a ruse and to steal a passage, as Arrian puts it. He sought at first to divert the attention of Porus by dividing his army into several columns with which he made frequent excursions in different directions, as if searching out a spot for easy passage across the river. At the same time he sent out foraging parties into the country and gathered provisions in large quantities, so as to lead the enemy to think that he intended to await a more favourable time when the melting of the snow on the mountains would stop, the river would be low and the crossing easier. The numerous feints of Alexander kept Porus at first perpetually on the move in the nights, and finally he became indifferent to the threats of crossing that never materialised. 'When Alexander had thus quieted the suspicions of Porus about his nocturnal attempts', he completed his plans for crossing the river at a point some sixteen miles above his camp. The spot chosen was completely screened from the view of Porus' camp by a remarkable bend in the river, a thickly wooded island in its middle and a bluff on the opposite bank. And

Porus' men had become so used to the noises on Alexander's side of the river that the actual preparations for the crossing were carried out with hardly any concealment and without the sentries of Porus suspecting anything unusual; a thunderstorm and a heavy downpour of rain also helped to drown the sound of arms and the shouting of orders.

The actual day chosen for the crossing was advanced by the news that Abhisares of the hill country was, notwithstanding his recent embassy to Takshaśilā, hastening with his army to the assistance of the Paurava, and it was important to force the encounter before the allies joined their forces.

Alexander laid his plans with care and precision. A strong division under Craterus and the troops of Takshaśilā were left behind in the main camp with orders to remain there as long as they saw the elephants on the opposite bank, but to attempt the passage of the river 'with all possible speed' whenever they should see the elephants withdrawn. Half way between the main camp and the island were posted the mercenary cavalry and infantry under three commanders, Meleager, Attalus and Gorgias, with instructions to cross to the other side in detachments as soon as they saw the Indians fairly engaged in battle. Alexander took the bulk of the army including the Companions under his own command and marched to the selected spot keeping at a considerable distance from the river bank to avoid detection by the enemy. Towards daybreak the storm subsided and the rain ceased. The army crossed over to the island in boats and skin rafts specially prepared for the cavalry, without being noticed by enemy sentries. Alexander himself crossed over in a thirty-oared galley accompanied by Ptolemy, afterwards king of Egypt, Perdiccas, the future regent, Lysimachus, later king of Thrace, and Seleucus who was to inherit Alexander's Asiatic empire; there also were the body-guards and one half of the hypaspists. The movements of the troops were concealed by the woody island, until, having passed it, they came within a short distance of the left bank. Then they were perceived by the Indian sentinels who rode off to convey the news to their camp. Meanwhile Alexander, who was the first to disembark, formed the cavalry into line as they came up and moved forward at their head; but he soon discovered that he had not yet reached the mainland, but was still on another island separated from it by a channel, usually shallow, but swollen into a formidable stream on account of the rain. A ford, barely passable, was at length found and the infantry crossed over breast-deep in water and the horses swam across with only their heads above the stream. On this occasion Alexander is said to have exclaimed: 'O Athenians! Can you believe what dangers I undergo to earn your applause?' Then crossing over, Alexander drew up his forces in order of battle. He posted the body-guards and cavalry on the right wing, and the horse-archers in front of them; next to these were placed the infantry with the archers and javelin-men at each extremity of the phalanx.

Having made these dispositions, Alexander led his 5,000 cavalry forward at a rapid pace; he asked the archers to hasten at the back to give support to the cavalry, while the infantry were to follow at ordinary marching pace in regular order. He decided to avail himself of his superior strength in cavalry, and was confident of defeating the entire army of Porus or keeping it engaged till the infantry came up; if, on the other hand, at the news of his marvellous crossing the enemy took to flight, he would be able to overtake and destroy the fugitives quickly. But the Paurava was no craven. When he received intelligence of the crossing, his first thought was to come up with the enemy, if possible, before he completed the landing; and he immediately sent one of his sons with 2,000 cavalry and 120 chariots to go and contest the passage. But Alexander had made even the final passage before he came up. When he saw the prince advancing, Alexander thought that Porus was approaching with his whole army and sent the horse-archers to reconnoitre. When he discovered the real strength of the advancing force he charged with all his cavalry and overwhelmed it; 400 Indians fell, Porus' son among them. The chariots were no help on ground loosened by the rain and fell into the hands of the enemy, horses and all. When the survivors went and reported to Porus that Alexander had himself crossed the river with the strongest division of his army, he was perplexed for a while by the necessity of meeting Alexander's attack and defending the passage of the river against Craterus at the same time. He took a quick decision, and leaving a part of his elephants to check Craterus, he advanced to the decisive conflict with Alexander with the bulk of his troops. Beyond the swampy ground near the river, Porus found a tract of sandy soil on the Karrī plain, suited to the movements of his forces, and there he drew up his army for the battle. He relied chiefly on his elephants and he placed them in the front of his line at intervals of a hundred feet; between and behind the elephants were ranged the infantry with huge bows capable of shooting long arrows with great force, though the looseness of the ground due to rain handicapped them badly on this occasion. One half of the cavalry was posted on each flank and the chariots in front of them.

Alexander, when he perceived the Indian troops drawn up in battle order, made his cavalry halt, to allow time for the infantry to come up and rest a while after their march, while he himself rode round the ranks considering the plan of attack to be followed. His aim was to make full use of the cavalry arm, in which he was superior, and to deprive Porus of the advantage he expected from the elephants and from his numerous infantry. He posted himself with the main body of cavalry on the right, and stationed Koinos with two squadrons on the left. He would begin the battle with an attack on the enemy's left wing, which he anticipated would draw out the enemy cavalry from the right for its protection, and in this case Koinos was to fall on their rear. His own phalanx commanded by Seleucus and others was not to take part in the action until they saw the Indian cavalry and infantry thrown into disorder by his cavalry charge. The course of the battle answered Alexander's expectations at every point. The 1,000 horse-archers were first ordered to deliver the attack and the shower of their arrows and the charges of their horses threw Porus' left wing into some confusion; Alexander then charged with the rest of his cavalry; the Indian cavalry of the right wing was summoned to the relief of the left and was taken in the rear by Koinos. Thus the Indian cavalry had to fight on two fronts, and the movements involved threw their ranks into confusion, and Alexander pressed his attack home before they could recover and complete their formation, whereupon they 'broke from their ranks and fled for shelter to the elephants as to a friendly wall'. The elephants were then urged against the Macedonian cavalry, but were soon met by the phalanx which advanced to take advantage of the confusion; but the shock of the charging elephants was too much even for the close formation of the phalanx and for some time wrought havoc among the Greek forces and afforded a chance to the Indian cavalry to rally and renew the attack. But another charge from Alexander's cavalry once more broke their ranks and drove them back upon the elephants. The engagement now became crowded into a narrow space, and the elephants being pressed from all sides became uncontrollable; many of them lost their drivers, and maddened by wounds, they turned their fury against friend and foe quite indiscriminately. The Macedonians who retained a wide and open field on the whole suffered less from the elephants as they eluded their attack by giving way when they charged, and followed them and plied them with darts when they retreated. At length many of the elephants were killed and the rest spent with wounds and toil, ceased to be formidable. Then Alexander ordered a general charge of horse and foot and the battle ended in a decisive victory for him. By this time the Macedonian divisions on the right bank had crossed over, and being fresh, were employed in the pursuit of the retreating Indians on whom they inflicted great slaughter.

The losses on the Indian side were indeed terrible; but the Greek accounts seem to exaggerate them while they are at great pains to conceal the losses on their own side. 'The loss of the Indians in killed', affirms Arrian, 'fell little short of 20,000 infantry and 3,000 cavalry, and all their chariots were broken to pieces. Two sons of Porus fell in the battle, and also Spitaces, the chief of the Indians of that district.....The elephants, moreover, that escaped destruction in the field were all captured. On Alexander's side there fell about 80 of the 6,000 infantry which had taken part in the first attack, 10 of the horse-archers who first began the action, 20 of the Companion cavalry, and 200 of the other cavalry'. Propaganda is not so modern an art as we may imagine! But the most decisive proof of the desperate nature of the struggle with the elephants and of the impression it produced on the minds of Alexander's generals is found in the course of subsequent events. The generals soon developed a stout opposition to further advance into India, and Seleucus, who had seen something of the Indian elephants in the battle of the Jhelum, when he became king was ready to cede whole provinces in order to secure an adequate number of these noble animals for his army.

Porus himself, mounted on a tall elephant, not only directed the movements of his forces but fought on to the very end of the contest; he then received a wound on his right shoulder, the only unprotected part of his body, all the rest of his person being rendered shot-proof by a coat of mail remarkable for its strength and closeness of fit; he now turned his elephant and began to retire. Alexander who had observed and admired his valour in the field was anxious to save his life and sent Taxiles after him on horseback to summon him to surrender; but the sight of this old enemy and traitor roused the indignation of the Paurava, who gave him no hearing and would have killed him, had not Taxiles instantly put his horse to the gallop and got beyond the reach of Porus'. Even this Alexander did not resent; he sent other messengers till at last Meroes (Maurya?) a friend of Porus, persuaded him to hear the message of Alexander. The Indian king, overpowered by thirst and fatigue, dismounted and took a draught of water; when he felt revived he allowed himself to be led to Alexander's presence. When the conqueror heard of his approach he rode forward with a few of the Companions to meet him and admired his handsome person and majestic stature. He saw too with wonder that Porus did not seem to be broken or abased in spirit, but advanced to meet him as one brave king would meet another after contending with him in the defence of his kingdom. Alexander, who was the first to speak, requested Porus to say how he wished to be treated. 'Treat me, O Alexander! as befits a king' was the answer of Porus. Pleased with it, Alexander replied; 'For mine own sake, O Porus! thou shalt be so treated, but do thou, in thine own behalf, ask for whatever boon thou pleasest' to which Porus said that everything was included in what he had asked. Alexander not only reinstated Porus in his kingdom, but added to it territory of still greater extent. Thus the Paurava took his place in the world-empire of Alexander for a time by the side of his old enemy, the king of Takshaśilā. Possibly Alexander meant that they should be a check on each other.

The actual date of this important battle is not free from doubt; the Greek texts are conflicting and modern commentators are also divided; the middle of May 326 B. C., rather than July, seems to have the best support.

Alexander honoured with splendid obsequies those who had fallen in battle, and made the customary offerings to the gods in acknowledgement of the victory and held the usual games and contests. He founded two cities, Nikaia, the city of victory, on the battlefield, and Boucephala on the opposite bank of the river, whence he had put out to cross the river at dawn and where Alexander's stalwart old horse Boucephalus had met his end. It was his fixed policy to knit the various provinces of his far-flung empire by means of these cities of European men. Craterus was left behind with a part of the army to build and fortify the new cities. Later, Alexander seems to have struck a coin to commemorate the battle, showing him on a galloping horse in pursuit of Porus' elephant; two specimens of the coin are known so far.[1]

After Jhelum

When Alexander took the field again with a select division of horse and foot, he invaded the land of the Glausai or Glauganikai (Glauchukāyanas) as they were called, a free tribe on the western bank of the Akesines (Chenab) living in thirty-seven cities of between five and ten thousand inhabitants each and a multitude of villages. These people were now placed under the rule of the Paurava against whom they had maintained their independence for so long. From here Taxiles, now reconciled to Porus, was sent back to his capital. The Rājā of Abhisāra, who could not join the Paurava before the battle of the Jhelum, now sent his brother with forty elephants and a money present to renew the protestations of his

1. See the Note on Early Foreign Coins in India (below).

friendship to Alexander and offer the surrender of himself and his kingdom into his hands; Alexander demanded the presence of Abhisares in person, adding that if he failed to come Alexander might go himself with his army to look for him. Envoys came also from another Porus across the Chenab, perhaps a relative, but no friend, of the great Paurava. Here too Phrataphernes, the satrap of Parthia, joined Alexander with the Thracian troops that had been left with him. At the same time urgent messages reached him from Śaśigupta at Aornos stating that the Assakenoi had risen in rebellion against their governor Nicanor and slain him; Tyriespes, the Iranian satrap of the neighbouring province on the west, and Philip, perhaps the same as was satrap of Takshaśilā, were asked to go and quell the insurrection and restore order. Here was a warning that the empire was becoming too unwieldy for effective control.

Keeping close to the hills to avoid wide crossings of the streams, Alexander still found the Akesines (Chenab) difficult to cross; it was July and the rains were in full swing; the strong current of the river over a rocky bed, somewhat less than two miles in width, caused some losses to Alexander in the crossing; it is said that the other Indian name of the river, Chandrabhāgā, sounded ominously in Greek ears.[1] And he had to leave Koinos behind to manage the rest of the transport across, and to send the Paurava home to recruit fresh troops and elephants and rejoin him with these. Alexander now pressed on to the next river, Hydraotes (Rāvi), 'not less in breadth than the Akesines, but not so rapid', leaving garrisons at suitable places along his route to secure his communications. From the banks of that river he despatched Hephaestion with enough troops into the territory of the younger Porus, who had abandoned his country with a handful of followers when he learned of the esteem of Alexander for the other Paurava. Hephaestion was to reduce the territory of the fugitive Porus and of all the independent tribes on the banks of the Rāvi, and add it to the kingdom of the great Paurava; he was also to build the walls of a city on the Chenab

1. Alexandrophagus, devourer of Alexander.

where Alexander was to settle some of his war-worn veterans on the return.

Alexander crossed the Rāvi and entered the land of the Kathaians (Kaṭhas), who were among the best fighters in the Punjab and had gathered their allies for the defence of their fortified capital, Sangala (not yet identified). These warlike Kshatriya tribes had proved their mettle a short time before against Porus and Abhisares when they marched against them; would they prevail against the new-comer from farther west? Within two days of his crossing the Rāvi, Alexander had received the submission of Pimprama (unidentified), the city of the Adraistai (Adhṛshṭas or, according to Jayaswal, Arishṭas). But the Kathaians of Sangala camped under shelter of a low hill outside the city and offered a determined resistance from behind a triple barricade of wagons. Finding his cavalry of no avail against the enemy, Alexander led the infantry on foot and after much hard fighting, compelled the Indians to seek refuge behind the city walls. Alexander now closely invested the city, and Porus joined him with a force of 5,000 Indians and several elephants; the besieged made a plan of escape by night across a shallow lake on one side of the city, but it was betrayed to Alexander, who fell upon the fugitives and forced them back into the city, after inflicting losses on them. Military engines then began to batter the walls, but before a breach was effected, the Macedonians carried the walls by escalade. The city was taken, many of the Kathaians were killed, and more taken prisoner. The desperate nature of the fighting is clear; the Greek accounts admit an unusually large number of slain and wounded in Alexander's army; and Alexander razed the city to the ground. The inhabitants of two neighbouring cities, the allies of the Kathaians, escaped a similar fate by abandoning their cities in good time.

On the Beas

Alexander asked Porus to garrison the country and himself pushed on to the Hyphasis (Beas), byond which, it was reported, lay an exceedingly fertile country inhabited by brave agriculturists enjoying an excellent system of government under an aristocracy which exercised its power with justice and moderation; besides, the land was well stocked with elephants of superior size and courage. While he was encamped on the Beas, Alexander was told by a chieftain named Bhagala (Pāṇini knew the name) about the extent and power of the Nanda empire, and Porus confirmed his statements. Such information whetted Alexander's eagerness to advance further; but his troops, especially the Macedonians, had begun to lose heart at the thought of the distance they had travelled from their homes and the hardships and dangers they had been called upon to face after their entry into India. And at the Beas the army mutinied and refused to march further. Alexander convoked an assembly of the officers and sought to rouse their enthusiasm by recounting the glory of their past achievements, by demonstrating how very near they had come to dominion over the whole world, what rich rewards awaited them at the completion of their task, and what dangers might imperil their young empire if they left some nations unconquered; he cajoled and flattered them,—all in vain. After a long and painful silence, Koinos summoned up courage to speak for the whole army. 'You see yourself', he said, 'how many Macedonians and Greeks started with you, and how few of us are left. From our ranks you sent away home from Baktra the Thessalians as soon as you saw they had no stomach for further toils, and in this you acted wisely. Of the other Greeks, some have been settled in the cities founded by you, where all of them are not willing residents; others still share our toils and dangers. They and the Macedonian army have lost some of their numbers in the fields of battle ; others have been disabled by wounds; others have been left behind in different parts of Asia, but the majority have perished by disease. A few only out of many survive, and these few possessed no longer of the same bodily strength as before, while their spirits are still more depressed. All those, whose parents are still living, have a yearning to see them—a yearning to see their wives and children—a yearning to see were it but their native land itself, a desire pardonable in men who would return home in great splendour derived from your munificence and raised from humble to high rank, and from indigence to wealth. Seek not, therefore, to lead them against their inclinations, for you will not find them the same men in the face of dangers, if they enter without heart into their contests with the enemy.' He exhorted Alexander to return home first, and then form a fresh expedition if he wished it. He also uttered an ominous warning against the visitations of the deity which no man can foresee and guard against. The army applauded the speech, Alexander resented it, and in his wrath announced that he was going forward himself with those who would follow him willingly while the rest might go home and tell their friends that they had left their king in the midst of his enemies. He withdrew into his tent and shut himself in for three days. The mood of the soldiers did not change, and Alexander recognised that after Jhelum and Sangala his army had no desire to meet another Āraṭṭa people across the Beas, who had more and better elephants than Porus. It was a severe blow to Alexander, who saved his face by offering a sacrifice preliminary to crossing the river and finding the omens unfavourable to the enterprise. He then proclaimed his decision to return, and the army received it with tears of joy and grateful shouts.

The Return

Alexander built twelve colossal altars to the gods who had led him thus far as a conqueror, and then, after a solemn sacrifice and games, he began to retrace his steps to the Rāvi and the Chenab. Plutarch records, it is not clear on what authority, that even in his day the kings of Magadha continued to hold these altars in veneration. All traces of them have disappeared long since.

The country west of the Beas was committed to the charge of Porus—'Seven nations in all, containing more than 2,000 cities'. While he was making preparations on the Chenab for his voyage to the sea, he received another embassy from Abhisares accompanied by Arsakes, ruler of the neighbouring country of Uraśa; Abhisares himself was ill and could not come, as the ambassadors Alexander had sent to him attested. Abhisares was now made satrap of his own dominions and Arsakes placed under him. Here too Alexander received welcome reinforcements, comprising 5,000 Thracian cavalry, 7,000 infantry sent by Harpalus, the king's cousin and satrap of Babylon, and 25,000 suits of armour inlaid with silver and gold which were at once distributed to the troops who badly needed them. After another sacrifice he recrossed the Chenab and reached the Jhelum where he repaired the damage caused by the rains to his two new cities and attended to other affairs of the country.

Somewhere near the land of the Kathaians lay the country of Saubhūti, the king who issued the well-known series of silver drachms bearing his name in Greek as Sophytes; the name of his country Subhūta is mentioned by Pāṇini. Its exact location is uncertain; Arrian puts it on the Hydaspes, while others place it farther East. Curtius records a dramatic interview between the tall and handsome Saubhūti and Alexander in which Saubhūti offered his submission to the conqueror, whom he entertained with splendour afterwards. The famous hunting dogs of his country were exhibited to the foreigners who were greatly impressed by them.

On the Jhelum Alexander completed his fleet by impressing all available country craft and constructing a large number of galleys, with the excellent timber that was ready, and the necessary transports for horses. In the end there were 800 ships in all. As these preparations were being made, Koinos fell ill and died, a loss both to Alexander and the army. Alexander took with him on the ships all the hypaspists, the archers, the Agrianians and the corps of the horse-guards. The rest marched in three divisions, Craterus on the right bank, Hephaestion with the elephants on the left, and Philip, satrap of the territory west of the Jhelum, following at an interval of three days; the Nysian cavalry were now sent back to Nysa. The naval squadron was commanded by Nearchus, Alexander's own ship being piloted by Onesicritus. The start was made early in November 326 with due solemnity and in proper order as Alexander poured libations out of a golden bowl to the Hydaspes, the Akesines and the Indus, and to Heracles and Ammon. The vast procession moved towards the sea as the wooded banks of the river echoed the shouts of the rowers and the beats of the oars. The people who had thronged the banks to see the strange spectacle followed the fleet to a considerable distance, for they had never before seen horses on board ship; and the extraordinary mixture of races and garbs among the crews must have furnished a picturesque sight.

On the third day Alexander halted at a place where Craterus and Hephaestion had pitched their camps each on his side of the river. All of them waited there for two days till Philip joined them and then he was sent off to the Akesines in advance, the other generals being instructed to follow him. The Malloi (Mālavas) and the Oxydrakoi (Kshudrakas) were getting ready to give a hostile reception to the invader, and Alexander wanted to press on quickly and attack them before they completed their dispositions. On the fifth day after starting again from that place, Alexander came to the confluence of the Hydaspes and the Akesines. The courses of rivers in the Punjab and Sindh have changed so completely that it is altogether impossible to follow the descriptions of the ancient historians with the aid of modern maps. The confluence of the two rivers which most probably occurred much earlier in their course in Alexander's time than at present, was a thundering rapid on a narrow bed full of dangerous eddies and whirlpools; the very noise of the waters unnerved the sailors and the best exhortations of the pilots were of no avail; many ships were damaged, and two of them sank with the greater part of their crew. But soon the river began to widen out and the fleet was moored in safety in a roadstead on the right bank, away from the current. The damaged crafts were repaired and Nearchus was ordered to sail downward till he reached the confines of the land of the Malloi where all the troops were to gather together and await orders.

Republican Tribes

Alexander himself landed with a body of picked troops and made an inroad against the Siboi (Śibis) and the Agalassoi (Agraśreṇis) to prevent their joining the powerful confederacy of the Malloi lower down the river. The Śibis, a wild people clad in skins and armed with clubs, who claimed descent from the soldiers of Hercules, made their submission when Alexander encamped near their capital. Their neighbours, the Agalassoi, were not so amenable; they had mustered an army of 40,000 foot and 3,000 horse and offered battle. They fought hard in the field and in the streets of their city, and many Macedonian soldiers fell; this roused the fury of Alexander, who set fire to the city and massacred large numbers of the inhabitants, condemning many others to slavery; a bare 3,000 sued for mercy and were spared.[1] Alexander then rejoined the fleet.

From his camp below the confluence of the Jhelum and the Chenab, Alexander planned a great drive against the tribal confederations of the Mālavas, and their allies, the Kshudrakas, who lived farther tot he East along the Beas. While he himself with his favourite troops would deliver the main attack, Hephaestion, who had gone in advance, and Ptolemy, who was to follow behind, would prevent the enemy's attempts to escape in either direction. Nearchus was to take the fleet to the next confluence of the Chenab with the Rāvi, where all forces were to assemble again at the end of the campaign.

Alexander struck across fifty miles of waterless desert and completely surprised the first city of the Mālavas he came against; the men, who were abroad in the fields unarmed, offered no resistance and were simply butchered; the rest were shut up in the city, guarded by a cordon of cavalry round the walls till the infantry came up. Then Perdiccas was sent forward to the next city, which he was to invest without attempting to storm the place till Alexander came up. The first city was now carried by assault, the citadel in the centre of it holding out somewhat longer; practically all the garrison were killed. Meanwhile Perdiccas reached the city against which he had been sent, and found it deserted; he rode in hot pursuit of the fugitives and overtook and killed some, but the bulk of them managed to escape him to the marshes of the river and beyond.

Soon Alexander came up and joined the pursuit; many of the Mālavas were overtaken and slain while crossing the Rāvi, but others made good their escape to a position of great natural strength which was also strongly fortified; here they were attacked by Peithon, who carried the fortress by assault

1. Diodorus xvii, 96

and made slaves of all who had fled to it for refuge. The next place to be attacked was a city of the Brahmins to which the Mālavas had flocked; here the resistance was desperate and most of the five thousand defenders sold their lives dear, only a few being taken prisoners. After a day's rest for the army, Alexander resumed the pursuit and, when he found the cities empty, he had the jungles scoured for fugitives, and his soldiers had instructions to kill everyone that was caught, unless he surrendered voluntarily. He himself marched against the chief city of the Mālavas; learning that they had recrossed the Rāvi and were ready to obstruct his passage, Alexander hastened to where they had dawn up in battle array, some 50,000 in numbers according to Arrian, on the right bank of the Rāvi; he plunged into the stream with his horse, and the Mālavas, not aware of the weakness of the force which Alexander took with him, withdrew from the bank without opposing the passage; when they saw the true position they returned to the fight. But Alexander kept them engaged with light charges till his infantry came up. The Mālavas now withdrew into the nearest stronghold, being hotly pursued by the enemy. In the assaults that followed the next day, the main walls of the city were yielded with little resistance; the citadel held out, and in the assault on it Alexander exposed himself in a way that nearly cost him his life; scaling ladders were few, and Alexander got up one of them, being the first to appear on the wall, a conspicuous target because of his shining arms; to escape the danger, he jumped within the citadel and only a few of his companions could join him there at once; they maintained an unequal contest for some time, but the arrows of the Mālavas killed some of them, and Alexander himself was deeply wounded in the chest, and fainted with loss of blood when the arrowhead was pulled out by Perdiccas. Possibly Alexander adopted the desperate expedient to keep up the morale of his troops in this difficult war. The danger to their king maddened the Greek troops and when they managed to gain the citadel by scrambling up the earthen walls and breaking in the gates, they did not spare man, woman or child.

When Alexander was still here, recovering from the wound, the rumour spread to the main camp that he had died of it. Even when he had himself conveyed to their midst in a few days, they still doubted if he was really alive; to carry conviction to his soldiers, he rode a horse when he should have been conveyed in a litter and walked some distance to his tent, and there was universal joy and relief in the camp. Curtius gives a long account (IX 6) of the generals' friendly impeachment of Alexander's rashness, and his defence; 'I measure myself not by the span of age, but by that of glory'.

What was left of the Mālava people after the decimation of the war sent in their submission now, and the Kshudrakas, who had been holding aloof so long as the swiftness of Alexander's movements left them no chance of going to aid the Mālavas, also sent their representatives with full authority to conclude a treaty with the invader. These ambassadors, a hundred in number, says Curtius, all rode in chariots and were men of uncommon stature and of a very dignified bearing. Their robes were of linen and embroidered with inwrought gold and purple. Alexander accepted their excuses and entertained them on a sumptuous scale before he sent them back; they returned in a few days 'with presents for Alexander which consisted of 300 horsemen, 1,030 chariots, each drawn by four horses, 1,000 Indian bucklers, a great quantity of linen cloth, 100 talents of steel, some tame lions and tigers of extraordinary size, the skins also of very large lizards, and a quantity of tortoise shells'. Alexander, demanded, according to Arrian, a thousand of their best men as hostages, and when they came, he did not like to keep them but sent them back. The two nations which had thus formally submitted were attached to the satrapy of Philip. But the campaign against the Mālavas was no unalloyed success. As a record of mere slaughter it stands out unique even in the blood-stained annals of Alexander's Indian campaigns. The deep wound in his chest, the result of a desperate expedient, left him weakened and indirectly hastened his end. The stout opposition encountered among the Brahmins of the Punjab and the cities of the Mālavas was indeed the beginning of the reaction that was soon to wipe out all traces of Alexander from India and to establish the empire of the Mauryas.

Voyage along the lower Indus

The progress of the flotilla down the Chenab and the Indus cannot be traced; nor can the confluences of the rivers mentioned by the Greek writers be identified. Arrian mentions the junctions of the Rāvi with the Chenab, and of the combined stream with the Indus. More ships were built, and more tribes submitted along the course, the Abastanoi, (Ambashṭhas), Xathaoi (Kshatriyas) and Ossadioi (Vasātis). The confluence of the Indus and the Chenab was fixed as the southern boundary of the satrapy of Philip; a city was founded there and d ckyards constructed. Complaints reached about this time against Tyriespes, the satrap of Paropamisadai, and he was replaced by Oxyartes, the father of Roxana, Alexander's favourite wife.

The country below the last confluence differed from the Punjab in its political and social conditions, which have been noted with surprise by the Greek writers. There were no free tribes here, but principalities ruled by kings whose Brahmin counsellors had great influence with them and the people. Alexander first sailed down the river to the 'royal seat' of the Sogdoi, where he founded another city with dockyards for the future trade of the city. He appointed Peithon, the son of Agenor, satrap of the lower Indus valley and the sea-board.

The greatest king of this region was known to the Greeks by the name Musicanus (Muchukarṇa ?). He did not offer his submission or even send presents, but when surprised by the sudden arrival of Alexander in his country, he adopted the course of prudence, tendered his submission and was confirmed in his territory though a garrison was installed in the citadel of his capital (Alor?), which Craterus was to fortify adequately. Alexander then took a number of cities with much booty, all from a chieftain named Oxycanus who was made prisoner. Sambus had abandoned his capital Sindimana when he heard that Alexander had made friends with his arch-enemy Musicanus; his relatives explained the situation to Alexander and offered presents, which were accepted. But the most irreconcilable enemies of the foreigners in this region were the Brahmins (Brāhmanako nāma Janapadaḥ- Patañjali) and one of their cities was carried by storm and all its inhabitants put to death. Meanwhile Musicanus, acting probably on the advice of his ministers, threw off his allegiance; Peithon who was sent against him suppressed the revolt with a strong hand. He destroyed some cities and placed garrisons in others; he took Musicanus captive and produced him before Alexander, who ordered that he should be executed along with his instigators.

Then came the ruler of Patala and the delta country and offered his submission. He was sent back to his capital with orders to prepare for the reception of the expedition. Diodorus states that in this region there were two hereditary kings and a council of elders; if that was so, one of them set out to meet Alexander and gain time, while the other was preparing for a flight; for Alexander found Patala totally deserted when he came to the city. From here, Craterus was sent away with a large section of the army with all the elephants by the route leading through the Mūla pass, Arachosia (Kandahar) and Drangiana (Seistan). With the rest of the army Alexander continued his course downstream and reached Patala in the middle of July 325 B. C.; when he found the city deserted, he sent his emissaries to overtake the fugitives and persuade them to return in safety to their lands and cultivate them as formerly, and so most of the people did return to their homes.

At Patala the Indus divided into two large rivers. Alexander foresaw a big future for the city and Hephaestion was directed to build a citadel and a harbour there. Alexander set out with some ships to explore the western arm of the river; the task was rendered difficult by lack of knowledgeable pilots, the whole country having been deserted by its inhabitants, and by the damages to his fleet due to a storm and the bore, the tidal wave that rushes with great violence up the mouths of some Indian rivers. Some native pilots were at last discovered and the vessels were steered to the open sea. Alexander offered sacrifices int wo islands in the river to some gods as prescribed by the Egyptian oracle of Ammon, and in the open sea he sacrificed bulls to the sea god Poseidona nd after pouring a libation he flung the golden goblet into the sea, praying for the safety of Nearchus and his fleet in the ensuing voyage. When he returned to Patala, he found that Peithon, who had been left behind to settle colonists in the newly fortified cities and suppress the last embers of rebellion, had arrived after completing the task.

Exploration and return to Babylon

Alexander now explored the eastern branch of the river, found that it gave easier access to the sea, and came by a large sized lake, on the shore of which he caused a harbour to be built, as a starting point for Nearchus; he ordered wells to be dug along the coast and provisions to be collected. The exact location of this lake is not easy to decide; it may have been the Rann of Cutch or the Samarah lake to the west of Umarkot. Alexander returned to Patala and completed his plans for leaving India. The Cretan Nearchus, who had successfully navigated the rivers during a long voyage of little less than a year, was to bring the fleet from the mouth of the Indus along the coast into the Persian Gulf andr ejoin him at the mouth of the Euphrates, while he himself would march with the army by land across Gedrosia keeping as close to the fleet as practicable; he is said to have chosen this difficult route because no one hadt raversed it except thel egendary Semiramis and Cyrus, who escaped with just a few followers and he wanted tos urpasst hem.

Nearchus was timed to start with the N. E. monsoon (late October); but the local tribes became threatening after Alexander's departure and he sailed down the eastern arm of the Indus late in September and had to cut his way across a sand bar at the western mouth; contrary winds detained him for twenty-four days at 'Alexander's harbour', somewhere near Karachi. When the monsoon arrived he sailed again, moving continuously along an unknown hostile coast where he had to land often for water and provisions. After traversing about a hundred m les, he came to a good harbour at the mouth of the Hab river; beyond it he coasted along the country of the Oreitai, and at a place called Kokala he came by a store of provisions deposited for the fleet by Alexander, and established contact with Leonnatus, who was fresh from an important victory against the Oreitai. There was an exchange of men between them, and the fleet was repaired and victualled before Nearchus sailed again.

Alexander started in September for his famous march through Southern Gedrosia (Mekran). His plan was to support the fleet, which needed support, by digging wells and forming depots of provisions at convenient points. When he reached the Arabios (Hab) he found the country deserted, as the Arabitai tribesmen had fled in terror. Crossing the river, he entered Las Bela, the land of the Oreitai, who offered a slight and ineffectual opposition to his progress. One of their villages, Rambakia, pleased Alexander by its situation and Hephaestion was instructed to colonise it with Arachosians (Curtius). When he passed on to the country of the Gedrosi, he appointed Apollophanes satrap over the Oreitai and left Leonnatus to reduce the country and help in thes cheme of colonisation. Leonnatus fought a pitched battle with the tribesmen, inflicting great losses on them,a nd the satrap designate, Apollophanes, was among those who fell on his side. Alexander with the rest of the army crossed into Gedrosia, and kept as close to the coast as possible to be able to serve his fleet. The route lay across a burning arid desert, and the obstacle of the mountain range ending in Cape Malan seems to have forced him into a more appalling region inland, up the valley of the Hingol. 'The blazing heat and the want of water', says Arrian, 'destroyed a great part of the army, and especially the beasts of burden, which perished from the great depth of the sand, and the heat which scorched like fire, while a great many died of thirst'. The guides lost the way, and marching was possible only by night on account of the day's heat; 'they ate the baggage-animals and burnt the carts for firewood'. At last they worked their way to the coast near the harbour of Pasni, where they found good drinking water. They reached Pura, the capital of the Gedrosians, sixty days after they had left the country of Oreitai, and then the army had some rest.

Alexander was advancing into Karmania, when tidings reached him that Philip, the satrap of the Indian country, had been murdered by his rebellious mercenaries; he heard also that the Macedonian body-guards of Philip had put his murderers to death. He could then do no more than send a message to Taxiles and Eudemus, a Thracian commander, asking them to assume charge of the province until he could send a satrap to govern it. About this time Craterus joined him with his division of the army and the elephants. Here also Alexander's anxiety about the fleet was allayed by Nearchus coming over to meet him and tell him of his strange encounters with whales and savages and of the safety of all the fleet except four vessels lost in the voyage. At the reunion all the past hardships were forgotten and some days were given to a round of feasting and sports. Then the army and the fleet proceeded to Susa, which they reached in the spring of 324 B. C. The death of Alexander in Babylon in the following year put an end to his project of world empire.

Results

The consequences of Alexander's invasion of India have been exaggerated out of all proportion by some writers and altogether denied by others. That Alexander meant to rule his Indian conquests as integral parts of his empire is clear from his division of the country into satrapies on the Persian model and from the great care he bestowed on the settlement of colonies of his followers at strategic points and on the location of dockyards and harbours along the Indus to foster the growing trade of the future. Arrian's account, as we have seen, enables us to distinguish five separate divisions of the conquered country; first there was the Paropamisadae with an Alexandria, under the Caucasus for its capital, ruled at first by Tyriespes and later by Oxyartes; the second was under Philip, the son of Machatus, at first satrap of Takshaśilā, in charge not only of the principality of Āmbhi but also of what had been the satrapy of Nicanor in the lower Kabul valley; to his charge was also given all the territory up to the Jhelum on the east and the confluence of the Indus and the Chenab in the south; the third province was the extended dominion of the Paurava where he was both king and satrap; the fourth was the satrapy of Peithon, the son of Agenor, which covered the Indus valley below the confluence and extended to the Hab on the west; lastly, there was the territory of Abhisāra in Kashmir in a somewhat less intimate relation to the empire. We can hardly doubt that, if Alexander had lived to a normal age, the connection of the satrapies with the rest of the empire would have been maintained and developed. As it is, we do not know if Aleexander even appointed a permanent successor to Philip as he intended. His generals recognised, soon after his death, that they were not equal to the task of maintaining their hold on all the territories that Alexander had brought under his sway; perhaps even Alexander felt the need for readjustments in the face of growing troubles in India after his return. In withdrawing from the Indian provinces and transferring Peithon to the west of the Indus in the second partition of the empire (321 B. C.) his successors evidently carried out what they knew to have been his own wish in the matter. The garrisons of European soldiers and the colonists in the different cities found their surroundings becoming more and more uncongenial and they rapidly faded from most of the stations. Only Eudemus at the head of the Thracian band of soldiers continued for some time as leader of the Hellenes in India; but even he quitted the scene by 317 B. C., taking with him the war elephants of Porus whom he had slain treacherously. Taxiles also disappeared from view soon after, we do not know how. And some years afterwards Seleucus surrendered his distant provinces to the Indian emperor in exchange for war-elephants.

But the invasion itself, though it lasted less than two years, was too great an occurrence to leave things just as they were. It showed clearly that an emotional love of independence was no match to the disciplined strength of a determined conqueror, though we should not fail to note that in this instance the states of North-Western India had to contend against one of the greatest generals of the world. It left the warrior tribes of the Indus river system weakened and broken, and thus paved the way for the easy extension of Mauryan rule. It demonstrated the need for a wiser political policy on the part of the Indian rulers. Who can doubt that the lessons of the invasion and the example of Alexander go far to account for the career of Chandragupta and the establishment of his empire ? At any rate the role of Taxiles does not recur in Indian history for the next fifteen centuries. Lastly, though India was not Hellenized at any time in the sense in which Western Asia was, there was much active contact between

India and the Hellenistic kingdoms, and in the realms of art, currency and astronomy India became a debtor; the fine silver coins of Sophytes with their Greek legends and their Attic weight standard are among the earliest witnesses to this development. On the European side, the expedition of Alexander brought a vast increase in the knowledge of India, which was for the most part carefully recorded by contemporaries, and availed of by later writers now accessible to us. 'Not a few of Alexander's officers and companions were men of high attainments in literature and science, and some of their number composed memoirs of his wars, in the course of which they recorded their impressions of India and the races by which they found it inhabited' (M'Crindle). Some wild tales indeed gained currency; but when all subtraction is made, the extent of new knowledge acquired was considerable. But even here exaggeration is easy; it has been said that the age of Alexander must take rank with that of Columbus as a time when a new world was discovered to Europe. But Alexander did not discover an unknown world; Greece and India had known each other for many generations, and trade contacts and other relations had long been established through the medium of the Persian empire. And Craterus in his journey from the Indus valley to Karmania evidently followed an already established route, though the navigation of the Indus, and the rounding of the coast of the Makran and the Persian Gulf by Nearchus, were a distinct gain to geography and trade, and the march of Alexander across Gedrosia a marvellous achievement of daring and leadership. The actual gain in the knowledge about India was much greater under Alexander's successors than in his own day; but he founded the empire which, even when it broke up, long retained in its parts, the impetus his genius had given it.

CHAPTER III

INDIA IN EARLY GREEK AND LATIN LITERATURE

1. *Introductory*

India and Greece met in the Persian empire some two centuries before the time of Alexander. Even earlier, Indian ideas seem to have travelled far into the West and influenced Pythagoras and his followers; true, we cannot now say by what channel this contact was made, but the similarities between Pythagorean thought and that of the Upanishads, and between the organisation and ceremonial of the Pythagorean fraternity and the ancient ascetic orders of India are too close to be treated as chance coincidences or the results of parallel developments. Aristoxenus (*c.* 330 B. C.), a Greek writer on harmonics and a pupil of Socrates, is known to have mentioned the visit of an Indian philosopher to Athens and the meeting between him and Socrates at which the scope of philosophy was discussed; and the celebrated simile of the rope and the snake, which is found in Sextus Empiricus and nowhere else in Greek or Latin literature, has been traced to Pyrrho, the founder of the Sceptic system, who accompanied Alexander to India.[1]

The accounts of any country and its people by foreign observers are of great interest to the historian of the country; for they enable him to know what impression the country made upon the minds of such observers and to estimate with greater confidence the part played by it in the general history of the world. And where, as in the case of ancient India, the native sources of history fail him partly or altogether at some points, the writings of foreigners gain great value in his eyes. Yet it is easy

1. Richard Garbe, *The Philosophy of Ancient India*, pp. 39—46, seems to me to give a much more balanced criticism of earlier writers, particularly of Leopold von Schroeder, than A. B. Keith, Pythagoras and the Doctrine of Transmigration, *JRAS*, 1909, pp. 569—606. See also Radhakrishnan, *Eastern Religions and Western Thought*, pp. 140—42. Like Garbe, I would restrict the scope of my observations to Pythagoras and his school. For Aristoxenus cited by Eusebius, see Rawlinson, India and Greece in *Ind. Art and Letters*, X (1936), pp. 57—8. For Pyrrho and Sextus Empiricus, S. J. Warren, Het Slang en Truw voorbeeld bij Sextus Empiricus en in Indie, *Versl. en Med. der kon. Akad. van Wetenschappen, Amsterdam*, IV, ix, pp. 230—244.

to exaggerate the value of the Greek writings on India. The Greek writers did evince a commendable interest in observing and recording facts; but they were also credulous purveyors of all the fable and gossip that came their way. The few who wrote before the invasion of Alexander did so mostly from hearsay and had little direct knowledge of India. The scientists and men of action who accompanied Alexander must have found most of their time taken up with planning, marching and fighting in a hostile and unknown country, and the wonder is that they succeeded in doing what they did to make India known to their countrymen; and the lands they traversed were but the fringe of Hindusthan far from the genuine centres of Hindu culture in the heart of the country. The ambassadors of the Hellenistic kings who came after Alexander, in particular Megasthenes, had better opportunities of studying the country and its people as their missions took them into their midst. But being ignorant of the language of the people, they must have depended on interpreters of sorts and experienced considerable difficulty in comprehending correctly what they saw and heard. The Chinese pilgrims of a later age who had command of the Sanskrit idiom were much better placed in this respect; but their interests were not so wide. Lastly, with very few exceptions, Herodotus being the most notable of them, all the original writings have perished, and we now depend on excerpts preserved by later writers and compilers, who, in turn, had access only at second hand to the matter they quoted. We lack the means of forming an independent integral judgment of most of our ultimate authorities. Nevertheless it is useful to study these excerpts with care, for much can be learnt thus of the geography, physical and human, of India as it was understood by contemporary Greek writers, of its fauna and flora, of its society, religious condition, and economic activity.

2. *Scylax*

The first Greek to write a book on India was the sea-captain Scylax of Caryanda whom Darius sent out *c.* 509 B.C. on a voyage of exploration to find out where the Indus emptied itself into the sea. He is said to have started from the city of

Kaspatyrus in the Paktyikan district, sailed down the stream to the sea, and after a voyage of thirty months, reached the place whence the Egyptian king Necho sent the Phoenicians to sail round Libya. 'After this voyage was completed', says Herodotus, 'Darius conquered the Indians, and made use of the sea in those parts'. Scylax's voyage might have taken him through the lower Kabul valley, parts of Kashmir and the bulk of the Indus country. We know little of Scylax's book; we do not hear of it as being a guide to Alexander in his voyage. It is certain however that Scylax started some of the fables about Indian peoples which coloured Greek traditional beliefs about India for many centuries ; there is a reference in Philostratus' Life of Apollonius of Tyana, to 'men that are shadow-footed or have long heads' and 'the other poetical fancies which the treatise of Scylax recounts' about peoples who 'didn't live anywhere on the earth, and least of all in India.' Aristotle cites Scylax's statement that in India kings had a marked superiority over those they governed.[1]

The antiquarian and geographer, Hecataeus of Miletus (B. C. 549-486)[2], might have used Scylax; he opens one of his works, *Inquiries*, with the admirable statement: 'What I write here is what I consider true; for the tales of the Greeks appear to me to be many and ridiculous.' From his other work, the *Geography*, some Indian names have survived: they are those of the river Indus; of two cities, Kaspapyros, a city of Gāndhāra, Multan according to another view, probably the same as Herodotus' Kaspatyrus, and Argante, a city in the valley of the Indus; and of some peoples, viz., the Opiai, the Kalatiai, the Sciapodes (the shadow-footed people of Scylax) and perhaps also the Pygmies. Beyond the Indus was a sandy waste, a statement in which Hecataeus is followed by Herodotus, their knowledge of India being mostly limited to the Persian part of it.

1. The chief reference to Scylax is Herodotus, IV 44. See Philostratus, *The Life of Apollonius of Tyana*, III, 47 and Aristotle, *Politics*, VII, 14, 3.

2. For Hecataeus of Miletus see *Cambridge Ancient History*. IV, pp. 518—19: Lassen, *Ind. Alt.*, ii, pp. 635—36. Foucher, *Ancient Multan*, in *Woolner Commemoration volume* (Lahore 1940) pp. 89—105 argues that Kaspapyros must be identified with Multan.

3. *Herodotus*

The references to India and Indians in Herodotus (B. C. 484-425)[1] place them in a clear light, and the monstrous races that formed the stock in trade of Greek writers on India before and after him do not make theira ppearance in his pages. India is to him the furthest region of the inhabited world towards the east, and Indians dwell nearest the rising of the sun. Of the Indians within the empire of Darius he observed that they were more numerous than any other nation known to him, and paid a tribute exceeding that of every other people, three hundred and sixty talents of gold-dust. But he knows that there were many other tribes of Indians, all of them dark-skinned, living a long way from Persia towards the south over whom King Darius had no authority. There were many tribes among Indians and they did not all speak the same language. Some were nomads, others not. Among the nomads were the Padaeans, who lived on raw flesh, including that of sick or old members of the tribe, who were offered in sacrifice to their gods—a practice attested by modern observers to have obtained till recently among some savage hill tribes. The same custom prevailed among the Kallatiai within the Persian empire. There was another tribe of marsh-dwellers who ate raw fish and wore garments of sedge. Herodotus' knowledge of the people across the Persian border was by no means confined to savages. 'There is another set of Indians whose customs are very different. They refuse to put any living animal to death, they sow no corn, and have no dwelling houses. Vegetables are their only food. There is a plant which grows wild in their country, bearing seed, about the size of millet seed, in a calyx: their wont is to gather this seed and having boiled it, calyx and all, to use it for food. If one of them is attacked with sickness, he goes forth into the wilderness, and lies down to die; no one has the least concern either for the sick or for the dead.' This is a very good account of the life of the forest-dwelling sages of India who used wild rice (*nīvāra*) for their staple food.

1. Herodotus, III, 38, 94, 98—106: VII, 65, 86: McCrindle, *Anc. Ind.* Sec. 1. The citations in the text are from Rawlinson's version, Everyman's Library Edn. Strabo, XV, 1, 56 (p. 59) for Megasthenes on cannibalism.

Within the Persian empire, the Indian tribes of Paktiyika (Pashtu country), who dwelt northward of all the rest of the Indians and resembled the Bactrians in their mode of life, were the most warlike, and from among them were selected the men who were sent to procure gold from the sandy-desert. Herodotus gives a full account of gold-digging ants of the size of dogs, which threw up mounds of the gold-dust that was collected and brought away by the Indians in camel loads during the hottest part of the day when the ants hid themselves to escape the heat; this story in some form became a permanent feature of all later Greek accounts of India; Nearchus averred that he saw the skins of these ants and that these resembled the skins of leopards;[1] Megasthenes connects the Derdai (Skt. Daradas, mod. Dards) with the gathering of ant-gold, and states that they diverted the attention of the ants by depositing the flesh of wild beasts in different places before beginning to remove the gold. Some ingenious scholars explain away the ants of the size of dogs by supposing that the ants are dervied from the name of gold *pipīlikā*, and that the native miners did keep formidable dogs which chased away the people who came to take the gold; such explanations raise more questions than they answer and are of no value. Herodotus adds that India got a small part of its gold supply from mining and both he and Megasthenes mention that some of it came from river beds.[2]

Herodotus notes that the beasts and birds of India were much bigger than those found elsewhere, except the horses, which were surpassed by the Median breed. He tells us of a

1. Strabo, XV, 44, in McCrindle, *Anc. Ind.*, p 51 where he gives references to several ancient authors mentioning the gold-digging ants: also his *Meg. and Arrian*, pp. 94—7. The *Mahābhārata*, (Cal. ed.), VII, 1860 also mentions them.

tadvai pipīlikam nāma uddhṛitam yat-pipīlikaiḥ
jātarūpaṁ droṇa-meyam ahārshuḥ puñjaśo nṛipāh

The Kumbakonam edition (II, 78, 80) reads wrongly *kuñjaśo* for *puñjaśo*. The remarkable identity in the expressions employed by Herodotus and in this verse should be noted. Modern scholars are generally inclined to trace to Indian sources most of the fabulous things narrated of India in the Greek books. Tarn, after Laufer, traces the ant-legend to Mongolian sources (*The Greeks in Bactria and India*, pp. 106—7). The Son river was called Eranoboas, Hiraṇyavāha, gold-carrier.

2. *Frag.* XXIX, pp. 78—9—Strabo, XV 1: 57. pp. 63—4. (The page references are, unless otherwise stated, to McCrindle's translations). Also Curtius, VIII, 9—*Alexander's Invasion*, p. 187.

Persian governor of Babylon who 'kept so great a number of Indian hounds, that four large villages of the plain were exempted from all other charges on condition of finding them in food'. The Indus was for him the only river, besides the Nile, that produced crocodiles.[1] Most interesting to the Greeks must have been his discovery that there were trees in India 'the fruit whereof is a wool exceeding in beauty and goodness that of sheep. The natives make their clothes of this tree wool'. 'The Indians in the army of Xerxes wore cotton dresses, and carried bows of cane, and arrows also of cane with iron at the point'. Some Indians with similar equipment rode on horses while others used chariots drawn by horses or wild asses.

4. *Ctesias.*

Ctesias the Cnidian, who wrote a book on India[2] was just one generation later than Herodotus. Ctesias spent seventeen years in the Persian court (*c.* 416-398 B. C.) as physician to the Emperor Artaxerxes Mnemon. He must have had numerous opportunities of hearing reports of India from Persian officials who visited the country and of meeting Indian merchants and ambassadors who came to the Persian court; and he obtained permission besides from the Persian king to consult the state archives. But his work has not survived except in an abridgement of Photius, a Patriarch of Constantinople in the ninth century A.D. (858-886), and a number of citations by earlier writers particularly Aelian and Pliny. In no respect does Ctesias mark an advance upon Herodotus, and almost all his statements can with perfect justice be characterised as tall lies. Even the few facts to be gathered from him—such as that all Indians were not black, that he had seen some white ones among them, and that Indians were noted for their sense of justice, their devotion to their king and their contempt of death—are too vague to be accepted with confidence, particularly from such a writer. He cannot be excused on the ground that Photius had a predilection for the fabulous and abridged his work laying stress unduly on the fabulous races and wonder-

1. I, 192 (hounds): IV, 44 (crocodiles).
2. McCrindle-*Ancient India as described by Ctesias the Cnidian,* Calcutta, 1882.

ful products of India that Ctesias had mentioned, and passing over the more valuable portions of his narrative; for no other writer found anything of value in him. The case is not much improved by our seeking to explain his dog-headed and dog-faced men, pygmies and such others by a reference to like monstrosities known to old Indian books. In fact Ctesias wrote himself down as a fibster when he described the Martikhora (man-eater), a creature of the size of a lion, with the face of a man, capable of shooting its poisonous stings from its tail to a great distance and thus killing every animal except an elephant, and added that he saw in Persia one of these monsters sent from India as gift to the Persian King !

In truth the period between Herodotus and Alexander is marked by a decided setback in the Greek knowledge of India. The Persians lost their Indian Satrapy after some time and Alexander did not come across Persian officials east of the Hindu Kush. Even Herodotus was perhaps not much read, and there is no evidence that Alexander knew of his account of Scylax's voyage. On the banks of the Indus he thought that he had reached he sources of the Nile, and on the banks of the Beas he told his soldiers that they were at no great distance from the Eastern Sea, i. e., the end of the earth in that direction.[1] It has been doubted if Alexander ever really heard of the Ganges or suspected the real extent of the contemporary empire of Magadha; the intention attributed to him of conquering the Prasii on the Ganges may well be a later legend; and possibly he knew of only the Sutlej and just one kingdom beyond, that of the Gandaridae, the conquest of which would bring him to the shore of the Eastern Ocean.[2]

5. *Historians of Alexander*

But the expedition of Alexander was the first occasion when the West began to hear a good deal about India that was based on the direct personal observation of the reporters. By that time the Greeks had begun to take an active interest in scientific pursuits, and Alexander was himself a disciple of one

1. Arrian, *Anabasis*, VI, 1 and V, 26: Strabo, XV, 1,25.
2. Cf. Tarn, *Cambridge Ancient History*, VI, pp. 410—11.

of the greatest masters of human knowledge. Though in his wars and campaigns the first place was given to military considerations, other interests of a wider character were by no means forgotten, and among his lieutenants and companions there were many scientists and literary men who later employed their pens in describing what they had seen and heard wherever they went no less than in celebrating the martial successes of Alexander. They were the first to communicate to the outside world more or less accurate knowledge of India, its physical features and products, its inhabitants and their social and political institutions. Three or four writers stand out among the contemporaries of Alexander because of the frequent references made to them by later writers. First is Nearchus, who in his account of his voyage in the Persian Gulf gave generally dependable information on many topics he happened to touch on. A Cretan by birth, he had been brought up at the Macedonian court and educated along with Alexander. His memoirs are no longer extant, but the works of Strabo and Arrian contain copious extracts from them. Then comes Onesicritus, the chief pilot of Nearchus' fleet, who wrote a life of Alexander which is now lost. He was a follower of the Cynic philosopher Diogenes, and was on this account chosen by Alexander as best fitted to initiate contact with the Indian sages of Takshaśilā. His love of the marvellous often led him into exaggerations and Strabo says tartly that 'he may as well be called the master fabulist as the master pilot of Alexander'.[1] Modern writers also differ in their estimates of his credibility. Aristobulus was another writer who accompanied Alexander and wrote a history of his wars which was one of the principal sources used by Arrian in his *Anabasis* and by Plutarch in his life of Alexander. His interest seems to have been mainly geographical; he is said to have begun writing his work very late in life when he was over eighty years of age, and the historical parts of his work seem to have suffered from the influence of a new rhetorical mode, and the Alexander myth that was already beginning to take shape. Among the contemporary historians of Alexander there was none to beat Kleitarchus;

1. XV, 129: *Anc. Ind.*, pp. 34—5: Breloer, *KS*, ii, p. 26.

he was the son of Deinon, a historian of Rhodes, and he accompanied the expedition of Alexander. His history of the expedition was full of invention and romance and was held in little esteem by those who came after him. One of Kleitarchus' stories preserved by Aelian (and Strabo) is to the effect that Alexander and his army were once, while marching through a jungle, thrown in to a panic by mistaking a group of big-sized apes for a hostile army.[1]

6. *Greek Ambassadors*

Subsequent to these writers came the ambassadors from the Hellenistic kingdoms to the Mauryan court, whose observations on India were based on a wider and somewhat closer knowledge of the country. Among them the most celebrated was, of course, Megasthenes. But there were also Deimachus, who resided for a long time in Pāṭaliputra, whither he was sent on an embassy by Seleucus to Amitraghāta (Bindusāra), the successor of Chandragupta; Patrocles, the admiral of Seleucus, who was sent out to explore the less known regions of Asia and whom Strabo described as the least mendacious of all writers on India whom he had consulted; Timosthenes, admiral of the fleet of Ptolemy Philadelphus, and Dionysius who, according to Pliny, was sent by the same ruler to the Indian King. But none of them seems to have added anything of real importance to what Megasthenes had stated about India. Megasthenes, in fact, marks the culmination of the knowledge which ancient Europe ever had of India. Writers who came after Megasthenes improved their knowledge of India's geography, but their account of Indian civilisation was accurate only in the measure in which they followed Megasthenes.

Megasthenes lived for some time with Sybyrtius, the Satrap of Arachosia, and from there Seleucus sent him out as ambassador to the court of Chandragupta, and he visited Chandragupta often during his stay at the capital; this was of course after the conclusion of the treaty of alliance between Chandragupta and Seleucus (305 B.C.).[2] Megasthenes evidently

1. *Anc. Ind. in Class. Lit.*, *pp.* 148—49.

2. Arrian (*Indica*, V) seems to say that Megasthenes visited Porus: but this has been rightly traced to a scribal error in the text of Arrian who

knew Kabul and the Panjab very well and travelled along the royal road from the frontier to the capital of the Mauryan empire. For his knowledge of the rest of India he depended on report. He wrote the *Indika*, a comprehensive work on India, apparently divided into four books describing the country, its soil, climate, animals and plants, its government and religion, the manners of the people and their arts. He sought to describe many things from the King's Court down to the remotest tribes. Many writers copied him assiduously in later times even as they cast aspersions on his veracity, as did Eratosthenes and Strabo.

Of the education and training of Megasthenes we know little. We may guess that he was an administrator and diplomat with a sober vision that sought to penetrate behind appearances and give a faithful report to his monarch of the strength and weakness of the neighbouring empire on the east. We do not know if he wrote out his work when he was in India or after his return to the West. Ina ny event his statements on the Indian State, Law and Administration must be interpreted with care in the light of his natural prepossessions as an official of a large Hellenistic State and it is probable that some of them included an argument, criticism, or correction due to what other Greek writers before him had stated on particular topics. Megasthenes has often been denounced as untrustworthy both by ancient and modern writers, but this charge applies, properly speaking, only to what he writes from hearsay, particularly on the fabulous races of India and on Herakles and the Indian Dionysus. Of the former the learned Brahmins of the country had a great deal to tell him, but he says that he did not set down everything he heard, which may be readily accepted in the light of the Purāṇic accounts of such races. Quite probably he fell into some errors, but as we can be certain in no instance that we have his very words before us, it is always doubtful if the mistake was made by Megasthenes or the writers who used his work. Let us also remember that these

might have said only that Chandragupta was greater than Porus, implying a comparison, quite natural to him, to the advantage of Megasthenes as against the earlier group of writers who accompanied Alexander. See McCrindle, *Megasthenes and Arrian*, p. 15. Lassen (ii, p. 668) accepts the interpretation of Arrian, *Anab.* V, 612, that Megasthenes visited India more than once.

writers extracted from Megasthenes just those data on India which they considered would be of interest to their readers or which lent themselves to attractive literary treatment calculated to amuse them. Of the manner in which the *Indika* of Megasthenes was used by these authors, Schwanbeck remarks: 'Since Strabo, Arrianus, and Diodorus have directed their attention to relate nearly the same things, it has resulted that the greatest part of the *Indika* has been completely lost, and that of many passages, singularly enough, three epitomes are extant, to which occasionally a fourth is added by Plinius.'[1]

7. *India : Size*

The statements of all ancient writers on the size of India and the length of its boundaries are but random guesses, and Strabo who has collected most of them, comments on their discrepancies and on the difficulty of being confident or precise in treating of Indian matters. Patrocles said that it was 15,000 stadia (1,724 miles) from the southernmost point of India to the most northerly, and this happy guess—it could not have been anything more—comes very near the truth, the real distance being 1800 miles. Other guesses are not so happy and need not be mentioned, though it may be noted that Megasthenes puts the length of the royal road he travelled by from the north-west to Pāṭaliputra at 10,000 stadia, and adds 6,000 stadia to it to arrive at the total breadth of the country, making a computation from the time taken in voyages from the sea up the Ganges to Pāṭaliputra. Eratosthenes, the President of the Alexandrian Library from 240 to 196 B.C., was the first

1. McCrindle, *Megasthenes and Arrian*, p. 19. Diodorus, native of Sicily, was a contemporary of Julius Caesar: his *Bibliotheke* comprised 40 books, some of them no longer extant: book II., chh. 35—42 epitomise Megasthenes: bk. XVII gives an account of Alexander's invasion, and XVIII and XIX contain short notices of India:—all translated by McCrindle in his works. Arrian (A. D. 132) wrote the *Anabasis* and *Indika*, using the contemporary account of Alexander and the work of Megasthenes. Strabo came from Amasia in Asia Minor, *c.* 64 B.C.—19 A.D., His *Geography* is a very comprehensive work: Bk. XV, chh, 1 and 2 are devoted to India and Ariana respectively, and are translated by McCrindle in his *Ancient India as described in Classical Literature*. Strabo drew his material mostly from the contemporaries of Alexander and from Megasthenes. Pliny he Elder, 23—79 A.D., wrote a cyclopaedic *Natural History* in thirty-seven books: the sixth book contains his geography of India, based mainly on the *Indika* of Megasthenes, translated by McCrindle, *ibid*.

real geographer of the Hellenistic age, who studied and arranged systematically all the geographical knowledge available in his day; but his conclusions on the position and configuration of India were far from correct. He thought that the country was of the shape of an irregular rhomboid with the Indus and the Himalayas for its shorter Western and Northern sides, measuring respectively 13,000 and 16,000 stadia; the longer sides each exceeded its opposite by 3,000 stadia. His orientation was completely wrong and he put the southern extremity of the peninsula farther east than the mouth of the Ganges. Some idea of the exaggerated notions entertained of the size of India may be had from Ctesias' opinion that India was not less than the rest of Asia; he was excelled by Onesicritus who regarded it as the third part of the habitable world, while Nearchus gathered that to traverse the plains only occupied a journey of four months.[1] The existence of Ceylon was vaguely known to Onesicritus.

Megasthenes greatly exaggerated the length of India from north to south, and put it at 22,300 stadia at its shortest.[2] But he is right in noting that India well nigh embraced the whole of the northern Tropic zone of the earth and in the extreme south the gnomon of the sundial may frequently be observed to cast no shadow or cast it to the southward (in summer) while the constellation of the Bear is by night invisible.[3]

8. *Climate*

In India's climate, the rains attracted their attention most, as they had not seen anything like them before. Aristobulus noted that rain fell for the first time after Alexander reached Taxila, and continued incessantly all the time he marched eastward to the Beas and back to the Jhelum; he knew that the monsoon (the Etesian winds as he calls them) brought the rain. The relatively very scanty rainfall of the lower Indus

1. Patrocles in Strabo, II, 1.2 (Falconer, i, p. 106): other writers in XV, i. 10—2 (*Anc. Ind. in Class. Lit.* pp. 15—19). See also *Megasthenes and Arrian. Frags* IV ff. Strabo, XV, 1, 15 (pp. 20—21) for Onesicritus on Ceylon (Taprobane).

2. *Frag.* VIII (p. 52).

3. *Frag.* I (Diod. II, 35), p. 30.

valley, which gets little benefit from either monsoon, did not escape him, and he notes that in the spring and summer of 325 B.C., Alexander spent nearly ten months on the voyage down the river 'without ever seeing rain even when the Etesian winds were at their height'. Eratosthenes speaks of the rains falling regularly every year both in summer and in winter.[1] He thought that the evaporation from the vast rivers was another cause of rain, besides the monsoons.

9. *Rivers*

The immensity of the Indian rivers, of the Indus and Ganges systems, is noted and commented on by Megasthenes. The Ganges 'which at its source is 30 stadia broad, flows from north to south, and empties its waters into the ocean forming the eastern boundary of the Gangaridai..........Another river, about the same size as the Ganges, called the Indus, has its sources, like its rival, in the north, and falling into the ocean forms *on its way* the boundary of India'. Besides these two great rivers and their tributaries, there were 'a great many others of every description',[2] and many of them were navigable. Arrian recognised, following Nearchus that the larger portion of India is a plain formed of alluvial deposits of the large rivers particularly the Indus and the Ganges.'[3] The erratic changes in the courses of the rivers of the Indus system were noticed by Aristobulus; once when he went on some business into the country he saw a tract of land deserted on account of the Indus having shifted its course into a new channel; there were the ruins of a thousand towns and villages once full of life.[4] During floods the rivers rose to considerable heights and inundated vast areas, the cities located on eminences being turned into islands for a time. When the water subsided and the

1. Strabo, XV, 1, 17 and 20 (pp. 21—3, 25).

2. *Frag.* I (pp. 33—4): Arrian, *Indika*, ch. 4 (pp. 186—94). Megasthenes records the fable of river Silas in which nothing would float and which petrified everything plunged in it. Fr. XXI-XXIV, pp. 65—6: 196—7.

3. Strabo, XV, 1, 16 (p. 21): Arrian's *Anabasis* Bk. V, ch. vi, pp. 88—90 of *Ancient India, Its Invasion by Alexander*.

4. Strabo, XV, 1, 19 (p. 25).

land but half dried, it was sown and planted with little labour and perfectly satisfactory results.[1]

10. *Fertility of Soil*

The soil was fertile and the greater part of it was under irrigation and bore two crops in the year both of fruit and grain. Rice, millet and sesamum were sown in summer; wheat, barley and pulse, in winter. Aristobulus noted that rice stood in water-logged fields and was sown in beds. Megasthenes traces the superior stature and the proud bearing of the people to the abundant means of subsistence at their command; he says that famine and scarcity were unknown in India. Sugar-cane is described as a reed yielding honey without bees, and the cotton plant continues to attract attention, Nearchus recording that fine webs were made from tree wool which was also used in a raw state by the Macedonians for stuffing mattresses and the padding of saddles.[2] Strabo preserves a description of the banyan tree by Onesicritus which is worth reproducing : 'there are some large trees from which branches grow out to the length even of twelve cubits. These branches then grow downwards as if they had been bent until they touch the ground. They next penetrate into the soil and take root like shoots that have been planted. Then they spring upwards and form a trunk, whence again, in the manner described, branches bend themselves downward and plant the ground with one layer after another, and so on in this order, so that from a single tree there is formed a long shady canopy like a tent supported by numerous pillars.' As regards the size of the trees, he states that 'their trunks could scarcely be clasped by five men'. Aristobulus stated that the shade of a single tree could shelter fifty horsemen from the noon tide heat, while Onesicritus put the number at four hundred; Nearchus said that even ten thousand men could rest under the shade of a single tree.[3] Many medicinal plants and roots, both salutary

1. *Ibid.*, 18 (pp. 23—24).
2. Meg. *Frags.* I, XI (pp. 31, 54—5). Strabo XV, 1,18 and 20.
3. Strabo, XV, 1, 21 (pp. 26—7). Arrian, *Indika*, xi (p. 210). Aśoka planted banyan trees on the roads: and there is an old Tamil verse which contrasts the tiny seed of the tree with its vast size capable of sheltering a whole army.

and noxious, were grown in India, and plants which yielded a great variety of dyes; Aristobulus noted that under the law any person who discovered a deadly substance without announcing its antidote at the same time rendered himself liable to the penalty of death, but one who discovered both got a reward from the king. India, like Arabia and Ethiopia, produced cinnamon, spikenard and other aromatics.[1]

11. *Minerals*

The mineral wealth of India is noted by Megasthenes. There was much gold and silver, and copper and iron in no small quantity, and tin and other metals employed in making articles of use and ornament, as well as the implements and accoutrements of war.[2] His observations on ant-gold and river-gold have been noticed already. Ceylon (Taprobane), he said, was more productive of gold and large pearls than India. He gave a good account of pearl-fishing, and stated that each shoal of oysters had a leader, to capture whom was to get the whole group. 'The fishermen allow the fleshy parts of such as they catch to rot away, and keep the bone, which forms the ornament; for the pearl in India is worth thrice its weight in refined gold.'

12. *Animals*

Among Indian animals the Elephant easily got the first place in the attention of almost every Greek observer.[3] The Indian elephants were seen to be larger and stronger than the African elephants, and Megasthenes thought that this was due to the Indian soil supplying food in unsparing profusion. The elephants of Ceylon were larger still. The longevity of an elephant's life was well known, though Onesicritus put it too high when he stated that they lived three hundred years, sometimes five hundred, and that they were very vigorous when

1. Strabo, XV, 1, 22(p. 28).

2. *Frag.* I (Diod. II, 36) p. 31: pearls, Frags. XVIII, L. B., (pp. 62, 114) and Arrian *Indika*, viii (p. 202).

3. *Frag.* I (Diod. II, 38) p. 35: *Ibid.* (Diod. II, 37) pp. 33—4: Strabo XV 1, 42 and 43 (pp. 49—50)—for one phrase here Bevan's translation is 'to sew beautifully' for McCrindle's 'to swim most admirably'-Arrian, *Indika*, XIII, XIV, pp. (213—4).

about two hundred. Arrian, obviously following Megasthenes, says more correctly that the longest lived animals attained an age of two hundred years, but many died prematurely of disease. The manner of hunting the elephant, described briefly by Nearchus and in greater detail by Megasthenes, was much the same then as the Keddah operations of today. The elephants were easily tamed and were naturally of a mild and gentle disposition, so as to approximate to rational beings. 'Some of them have taken up their drivers who have fallen in battle, and carried them off in safety from the field. Others have fought in defence of their masters who had sought refuge by creeping between their forelegs and have thus saved their lives. If in a fit of anger they kill either the man who feeds them or the man who trains them, they are so overpowered with regret that they refuse food and sometimes die of hunger'. 'They even learn to throw stones at a mark, to use weapons of war, and to swim most admirably.' Nearchus spoke of chariots drawn by elephants as a most valued possession, and made the curious statement that a woman who won the present of an elephant from her lover was highly honoured and no one thought of blaming her for sacrificing her virtue for such a prize.[1] And Strabo remarks that this contradicts Megasthenes' statement that private persons were not allowed to keep a horse or an elephant, as they were the property of kings only. The elephant corps was a great asset in war and the possession of a vast force of the largest sized elephants by the Gangaridai[2] made them the most dreaded of all the Indian states.

Next to the elephants, we find monkeys and snakes figuring prominently in the Greek accounts. In the forests on the banks of the upper Jhelum long-tailed apes of an uncommon size were found in vast numbers, and Kleitarchus' famous story of Alexander's strange encounter with a troop of them has been noticed above. They were quick to imitate everything they saw and were therefore easily caught by hunters washing their eyes with water in their presence and then leav-

1. Strabo, XV, 1, 43(p. 50) : Arrian, *Indika,* XVII, p. 222.

2. The Gangaridai and the Prasii (Prāchyas) are often mentioned together by the Greek writers and must be taken to apply to the people of the valley of Lower Ganges.

ing pots of bird-lime behind which sealed the eyes of the apes when they came and smeared their eyes with it; an alternative method was the use of baggy trousers smeared inside with bird-lime. Different varieties of monkeys were known to Megasthenes and described in detail by him as may be seen from extracts preserved by Aelian. One of these varieties so resembled men in appearance that they could easily be mistaken for ascetics, and in an Indian city called Latage they were provided every day with a regular meal under the King's orders after which they quietly withdrew to the forests without causing any damage or injury. Of another type in the eastern Himalayas we read: 'If these creatures are left unmolested, they keep within the coppices, living on wild fruit; but should they hear the hunter's halloo and the baying of the hounds they dart up the precipices with incredible speed, for they are habituated to climbing the mountains. They defend themselves by rolling down stones on their assailants, which often kill those they hit. The most difficult to catch are those which roll the stones. Some are said to have been brought, though with difficulty and after long intervals, to the Prasii, but these were either suffering from diseases or were females heavy with young.[1] Arrian remarked that the knowledge of the apes of the Indian forests was so common in his time that he did not think it necessary to say much regarding their size or the beauty which distinguishes them or the mode in which they are hunted.[2]

The smaller poisonous varieties of the snakes, spotted and nimble in their movements, were noticed by Nearchus who expressed his surprise at the multitude and malignancy of their tribe.[3] When the rivers rose in flood and filled the plains with water, they invaded the dwelling houses in villages, and on this account the people had to raise their beds to a great height from the ground, or even to abandon their homes through the presence of these pests in very large numbers. 'In

1. Strabo, XV, 1, 29 (p. 36): Meg. *Frags.* XIII, XIII B (21), (pp. 57—8. 60—61).

2. *Indika*, XV (p. 218).

3. Strabo, XV, 1, 45(pp. 51—2): Arrian, *Indika*, XV (pp. 218—19). The device of raised beds as protection against reptiles was noted by Marco Polo in South India in the 13th century A. D.

fact, were it not that a great proportion of the tribe suffered destruction by the waters, the country would be reduced to a desert. The minute size of some and the immense size of others are sources of danger; the former, because it is difficult to guard against their attacks, the latter by reason of their strength, for snakes are to be seen of sixteen cubits in length'. There were snake-charmers moving about the country and they were able to cure snake-bites, and Alexander collected round him for the benefit of his army a group of the most skilful among the snake-charmers. The longest snake seen by Aristobulus was nine cubits and a span in length, but Onesicritus[1] stated that Abisares, King of the mountain country, kept two serpents one of which was 80 cubits in length and the other 140. Megasthenes knew of pythons that could swallow stags and bulls whole. He also speaks of flying serpents, two cubits in length, which flew by night and dropped a poisonous secretion which blistered the skins of persons on whom it fell. There were also winged scorpions of an extraordinary size.[2]

Hunting dogs of astonishing strength and courage were noticed by the companions of Alexander in the country of Sophytes, and Alexander received one hundred and fifty of them as a present from him. A curious incident in Sophytes' court is related at some length by almost all the writers and here is Strabo's version of it : 'To prove their mettle, two of these dogs were set on to attack a lion, and when these were overpowered, two others were set on. When the contest was about equal, Sophytes ordered a man to seize one of the dogs by the leg and to drag him way, or if he still held on, to cut off the limb. Alexander at first refused to let the dog be so mangled, as he wished to save its life, but when Sophytes said, "I will give you four instead of it", he consented, and saw the dog allow its leg to be cut off by slow incision rather than let go its hold[3]'. It was believed that tiger blood ran in the veins of these dogs !

1. Strabo, XV, 1, 28(p. 34). It is this statement of Onesicritus for which Strabo characterises him as a 'master fabulist' as well as the master pilot of Alexander.

2. *Frags.* XII and XVI(pp. 56—61).

3. Strabo, XV, 1, 31 and 37, (pp. 38—39, 46). Note 1 on p. 39 gives references to other accounts. Meg. *Frag.* XII (p. 56).

The tiger itself the Greeks naturally had little chance of coming across. Nearchus saw the skin of a tiger, but not a live animal. He heard, however, that it equalled in size the largest horse, but for swiftness and strength no other animal could be compared to it ; that the tiger when it encountered the elephant, leapt upon the head of the elephant and strangled it with ease ; and that the animals usually seen and designated tigers were but jackals with spotted skins and larger than other jackals—which, of course, is a quaint description of leopards. According to Megasthenes the largest tigers were found in the country of the Prasii, almost twice the size of lions. He once saw a tame tiger led by four men, seizing a mule, overpowering it and dragging it to him, all by its hind leg ; such was the strength of the animal[1].

Megasthenes noted that some animals known only in a tame state in Greece were found also in the wild state in India, such as sheep, dogs, goats and oxen. The one-horned horse or *kartazon* of which a somewhat minute account is preserved by Aelian is generally taken to be the rhinoceros[2]. Nearchus came across whales of enormous size in his voyage before he entered the Persian Gulf, and Aelian probably follows Megasthenes in his interesting description of these monsters 'five times larger than the largest elephant'. The rib of a whale was as much as twenty cubits and its lip fifteen cubits[3].

Among the birds, parrots and peacocks attracted particular notice. Arrian criticises Nearchus for writing at length about parrots as if they were a curiosity and saying that they were indigenous to India ; but Aelian's account, doubtless based on Nearchus and other writers, is not devoid of interest : 'There are, I am informed, three species of them, and all these, if taught to speak, as children are taught, become as talkative as children, and speak with a human voice ; but in the words they utter a bird-like scream, and neither send out any distinct or musical notes, nor being wild and untaught are able to talk'. The same

1. Arrian. *Indika*, XV (p. 217): Strabo, XV, 1, 37, (p. 45)—Meg. *Frag.* XII, (p. 56).

2. Meg. *Frag.* XV, XVB (pp. 58—60): Strabo, XV, 1, 56 (p. 59 and *n.* 3)

3. Strabo. XV, 1, 11—12 (p. 91): Meg. *Frag.* LIX (pp. 164—65).

writer observes that the peacocks of India were the largest anywhere met, and Alexander was so charmed with their beauty that he threatened the severest penalties against any one who should kill a peacock[1].

Having gained some idea of what the Greeks knew of India's natural phenomena, we may now turn to their accounts of its humanity, social institutions and polity, and here Megasthenes is our leading authority, the attention of earlier writers having been confined to the North-west and to local customs and institutions in that part of the country. India, being of enormous size when taken as a whole, was, according to Megasthenes' information, peopled by races both diverse and numerous, not one of which was originally of foreign descent, all being evidently indigenous. Moreover, India neither received a colony from abroad, nor sent out a colony to any other nation[2]. These are statements of some historical value ; the memory of the incoming of Aryans had completely faded out, and quite probably, the movement of colonisation to the Eastern lands, Indo-china and Malaysia, had not yet begun. But the contact with the Hellenistic kingdom was already established, and the time was not distant when Asoka's zeal for Dhamma would carry the name of India far and wide to the West certainly, and possibly to the North and East as well.

13. *Legends.*

Though Megasthenes seems to have introduced his account of the legends centring round Dionysus and Herakles with the observation that he heard them from 'the men of greatest learning among the Indians', it is obvious that all the versions of these stories now accessible to us have been thoroughly edited from the Greek point of view. We may be sure that no Indian scholars ever spoke of Dionysus and Herakles under those names, and that, if anything, Megasthenes took some things that he heard to be the same as some other things known to him better, and made his own identifications before setting down his thoughts. Let us remember also that the vainglorious credulity of Alexander

1. Arrian, *Indika*, XV (p. 218): Meg. *Frag.* LIX (p. 159): Aelian, V, 21 (*Anc. Ind. in Class. Lit.*, *p.* 139, and *n.* 1).

2. *Frag.* I (Diod. II, 38), xlvi (Strabo, XV, 1, 6), *Meg.* pp. 35, 107—8.

had given a good start to these legends with the earlier writers, with whose works Megasthenes was very well acquainted. Dionysus figures in these legends as the conqueror and civiliser of India and its first ruler, the founder of cities, the teacher of industrial arts, and the establisher of religion and polity. The Oxydrakoi claimed to be descended from Dionysus, the vine grew in their country and they displayed great pomp in their processions, and their kings set out on their military expeditions in the Bacchic manner ; from these facts, modern scholars have inferred that Dionysus of these narratives was a Greek representation of the Indian god Śiva. It is difficult either to confirm or contradict this opinion, but it is clearly wrong to think that Herakles represents Kṛishṇa. There can be no doubt that some elements of Kṛishṇaism are mixed up here, for Arrian remarks : 'This Herakles is held in especial honour by the Sourasenoi (Śūrasenas) who possess two large cities, Methorā (Mathurā) and Cleisobora (Kṛishṇapura ?), and through whose country flows a navigable river called Iobanes (Yamunā).' But the mention by Megasthenes of his daughter Pandaia and of the Pāṇḍya kingdom in the south over which she was set to rule, and some other traits, particularly the Sibai (Śivas) claiming descent from Herakles, bring him once more into the cycle of Śaiva legends. Arrian gives the curious information, which doubtless he owes to Megasthenes, that from Dionysus to Sandrakottos the Indians counted 153 kings and a period of 6042 years broken by three periods of republican rule, and that Herakles came fifteen generations after Dionysus—figures which do not tally with any known Purāṇic reckonings which they resemble so much. Herakles is also said to have founded 'no small number of cities, the most renowned and greatest of which he called Palibothra'[1].

14. *People*

The Indians, says Arrian, are slender and tall in person, and of much lighter build than other men.[2] Though some of

1. Meg. *Frag.* 1 (Diod. II, 38—9). pp. 36—40: Fr. XLVI (pp. 107—111)—Strabo, XV, 1, 6—8 (pp. 11—14): Fr. LVIII (pp. 158—9): Arrian *Indika,* VII ix, (pp. 198—204).

2. *Indika,* xvii (p 221): also *Inv. of India by Alexander,* p. 85 on the stature of men in the Indus Valley.

them are dark in complexion, they neither have wooly hair, nor complexions so intensely dark as the Ethiopians, and the reason for this is found in the humid atmosphere of India.[1] Indians seldom suffered from disease and enjoyed long lives (Onesicritus gives 130 years, and even more) as they lived frugally and abstained from wine though they drank rice-beer commonly enough.[2] In the dominions of King Sophytes every new born baby was inspected when it was two months old by State officials and if any defect or deformation in its limbs was discovered it was ordered to be killed. 'In contracting marriages they do not seek an alliance with high birth, but make their choice by the looks, for beauty in children is a quality highly appreciated.' Curtius and Diodorus both give substantially the same account of this matter, obviously derived from a common source; we see from Strabo,[3] who says the same things of Kathaians, that Onesicritus is the authority for these statements. But we cannot be sure whether he wrote down exactly what he saw in India, or idealised it in the light of very similar Spartan institutions known to him. He also stated that the handsomest man was chosen as king among these peoples, and that they sought to embellish the beauty of their persons by dyeing their beards and their garments with the colours of surprising beauty which the country produced. Megasthenes attributed the great artistic skill of the Indians to the pure air they inhaled and the very finest water they drank.[4]

1. Strabo, XV, 1, 24 (pp. 29—30): Arrian, *Indika*, vi (pp. 197—8).

2. Strabo, XV, 1, 45 (p. 52)—Meg. *Frag.* XXVIII (p. 69): also Strabo, XV, 1, 34 (p. 41), Arrian, *Indika, XV*. (p. 219).

3. Curtius, IX, i (p. 219): Diod. XVII, 91 (pp. 279—80): Strabo, XV, 1,30 (p. 38). Here is Curtius' description of Sophytes and his sons as they came out of their capital city to meet Alexander; 'He was distinguished above all the other Indians by his tall and handsome figure. His royal robe, which flowed down to his very feet, was all inwrought with gold and purple. His sandals were of gold and studded with precious stones, and even his arms and wrists were curiously adorned with pearls. At his ears he wore pendents of precious stones which from their lustre and magnitude were of an inestimable value. His sceptre too was made of gold and set with beryls' (IX, 1, p. 220). Arrian, *Indika*, XVI (p. 220) cites Nearchus on Indians dyeing their beards. Some other writer cited by Strabo, XV, 1, 71 (pp. 76—7) asserts that Indians always wore white, contrary to what is said by others: he adds that they wore long hair and beards, and plaited the hair and bound it with a fillet.

4. Diod. II, 36 (p. 31).

15. *Taxila*

Taxila (Takshaśilā) was the first large city seen by Alexander and his companions after they had crossed the Indus into India proper, and in this friendly city they spent some days somewhat free from the warlike atmosphere of a military camp. It is worth our while, therefore, to gain some idea of the impression produced by this very populous and wealthy city and its institutions on the minds of the Greeks before we proceed to consider the more systematic account of Megasthenes, or rather what has survived of it. We may also review the details relating to other states and peoples in the North-west of India.

Taxila was a large city governed by good laws. The surrounding country was thickly peopled and extremely fertile, and the wealth of the city and its ruler might be judged from the presents offered to Alexander and his friends by Taxiles. Some strange and unusual customs of Taxila are noticed by Aristobulus. Those who, from poverty, were unable to marry off their daughters, exposed them in the flower of their youth for sale in the market place, advertising them by the sound of war-drums and conches ; a prospective husband was allowed to inspect the back of the girl first, then her front, and if there was mutual agreement, the alliance followed. Another custom was to throw out the dead to be devoured by vultures, doubtless a trace of Iranian influence. Polygamy was not unknown here as elsewhere, and Satī was practised among Taxilans, and the widow who refused to burn was held in contempt.[1] Satī was observed among the Kathaians also, and Strabo is frankly sceptical of Diodorus' reason for the practice, namely that it was meant to check women seeking to dispose of their husbands by poison when they happened to fall in love with younger men.[2] From Diodorus, however, we get one of the earliest and most vivid descriptions of the actual scenes that marked such occasions. An Indian commander in the Army of Eumenes was killed in battle in Iran in 316 B.C. ; he had two wives and both

1. Strabo, XV, 1, 28 (pp. 33—4): *ib.*, 62 (p.69).

2. Strabo, XV, 1, 30 (p. 38): Diodorus XIX, 33—4 (pp. 202—4). McCrindle's translation of the extract from Diodorus has been slightly altered in the light of Bevan's version at *CHI*, I p. 415. See also Diod. XVII, ch 91 (p. 279 of *Invasion* and *n*. I—i)

offered to burn themselves on his pyre ; the matter was taken to the Greek generals who decided in favour of the younger wife burning, as the elder one was with child. 'Whereupon the one who lost her cause went away weeping and wailing, rent the veil from her head; and tore her hair as if some terrible news had been told her. The other, overjoyed at her victory, set forth for the funeral pile, crowned with fillets by the women who belonged to her,and decked out splendidly as for a wedding. She was escorted by her kindred setting forth in song the praises of her virtues. When she came near to the pyre, she took off her adornments and distributed them to her servants and friends leaving them as memorials of her, as it were, to those who had loved her. Her adornments consisted of a multitude of finger-rings, set with precious stones of divers colours ; upon her head there was no small number of little golden stars, between which were placed sparkling stones of all sorts ; about her neck she wore several necklaces each a little larger than the one above it. At length she took farewell of her domestics, and was assisted by her brother to mount the pyre, and, to the great admiration of the crowd which had gathered together to see the spectacle, she made her exit from life in heroic style. For the whole army under arms marched thrice round the pile before fire was set to it, and the victim, having meanwhile laid herself by her husband's side, scorned to demean herself by uttering shrieks even when the flames were raging round her. The spectators were moved, some to pity and some to exuberant praise, while there were not wanting Greeks who condemned the custom as savage and inhumane.'

16. *Sages.*

The Greeks first met Indian sages in the neighbourhood of Taxila, and there are many versions of their meetings with tangible variations that puzzled even Strabo and still continue to vex scholars who study accuracy in such far off things. Nearchus, Onesicritus and Aristobulus all gave their own accounts, and Megasthenes worked them up with the aid perhaps of yet other accounts of which we know nothing ; all this is clear from Strabo. Arrian and Plutarch give an account of Alexander's interview with the sages which took place more likely in Taxila rather than in the country of Sambos and after his revolt.[1] Nearchus' account of the sages is brief, but illuminating as explaining the basis of some of Megasthenes' statements on Indian social organisation. 'Some of the Brahmanes take part in political life, and attend the kings as counsellors. The others are engaged in the study of nature. Kalanos belongs to the latter class. Women study philosophy along with them, and all lead an austere life.' Kalanos (Kalyāṇa ?) of Taxila was the one who allowed himself, as Plutarch narrates, to be persuaded by Taxiles to visit Alexander, accompanied him to Persia, and there, disregarding the entreaties of Alexander, burnt himself alive when he fell ill for the first time in his seventy-third year. There was unanimity among the philosophers regarding the propriety of self-immolation, and Megasthenes noticed this. Aristobulus appears to have noticed the difference between *sanyāsins* and *vānaprasthas* as he says that of the two Brāhmaṇa sages the saw, the elder had his head shaved, but the other wore his hair. Both of them were followed by their disciples. He may be right in saying that they spent their spare time in the market place, and got their food free, but that this was a privilege they enjoyed in return for their being public counsellors can hardly be accepted as a correct statement. They came to Alexander's table, took their meal standing, and exhibited feats of endurance like lying in the sun or standing on one leg for a whole day. Onesicritus states that Alexander sent him to the sages in the first instance as he heard they went about naked and did not accept invitations from other persons. He found at a distance of less

1. Nearchus in Strabo, XV, 1, 66 (p. 72): Onesicritus *ib.* 63—5 (pp. 69—72). Aristobulus, *ib.* 61 (pp. 68—9): Megasthenes, *ib.* 58—60 (pp. 64—67)—*Frag.* XLI (pp. 97—103). Plutarch, chh. 64—5 of his Life of Alexander for which see McCrindle, *Ivasion*, pp. 313—15. Also a short account of Curtius, VIII, ch. ix (p. 190). Diodorus, XVII, ch. 107 (p. 301) on self-immolation of Kalanos; also Strabo, XV, 1, 68 (pp. 73—4). Lastly, McCrindle, *Invasion*, pp. 386—92 on Kalanos. For a recent criticism, somewhat too subjective, of these accounts, see Tarn, *The Greeks in Bactria and India*, pp. 428—31, who discounts Onesicritus completely and says ; 'Onesikritos indeed put out a story that Alexander had not talked to the men himself but had sent *him* to do it: but he could do no better than make one of his Indians give the ordinary Greek account of the Golden Age and the other talk a few cynical common places, and his version never exercised any influence'. Plutarch (ch. 65, opening sentences) believed that Alexander met the sages himself and also sent Onesicritus to them.

than three miles from Taxila, fifteen men standing in different postures, and among them Kalanos and Mandanis (or Dandamis as in other texts). Kalanos gave a general account of the golden age in the past, but would not proceed further unless the Greek visitor stripped and lay down naked on the same stones with himself. The older and wiser Mandanis rebuked Kalanos for his insolence, and was more accommodating to the guest's curiosity and they compared notes on the ideas of Greek and Indian philosophers. Mandanis approved much that he heard from Onesicritus of Greek philosophy as taught by Pythagoras, Socrates and Diogenes, but criticised the Greeks for preferring custom to nature and refusing to give up clothing. Conversation was not easy as it had to be conducted through three interpreters who understood nothing of what they were asked to translate. 'One might as well expect water to flow pure through mud' said Mandanis. Alexander is said to have met no fewer than ten of these philosophers and propounded hard questions to them ; they answered them to his satisfaction and he rewarded them duly.

17. *Philosophers*

Megasthenes has much to say on Indian philosophers ; he must have gained his knowledge from previous writers as well as from personal observation. His distinction between those who inhabited the mountains and worshipped Dionysus, and those who lived in the plains and worshipped Herakles is not easily understood, and Strabo himself remarked : 'These accounts are fabulous, and are contradicted by many writers.' His account of the Brāhmaṇas and Śramaṇasis much more valuable, though there is room for doubt about what exactly he meant by these terms. The Brāhmaṇas, he says, were held in higher esteem and had a more consistent dogmatic system. The pre-natal ceremonials (*saṁskāras*), the stages of life (*āśramas*) and the rules and practices governing them, the relative freedom from restraint enjoyed by the *gṛihastha* (house-holder) were all known to Megasthenes, though on some matters he seems to portray theory rather than actual fact, as when he says that the Brāhmaṇas marry as many wives as possible to secure good progeny ; or when he gives the period of study as thirty-seven years. Their philosophy and cosmogony which had some things in common with Greek teaching on the subjects are also briefly expounded by him. He says that women were kept out of philosophical studies for fear of the bad women divulging the secret lore to unworthy people, and the good ones deserting their husbands for a life of asceticism ; but here he is contradicted by Nearchus, though on this matter quite possibly both theory and practice differed in different localities. This account of the Brāhmaṇas then is reasonably accurate and interesting as a record of the impression produced by them in the mind of an observant foreigner. But the description of the Śramaṇas is not a little puzzling, because while the name generally indicates Buddhist ascetics, there is little in the description itself which will not apply to Brāhmanical ascetics. Here is the account as reproduced by Strabo : 'Of the Sarmanes the most highly honoured are the Hylobioi. They live in forests, subsist on leaves and wild fruits, wear garments made from the bark of trees, and abstain from wine and commerce with women. The kings consult them by messengers regarding the causes of events, and use their mediation in worshipping and supplicating the gods. Next in honour to the Hylobioi are the physicians, for they apply philosophy to the study of the nature of man. They are frugal in their habits, but do not live in the fields. Their food consists of rice and barley-meal which every one gives who is asked, as well as every one who receives them as a guest. By their knowledge of medicine they know how to make marriages fertile and how to procure male or female children as may be desired. They effect cures rather by regulating diet than by the use of medicines. The remedies in most repute are ointments and plasters. All others they suppose to partake largely of a noxious nature. Both this class and the other class of persons practise fortitude as well by undergoing active toil as by enduring suffering, so that they will remain motionless for a whole day in one fixed posture. Besides these there are divines and sorcerers and those who are conversant with the rites and customs relating to the dead, who go about villages and towns begging. Those who are more cultured than these, even they allow themselves to make use of popular ideas about hell which seem to make for godliness and purity of life. Women study philosophy with some of the Sarmanes, on the condition of observing sexual continence like the men.' The name 'forest-dwellers' (Hylobioi) does create a doubt if Megasthenes had the *vānaprasthas* in mind ; but the Buddhist monks also shunned cities and villages and dwelt in forests ; and the term Sarmanes (Śramaṇas) as well as the social services described, such as healing the sick and preaching to the people seem more appropriate to the Buddhist monks than to Brahman ascetics ; again women were admitted more readily into the order of *bhikkuṇis* than among Brahmanical ascetics. If this reasoning is correct, we have here one of the earliest accounts of the Buddhist order of monks, and it is to be noted that when Megasthenes wrote, they did not yet command as much esteem in Society as the Brāhmanas. Asoka's labours for the cause of Buddhism lay still in the future ; but the *bhikkus* were already making a name for themselves by their zeal in the practice of Dhamma.

18. *North-Western India.*

To return to the notices of the North-west by Alexander's contemporaries. Nearchus noted that the laws of Indians differed from those of other nations and were not committed to writing, a statement obviously inspired by the name *smṛiti* (memory) for the law codes, and repeated by Megasthenes also. Among certain tribes, Nearchus observed, a girl was given away as the prize to the victor in a boxing match. Among others land was cultivated in common by a number of families who shared the produce in harvest time according to needs for the ensuing year, and then destroyed the remainder so as to encourage industrious habits and discourage idleness[1]. The dress worn by the Indians was made of cotton of a brighter white colour than any cotton found elsewhere, or appeared so in contrast to their dark complexion. 'They wear an under-garment of cotton which reaches below their knee half-way down to the ankles, and also two upper garments of which they throw one over their shoulders, and twist the other in folds round their head. The Indians wear also ear-rings of ivory, but only the

1. Strabo, XV, 1, 66 (p. 72). *Ib.* 53 (pp. 55—6) for Megasthenes on absence of written laws. Both Nearchus and Megasthenes knew that writing was well known in India and used for other purposes.

rich ones....Such Indians as are thought anything of use parasols as a screen from the heat. They wear shoes made of white leather, and these are elaborately trimmed, while the soles are variegated, and high healed to make the wearer seem so much the taller[1].'

19. *Arms*

Arrian give a fairly detailed account of the arms and outfit of the Indian soldiers, based on the authority of Nearchus[2]; "The foot soldiers carry a bow made of equal length with the man who bears it. This they rest upon the ground, and pressing against it with their left foot, thus discharge the arrow, having drawn the string far backwards far the shaft they use is little short of being three yards long, and there is nothing which can resist an Indian archer's shot,—neither shield nor breast-plate, nor any stronger defence if such there be. In their left hand they carry bucklers made of undressed ox-hide, which are not so broad as those who carry them, but are about as long. Some are equipped with javelins instead of bows, but all wear a sword, which is broad in the blade, but not longer than three cubits ; and this, when they engage in close fight (which they do with reluctance), they wield with both hands, to fetch down a lustier blow. The horsemen are equipped with two lances like the lances called *saunia*, and with a shorter buckler than that carried by the foot-soldiers. But they do not put saddles on their horses, nor do they curb them with bits like the bits in use among the Greeks or the Kelts, but they fit on round the extremity of the horse's mouth a circular piece of stitched raw hide studded with pricks of iron or brass pointing in-

1. Arrian, *Indika*, XVI (pp. 219—20). McCrindle's translation modified in the light of Bevan's version in *CHI*, I, p. 412. Curtius, Bk, viii, ch. 9 has the following : 'The character of the people is here, as elsewhere, formed by the position of their country and its climate. They cover their persons down to the feet with fine muslin, are shod with sandals, and coil round their heads cloths of linen (cotton). They hang precious stones as pendants from their ears, and persons of high social rank, or of great wealth, deck their wrist and upper arm with bracelets of gold. They frequently comb, but seldom cut, the hair of their head. The beard of the chin they never cut at all,but they shave off the hair from the rest of the face, so that it looks polished.' Also Strabo, XV, 1, 54 (p. 57)—Meg. Fr. XXVII (p. 70).

2. Arrian, *Indika*, XVI (pp. 220—1): cf. Strabo, XV, 1, 66 (pp. 72—73), much briefer.

wards, but not very sharp; if a man is rich he uses pricks made of ivory. Within the horse's mouth is put an iron prong like a skewer to which the reins are attached. When the rider, then, pulls the reins, the prong controls the horse, and the pricks which are attached to this prong goad the mouth, so that it cannot but obey the reins.'

The chariot and the elephant played an important part in Indian warfare. The chariot was drawn by four horses and carried six men—one archer and shield bearer on each side besides two charioteers who were also men-at-arms ; when the fighting was at close quarters, they dropped the reins and took part in the combat[1]. Aelian says, however, that the chariot carried only two men beside the charioteer ; this may have reference to chariots of smaller size. The same writer says that each elephant carried three archers besides the driver[2]. According to Curtius, an image of Hercules was borne in front of the line of the Paurava's infantry in the battle of Jhelum, and this acted as the strongest of all incentives to make the soldiers fight well[3].

20. *Skill in arts.*

Nearchus testifies to the ingenuity of Indians in works of art by citing their facility in the imitation of the sponges, curry-combs, oil-flasks and such other articles which they saw the Greeks using. Cloth was used for writing on. Copper was used fused but not wrought, with the result that vessels broke like earthenware if they fell to the ground. Prostration before kings and noblemen was unknown ; only hands were raised in salutation[4]. According to one of Strabo's sources, it was a great occasion when the king washed his hair, and the courtiers vied with each other in sending costly presents ; this seems to be a reference to the *abihsheka* of the king soon after his accession. In the processions at festivals many elephants

1. Curtius, viii, 14, (*Invasion*, p. 207).
2. Meg. *Frag.* XXXV, p. 90.
3. Curtius, *Ibid* (p. 208).
4. Strabo, XV, 1, 67 (p. 73). Curtius, viii, ch. 9, says that the tender side of the barks of trees received written characters like paper—*Invasion*, p. 186.

adorned with gold and silver were in the train, as well as four-horsed chariots and ox-waggons. There followed hosts of attendants in holiday attire carrying basins, goblets and other vessels of silver and gold some of them set with precious gems. Animals and birds also formed a feature. Kleitrachus mentioned four wheeled carriages carrying whole trees from which were suspended cages with tame birds of bright plumage and fine song.[1]

Peculiar usages

Onesicritus noted a number of usages peculiar to the kingdom of Musikanos in Sindh. They had a common meal which they ate in public as did the Lacedemonians, their food consisting of the produce of the chase. They used neither gold nor silver though they had mines of these metals. They had no slaves. and employed instead young men in the flower of their age, as the Cretans employed Aphamiotai and the Lacedemonians the Helots. They studied no science but medicine with any care, for they regarded the excessive pursuit of any art, as war for instance, to be a wicked thing. They had no actions at law but for murder and outrage ; in contracts and other matters of mutual trust, if one of the parties broke faith the other must endure it and blame himself for trusting the wrong man and not engross the attention of the citizens with his law-suits[2].

21. *Slaves*

Some of these statements particularly those relating to slavery and law-suits, were repeated by Megasthenes with a much wider application. His statement on slavery has been extracted by Diodorus, Arrian, and Strabo[3]; we may reproduce Arrian's as being the clearest and most complete of them ; 'All the Indians are free, and not one of them is a slave. The Lakedaemonians and the Indians are so far in agreement. The Lakedaemonians, however, hold the Helots as slaves, and these

1. Strabo *Ibid.* 69 (pp. 75—6) King's washing his hair is interpreted *abhisheka* by Jayaswal, *JBORS*, II, p. 99.
2. Strabo *Ibid*, 34 (p. 41).
3. Diod. II, 39 (p. 40): Arrian, *Indika*, X—*Frag.* xxvi (pp. 68—9 and 206—8): Strabo, XV, 1, 54 (p. 58).

do servile labour ; but the Indians do not even use aliens as slaves, and much less a countryman of their own.' To understand this statement in its proper sense, we should remember that Megasthenes had Onesicritus before him ; and we find him deliberately extending to all India a statement that his predecessor made particularly of one country visited by him, and equally deliberately correcting or contradicting him in regard to Helotry. Megasthenes says in effect, that there are no slaves in India as Onesicritus knew, but his comparison of the Indian servants to Helots is wrong, for the Helots were put to servile labour and were in fact slaves. Obviously Megasthenes is here thinking of slavery in its full legal and political implications according to which the slave was the chattel of his master with no rights of any kind whatsover. And by a close study of the rules of the *Arthaśāstra* on *dāsas* and *karmakaras*, serfs and hired labourers, Breloer has shown that *dāsas* were not slaves in this sense ; for they could not be employed in unclean work—servile labour as Megasthenes would call it, and they could hold and transmit property and regain their freedom by right under certain conditions. And this appears to be the correct meaning of the text before us. Megasthenes was neither misled by the mildness of Indian slavery into denying its existence, nor was he idealising Indian conditions for the edification of the Greeks, but simply stating and interpreting a fact as he saw and understood it, incidentally commenting on the view of another writer known to him[1].

22. *Deposits*

Regarding law-suits, Strabo is our only source of ascertaining what Megasthenes said, and he is known often to abridge his original very considerably. Strabo writes : 'The simplicity of their laws and their contracts is proved by the fact that they seldom go to law. .They have no suits about pledges or deposits, nor do they require either seals or witnesses, but make

1. Breloer, *Kautalya Studien*, II, Pt. i, pp. 11—69. *Contra*. Stein, *Megasthenes und Kauṭilya*, pp. 109 ff. where the argument is built on the assumption *dāsa*-(Gk.) doulos—slave. J. J. Meyer has found fault with Breloer for assumig too much knowledge of Greek law on the part of Megasthenes, but his criticism carries no conviction to me. ZII, 7, pp. 194-204 and Breloer's rejoinder, pp. 205—32.

their deposits and confide in each other[1].' This statement, which again follows the account of Nearchus, has been explained by Breloer on the assumption that the Greek writers were thinking of the elaborate Greek procedure regarding deposits which invariably needed a written document, six witnesses and a seal, and of the form of private suit (*dike*) in connection with such pledges and deposits. Witnesses and seals are, of course, known to Indian law, and the *Arthaśāstra* is no exception here. But when there is a proper meaning that we can find for the statements we get at second hand, it would be well to accept it and acquit the Greek writers of misunderstanding Indian conditions or of idealising them[2].

23. *Seven classes of the people*

Perhaps the best known section of Megasthenes is his account of the seven 'tribes' or classes of India. They are : (1) The philosophers, (2) cultivators, (3) herdsmen and hunters, (4) artisans and traders, (5) fighters, (6) overseers (Ephors or Episcopoi) and (7) councillors and assessors[3]. Megasthenes, like Nearchus, mentions two types of Brahmins—those engaged in the study of nature and practice of religion, and those who took part in political life and advised the king as counsellors. Both these classes were numerically small, but highly respected for their learning and character. The class of philosophers included two types ; first the officiating priests (*purohitas*) who conducted religious ceremonials, public and private, in return for *dakshiṇā*, were exempt from labour and taxation, and predicted the fortunes of every year at its commencement ; then there were the ascetics (*sanyāsins*) who have been mentioned already. The seventh class provided the *mantrins*, the judges, treasurers and generals for the army. The second class of culti-

1. Strabo, XV, 1, 53 (p. 56)=Meg. *Frag.* xxvii (p. 70) Also *Frag.* xxvii B and C (p. 73).

2. Breloer, *op. cit.*, pt. ii, pp. 70—158. *Contra.* Stein, *op. cit* pp. 204—5.

3. Diodorus, II, 40—41 (Meg. pp. 40—44);Arrian, *Indika*, XI—XII (pp. 208—13); Strabo, XV, 1, 39—41 and 46—49 (pp. 47—8 and 53). Also Diod. II, 36 (p. 33) for immunity of cultivators from ravages of war. Monahan, *Early History of Bengal*, p. 153, refutes Stein's doubts over this question.

vators formed the bulk of the population ; they were exempt from fighting and other services, devoted the whole of their time to tillage, and were of a mild and gentle disposition. They lived in the country and avoided towns as much as possible. In times of war, they were allowed to go about their occupation undisturbed by the surrounding conflict. In the words of Arrian : 'In times of civil war the soldiers are not allowed to molest the husbandmen or ravage their lands : hence, while the former are fighting and killing each other as they can, the latter may be seen close at hand tranquilly pursuing their work,—perhaps ploughing, or gathering in their crops, pruning the trees, or reaping the harvest.' This does not seem to be an idealised picture, but a matter of general practice and common knowledge in ancient India ; witness the telling simile in an old Buddhist commentary which says that philosophers while destroying the opinions of their adversaries must carefully respect the principles of logic which are useful to all, just as kings, while destroying the soldiers of their enemies, respect the field labourer who is the common help of both armies[1]. The cultivators paid a determinate share of the produce to the state by way of rent for the land they cultivated but did not own. On this important subject[2], we may set down the actual words of the Greek authors. Arrian says simply : 'they cultivate the soil and pay tribute to the kings and the independent cities'. Diodorus is more elaborate, but by no means more helpful ; he says : 'They pay a land-tribute to the king, because all India is the property of the Crown, and no private person is permitted to own land. Besides the land-tribute, they pay into the royal treasury a fourth part of the produce of the soil'. Lastly, Strabo has this : 'The whole of the land belongs to the Crown, and the husbandmen till it on condition of receiving as wages one-fourth of the produce.' We notice marked differences in these extracts from Megasthenes by the three writers. Arrian is silent on state ownership and says that the payment for land was of the same order in monarchies and in free cities (republics), which should

1. The citation is from *Abhidharmakośavyākhyā*—see Breloer, i. p. 118, n. Also *IHQ*, ii, (1926), p. 656.

2. U. N. Ghosal, *Ownership of Land in Ancient India*, *IHQ*, ii (1926), pp. 198—203. Also *post* chapter on Mauryan Polity.

be deemed enough to silence all attempts to restrict the application of our texts to the royal domain ; Diodorus mentions the payment of a quarter share of the produce to the state *in addition* to the tribute, while Strabo says that three-fourths were given up to the state, only a quarter going to the cultivator as wages. It may well be doubted whether these differences in the rate of land tax or rent may be properly explained as due to differences in the conditions under which cultivation was carried on under a sharing system, the landlord contributing only the land in some cases, but cattle, plough, manure and so on in different degrees in other instances. The *Arthaśāstra*, however, knows these differences, and Breloer has argued that the Mauryan polity was based on a close supervision and regulation of all agriculture and industry in the land by government agency[1]. In Taxila alone soldiers outnumbered husbandmen, as the king was at war with two of his neighbours, as he told Alexander[2].

The *third* class, shepherds and hunters, lived a nomadic life in forests, cleared the land of wild beasts, birds that devour seeds sown, and other pests, received an allowance of corn from the king for the service, and paid him tribute in cattle. The *fourth* class of artisans and traders paid taxes from their earnings, except armourers and shipwrights who received subsidies. The *fifth* class, warriors, less numerous only than the cultivators lived a life of ease and enjoyment in peace; they received a handsome pay out of which they maintained all the servants they required for cleaning their arms, keeping their horses, driving their elephants and chariots and attending on them at home and in camp. The *sixth* class evidently includes both officials openly employed for the supervision of the work of the different departments, the *Mahāmātras* and *Adhyakshas*, and the numerous spies (assisted by the courtesans) who were engaged in the constant communication of secret information about all men and things to the king and, in republics, to the magistrates.

1. Breloer, *KS*, i, pp. 77—93 ; *contra.* Stein, *op. cit.*, pp. 126—9.

2. 'When Alexander asked him whether he had more husbandmen or soldiers, he replied that as he was at war with two kings he required more soldiers than field labourers.' Curtius, viii, ch. 12 (*Invasion*, p. 202.).

24. *Marriage and occupation rules.*

Diodorus concludes his summary of this class-organisation with the following observations : 'Such, then, are about the parts into which the body politic of India is divided. No one is allowed to marry out of his own class, or to exercise any calling or art except his own : for instance, a soldier cannot become a husbandman or an artisan a philosopher.' Arrian has also similar remarks at the end with this addition : 'It is permitted that the sophist only be from any class ; for the life of the sophist is not an easy one, but the hardest of all.' By sophist of course an ascetic is meant here. Strabo also gives these restrictions regarding marriage and occupation, but adds that the philosophers are exempt from them on account of their superior merit. The stress laid on endogamy and the adherence to one's own occupation (*svadharma*), the only exception being in favour of the Brahmin, clearly indicate that Megasthenes did mean to describe the caste-system as we should now call it ; but these restrictions obviously had no meaning with reference to some of his classes, particularly the sixth and seventh[1]. Either he did not hear of the theory of the four *varṇas*, or was carried away by a desire, natural in a Hellenistic Greek, to establish a similarity between Egypt and India in social organisation[2]. Allowing for all its inaccuracies, there is still much in Megasthenes' picture that is true to reality and is borne out by Indian literary works including the *Arthaśāstra.*

25. *Food and drink.*

The Indians, says Megasthenes, lived frugally, and, being simple in their manners, led happy lives. Their staple food was rice, and there was no common meal hour, each one taking

1. Breloer has argued that Megasthenes must have applied the term *mesos* to the classes, and used *genos* only in the statement on endogamy, that Diodorus and Strabo kept up this distinction, while Arrian has caused confusion by applying the term 'genos' to the Seven classes. In other words, the rule regarding endogamy is a piece of family law that stands apart from the division of the population into seven classes. *ZDMG*, 1934, p. 137. But I hesitate to accept this ingenious argument. Breloer has also sought to show on the strength of Pliny, VI, 19 (22) sec 66 and Solinus 52, 9 that Megasthenes made up his seven classes from the five of Taxila polity mentioned by an earlier writer, most probably Onesicritus, and that Herodotus' classes of Egypt had little to do with it. *Ibid* pp. 147—64.

2. 'The Egyptians are divided into seven distinct classes—these are the priests, the warriors, the cowherds, the swineherds, the tradesmen, the interpreters, and the boatmen'. Herodotus, II, 164.

his food by himself when he felt inclined ; 'the contrary custom would be better for the ends of social and civil life'[1]. At supper a table was placed before each person and a golden bowl on it ; into this they first put boiled rice and then they added many dainties prepared in the Indian way[2]. They drank wine only at sacrifices, at which they did not stab the victim, but strangled it in order that only what is entire may be offered to the deity.

26. *Crime and Punishment.*

Theft was of rare occurrence, and in Chandragupta's camp of 400,000 men, the thefts reported on any day did not exceed 200 drachmae (about Rs. 100)[3]. Love of finery and ornament was indulged in by those who could afford it. They had their bodies massaged by means of smooth rollers of ebony ; they wore robes worked in gold, ornaments set with precious stones, and flowered garments of the finest muslin. They married a number of wives, some for children and others for pleasure[4]. The code of punishments was severe, and threatened mutilation for bearing false witness, and death for causing the loss of the hand or eye of the artisan. In other cases of bodily injury, the offender not only paid the penalty according to *lex talionis* but had his hand cut off as well. Indians were peculiarly distinguished among the nations as lovers of dance and song ; they reared no costly monuments for the commemoration of the dead, but celebrated their virtues in song[5].

27. *Pāṭaliputra*

India was a land of many towns, and Megasthenes was aware of the difference in administrative organisation between town

1. *Frag.* XXVII (pp. 69—70)=Strabo, XV, 1, 53—4 (pp. 55—8).
2. *Frag.* XXVIII (p. 74).
3. One sentence of strabo is usually translated : 'Their houses and property are for the most part unguarded'. But Breloer questions the correctness of the text and holds that the last word should properly read 'guarded', implying a contrast between the stronger closed part of a house and its more open portions—a plan of house building imposed by the climate and prevailing even now. *KS*, ii, p. 9.
4. Purchase of wives from their parents in exchange for a yoke of oxen is mentioned in this context as a universal rule ; but this is surely due to some misunderstanding on the part of Megasthenes or Strabo. The prescription is known to Indian law-books and applies only to the *ārsha* form of marriage.
5. Arrian, *Anabasis*, vi, 3, (*Invasion*, p. 136) , *Indika*, X (p. 204)=Meg. *Frag.* XXVI (pp. 67—8).

and country. Cities situated on the banks of rivers or on the sea coast were built of wood as they were liable to frequent damage from rain and flood, while those standing on commanding situations or lofty eminences were built of brick and mud. Pāṭaliputra at the confluence of the Ganges and the Son was the largest Indian city[1]. The palace of Chandragupta, 'the greatest of all the kings of the country', far surpassed those of Susa an Ekbatana in its splendour and magnificence. In its parks were kept tame peacocks and pheasants. There were shady groves and meadows planted with trees the branches of which were cunningly interwoven by the art of the horticulturist. And the trees were kept ever green and never seemed to grow old or shed their leaves. Some were native to the soil, others brought from other lands with great care for their beauty, but the olive was not among them. Birds were there, not confined, but coming of their own accord and making their nests and forming lairs on the branches of the trees. Parrots were native to the land and were maintained in large numbers, as they were valued for their capacity to imitate human speech ; they often hovered in groups round about the king. In the palace grounds there were artificial ponds of great beauty filled with fish of enormous size but quite tame. No one had permission to catch them ; but the king's sons, when they were children, learned to fish and to swim at the same time in these tranquil ponds, learning also how to sail their boats[2].

1. Meg. *Frag.* XXV (pp. 66—7)=Strabo, XV, 1, 35—6 (pp. 42—4) : *Frag,* XXVI (pp. 68—9)=Arrian *Indika,* X (pp. 204—6). Also Pliny at *Meg.* p. 139. Details reproduced in Chapter on Chandragupta.

2. Aelian, XIII, Ch. 18 (*Anc. Ind. in Class. Lit.*, pp. 141—2). Curtius, viii, 9, on the King and the palace may be cited here for comparison: 'The luxury of their kings, or as they call it, their magnificence, is carried to a vicious excess without a parallel in the world. When the king condescends to show himself in public his attendants carry in their hands silver censers, and perfume with incense all the road by which it is his pleasure to be conveyed. He lolls in a golden palanquin, garnished with pearls, which dangle all round it, and he is robed in fine muslin embroidered with purple and gold. Behind his palanquin follow men-at-arms and his body-guards, of whom some carry boughs of trees, on which birds are perched trained to interrupt business with their cries. The palace is adorned with gilded pillars clasped all round by a vine embossed in gold, while silver images of those birds which most charm the eye diversify the workmanship. The palace is open to all comers even when the king is having his hair combed and dressed. It is then that he gives audience to ambassadors, and administers justice to his subjects. His slippers being after this taken off, his feet are rubbed with scented ointments. His principal exercise is hunting ; amid the vows and songs of his courtesans he shoots the

28. *Women in the Palace*

The king's personal wants were attended to by women. The bodyguards and soldiery were posted outside the palace gates. The statements that a woman who killed the king when drunk became the wife of his successor, and that the king might not sleep during day, and was obliged to change his couch often by night with a view to defeat plots against his life, must be treated as curious gossip rather than be accepted for facts as some writers do. On the other hand, the role of women in the personal service of the king is well attested in Indian literature, and Kauṭilya lays down many precautions to be observed as a routine for ensuring the personal comfort and safety of the king (*ātmarakshitakam*). The king spent much time outside his palace hearing and judging cases, and he did this even while he was being massaged. He went out for offering sacrifice, and for the chase. The hunting procession was a somewhat Bacchanalian display. 'Crowds of women surround him, and outside of this circle spearmen are ranged. The road is marked off with ropes, and it is death, for man and woman alike, to pass within the ropes. Men with drums and gongs lead the procession. The king hunts in the enclosures and shoots arrows from a platform. At his side stand two or three armed women. If he hunts in the open grounds he shoots from the back of an elephant. Of the women, some are in chariots, some on horses, and some even on elephants, and they are equipped with weapons of every kind as if they were going on a campaign[1]'. Curtius gives a more rhetorical account of the king and his doings.

game enclosed within the royal park. The arrows, which are two cubits long, are discharged with more effort than effect, for though the force of these missiles depends on their lightness they are loaded with an obnoxious weight. He rides on horse-back when making short journeys, but when bound on a distant expedition he rides in a chariot (howdah) mounted on elephants and, huge as these animals are, their bodies are covered completely over with trappings of gold. That no form of shameless profligacy may be wanting, he is accompanied by a long train of courtesans carried in golden palanquins and this troop holds a separate place in the procession from the queen's retinue, and is as sumptuously appointed. .His food is prepared by women, who also serve him with wine, which is much used by all Indians. When the king falls into a drunken sleep his courtesans carry him away to his bedchamber, invoking the gods of the night in their native hymns" (*Invasion*, pp. 188—190).

1. Meg. *Frag.* XXVI (pp. 71—2)=Strabo, XV, 1, 53 (p. 58).

29. *Administration*

The administrative organisation of the Mauryan state is described by Megasthenes under three heads : (1) rural administration, (2) city administration and (3) military administration[1]. The distinction between town and country for administrative purposes was well established in Indian polity, as is clear from the constant references to *paura* and *jānapada* in literature ; and as the Mauryan empire was the nearest approach to a war-state ever attained in India, army administration attracted the special attention of an observer of the type of Megasthenes. The picture he presents is that of a highly organised and efficient bureaucracy engaged in regulating activities in almost every important sphere of national life.

The officials of the rural branch so to say, to whom Megasthenes applied the general designation *agronomoi*, supervised irrigation and land-measurement, hunting and enforcement of forest laws and all the occupations connected with agriculture mining, carpentry and metal industries. They also collected taxes and maintained the roads, setting up mile-stones indicating distances at every ten stades (a little over a mile). This seems to be a summary account of the duties of a large number of officials rather than of the activities of a single board[2].

Those in charge of the city (the *astynomoi*) were divided into six bodies of five each. Their functions were respectively (1) supervision of industrial establishments ; (2) care of foreigners including provision of lodging and assistants who would watch their doings, attention to sick persons and burying the dead[3] ; (3) census of population and property ; (4) control of trade

1. Meg. *Frag.* XXXIV (pp. 86—9)=Strabo XV, 1, 50—2 (pp. 53—5). McCrindle's translation saying that the first class of officers 'have charge of the market' is now seen to be a mistake due to the word *agoronomoi* having somehow crept into Strabo's text in the place of *agronomoi* which is obviously required by the context. Cf. Stein, *Op. cit.*, pp. 233—4. Monahan *Early History of Bengal*, pp. 160—61, traces analogies in detail between Megasthenes and Kauṭilya in the administrative organisation of town and country.

2. *Contra* Stein, *Op. cit.*, p. 235.

3. Cf. Meg. *Frag.* I—Diod. II, 42 (pp. 44—5). 'Among the Indians officers are appointed even for foreigners, whose duty is to see that no foreigner is wronged. Should any of them lose his health, they send physicians to attend him, and take care of him otherwise, and if he dies they bury him, and deliver over such property as he leaves to his relatives. The judges also decide cases in which foreigners are concerned, with the greatest care, and come down sharply on those who take unfair advantage of them.'

and commerce, regulation of weights and measures, and marking with the official stamp articles passed for sale[1], no one being allowed to deal in more than one commodity except on payment of a double-tax ; (5) similar duties regarding manufactured goods, the traders being required strictly not to mix new goods with old ; (6) collection of the tax of ten per cent on sales, the penalty for evasion being death. The six bodies acted together in general matters like the maintenance of public buildings, regulaion of prices, and care of markets, harbours and temples.

This account of city-government does not correspond *prima facie* to anything known from Indian sources. It has been pointed out[2] rightly that while in the pages of the *Arthaśāstra* we come across individual officials in charge of more or less the same duties as are discharged by some of the boards of Megasthenes' account, there is no trace whatever of a body of thirty dividing into six pentads ; and as the same arrangement recurs in his description of military administration, it has been suggested that Megasthenes gave a schematic and idealised account far removed from realities. On the other hand, urban administration has always been different from rural, and there is evidence that at the time of Alexander's invasion some of the larger cities had an administrative system very like what Megasthenes has detailed. Thirty deputies from Nysa accompanied Akouphis on his visit to Alexander; and, 'from the Oxydrakai came the leading men of their cities, and their provincial governors, besides 150 of their most eminent men, entrusted with full powers to conclude a treaty[3]'. It is possible that in these republican cities, the entire aristocracy had a voice in government and the executive work was carried on by groups of five ; for the *pañchāyat* is after all a very widespread Indo-Aryan institution[4]. The rise of the Mauryan empire did bring about a considerable change, and it is possible that Megasthenes was either not fully abreast of the new situation, or probably his account is coloured by his knowledge of the historians of Alexander.

1. I follow here Smith's correction of McCrindle—See *Aśoka* (3rd edn.) p. 88, *n.* 1.
2. Stein, *Op. cit.*, pp. 248—66).
3. Arrian, *Anabasis*, V, 1 (*Invasion*, p. 79) : ib. vi, 14 (p. 154).
4. Breloer, *ZDMG*, 1935, pp. 61—7.

Lastly the war office comprised a board of thirty, functioning in six divisions of five members each. The first division was the admiralty ; the second, transport and commissariat providing, among other things, servants to beat the drum, and groom the horses, and mechanists to tend the machines; the remaining four were respectively in charge of infantry, cavalry, war-chariots and the elephants. There were royal stables for the horses and elephants and an arsenal for the arms, 'because the soldier has to return his arms to the magazine, and his horse and his elephant to the stables'. Horses were broken in by professional trainers forcing them to gallop round and round in a ring, especially when they saw them refractory ; the *Arthaśāstra* devotes whole sections to a description of the movements to which the war horses and elephants should be trained, besides describing their proper care in considerable detail[1].

1. Meg. *Frag.* XXXV (p. 89). *AS.* ii, 30—31.

APPENDIX TO CHAPTER III

EARLY FOREIGN COINS IN INDIA

(*Nanda-Maurya Period*)

The coins current in India before her contact with the Greeks were of the variety usually described as punch-marked and cast[1]. Their manufacturing technique widely differed from that of the Greek coins, and it has been almost unanimously accepted that it was invented by the early Indian moneyers, without the aid of any outside influence[2]. Though numismatists differ about the earliest date of the circulation of these indigenous coins, there is no doubt now that many of them passed current during the Nanda-Maurya period, being introduced in India at a much earlier time. Other types of coins which also passed as currency in the extreme north of India during this period were those issued by the Achaemenid Persian rulers of this region. The Persian emperors from Darius I onwards usually struck two types of coins, viz., the darics and the sigloi, the former being of gold and the latter of silver. The name 'daric' is evidently derived from that of Darius Hystaspes whose Indian conquests included the whole of the Indus valley while

1. The name 'punch-marked' is given to a large mass of early Indian coins, mostly in silver and comparatively infrequently in copper, on account of the various symbols being punched on metal blanks of different shapes, sizes and weights. It was at first suggested by numismatists that these coins were private issues, various moneyers or shroffs being held responsible for their manufacture: according to this view the symbols on their surface were nothing more than the hall-marks of the different individuals through whose hands the coins passed in the course of trade and commerce. But this view has given place to the more probable one of their having been issued by a centra authority. Uninscribed cast copper pieces bearing such symbols as elephant, tree in railing, mountain &c., are some of the commonest coins of ancient India, and belong probably to the same period in which the punch-marked coins are to be dated. For a full treatment of these varieties of the earliest indigenous coins of India, the reader is referred to J. Allan's *Catalogue of the Coins of Ancient India*, Introduction, parts ii-iv.

2. M. Decourdemanche, however, was of opinion that most, if not all, of the punch-marked coins belong to the Achaemenid monetary system, these being nothing but a variety of the Indian issues of the Achaemenid Persian emperors: *Journal Asiatique*, 1912, pp. 117—132. D.R. Bhandarkar opposes this view; cf. *Carmichael Lectures*, 1921, pp. 118—22. J. Allan thinks that the thick silver bent bars with devices on their concave side, found in some parts of north-western India, 'are struck on a Persian standard and represent double sigloi or staters, half and quarter sigloi, *CAI*. p. xvi, 1—3.

'siglos' is based on 'shekel', a kind of weight standard adopted by the Persians from the ancient Babylonians. On the obverse of the former, the Persian emperor armed with a bow and a spear is shown in a running posture, while the reverse contains an irregular oblong incuse. The Persian silver coins bear almost identical devices, but several of them have peculiar countermarks both on the obverse and the reverse, which according to some scholars emphasise their definite Indian association[1]. The darics are about 130 grains (8.42 grammes) in weight, while the maximum weight of the sigloi, twenty of which were equal in value to a daric, was 86.45 grains (5.6 grammes). It was previously held that both these varieties of silver and gold Persian coins were actually minted in India, and passed current there side by side. But a more acceptable suggestion has been made not very long ago that the relative cheapness of gold in this country would make it uneconomical for the Persians to mint any gold coins here for circulation ; in fact, it would tend to draw outside the country any darics which might have been brought there in course of trade and commerce[2]. This view has been supported by the non-discovery of the darics here in any quantity, and the comparative frequency of sigloi in the Indian soil.

But according to Schlumberger silver sigloi are only sparingly found in the eastern parts of the Achaemenid empire and it has been shown that they were issued chiefly for the western cities.[3] It is strange, however, that the Achaemenids who coined silver for one area did not do so for the other. It may reasonably be suggested that the so-called bent bar coins and other pieces of smaller denominations bearing

1. Rapson held this view; he recognised some symbols thus countermarked as similar to those found on Indian punch-marked coins, and other marks he explained as resembling several Brāhmī and Kharoshṭhī letters: *JRAS*. 1895, pp. 865. ff. E. Babelon attributed these countermarks to other countries of Asia, such as, Lycia, Pamphylia, Cilicia and Cyprus; *Les Perses Achemenides* p. xi. G. Macdonald says 'that the results of the most recent in vestigation (Hill, *JHS*. 1919, pp. 125 ff.) rather tend to bear out his opinion' though he does not ignore the noteworthy similarity between them and the Indian punchmarks; *CHI*. I, 344.

2. *CHI*. I, 342—43. The ratio between gold and silver in India as we know from Herodotus, 'was not higher than 1:8' as compared with the form of 1: 13. 3 maintained by he Imperial mint'.

3. R. Curiel and D. Schlumberger, *Trisors Monetaires d' Afghanistan*, Paris 1953, p. 3A.

similar marks were struck for the eastern region with their knowledge and consent.[1] Side by side with this class of money, which served the needs of some peoples and areas in the east, there also circulated in large numbers the silver coins of the various cities of Asia minor. The Athenian "owls", together with the issues of other Greek cities, which have been found in Afghanistan[2] must have been brought there by the Greeks both as settlers and traders. Undoubtedly there was a continuous flow of such coins from the west, as it is probable that pieces of similar character were also struck locally.[3]

As the Achaemenid power declined, local satraps became virtually independent and we get such money as the coins called "imitation owls" and "eagles", and the issues of a certain Sophytes. Typologically they seem to form a single group, one series being linked with the other by features of type and fabric and they apparently conform to an independent system of metrology which may have arisen from local custom and the exigencies of trade.

It will be of interest now to study in brief the special features of these imitations of owls, some of which according to most numismatists were actually minted in the extreme northwest of India or just outside. The original 'owls' of Athens were beautifully executed silver coins of various denominations usually tetradrachms, which bore on the obverse the head of Pallas Athene, the tutelary deity of the city, and on the reverse the figure of an owl, the birds sacred to the goddess, with the legend AΘE usually in the right field. These coins were so much in demand among the people of the Aegean world and among those of the

1. A.K. Narain, *The Indo-Greeks*, p. 4. fn. 1.

2. 'Enquiry has failed to bring to light any trustworthy records of the actual discovery of "owls" in India': this remark in CHI, p. 387, is true to this day. But we are concerned here with areas in Afghanistan where these coins have been found; Cunningham, JASB, 1881, pp. 169-82, 186 & c, and Schlumberger, loc. cit. PP. 46 ff.

3. This appears to be clear not only from the 'taurine', 'caduceus', and other symbols which sometimes appear on 'owls' but from the coins bearing AI-instead of AΦE, which B.V. Head interprets as perhaps referring to the Aigloi, whom Herodotus, iii 92, mentions as dwelling to the north of the Bactrians. Cf. also Macdonald, CHI, P. 387; Schlumberger (op. cit., p. 4), however, thinks that they denote some satrapal name.

middle and near east, that Athens had to supply the specie from her own mint. When Athens lost her political importance as a result of her debacle in the Peloponnesian War and the subsequent Macedonian hegemony, her mint was closed, and imitations of the above type of the Athenian coins were made in large numbers in the countries which once used to import the Athenian originals. These imitations can be divided into two-well-defined classes, the first closely approximating to its prototype. The second class softer in style usually bears the monogram M behind the head of Athene on the obverse and a bunch of grapes over the back of the bird on the reverse. The most characteristic feature which, however, distinguishes the second class from the first is that the obverse and reverse devices of the former are finely adjusted (↓ ↑), whereas in the case of the latter no such adjustment seems to have been made; this nice fixity of position of one die in relation to that of the other may point 'to the employment of a hinge or of some equally effective contrivance' (Macdonald). Moreover, the first class usually consists of tetradrachms, while the second also contains drachms and didrachms. These smaller denominations, again, are not based like the higher ones on the Attic standard of weight, a drachm according to which weighed 67.2 grains (4.37 grammes), but on one in which the same would weigh no more than 58 grains (3.75 grammes). These numismatic peculiarities of the second class of the imitations place them alongside 'another set of drachms and diobols which are struck from regularly adjusted dies (↓ ↑), but in which the place of the Athenian owl is taken by an eagle, looking backwards' (Macdonald). On this latter class of coins, the bunch of grapes behind the owl's back is in one case accompanied by a caduceus. These latter sets of imitation of the Athenian 'owls' were undoubtedly the prototype of Sophytes' coin discussed above, and this is one of the principal reasons which have led numismatists to infer that 'at least the smaller Athenian imitations were not unfamiliar in the north of India'[1].

The silver coins which were issued by one Sophytes, may also be considered here. This Sophytes has been identified by some scholars with Sopeithes of Arrian (vi, 2, 2) and Strabo (xv. 699), who ruled over territories in the Salt Range region, Punjab, at the time of Alexander's invasion

1. CHI. 1, 387-88.

and Sopeithes was taken to be the Greek form of the Indian name Saubhūti.[1] But R.B. Witehead has questioned the identity of Sophytes and Sopeithes. He further suggested that Sophytes was an eastern satrap in the last quarter of the fourth Century B.C. ruling somewhere in the Oxus region where his coins were originally minted—(*Numismatic Chronicle*, 1943). There is no record of an actual discovery of any of these coins in Indian soil, but J. N. Banerjee thinks that there is also no clear proof of Sophytes' connection with the Oxus region. Arrian and Strabo are explicit about the existence of one Sopeithes (most probably the Greek transliteration of some such Indian name as Saubhūti) and Banerjea feels it tempting to connect it with the name Sophytes, the issuer of the coins in question (*JNSI* VII, pp. 23-6). A.K. Narain has re-examined the problem of the identification of Sophytes and he supports Whitehead in rejecting the Indian origin of Sophytes.[2] According to him Sophytes, whose name does not seem to be Greek, and who minted coins without any royal title, may well have been an eastern satrap under Achaemenid rule, a Greek (or a Graeco-Iranian) with the semblance of an Iranian name.[3] The obverse of these coins shows the head of the king to right within dotted border, wearing close-fitting helmet and cheek-plate, the former adorned with a wreath of olive leaves; on the reverse is shown a cock to right with a caduceus on the left field and the Greek legend ΕΩϕΥΤΟΥ on the right, all inside a border of dots. The coins are struck from regularly adjusted dies (↓ ↑) and usually bear a monogram consisting of the Greek letter M or MN; their approximate weight is 58 grains. The discovery of a unique trihemiobol, now in the Berlin Museum, bearing the helmeted head of Athena in place of that of Sophytes, apart from most other numismatic features, definitely proves its connection with the Athenian 'owls'. The weight of Sophytes' coins, which according to earlier numismatists was derived from the Indian *dharaṇa* or *purāṇa* (silver punch-marked coins weighing 32 ratis, roughly 58 grains) has now been shown

1. D.R. Bhandarkar attempts to prove that Sophytes was really a Hinduised Greek: for his arguments, cf. CL. 1921, pp. 30-1.

2. *JNSI*, 1949, pp. 93-99.

3. *The Indo-Greeks*, p. 5.

by Macdonald and others to be the same as that of the imitations; it has been described as a lighter Attic standard sometimes adopted by moneyers in their issue of such coins in east. An earlier view regarding the prototype of Sophytes' coins, even now not completely abandoned, is that they were imitated from a certain type of Seleucus' coins; in fact such was the close similarity between the obverse of this issue of Seleucus I and that of the coins Sophytes, that some numismatists were tempted to connect the two sets of coins in this manner. It is more correct to accept the view suggested by Rapson long ago that both were derived from the imitations of the Athenian 'owls'.[1]

No coins of any Greek prince, however, could have been in circulation in India before Alexander invaded the country. It is presumed that even during the period of his short stay there in the course of his conquests in the north-western regions, he could hardly have found any time to issue coins in his newly acquired territories. A copper coin of squarish shape bearing the name of Alexander, which was supposed at first to be his Indian issue, has been long since declared to have no connection with India[2]. But two silver coins (tetradrachms) bearing the name of Alexander and one silver coin, that of Philip Aridaeus, were discovered by Marshall in the course of his excavations at the Bhir Mound site Taxila[3]. These coins 'bear on the obverse head of Alexander wearing the lion skin, and on the reverse Zeus seated on a throne with the eagle on his right hand and the

1. P. Gardner (BMC. p. xx) and several other older numismatists held the view; it has also been supported by C. Seltmen in his *Greek Coins*, pp. 228-29, pl. LII. 3, and pl. LV. 6. But Rapson correctly suggested long ago that 'both of these classes may have been derived from the same originals—the imitations of the Athenian coins made in India; IC. p. 4.

2. P. Gardner thought that there were a few such pieces of Alexander's Indian money: *BMC*. xviii. But realy the piece, now in the collection of the Berlin Museum, is unique. The shape which is the only reason for associating it with India might have been an accidental freak, 'the result of awkward handling by some workman at a western mint'. Macdonald refers to a group of tetradrchms with Zeus' head on the obverse and the eagle on a thunderbolt accompanied by the legend AΛEΞAN△POY on the reverse, as having some connection with the east, if not actually with India : *CHI*. I 388—89. The presence of a satrapal tiara on the right field of the reverse sides of these coins proves that they were satrapal issues.

3. *ASR*. 1924—25, pp 47—8, pl. ix. These coins were found in a small earthen jar which also contained as many as 1167 silver punch-marked and bent-bar-type of Indian coins, and one Persian siglos.

sceptre in left'. Though they have different legends and monograms, they are closely similar to one another. On one of the coins of Alexander, the legend ΒΑΣΙΛΕΩΣ ΑΛΕΞΑΝΔΡΟΥ can be distinctly read. Their freshly-minted condition and the fact that they were recovered from a stratum, assigned by Marshall to the 3rd or 4th Century B.C., may lead one to suppose that they were actually minted in India. But this first recorded find of such coins in India is still unique and the coins could have been brought here from outside.

The troubles which Alexander's officers left in charge of his Indian conquests had to encounter in mainiaining their transitory hold on these regions did not allow them to issue coins in any number in the name of their master[1]. But a few interesting coins of Greek technique belonging to the latter half of the 4th century B.C. have been discovered, which, though all of them were not found in India, seem to have Indian association. Among them mention may be made first of the few unique silver decadrachms issued by Alexander himself from his Babylonian mint, which were distinctly of a commemorative character. The obverse shows an elephant with two riders followed by a warrior on a prancing horse, while the reverse contains the standing figure of Alexander shown as the god Zeus. The obverse device has been explained by numismatists as the artist's version of Alexander's battle with Porus, the Macedonian emperor on horseback attacking with his lance Porus riding on the elephant, while a second person, the driver of the elephant, turns to throw a javelin at the pursuer. The reverse depicts Alexander dressed in a Macedonian cloak with a composite helmet on his head, his fight hand holding a thunderbolt and his left a spear ; Nike is shown in the top left field, about to place a wreath on his head. The monogram on the lower left field of the reverse is ΑΒ which may either stand for ΒΑΣΙΛΕΩΣ ΑΛΕΞΑΝΔΡΟΥ, or may more probably be a contraction for Babylon, one of the mint cities of Alexander.

1. Macdonald's description of a few such imitations of the Athenian 'owls' which might have been minted in the extreme north-west of India, may be noted in this connection : *CHI.* I, 388. They are the same as referred to in the previous foot note.

Several Greek coins[1] issued in Syria and in the adjacent countries to its east, some bearing the name of Seleucus I and others those of Seleucus I and his son Antiochus I jointly require a brief notice here on account of their Indian association of a somewhat remote character. The first group of these have on the obverse the head of a horned horse to right inside a dotted border, while their reverse shows an Indian elephant. Another class of coins in the same series bear a laureate head of Zeus on the obverse and Pallas Athene driving in a chariot drawn by four elephants on the reverse. The Greek legend ΒΑΣΙΛΕΩΣ ΣΕΛΕΥΚΟΥ on the reverse side of both the classes proves that they were issued after 306 B.C. when Seleucus I assumed the royal title for the first time. A few of the latter class of coins, coarser in style and execution, are usually collected from the extreme north and north-west of India, showing thereby that though they were not actually minted in India, they might have been in circulation in this region. The other group of Greek coins, more or less similar in type to the second class of such coins just noticed,—on the reverse is shown a fighting Athena riding in a car drawn by either two or four elephants, bear the Greek legend ΒΑΣΙΛΕΩΣ ΣΕΛΕΥΚΟΥ ΚΑΙ ΑΝΤΙΟΧΟΥ. The elephant device in all the above types of coins seems to have some remote connection with one of the terms of the treaty concluded by Seleucus I with Chandragupta Maurya ; according to it the former bartered away the provinces of Paropanisus, Aria, Arachosia and Gedrosia along with his claims to the Punjab and other Greek conquests in northern India for five hundred war elephants. This particular war arm proved so decisive a factor at the battle of Ipsus where Antigonus the formidable rival of Seleucus was overthrown, that it became one of the favourite dynastic devices of the Seleucidae. The head of a horned horse, another favourite device of the same, was perhaps commemorative of Bucephalus, the famous charger of Alexander the Great, in whose honour the Macdonian emperor founded a city named Bucephala on the bank of the Jhelum in the Punjab.

1. These are usually tetradrachms ; coins of lesser denominations, however, are not unknown.

Most of the Greek coins discussed above are extra-Indian in character, from the point of view of their provenance ; but almost all of them have some association, near or remote, with the country. The hoards of Greek coins, however, that were actually minted here and which passed as currency in the extreme north and north-west were the ones issued by the Greek rulers of Bactria and India. These Bactrian Greeks at first owed allegiance to Seleucus I and his successors, and it was under Antiochus Theos (Antiochus II), the grandson of Seleucus I, that one Diodotus, the Greek satrap of Bactria, threw off the Syrian yoke sometime in the middle of the third century B.C. Justin says that this Diodotus died shortly after the assumption of independence and was succeeded by his son of the same name. The second Diodotus issued coins bearing his name and the device of Antiochus II. But these coins as well as those of Euthydemus I who dispossessed him of the throne of Bactria, were all issued outside India. The coins of the immediate successors of Euthydemus I, viz., Demetrius and others were mostly non-Indian issues ; a few of them were, however, actually minted in this country, when Demetrius carried the Bactrian Greek arms into India and conquered some parts of it. Eucratides who was a supplanter of Demetrius in Bactria and the head of a rival branch of the Greek princelings contending with Demetrius' successors for possessions in the extreme north and north-west of India, issued a large number of coins many of which were of Indian origin. The coins of the host of the Indo-Greek rulers, mostly belonging either to the house of Euthydemus I or to that of Eucratides, were all minted here, because these Greek princes who had long been driven out of Bactria by the Sakas had made their home in India. The story, however, of these Bactrian and Indo-Greek princes and their coins, though begining in the latter part of the Maurya age, really falls within the Śuṅga and Kāṇva periods.

CHAPTER IV

CHANDRAGUPTA AND BINDUSARA

In a previous chapter we traced the expansion and consolidation of the Magadhan empire under the Nandas. The New Monarchy was exposed to a two-fold danger. On the one hand there were symptoms of popular disaffection with the regime which did not augur well for the future. Besides this there appeared on the north-western horizon the spectre of foreign dominion. Alexander, it is true, had to retire from the Beas but his "successors" inherited his ambition and some of his plans. The lament was no doubt heard that the pursuit of Alexander's policy and retention of his conquests required "royal troops under the command of some distinguished general"[1]. Neither of these conditions could be fulfilled for some time after Alexander's death. The Macedonian Regents[2] from 323 to 317 B.C. had to be content with a sort of condominium on the Indian borderland. It did not, however, take long to consolidate the *Yavana* forces in Western Asia under a new leader so that Indians had once more to prepare themselves for their fiery onset.

Many of the prominent figures that strutted on the Indian stage in the twenties of the fourth century B.C.—Agrammes, Āmbhi, Porus, to name only a few—did not show any proper realisation of the problems that faced their country, or the destiny that awaited her. To preserve and augment the nascent empire of Magadha, to deal effectively with the foreign menace, to "unify the innumerable fragments of distracted India" and bring the ideal of the *Chakravartin* into the realm of practical politics, to inspire Indians with a zeal for mighty endeavour in

1. McCrindle, *Ancient India as described in Classical Literature*, pp. 201—2.

2. It is an interesting question whether Macedon, the home of Alexander and many of his "successors", was known to Indians. The *Adina-puṇyāvadāna* (No. 52) of the *Avadāna-kalpalatā* of Kshemendra refers to a city styled Madhuka in the published Sanskrit text. The name is however given as Māshūdana in the Bengali version by Mr. S. C. Das. The second name, if authentic, may be reminiscent of Macedon.

various fields of activity and bring her politically and socially into close touch with the outer world—all this required a man of heoric proportions. Such a man did not take long in coming. If Plutarch and Justin are to be believed there appeared before Alexander in the Punjab (326—25 B.C.) a 'stripling'[1] of humble birth about whom tradition records signs and portents significant of an august destiny[2]. He conceived the grand design of reversing the condition of things that must have filled the mass of his countrymen with despair. For nearly a quarter of a century he did bestride the Indian world like a colossus. For generations the country had to follow in the lines laid down for her by Chandragupta.

The success of the new Indian leader has been immortalised by a grateful posterity. Fragments of the cycle of legends of which he is the hero survive even in the works of Latin historians. In our own country we have lauds, tales, plays, even philosophical dissertations in Sanskrit, Pali, and Prākṛit in which writers eulogise the hero in whose arms the earth harassed by barbarians found a refuge, who nearly succeeded in bringing about the unification of "Jambudvipa". Unfortunately very little is recorded about the life and career of this remarkable man, which bears the stamp of unassailable authenticity. One searches in vain for his very name in the inscriptions of his grandson. The *Mahābhāshya* of Patañjali has interesting references to *Chandraguptasabhā*[3] and to Amitraghāta[4], possibly the son of Chandragupta, but records nothing about the deeds of the earliest of the Mauryas. Much that is known about him belongs to the domain of folklore. A *Chandraguptakathā*—the nucleus of *Chāṇakya-Chandragupta-kathā* of mediaeval times—must have come into existence before the beginning of the Christian era, as is apparent from the marvellous episodes that have found their way into the narrative of Justin who abridged the Latin history of Pompeius Trogus, a contem-

1. *Plutarch's Lives* (Loeb), Vol. VII, Life of Alexander, Chap. 62 ; p. 403 ; McCrindle, *Invasion of Alexander*, p. 311 for Plutarch ; p. 327 for Justin.

2. Cf. *bāla eva hi lokena sambhāvitamahodayaḥ* ; in *Mudrārākshasa* (ed. by Haridās Siddhāntabāgis-Bhattāchārya), p. 452 ; *Pariśishṭa Parvan* (e.d. by Jacobi, 2nd Ed.), VIII. 243 ; also Justin McCrindle *Invasion*. p. 327.

3. I. 1.9.

4. III. 2.2.

porary of Augustus. Fragments of the story have also been preserved by the Buddhists in the *Milinda-Pañho* and the *Theragāthā Commentary*[1] and by the Jains in certain mediaeval epigraphs of Mysore besides other documents. Curiously enough Chandragupta is ignored in the *Asokāvadāna* though we have notice of his son Bindusāra. The Tamilian reference to "Vamba Moriyār" may also have been connected with the Chandragupta saga. Fuller details are given in Hemachandra's *Pariśishṭaparvan*, the *Mahāvaṁśa Ṭika*, Burmese legends[2] and the Kashmirian versions of the *Bṛihat-Kathā*. There is a dramatic rendering of one form of the legend by Viśākhadatta. The central theme of the story is hinted at in the *Chaṇḍakauśika*[3]. Certain additional details are found in the commentary on the *Vishṇu Purāṇa* and that of Dhuṇḍirāja on the *Mudrārākshasa* of Viśākhadatta.

To narrate the true story of Chandragupta one cannot rely entirely on the *Kathā* but has to piece together scraps of information obtainable from inscriptions, classical sources, genealogical lists preserved in Indian and Cylonese chronicles and certain incidental notices.

The epigraphic records of Aśoka and Daśaratha, while of value as a source of information regarding spiritual ideals, state of religion, internal organisation and social life in the early Maurya epoch, do not mention specific events that may be referred with precision to the reign of either Chandragupta or his son Bindusāra. Far different in character is the Junagadh Rock inscription of Rudradāman which not only specifically names the first Maurya but affords an interesting glimpse of the extent of his conquests and methods of administration. For fuller notices of Chandragupta's career we have, however, to turn to Greek and Latin writers of the Hellenistic period and the early centuries of Imperial Rome. Among classical sources an important place should be given to notices of friendly intercourse between the first two Mauryas and their Syrian contemporaries for which we are indebted to Athenaeus who quotes from Phylarchus and Hegesander[4]. There was an exchange of

1. Malalasekera, *Dictionary of Pali Proper Names*, I, 846.
2. Bigandet, *The Life or Legend of Gaudama* II, 12 ff.
3. Quoted in the *Kāvyamīmāṁsā* (3rd ed.), p. XIII.
4. McCrindle, *Invasion*, pp. 405, 409 n.

embassies as well as correspondence between the Indian and certain Hellenistic courts. The names of three of the Hellenic envoys have survived, namely, Megasthenes, Daimachus and Dionysius. As is well known the *Indika* of Magasthenes constitutes in some respects the most valuable source of information regarding Chandragupta and his times. But the fragments that survive in the books of Diodorus, Strabo, Arrian, Pliny and others throw more light on internal government and manners and customs of the people than on the political transactions of the age. For the events that followed the death of Alexander and led up to the rise and expansion of the Maurya empire reliance has to be placed mainly on the XVIII and XIX Books of the *Universal History* (*Bibliotheke*) of Diodorus Siculus, the *Life of Alexander* by Plutarch, Justin's Epitome of the *Historia Philippicae* of Pompeius Trogus (Book XV), the *Syriake* of Appian (Book XI. 9.55) and certain passages from the *Geography* of Strabo and the *Natural History* of Pliny. The Purāṇic and Ceylonese chronicles have nothing to say regarding Chandragupta's relation with the Hellenic powers. But they notice the dynastic change in Magadha and give information regarding the king's lineage not known from classical sources. The Chroniclers whose extant works cannot be dated earlier than the Gupta Age could not escape from the influence of the *Chāṇakya-Chandragupta-Kathā* which must have reached a highly developed form in their days. In their accounts the figure of Kauṭilya, unknown to earlier texts, makes its appearance as that of the leading actor in the drama of events that leads to the supersession of the Nandas by Chandragupta. This is in striking contrast with the facts recorded by Justin, following Trogus, according to which Chandragupta plays the leading role in the dynasiic revolution among Indians and Kauṭilya is not even alluded to.

Among the sources of the Maurya period mention is often made of the *Kauṭilīya-Arthaśāstra*. The copious information obtainable from this work relates more to ideals and methods of administration, social life etc., than to external political facts ; it is also a matter of controversy how far the famous treatise can be regarded as a genuine product of the Maurya Age.

Before we proceed to sketch the life and career of Chandragupta on the basis of the sources indicated above, it may not be out of place to say a few words about the vexed question of chronology.

Attempts have been made to determine the chronology of the Mauryas in general, and Chandragupta in particular, with the help of Jain and Buddhist tradition. Hemachandra informs us in the *Pariśishṭaparvan*[1] that the accession of Chandragupta took place 155 years after the liberation of Mahāvīra. This statement is confirmed by Bhadreśvara in his *Kahāvali.*[2] Merutuṅga, however, in his *Vichāraśreṇi*[3] refers to other sources which place the event 60 years later in 215 A.V. Apart from the lack of unanimity among these Jain writers, the date of Mahāvīra's liberation is itself a matter of controversy, and it is not safe to to build a chronological edifice on such foundations. The memorial verses quoted by Merutṅga give other details which put the interval between the accession of Chandragupta and the end of Śaka rule and the foundation of Vikrama era at 255 years[4] This would place the accession of the first Maurya in 313 B. C.—a result that closely approximates the epoch of the Seleucidan era, and has, therefore, found favour with some scholars. It should, however, be noted that the Jain writers are apparently referring to Chandragupta's rule in Avanti, and not Magadha or the Punjab, and that part of the chrolonological tradition embodied in the memorial verses is contradicted by Bhadreśvara and Hemachandra. Moreover, the date 313 B.C. for Chandragupta does not accord with Buddhist tradition which puts his accession 162 years after the *Parinirvāṇa* of the Śākya Sage, that is, 382 B.C., if we accept the Ceylonese epoch (544 B.C.) of the Great Decease, and 324 B.C., if we prefer the Cantonese tradition (486 B.C.) for the passing away of the Enlightened One. The earlier date is no doubt opposed to classical evidence, but the date 324 B.C. is not irreconcilable with the testimony of Greek and Latin writers. The figures given by Buddhist chroniclers are, however, as much open to comment as the data of Bhadreśvara, Hemachandra and Merutuṅga. We have, therefore, to turn to the clues furnished by

1. Ed. Jacobi p. xx ; Text, VIII. 339.
2. *Ibid.* p. xx.
3. *Ibid.* p. xx.
4. Ind. Ant. 1914 pp. 118 f. Jacobi, *Kalpasūtra of Bhadrabāhu*, Leipzig, 1879, p. 7 :

classical accounts supplemented by the testimony of Aśokan inscriptions.

The classical writers refer to several famous episodes in the career of Chandragupta with hints as to their chronological sequence. He met Alexander while yet a 'stripling' and not yet 'called to royalty' (326—25 B.C.)[1] and mounted the throne of India 'not long afterwards'[2] by instigating the Indians to overthrow the existing government, or according to another interpretation, soliciting the Indians to support his new sovereignty[3]; *thereafter*[4] he prepared to attack Alexander's prefects ; the latter were put to death and the yoke of servitude was shaken off from the neck of India 'after Alexander's death' (i.e., after 323 B.C.).[5] Chandragupta was reigning over India when Seleucus was laying the foundation of his future greatness.[6] (The famous Macedonian general acquired the satrapy of Babylon for the first time in 321 B.C., regained control of the city and founded an era in 312 B.C., and assumed the title of king in 306-5 B.C.). After subduing the Bactrians he passed over into India, concluded a treaty with Chandragupta and then returned home to prosecute the war with Antigonus (before 301 B.C).[7] Appian, who also refers to the war which Seleucus waged with Chandragupta, besides other events, mentions the understanding with the Indian

1. Plutarch, Op. cit Ch. LXII. (Loeb Classical Library), translated by Perrin ; Justin, *Inv. Alex.* p. 327.

2. Plutarch; *op. cit.* LXII, p 401.

3. Just in, *Inv. Alex.*, p. 328; Watson's translation of Justin, p. 142.

4. Justin uses the words "having thus won the throne" once again after mentioning the fight with the prefects. This has led scholars including Tarn (*Greeks in Bactria and India*, p. 47 n2) to surmise that the acquisition of his kingdom by Chandragupta *followed* the war with Alexander's satraps, the last of whom, Pithon did not leave India till 316 B. C. But the words "having thus won the throne" are not to be construed merely with the preceding sentence describing incidents in connection with the war with the prefects. They refer also to the events that preceded the clash of arms with the Macedonian commanders, and in fact, sum up the whole episode relating to the rise of Chandragupta. For a similar summing up of the exploits of Seleucus, see Appian, *Syrian Affairs*, XI 9.55 referred to above. In the detailed account given by Justin we are expressly told that Chandragupta was stimulated to aspire to royalty by an incident that happend immediately after his flight from Alexander's camp in 326/25 B.C. The use of the term *deinde* (thereafter) after "new sovereignty" suggests that the Macedonia War came *sometime after* the change of government among Indians. In the *Mudrārākshasa* too the total destruction of *Mlechchha* chieftains and troops follows the dynastic revolution in Magadha (*Indian Culture*, II.. p. 561 f.)

5. Justin. *Inv,Alex.*, 327.

6. *ibid.*, 328.

7. *ibid.*. 328.

king about the marriage relationship and adds that "some of the exploits were performed before the death of Antigonus and some afterwards"[1] i.e., after 301 B.C. That these operations cannot have reference merely to dealings with Chandragupta but include also events outside this country, that find mention earlier in Appian's narrative, e.g. the war with Syrian clans, is clear from other sources, such as the narrative of Justin who dates the treaty between the Syrian and Indian monarchs before the clash of arms of Seleucus with Antigonus. In fact Appian here sums up the career of Seleucus as a Nicator.

How long Chandragupta lived after the war with Seleucus cannot be precisely determined from Greek sources. His grandson Aśoka is known to have been a contemporary of Magas of Cyrene who died not later than 259—58 B. C. according to the evidence of Porphyry, which seems to be confirmed by the testimony of Callimachus, a contemporary poet, of Polybius (X. 22) and of coins.[2] The acceptance of this date implies that the XIII Rock Edict of Aśoka cannot be dated later than 259—58 B.C. as it speaks of Magas as alive. As rescripts of morality began to be written when Aśoka was anointed twelve years, his coronation could not have taken place after 270—69 B.C. The death of Chandragupta and the reign of his son Bindusāra must, according to the evidence we have cited, fall between the Seleucidan war and 270—69 B.C. Tradition assigns a period of 24 years to the reign of the first Maurya, 25, 27 or 28 years to Bindusāra, and 4 to the interval between the accession and the coronation of Aśoka. If we accept the mean figure 27 for Bindusāra, a period of 55 years must have intervened between the accession of Chandragupta and the coronation of his grandson. The former event took place according to this calculation not later than 270-69+55=325-24 B.C. An early date for the rise of Chandragupta is suggested by the fact that at the time of the partition of Triparadeisos (321 B.C.) Antipater had to give the kingdoms that lay along the Indus and the Hydaspes (Jhelum) to Indian *Rājās* "for it was impossible to remove these kings without royal troops under

1. *Roman History*, Vol. II., Book XI. 9.55, p. 204. (Loeb Classical Lib. translation by White.
2. Tarn, *Antigonos Gonatas*, pp. 449 ff.

the command of some distinguished general.[1]" The inadequacy of "royal troops" and the absence of "distinguished general" are inexplicable unless the more important among the prefects of Alexander had already been put to death or expelled. That achievement is ascribed by the Latin historians solely to Chandragupta who, and not Āmbhi or the Paurava, "was the leader who achieved their (i.e., Indians') freedom"[2]. It is true that the great liberator is not mentioned in connection with the partitions of Babylon and Triparadeisos. But we have similar reticence in regard to Eudemos who had been directed along with Taxiles to assume the administration of the province governed by Philippus as early as 324 B.C.[3] He survived Porus, and clung to some part of India till about 317 B.C.

Greek and Latin writers frequently corrupt the name of Chandragupta. It was Sir William Jones who solved the puzzle and found in the appellations used by the classical historians and geographers variant forms of the name of the first Maurya as known from Indian sources. Writers of our own country, too, sometimes use epithets which require a few words of comment. As is well known the name of Chandragupta does not find a place in the epigraphs of his descendants. It, however, is distinctly referred to in the Junāgaḍh Rock Inscription of Rudradāman I. It is also known to Patañjali and a host of Indian bards and chroniclers, playwrights, poets and even philosophers. Among classical writers the nearest approximation to the correct name (*Sandrokoptos*) is made by Phylarchus, who is quoted by Athenaeus[4]. Strabo, Arrian and Justin have Sandrocottus. Appian and Plutarch corrupt it into Androcottus. In the *Mudrārākshasa* we have the cognomens Chanda-Siri (Chandraśrī), Piadaṁsaṇa (Priyadarśana) and Vṛishala[5]. Chandraśri is of course the shortened form of the name Chandragupta with the addition of the honorific Śrī[6]. The attribution

1. Dio. XVIII. 39; *McCrindle Ancient India in Classical Lit.* p. 211—12.
2. *Inv. Alex.* p. 327.
3. *Inv. Alex.*, p. 177 Smith, Aśoka, (3rd ed.) p. 12.
4. Strabo says that Sandrokottus adopted the surname Palibothros (*Pāṭaliputraka* ?), *Megasthenes and Arrian*, p. 66.
5. Haridas Siddhantabagis edition, pp. 42, 374.
6. The usual practice is to put the honorific before the name. For a contrary usage, of. Aśokaśri in *Pariśishṭaparvan*, Khāravelaśri, Veda or Skandaśrī, Skandaśrī, Śaktiśrī, Balaśari in inscriptions, and Yajñaśrī in the Purāṇas etc.

to Chandragupta of the appellation Piadaṁsaṇa, if based on correct tradition, is of great interest as it is generally known as an epithet of his famous grandson, Aśoka, and his common designation in inscriptions. As a title of royalty it finds mention in the *Vishṇudharmottara* as quoted in the *Rājadharmakaustubha* of Anantadeva[1]. But its use does not appear to have been so common in early times as that of Devānaṁpiya. Vṛishala is taken by some to hint at Chandragupta's extraction from the Śūdra line of the Nandas. But the cognomen is used in the epic and law books also of *Kshatriyas* and others who deviated from orthodoxy. An ingenious suggestion has been made in recent times that the expression really stands for *basileus*[2], the Greek word for king. There is, however, no suggestion in Indian literature that Vṛishala is a royal epithet. The word has a social and no political significance, and is often applied to non-royal personages, particularly wandering teachers and ascetics like the Buddha[3].

Regarding the ancestry of Chandragupta Indian writers have not preserved any unanimous tradition. There is no doubt agreement in regard to the name of the the family to which he belonged, which is invariably given as Maurya. But the origin and derivation of the word present a problem which requires elucidation. The Brāhmanical commentators like Dhuṇḍirāja and the annotator of the *Vishṇu Purāṇa* derived the expression from Murā, supposed to be the wife of a Nanda king, and grandmother or mother of the first Maurya. There is, however, no warrant for this view in early texts. The Purāṇas make no mention of Murā and do not refer to any dynastic connection between the Nandas, who were of Śūdra extraction, and the Mauryas. No doubt they say that after the extermination of all Kshatriyas by Mahāpadma Nanda, kings will be of Śūdra origin. This cannot however be taken to imply that all the post-Mahāpadman kings were Śūdras as some of them, e.g., the Kāṇvas, are distinctly styled *dvija*. In some Purāṇic texts

1. Kamal Krishna smritirtha's ed. p. 43
2. I.H.Q., XIII (1937), p.651.
3. *Kauṭilīya Arthaśāstra* (Text), p. 199 R. K. Mookerjee, *Hindu Civilisation*, p. 264.

the reading is *Śūdra-prāyāstv adhārmikāḥ*[1]. *Śūdra*-like and irreligious are not an inapposite description of several members of the Maurya family who showed predilection for Jainism and Buddhism. One text, the *Mārkaṇḍeya Purāṇa*, goes so far as to brand the Mauryas as *asuras*[2]. *Suradvish*, it may be remembered, is used by the *Bhāgavata Purāṇa* in reference to people beguiled by the Buddha[3]. The earliest authorities to claim a Nanda origin for the first Maurya are the *Mudrārākshasa* and the mediaeval versions of the *Bṛihat-kathā*. It is, however, to be noted that the Greek accounts do not suggest any blood relationship between Chandragupta and Agrammes, the Nanda contemporary of Alexander. The former is mentioned by Justin as "born in humble life[4]." The reference, to our mind, points to the fact that Chandragupta was not born in the purple and was not a scion of the royal line which he overthrew. It is significant that Plutarch includes "Androkottos" among the persons who, according to several historians, disclosed to Alexander the meanness of the origin of the contemporary ruler of the Prasii, apparently the last Nanda king. It does not seem probable that people who sneered at the "barber" line of Magadha could themselves claim no higher status in society.

Buddhist writers do not regard Maurya as a metronymic. They invariably represent it as the name of a clan[5] the members of which ranked as Kshatriyas since the days of the Buddha. Even Kshemendra who speaks of Chandragupta as *pūrvanandasuta* in his version of the *Bṛihat-kathā*, distinctly mentions Aśoka as born in the Solar Race in the *Avandānakalpalatā*[6]. The latter view accords with the testimony of several mediaeval inscriptions[7]. The antiquity of Moriya or Maurya as a clan name is clear from the *Mahāparinibbāṇa Sūtta* which represents the people in question as Kshatriyas and rulers of the little

1. Pargiter, *Dynasties of the Kali Age*, p. 25.
2. 88. 5.
3. I. 3. 24.
4. *Inv. Alex.* p. 327.
5. For traditional Buddhist accounts of the origin of the name, see Malalasekera, *D.P.P.N.*, II. 673.
6. Story No. 59, v. 2. 'Saurya' Kula may be regarded by some as a mistake for Maurya Kula, (ii. p. 209). but the supposition loses its force when later on in the same story we find Saurya and Maurya together in the passage—*Sphita Saurya-Maurya-Mahāvaṁśavanapañchānana Śrimad-Aśokadevaḥ*.
7. *Ep. Ind.* II, p 222

republic of Pipphalivana, probably lying between Rummindei in the Nepalese Tarai and Kasia in the Gorakhpur District[1]. Some recent writers seek to connect the first Maurya with Gandhāra and its neighbourhood on the basis of evidence which does not bear scrutiny[2]. The suggested identification of Chandragupta with Sisikottos is not borne out by Greek evidence. The treatment of the two eminent men by Alexander is different, and there is nothing to show that Sisikottos was a mere stripling when he met the Macedonian king for the first time. Equally implausible is the attempt to connect Śakuni, whom the Kāshmir Chronicle represents as the great-grand-father of Aśoka, with Śakuni of Gandhāra, famed in the *Mahābhārata*[3]. Śakuni is by no means an exclusive desigation of Gandhārian princes as it occurs in the Purāṇic list of Videhan kings[4]. In *Mudrārākshasa*, Act V, the Gandhāras are actually found arrayed against Chandragupta.

History does not record when the founder of the Maurya dynasty was born. As he was a mere stripling when he saw Alexander in 326—25 B.C. his birth could not have taken place before the middle of the fourth century B.C. Certain writers, as has already been noted above, record traditions that he was of royal extraction. The *Bṛihatkathā* and the *Mudrārākshasa* connect him with the Imperial Nanda dynasty of Magadha, and Buddhist commentators with the ruling family

1. *P. H. A. I.*, 4th ed., pp. 160, 217.
The names Morieis, Merues and Moeres are known to classical writers (*C.H.I.* I. p. 470 ; McCrindle *Inv. Alex.* pp. 108, 256). But their connection, if any, with Sandrocottus is not clear. If Morieis is a tribal name it may well stand for Moriya or Maurya.
Mauryaputra of *Mudrārākshasa* (II, 6, p. 99) may simply mean, 'belonging to the Maurya clan'. Cf. Śākyaputra, Nātaputta. It is by no means an exclusive designation of Chandragupta. The *Kalpasutra of Bhadrabāhu* ed. by Jacobi (p. 28) refers to a Mauryaputra Kāśyapa as one of the eleven gaṇadharas. Cf. also *Abhidhānachināmaṇi* I. 32.

2. Gandhāra Origin of the Maurya Dynasty and Indentification of Chandragupta with Sasigupta, by H. C. Seth. In *Indian Culture*, X. pp. 32n, 34, it is said that "Chandragupta was a man of the *Uttarāpatha*" and that "Hwen Thsang narrates a legend (Beal, *Buddhist Records*, I., p. 126 *Sic.*,) which connects the Śākya-Mauryas with the country of Udyāna". The passage on which the last statement is based is not quoted. The pilgrim's story (Beal, I. 128) simply mentions Udyāna as a place of refuge of a Śākya fugitive. The evidence hardly suffices to represent either the Śākyas or Chandragupta as "men of the Uttarāpatha." Is it suggested that *Mayūra-rāja* (king of peacocks) on p. 126 is to be taken to refer to Chandragupta ?

3. Seth, *op. cit.*, p. 15.

4. *Vāyu Purāṇa*, 89, 29.

of Moriyanagara, perhaps identical with Pipphalivana of early Pāli texts, members of which had to take shelter in Pupphapura (Pāṭaliputra) when the last monarch of the line had been put to death by a certain powerful Rājā. The queen consort of Moriyanagara, we are told, gave birth to Chandragupta, and the child is said to have been reared by a herdsman and a hunter[1]. A variant form of the story is given by the Burmese[2]. The foundation of the Maurya city (Moriyanagara) is there attributed to princes of Vaiśālī that had escaped from the massacre of Adzatathat (Ajātaśatru). According to Jain tradition recorded in the *Pariśishṭaparvan*[3], however, Chāndragupta was born of the daughter of a peacock-tamer (Mayūraposhaka) who lived in an obscure village. The sources of Trogus and Justin knew Chandragupta as a *novus homo*, a man "born in humble life". This does not accord with the tradition regarding his imperial pedigree, though it may well be reconciled with the story that his family, though sprung from a ruling *Kshatriya* clan, had fallen on evil days. Justin's reference to the hero's encounter with "a lion of enormous size" and "a wild elephant" of monstrous shape further shows that the *Chandraguptakathā* known to the Latin historians of the early century of the Christian era, might not have been altogether ignorant of Chandragupta's traditional association with hunters and tamers of the wild denizens of the forest. Little that is historical can, it has to be conceded, be extracted from these legends.

It should, however, be noted that all our authorities agree that the Mauryas hailed from Eastern India, the land of the Prasii. Young Chandragupta's detestation of the Prasian contemporary of Alexander, to which Plutarch bears witness, is in conformity with the tradition that the poor plight in which the Maurya family found itself in the twenties of the fourth century B.C. was due, in large measure, to the agressive policy of neighbouring rulers, particularly the imperialists of Magadha.

1. *Mahawanso* (Turnour) I. p. xl.
2. Bigandet, *Life or Legend of Gaudama*, II. p. 126.
3. (Text) VIII. 231 ; cf the Buddhist tradition connecting the name Moriya with *mora* (peacock), Malalasakara, *Dictionary of Pali Proper Names* II. 673.

Chandragupta's first emergence from obscurity into the full view of history occurs in 326—25 B.C. when he met Alexander. The fact is recorded by two of the classical writers, viz., Justin, who draws upon the history of Trogus, and Plutarch. The young Maurya might have acquainted the Macedonian invader with conditions in Eastern India. "Alexander", he is reported to have said in later times, "narrowly missed making himself master of the country, since its king was hated and despised by his subjects for the weakness of his disposition and the meanness of his origin.[1]" Details of the original speech and the manner in which it was delivered are not recorded. But we are told by Justin that its tone gave offence to the Macedonian king who gave orders to kill the Indian lad. The latter sought safety by a speedy flight[2]. Curiously enough some modern editors emend the text of Justin and propose to read *Nandrum* in place of *Alexandrum*. The name Nanda, however, is not known from any other classical source, and Plutarch, who also refers to the meeting between Alexander and "Androcottos", makes separate mention of the king or kings of the Prasii. Classical writers record other instances of Alexander's impatience with boldness of language. The cases of Cleitus and Callisthenes may be recalled in this connection[3].

The narrative of Justin leaves the impression that after his departure from Alexander's camp Chandragupta retired to a forest tract, drew together a body of armed men and 'solicited the Indians to overthrow the existing government.' and support a new sovereignty[4]. Modern translators of Justin's text characterise the warriors who gathered round the Maurya as a band of robbers. But the original expression used by the Latin historian has the sense of mercenary soldier, hunter, as well as robber. The former senses are in consonance with Indian tradition. According to the story told in the ***Pariśishṭaparvan***. troops were levied for Chandragupta with wealth procured by

1. Plutarch, (Loeb.) p. 403; McCrindle, *Inv. Alex.*, p. 311; cf. also Curtius and Diodorus in *Inv. Alex.* pp. 222, 282.
2. *Inv. Alex.*, p. 327.
3. Cf. Grote, *History of Greece*, (E.L.S.), XII., pp. 140ff, 147ff.
4. Justin, *Inv. Alex.*, p. 328 : Watson's translation, p. 142. "The new sovereignty" of Justin reminds us of the words *Maurye nave rājani* of the *Mudrārākshasa*, Act. IV., p. 278.

metallurgy or mineralogy (*Dhātuvāda*) for the purpose of uprooting Nanda[1]. The purpose of the levy stated in the Jainta text is important. In the light of this evidence 'the overthrow of the existing government' alluded to by Justin, can well be taken to refer to the subversion of the rule of the Nandas. As a matter of fact Justin in the earlier part of his narrative apparently draws a distinction between this event and the war with the prefects of Alexander, preparations for which were made *thereafter* (*deinde*). According to a subsequent passage, however, the winning of the throne and reigning over India seem to follow and result from the fight with the Macedonian commanders. The problem is not free from difficulties and our views have been stated in connection with the chronology of Chandragupta.

If the "overthrow of the existing government" does not refer to the fall of the Nandas, but only to the destruction of the Macedonian domination in the Indus valley, we shall have to assume that the classical writers, who recounted the story of the rise of Chandragupta, knew nothing regarding the fate of Agrammes, about whom they speak so much, and were ignorant of the dynastic revolution that gave Chandragupta the throne of Pāṭaliputra and the crown of Prasii. It is not very probable that the *Chandragupta Kathā* on which they must have drawn for some of their thrilling episodes, had no reference to the tragic end of Alexander's Magadhan contemporary who was "detested and held cheap by his subjects."

Be that as it may, for details of the momentous events that led to the supersession of the Nandas by the Mauryas we must turn to Indian chroniclers and story-tellers. No contemporary account has survived. The traditional story is told differently by different writers. In some cases only fragments have survived. One of the earliest of these, which lies embedded in the *Milinda Pañho*,[2] preserves its heroic character as a tale of war between the contending forces of the Nandas and the Mauryas. The lustre of Chandragupta is, as in the narrative of Justin, yet undimmed by that of an all powerful chancellor. His

1. Jacobi's edition, 2nd. ed., p. lxxiv : Text. VIII. 253-54.
2. S.B.E. XXXVI., p. 147. It is interesting to note that the Ceylonese commentator turns Nanda into "Nandagutta of Brāhmaṇa caste" (*Ibid* n. 3).

opponent Bhaddasāla is a brave soldier, a general of the Nandas, not an astute minister. The accounts of the Purānic genealogists, the chroniclers of Ceylon and the *Nītisāra* of Kāmandaka are still marked by comparative simplicity. They relate how the Nandas were uprooted and the "earth passed to the Mauryas[1]". But the credit for the achievement, for "anointing the glorious youth Chandragupta as king" over the earth (or Jambudvīpa) is given to a minister, the *Brāhmaṇa* Kauṭilya, Chāṇakya or Vishṇugupta. The treatise on statecraft ascribed to the latter goes so far as to omit in this connection all explicit reference to Chandragupta[2].

We have further embellishment in the *Mudrārākshasa* which competent critics are inclined to assign to the ninth century A.D[3]. Kauṭilya is now definitely the leading actor in the drama. The Nanda king who falls a victim to his wrath is named Sarvārthasiddhi, and the family is referred to as of noble birth (*abhijana*[4]). *Mlechchha* chieftains, Parvata, Parvataka, Parvateśvara or Śaileśvara, his brother Vairodhaka, son Malayaketu and Meghāksha or Meghanāda, king of the Persians, take part in the dynastic quarrel along with hordes of Śakas, Yavanas, Kirātas, Kambojas, Bālhikas, Khasas, Hūṇas and others. The barbarians appear at first as allies of Chandragupta. But when promises made to them are evaded, and Parvata and his brother fall victims to Chāṇakya's cunning, Malayaketu turns against the Maurya and joins the Nanda minister Rākshasa. The storm that threatened to burst upon Chandragupta was averted by jealousies and quarrels among his enemies. The *Mlechchha* forces dispersed and the discomfiture of Malayaketu as well as Rākshasa was complete. In the play the battle of intrigue proves more efficacious than the arbitrament of the sword. None of the Mlechchha chieftains have names which can be regarded as standing for genuine Greek or Persian

1. The reference to the Āraṭṭas equated with the "band o frobbers" of Justin, that some recent writers find in the Purānic texts is due to a misreading (Pargiter, *DKA*, p. 26 n 35.).
2. *Arthaśāstra,* Bk. XV., concluding verse.
3. Keith, *Sanskrit Drama*, p. 204.
4. *Mudrarākshasa* p. 386.

originals and the appearance of the Hūṇas in connection with the Magadhan conflict of the fourth century B.C. exposes the true character of several incidents narrated in the play. The identification of Parvataka with Porus, proposed by some writers,[1] has little to support it. Parvataka and his family are clearly branded as *Mlechchha* in the play, and their forces as *Mlechchha- bala*; on the other hand the Purus or Pauravas could claim an illustrious Vedic and epic ancestry. The territory over which Parvataka ruled is described by Jain writers as *Himavatkūṭa*,[2] while Porus ruled at first the country between the Jhelum and the Chenab to which were added territories stretching as far as the Hyphasis or Beas and the Indus. In the *Mudrārākshasa* one Sindhusena or Susheṇa appears as the prince of the Indus region. Lastly, Parvataka is slain by a poison maiden (*Vishakanyā*) as a result of Kauṭilya's intrigue, while Porus is killed by Eudamus, according to one reading of the text of Diodorus, and by Alexander himself according to Pseudo-Callisthenes.[3]

The Kashmirian redactors of the *Bṛihatkathā* show their independence of the tradition followed by the play by introducing a Yogananda, a Nanda produced by magic, that is, by the entry of an adept in that art into the body of the genuine (*pūrva*) Nanda. They also attribute to Śakaṭāla, the minister of the real Nanda, the destruction of the son of the supposititious king, and the bestowal of the royal dignity upon Chandragupta, child of the genuine monarch. Chāṇakya, according to this version, is simply a protege and an instrument of Śakaṭāla.[4] The real Nanda king is now definitely described as a Śūdra.

Fresh accretions to the tale are met with in the *Pariśishṭa-parvan*, the *Mahāvaṁśa Ṭīkā*, and the legend of the Burmese

1. *C.H.I.*, I., 471 : "Identification of Parvataka and Porus." H. C. Seth.

2. *Pariśishṭaparvan* (Op. cit., VIII. 297—98 (p. 222). Jacobi has the following note on Parvataka : 'In the list of the kings of Nepal, according to the Bauddha Pārvatīya Vaṁśāvalī (*Ind. Ant.*, Vol. XIII., p. 412) the 11th king of the 3rd dynasty, that of the Kirātas, is Parba, apparently our Parvata; for, in the reign of the 7th king, Jitedāsti, is placed Buddha's visit to Nepal, and in that of the 14th, Sthunka, Aśoka visited the country." (*Ibid.* p. lxxv, n1.)

3. Smith, *Aśoka*, (3rd ed.), p. 12 n ; McCrindle, *Ancient India in Classical Literature*, p. 178.

4. Text, Nirnaya Sagara Press, *Kathāpiṭhalambakaḥ Tarangas* IV and V ; Penzer's edition of Tawney's translation, Vol. I., p. 40—57.

Buddha.[1] We have different versions of the story of the initial failure of Chāṇakya and Chandragupta in their attack on the Nanda dominions, and their ultimate success due to experience gathered on the spot. According to the Buddhist version the last of the Nandas is put to death. But in the narrative of Hemachandra he is permitted to leave his kindgom.[2] There is lack of agreement in regard to another important matter. The *Mahāvaṁśa Ṭikā* definitely assigns Chāṇakya to the city of Taxila.[3] On the other hand, Hemachandra seems to suggest in the *Abhidhānachintāmaṇi*[4] "that Kauṭilya, son of Chaṇaka was a Dramila" i.e. an inhabitant of South India. But as the lexical verse indentifies him with Vātsyāyana, Mallanāga, Pakshilasvāmin as well as Vishṇugupta, little importance attaches to its testimony. Curiously enough the *Pariśishṭaparvan*[5] mentions Golla-*vishaya* as the home-land of the famous minister. The identity of the place is not known.

The overthrow of the Nandas rid the Magadhan empire of a dynasty that, in spite of its great services, had failed either to secure the good will of the subjects, or to show any intelligent grasp of the policy to be pursued towards the invaders in the North-West. The new regime had to justify itself by efficient administration, by promotion of the welfare of the people, and securing their protection against the *Yavana* menace. Regarding some of the methods adopted by Chandragupta opinions may differ. According to Justin "he oppressed with servitude the very people whom he had emancipated from foreign thraldom"[6] We do not know how far the remark applies to the Magadhan provinces. The judgment is of too sweeping a character to be supported by all other available evidence. We shall not enter here into the details of the Mauryan polity which will be dealt with in a later chapter. The emancipation of the Indians from foreign thraldom, to which the Latin historian refers, was

1. *Pariśishṭaparvan* Canto VIII; *Mahāwanso* (Turnour) pp. xlff. Bigandet, *op. cit.* II., 126 ff.
2. *Pariśishṭaparvan,* VIII 315 f., p. lxxvi.
3. *Mahāwanso* (Turnour) p. xxxixf
4. III. 517.
5. VIII. 194.
6. McCrindle, *Invasion,* p. 327.

in itself no mean achievement. We now turn to this famous episode in the career of Chandragupta.

The liberation of the land of the five rivers and the border country from the Macedonians was a long process. It required two wars to expel the prefects of Alexander and hurl back the battalions of one of the most ambitious and capable of his successors. The great Macedonian king and conqueror wanted to incorporate the territories he had conquered in India permanently into his empire. He made elaborate arrangements or their defence and administration. Garrisons were posted in several places, colonies planted, cities fortified at important stategic points and dock-yards constructed. Satraps recruited from Indians as well as Macedonians and allied peoples from the West were appointed to assume the administration of some of the conquered provinces. Certain areas were, however, left under the control of Indian *Rājās*.[1]

Alexander died in 323 B.C. His successors, who met to partition the Macedonian empire at Babylon on the day after his death, and again at Triparadisus in Syria towards the end of 321 B. C., had no desire to withdraw altogether from the Indian provinces. They could not however be blind to certain new developments. The Macedonians were torn by internal dissensions and their ranks were getting thinner in India. Antipater, regent of Macedonia from 321 to 318 B.C., managed to retain control over the satrapy of India which "bordered on the Paropanisadae" which he gave to Pithon in 321 B.C. "Of the adjacent kingdoms he gave that which lay along the Indus to Porus, and that along the Hydaspes (Jhelum) to Taxiles (Āmbhi), for it was impossible to remove these kings without royal troops under the command of some distinguished general."[2] Smith seems to think that the names of the *Rājās* have been interchanged.[3] This is not improbable. But it is well to remember that the city of Taxila did not lie far from the Hydaspes, and Porus might have been given charge of a part of the Indus valley over which Eudamus, the Thracian, exercised sway as one of the joint successors of Philippus.

1. See ch. III above.
2. McCrindle, *India as described in Classical Literature*, pp. 201—2.
3. *Aśoka*, (3rd ed.), p. 12n.

Eudamus was probably disfavoured as a partisan of Eumenes, a rival of Antipater.[1] It is significant that according to a reading of a passage of Diodorus, Eudamus is said to have seized a number of elephants after the death of Alexander, having treacherously slain Porus.[2] The hostility to Porus is explicable if the Indian Rājā had been granted favours by the Regent in Macedon at the expense of the Thracian commander. Eudamus had however soon to leave India to help Eumenes in his fight against Antipater. The event is usually dated in or about 317 B.C. and must in any case have preceded the execution of Eumenes in 316 B. C. Pithon, who favoured the side of Antigonus,[3] another great general who claimed a share of Alexander's inheritance, left India about the same time in 316 B.C.[4] and was slain in the battle of Gaza four years later.[5]

The leading part in the destruction or expulsion of Alexander's commanders in India is, as already stated, assigned by Justin to Chandragupta. The earlier attempt of Samaxus, the Assakenians, the Brāhmaṇas of the Lower Indus valley, and Musicanus (Mousikanos) had ended in failure. The process of liberation is likely to have begun before the Partition of Triparadisus when the lament is already heard about the growing power of the Indian Rājās and the absence or at least inadequacy of royal "troops under the command of some distinguished general." "It seems however that the country" "emancipated from foreign thraldom" did not stretch at first beyond the Hydaspes (Jhelum) in the north-west. The Macedonian Regent claimed to dispose of territories extending eastwards as far as that river in 321 B.C. But soon the Magadhan frontier reached the Indus. According to a fragment quoted by Pliny, possibly from Megasthenes, "the Indus skirts the frontiers of the Prasii"[6] that is, the Magadhan empire, doubtless during some part of the reign of Chandragupta as of his predecessors did not control any part of the Punjab, and his successors seem to have exercised sway over the province as far as the

1. McCrindle, *Invasion* p. 389.
2. Smith, *Aśoka*, (3rd ed.), p. 12n.
3. McCrindle *Invasion*, p. 400.
4. Tarn *Greeks in Bactria and India*, p. 47 n 2.
5. McCrindle *Invasion*, p. 400.
6. McCrindle, *Ancient India as described* by *Megasthenes and Arrian* p. 143.

north-western mountains. The Indians whose territory "bordered on the Paropanisadae" (in the Kabul valley) are known to have been under Pithon till c. 316 B.C. The district to which Eudamus clung, after the partition of Triparadisus which ignored him, may also have lain, like that of his predecessor Philippus, partly at any rate, beyond the Indus. These commanders had been partisans of Antigonus and Eumenes respectively. The execution of Eumenes in 316—15 B.C.[1] and the exhaustion of Antigonus in the war of 315 to 312—11 B.C.[2] left the way clear for Seleucus who returned to Babylon in 312—11 B.C., and soon made himself master of "the whole region from Phrygia to the Indus".[3] Appian, to whom we are indebted for the information conveyed by the last few words, seems clearly to suggest that the Indus formed the boundary between the dominions of Seleucus and Chandragupta before the two kings came to blows. The former is said to have "*crossed the Indus* and waged war with Androcottus, king of the Indians, *who dwelt on the banks of that stream.*"

It is a matter for surprise that the classical writers who have so much to say regarding the Indian campaigns of Alexander should preserve reticence in regard to the details of the famous struggle to which Appian refers. Even the date of the war and its total duration are not known for certain. Appian informs us that the fight went on "until they (i.e., the Syrian and Indian Kings) came to an understanding with each other and contracted a marriage relationship (*kedos*)." He adds that some of the exploits of Seleucus were performed "before the death of Antigonus (at Ipsus, 301 B.C.) and some afterwards."[4] The "understanding" or treaty with Chandragupta and "settlement of affairs in the East" are definitely dated by Justin before Seleucus' return home to prosecute the war with Antigonus.[5] Pliny refers to the opening up of India with its numberless nations and cities by the arms of Alexander,

1. *Inv. Alex.* p. 385, *Companion to Greek Studies* p. 110.
2. *Companion,* p. 110.
3. Appian, *Roman History,* Vol. II. (Loeb Library)—*Syr.* XI. 9.55.
4. Appian, *Ibid.*
5. *Inv. Alex.,* 328.

Seleucus and Antiochus, but gives no details that might have thrown light on the war with Chandragupta.[1]

While the war itself received scant attention at the hands of the historians, the "understanding" seems to have attracted greater notice. Plutarch tells us that Chandragupta "made a present to Seleucus of five hundred elephants."[2] Fuller information is given by Strabo who says :

"Along the Indus are the Paropamisadae, above whom lies the Paropamisus mountain ; then, towards the south, the Arachoti ; then next, towards the south, the Gedroseni, with the other tribes that occupy the seaboard ; and the Indus lies, latitudinally, alongside all these places ; and of these places, *in part*, some *that lie along the Indus* are held by Indians, although they formerly belonged to the Persians. Alexander took these away from the Arians and established settlements[3] of his own, but Seleucus Nicator gave them to Sandrocottus, upon terms of intermarriage (*epigamia*) and of receiving in exchange five hundred elephants."[4]

In another passage we are informed that "the Indus River was the boundary between India and Ariana, which latter was situated next to India on the west and was in the possession of the Persians at that time (i.e., at the time of Alexander's invasion) ; for later the Indians also held much of Ariana, having received it from the Macedonians."[5]

Diplomatic relations were also established between the contracting powers, for Strabo refers to the sending of Megasthenes to the court of Chandragupta at Pāṭaliputra.

The details of the "understanding" to which Strabo bears witness leave no room for doubt that Seleucus could not make much headway. Even royal Macedonian troops under a dis-

1. McCrindle, *Ancient India as described in Classical Literature*, p. 107. The journeys made from the Beas for Seleucus Nicator, to which Pliny bears witness, may, as pointed out by Macdonald, refer not to reconnaissances made during a campaign, but to information gathered subsequently by Greek envoys accredited to the Court of Pāṭaliputra (*Megasthenes and Arrian*, 1926, 129 ff., *Camb. Hist. Ind.* I. 430.).

2. Plutarch, *op. cit.* Ch. LXII.

3. Governments or provinces according to Tarn (*Greeks in Bactria and India*, p. 100.

4. *Geography* (Loeb. Library) translated by H. L. Jones, (XV. 2. 9), p. 143.

5. *Ibid.* p. 15 (XV. i. 10).

tinguished commander failed to dislodge the king of the Prasii from the Punjab. On the contrary, the invader had to give up some of the Macedonian possessions on the Indus "receiving in exchange the comparatively small recompense of five hundred elephants." In regard to the extent of the territory surrendered by Seleucus and the nature of the marriage compact of which, according to Strabo, the cession was in part the consequence, there has been considerable difference of opinion. Smith believed, on the strength of a passage of Pliny, that the countries ceded included the four satrapies of Gedrosia, Arachosia, Aria, and the Paropamisadae.[1] Pliny however simply says that "numerous authors include in India the four satrapies" in question.[2] He may have been referring to conditions not in the days of Seleucus and Chandragupta, but in some later epoch, e.g., that of the monarchs of the Scytho-Parthian dynasties who reigned previous to A.D. 77.[3] The words used by Strabo "and of these places, *in part*, some that lie along the Indus are held by Indians" do not convey the idea of a complete abandonment of the Satrapies in question including even Aria. Tarn is inclined to think that only those parts of the three satrapies of Paropamisadae, Arachosia and Gedrosia *which lay along the Indus* were ceded by Seleucus. In Gedrosia the district ceded was, in his opinion, that between the Median Hydaspes (identified with the Purali) and the Indus. Of the satrapy called Paropamisadae Chandragupta got, according to this view, only Gandhāra between the Kunar river and the Indus. The boundary in Arachosia is not precisely defined but it is suggested that what Chandragupta got lay east of a line starting from the Kunar river to somewhere near Quetta and then going to the sea by Kalat and the Purali river.[4] The contention of Tarn cannot however be accepted

1. *E.H.I.*, 4th ed. p. 159.
2. *Megasthenes and Arrian*, p. 156 ; *E.H.I.* 4th ed. p. 159.
3. Pliny's information was not solely drawn from the contemporaries of Alexander and Seleucus. He refers to the opening up of India by the arms of Antiochus as well as Alexander and Seleucus. He utilised the evidence not only of " old writers " but of ambassadors who came to the early Roman emperors (Mc Crindle *Ancient India as described in Classical Literature*, pp. 103, 107). He speaks of a discovery of a shorter route to the Indian ports by a merchant (p. 111) in comparatively recent times.
4. Tarn, *Greeks in Bactria and India*, p. 100.

In regard to one point he is definitely wrong. The V and XIII Rock Edicts of Aśoka count among the north-western tribes who were included within the *rāja-vishaya*, and were subject to the jurisdiction of imperial officials, not only the Gandhāras but the Yonas. Association with the Kambojas and the Gandhāras suggests that these Yonas are the people of that name mentioned in the *Mahāvaṁśa* whose city Alasanda had been identified by Cunningham and Geiger with Alexandria in the country of the Paropamisadae near Kabul[1]. When Strabo says that "the Indians held *much* of Ariana, having received it from the Macedonians", it is difficult to believe that he means only the comparatively narrow strip of territory that lay to the west of the Indus and east of a line drawn from the Kunar to the Purali. And the discovery in 1958 at Kandahar of a bilingual (Greek and Aramaic) edict of Aśoka is clear proof of the extent of territory ceded by Seleucus and its continuance in the Mauryan Empire in Aśoka's reign.

In regard to the marriage compact Macdonald draws a distinction between the terms *kedos* and *epigamia* used by Appian and Strabo respectively. The former, we are told, would signify an actual marriage, while the latter probably implied only "a convention establishing a *jus connubii* between the two royal families".[2] It is observed in this connection that there was no room in the family circle of Seleucus for any actual marriage relationship. Both the expressions used by our authorities may, however, signify a "connection by marriage," though the word used by Strabo has also the sense of "right of intermarriage between states."[3] The cession of territories "upon terms of intermarriage (*epigamia*)" implies that the marriage did take place, the lands in question being possibly treated as the dower of the Seleucid princess like the Kāśi village in the Buddhist story of Kosalā devī, and Bombay in the case of Catherine of Braganza[4].

By his victory over the Nandas and the Macedonians Chandragupta became master of the extensive region stretching

1. Cunningham, *Ancient Indian Geography*, p. 18 ; Geiger *Mahāvaṁsa*. p. 194.
2. *Camb. Hist. of India*, Vol. I., p. 431.
3. Liddell and Scott., *Greek-English Lexicon*, pp. 626, 946.
4. See on this point the observations of Tarn, *Greeks in Bactria and India* p. 174n.

from Magadha and Bengal to the easternmost satrapies of Ariana. The king of Pāṭaliputra and the Prasii dominated not only "the whole tract along the Ganges",[1] but the countries on the Indus that had once acknowledged the sway of the Persians and Alexander. Unfortunately the classical writers do not say much about any further extension of the Magadhan dominions in the interior of India. We have only the vague statement of Plutarch that "with an army of six hundred thousand men (Chandragupta) overran and subdued all India."[2] The conquest and subjugation of one important province, that of Surāshṭra or Kāthiawār in the extreme west, is however clearly attested by the Junāgaḍh Rock Inscription of Rudradāman which refers to Chandragupta's *Rāshṭriya* or High Commissioner Pushyagupta, the Vaiśya, who constructed the famous Sudarśana Lake. The incorporation of this country within the Magadhan empire implies control over Avanti or Malwa. The 'Muriyas' or Mauryas are actually included by Jain writers among the successors of Pālaka of Avanti[3]. Ujjain, the capital of the province, long remained the seat of a Maurya viceroyalty. In the days of Aśoka, grandson of Chandragupta, the Maurya frontier reached North Mysore. As the only specific conquest claimed by that emperor is that of Kaliṅga, the extension of the empire beyond the Tuṅgabhadrā must be due to one of his predecessors. Certain mediaeval inscriptions speak of parts of Mysore being protected by Chandragupta.[4] The evidence is late and too much cannot be built on it. It should however be noted that a number of Tamil authors, usually assigned to the early centuries of the of the Christian era, make allusion to the "*Moriyar*" having crossed a mountain with snow-capped peaks towering to the skies, and these allusions will be discussed elsewhere in the section on South India. In the third century B.C. the Chitaldrug district marked the furthest limit of the Maurya empire in the South. But

1. *Megasthenes and Arrian* p. 141. That the king of the 'Palibothri' (Pāṭaliputra) referred to in the Fragment is Chandragupta is clear from the description of the standing army which follows the account of the people and the capital city.

2. Plutarch, *op. cit.*, Ch. LXII.

3. Jacobi, *Kalpasūtra of Bhadrabāhu*, 1879, p. 7 ; *Pariśishṭaparvan*, Jacobi, 2nd. ed., p. xx.

4. Rice, *Mysore and Coorg from the Inscriptions*, p. 10.

posterity ignored these limitations and loved to regard the hero who had overthrown the Nandas and given protection to the earth harrassed by the *Mlechchhas* as "king over all Jambudvīpa", sole monarch of the country that extends "from the lord of the mountains (*Śailendra*, i.e., the Himalayas), cooled by showers of the spray of the divine stream (Ganges) playing about among its rocks, to the shores of the Southern ocean (*dakshiṇārṇava*) marked by the brilliance of gems flashing with various colours."[1] These words find an echo in the statement of Plutarch quoted above, thus pointing to the prevalence, as early as the beginning of the Christian era, of the tradition of Chandragupta's universal rule—the realisation of the ideal of a united India under an *Ekarāṭ* or *Chakravartin* to which the *Brāhmaṇas* and the *Nikāyas* give eloquent expression.

The political and military record of Chandragupta, brilliant as it is, does not sum up all his achievements. The great soldier who had liberated one part of his country from an unpopular dynasty, and another from foreign yoke, the architect of an empire embracing the greater part if not the whole of India, was as "strenuous in the arts of peace as in the arts of war." The conqueror of Bhadrasāla and Seleucus, master of a host of 600,000 foot-soldiers, 30,000 cavalry, 8,000 or 9,000 elephants[2], wore the velvet glove as soon as conditions permitted. Great though he was as a war-leader, he had no inordinate passion for the sanguinary revelries of the battle-field. He set out to accomplish the unity of India, but beyond its borders he never cast his covetous eyes. The statement of Arrian, who apparently quotes from Megasthenes, that "a sense of justice, they say, prevented an Indian king from attempting conquest beyond the limits of India[3]" perhaps reflects one of the fundamental principles of Mauryan foreign policy as laid down by the founder of the line and upheld by his successors.

The conquests of Chandragupta brought India into closer touch with the outer world, particularly with the countries of the Hellenic West. We have noted above that the clash of arms with the *Yavana* king of Western Asia was followed by

1. *Mudrārākshasa*, Act. III., verse 19.
2. McCrindle *Ancient India as described by Megasthenes and Arrian*, pp. 141, 161.
3. *Ibid.* p. 209.

the establishment of an intimate relationship of a personal character between the ruling houses of Pāṭaliputra and Babylon-Seleucia. A lady of the Seleucid family probably graced the royal palace of the king of Prasii, and a Greek envoy adorned his court. The consideration thus shown did not remain unreciprocated. We are informed by Athenaeus on the authority of Phylarchus that the Indian king sent sundry presents to Seleucus which included certain powerful aphrodisiacs[1]. Chandragupta's respect for Hellenic genius is also illustrated by the story that he did honour to the altars of Alexander[2] Diodorus speaks of a Greek author named Iamboulus who was made a slave by the Ethiopians and was later ship-wrecked on the shores of India and carried to the "king of Palibothra who had a great love for the Graecians[3]." It is, however, difficult to determine whether we have here an allusion to Chandragupta's phil-Hellenism, or, a reference to the liking that his son and successor had for Greek sophists. It is interesting to note in this connection the presence of a considerable number of foreigners in the metropolitan city of Pāṭaliputra. A special board of municipal officers engaged itself in looking after their safety and comfort. Special arrangements were also made to meet their judicial needs[4]. Arrian informs us that "the Indians do not use aliens as slaves."

In civil government Chandragupta showed an aptitude which placed him far above the ordinary warrior-king. The selection of councillors from men respected on account of their high character and wisdom, an equitable system of judicial administration, efficient management of municipal affairs, development of roads and irrigation works, concessions to husbandmen and artisans, encouragement of passenger traffic and commerce, and perhaps also the suppression of piracy, by a board of admiralty, limitation of slavery, and many other measures to promote the prosperity and civilization of the people, do not support the stricture of Justin that he "changed

1. McCrindle, *Invasion* p. 405.
2. Smith, *E.H.I.* p. 125n.
3. *Ancient India in Classical Literature*, p. 204-5.
4. *Megasthenes and Arrian*, pp. 42, 68.

the name of freedom to that of bondage" and oppressed his countrymen. The judgment of the Latin historian may have been based on the strict discipline that he enforced, and the severity of the penal code which permitted mutilation. We shall not deal in detail with these and other matters relating to Maurya polity as they will receive attention in a later chapter. We shall content ourselves with a brief notice of the king and his court.

The monarch usually resided in the famous metropolis of Pāṭaliputra, known to the Greek and Latin writers as Palibothra, Palibotra and Palimbothra.[1] But on occasions he must have moved about from place to place like Harsha. Appian's reference to Androcottus as the king of the Indians, who *dwelt* on or about the Indus,[2] suggests that the emperor might have used some city on or near that river as an alternative capital or at least as a 'camp of victory' (*jayaskandhāvāra*). The classical writers have left interesting accounts of the Maurya metropolis in the land of the Prasii. Pāṭaliputra, we are told was a large and wealthy city, situated at the confluence of the Erannoboas (Hiraṇyavāha or Son) and the Ganges, stretching in the form of a parallelogram. Its "inhabited quarters" covered an area 80 stades (9 miles 352 yards) in length and 15 stades (1 mile 1270yards) in breadth. It was enclosed by a wooden wall[3] pierced with loopholes for the discharge of arrows and crowned with 570 towers, apparently for keeping watch. The approaches to the city consisted of 64 gates. Running along the wall, but outside it, was a gigantic trench fed by water introduced from the neighbouring rivers, 6 *plethra* (200 yards) wide and 30 cubits deep, constructed for the purpose of defence as well as reception of sewage. Sumptuous palaces adorned the city, which housed a numerous population, including a large

1. The foundation of the city, as is well, known, is ascribed by Indian writers to Udāyi, son of Ajātśatru. Curiously enough a tradition quoted by Diodorus, presumably on the authority of Megasthenes (McCrindle, *Ancient India as described by Megasthenes and Arrian*, p. 37), gives the credit to Heracles.

2. Appian, *op. cit.* XI. 9. 55.

The capital of *Uttarāpatha* (the Indus Valley and the Borderland) in the Maurya period is known to have been at Taxila. It is not improbable that Appian alludes to the residence of Chandragupta in this city.

3. Cf. Patañjali IV. 3. 2. "*Pāṭaliputrakāḥ prāsādāḥ Pāṭaliputrakāḥ prākārā iti*"

number of foreigners. The care of the metropolis was entrusted to a corporation of 30 members (*astynomoi*).[1]

If Aelian is to be believed the royal palace "where the greatest of all the kings" of India resided was a marvel of workmanship with which "neither Memnonian Susa with all its costly splendour, nor Ekbatana with all its magnificence, can vie." Parks, resonant with the melodious notes of peacocks and pheasants, shady groves and ever green trees "set in clumps and branches woven together", some of which were brought from distant lands, lovely tanks abounding in tame fishes, and with little princes fishing, playing and swimming in them — were all calculated to lend charm to the scenery.[2] The majesty and beauty of the palace befitted the residence of a mighty monarch, and its dweller is revealed to us as a man of fine aesthetic sense with "a genuine joy of life and love of nature" not usually associated with a stern soldier. Excavations have brought to light the ruins of Maurya buildings at the village of Kumrahar, not far from the modern city of Patna. The wooden structures, especially fragments of timber palisade, probably date back to the reign of Chandragupta.[3]

Among the inmates of the palace the consorts of the great king claim special attention. One of them, if we accept the traditional interpretation of the treaty between Chandragupta and Seleucus, must have been a Seleucid princess.[4] Jain tradition refers to the name of another lady called Durdharā, represented as the mother of Binduasāra.[5] Burmese legends do not mention the name, but assign to the mother of Chandragupta's successor a Maurya lineage and the chief place among the queens.[6] The queens of the first Maurya are rather

1. McCrindle, *Megasthenes and Arrian*, pp. 37, 65f, 67f. 87, 209f.
2. Cf. Rock Edict II of Aśoka for importation of herbs, roots and fruits.

Monahan, *Early History of Bengal*, p. 177 ; *C.H.I.*, I., p. 411f ; McCrindle, *Ancient India in Classical Literature*, p. 141f.

Curtius in his *History of Alexander* (*Inv. Alex.*, pp. 188f) describes an Indian palace which is taken by some to be that of Chandragupta. But as has been pointed out by Monahan (*op. cit.* p. 178), it is not clear whether we have here a description of the court of the Imperial Mauryas or of some minor potentate.

3. Monahan, *op. cit.* pp. 173f ; Smith *E.H.I.* (4th edn.) p. 128n.
4. Cf. the views of Tarn, one of the most recent writers on the subject, *Greeks in Bactria and India*, p.174n.
5. *Pariśishṭaparvan*, pp. lxxix, 234 (VIII. 439).
6. Bigandet, *op. cit.*, p. 128.

shadowy figures, and we do not know whether like the wives of Chandragupta's Hellenistic contemporaries they played any conspicuous part in public life, court ceremonial, and policy. The sons of the king find mention in a passage of Aelian noted above as engaged in fishing, playing and swimming in ponds within the palace grounds. We do not know if these youngsters included the famous Bindusāra whose name and that of Siṁhasena among those of the sons of Chandragupta have been transmitted by tradition.[1]

Besides these members of the royal family, there was a host of women "bought from their parents" who took care of the king's person inside the palace, and even accompanied him on hunting expeditions.[2]

We have interesting glimpses of the private life of the king. He sometimes permitted himself to indulge in drinking[3], in all probability at sacrifices, but never to an excess as he might fall a victim to foul plots of ambitious women. He did not sleep in day time, and even at night he had to change his bed occasionally as a precaution against attempts on his life[4].

The court of Chandragupta was no less imposing than his palace. In later times the grammarian Patañjali could still recall the *Chandragupta-sabhā*[5]. Here the king conferred with his councillors and assessors who excelled in wisdom, received ambassadors, listened to the reports of the *episkopoi* who inquired into and watched all that went on in his vast dominions, and administered justice to his subjects even when the time came for attending to his person, that is, when he was to be rubbed with cylinders of wood[6].

The prominent figures of the *sabhā*, who were outside the class of diplomats, are known more from tradition than from documents of unassailable fidelity. Mention is no doubt made in an inscription of the Rāshṭriya Pushyagupta, the Vaiśya, who was put in charge of an important province. It is,

1. Siṁhasena may have been only an epithet of Bindusāra.
2. *Megasthenes and Arrian*, p. 70f.
3. Cf. Bindusāra's letter to Antiochus Soter, asking the latter to buy for him sweet wine. (*Inv. Alex.* 409n).
4. *Meg. and Arr.* p. 70f.
5. I. I. IX.
6. *Megasthenes and Arrian*, pp. 41, 70f, 85, 217f.

however, not known definitely whether he graced at any time the central *darbār* of his sovereign.

Tradition has preserved for us the names of several persons who are reputed to have attended the court of Chandragupta. Among these the place of honour should be given to the celebrated Kauṭilya or Chāṇakya, the all-powerful chancellor of the Maurya empire. We have already referred to the famous work on statecraft attributed to him. The contemporaneity of the king and his famous minister, though not proved by irrefragable evidence, is rendered possible by the unanimity of traditions to that effect recorded in the works of Indian, Ceylonese and Burmese writers of different persuasions. A second minister of Chandragupta, according to Buddhist legends, was a Jaṭilian, Maniyatappo by name, mentioned in the *Mahāvaṁśa Ṭīkā*[1].

Among other personages who figured in the *Sabhā* mention may be made of envoys who came from foreign courts. Of these the most celebrated was Megasthenes. He brought his credentials from Seleucus and resided long enough in Pāṭaliputra to observe things for himself. He wrote a book on India but unfortunately this interesting work has been lost. Only fragments have survived in the quotations of later classical writers.

If tradition is to be believed, the court of the first Maurya, like that of many of his successors who wore the imperial crown of India, opened its portals to a third group of personages, besides ministers and diplomats, viz., religious teachers. Jain writers emphasise that in his later days Chandragupta came into intimate touch with pontiffs of their faith, the most eminent among whom was Bhadrabāhu who is reported to have died in 170 A.V., i.e., 15 years after the accession of the first Maurya according to one reckoning[2]. He was the reputed author of the *Kalpasūtra* and other works. According to the *Rājāvalīkathe* he was born in a Brāhmaṇa family at Koṭikapura in Puṇḍravardhana[3].

1. Turnour, *op. cit.*, p. xlii.
2. *Pariśishṭaparvan*, pp. vii, xx, 248 (IX. 112).
3. *Ind. Ant.*, 1892, p. 157.
Fleet (*Ibid.*) pp. 156ff : *J.R.A.S.* 1909, p. 23n) is sceptical about the Jain story. Jacobi (*Pariśishṭaparvan*, pp. vi—vii : *Kalpasūtrā* p. 22) thinks that some works, e.g., the *Niruktas*, attributed to the sixth Patriarch, who died in 170 A.V., really proceeded from the pen of a late namesake. According to him the *Samacharis* may be regarded as the work of the great Bhadrabāhu.

The king, says Strabo, left the palace usually on four occasions, viz., to lead the army in person in time of war, to administer justice, to offer sacrifice, and lastly, to go to the chase. Hunting was a favourite pastime. The king marched out of the palace to the accompaniment of drums and gongs, and was surrounded by a host of armed women who rode "some on chariots, some on horses and some even on elephants". Spearmen were posted to protect the whole company. The king hunted in fenced enclosures, either from a platform in his chariot or from the back of an elephant[1].

On occasions he seems to have attended public spectacles. One such show is referred to by Pliny (on the authority of Megasthenes) in which foals of *kartazons*—a kind of one horned animal, probably the rhinoceros,—were set to fight each other[2]. Some of the facts mentioned by the classical writers receive confirmation from the inscriptions of Aśoka. The predecessors of that king, we are told, went on *vihāra-yātrā*, an important feature of which was hunting. They also celebrated *samājas* which may be compared with the public spectacles of Pliny.

In a passage of Strabo[3] reference is made to a great festival on the occasion of the hair-washing ceremony of the Indian king when the people brought him costly presents and made a display of their wealth. Certain writers are inclined to think that the Greek geographer got his information from Megasthenes, and that therefore the ceremony pertains to the court of Pāṭaliputra. They further urge that the festival was borrowed from Persia and regard it as a proof of India's indebtedness to Persian culture. It may however be pointed out that Strabo introduces the passage in question with the words "the following statements are made by *historians*", and makes special mention of Clitarchus[4]. The festival in question might, therefore, have been current even before Chandragupta. At any rate there is little warrant to connect it definitely with the court of Chandragupta at Pāṭaliputra.

1. *Megasthenes and Arrian* p. 71.
2. *Ibid.* p. 58.
3. XV. I. 69.
4. Author of a *Life of Alexander*, and a contemporary of that king. (cf. *Inv. Alex.* pp. 8, 10 : *C.H.I.*, 399, 675) Jayaswal in *J.B.O.R.S.*, II., p. 98. misses the reference to Clitarchus.

The personal gifts of Chandragupta were of a varied kind. Reference has been made to his interpidity and ability as a soldier, vigour and wisdom as an administrator, to his keen sense of beauty and love of nature. To these he added a wide intellectual curiosity and, according to traditional accounts, a deep interest in religion. These were probably imbibed from contact with philosophers. Megasthenes tells us that it was a general practice among Indian kings to consult through messengers a class of philosophers called the Hylobioi—a section of the Sarmanes (*Śramaṇas*)—who dwelt in the woods and lived a life of continence. The questions regarding which rulers sought illumination related to the cause of things and other matters. The services of these philosophers were also employed for the worship or supplication of deities[1]. Again, at the beginning of the year a great Synod of philosophers was called by kings in order that they might communicate useful suggestions in writing concerning *the improvement of crops or the cattle or the promotion of public interest*[2]. It will perhaps not be unreasonable to surmise that the Greek envoy learnt about some of these things from what actually came under his observation at Pāṭaliputra.

The king who conversed with philosophers, to benefit by their wise counsel, included within the range of his interest, even wild races. This is well illustrated by stories about the Astomi, who lived near the source of the Ganges and were brought to the court, and the Enotokoitai who died on the way as they refused to take food[3]. These stories may not be worthy of credence in all their particulars. But they prove that the classical writers credited Chandragupta with an amount of curiosity, not unworthy of a modern anthropologist.

The reign of Chandragupta was not altogether devoid of literary interest. We have already seen that tradition associates

1. McCrindle, *Megasthenes and Arrian*, pp. 102ff. Next in rank to the Hylobioi were the physicians who lived indoors, and effected cures by regulating diet rather than by the use of medicines. Among philopsophers there were some women. Medicine received attention along with philosophy.

2. *Ibid.*, pp. 38, 83, 214. Or, according to another interpretation, *prosperity of either fruits or living beings or concerning government. Geography of Strabo* (Loeb), VII, p. 69.

3. pp. 75, 80.

the authors of the *Kauṭilīya Arthaśāstra* and the Jaina *Kalpasūtra* with his court. The existence of a body of literature including *Suttas*, *gāthās*, and *apadānas* in the early Maurya period is vouched for by the inscriptions of Aśoka[1]. The reference to the story of Herakles and Pandaia[2] in the fragments of Megasthenes points to the popularity of epic tales (*ākhyānas*) in some shape. In explaining the statement of Megasthenes that the Indians had no written laws Bühler suggested that the Greek envoy took the term *Smṛiti* used by his informants in the sense "memory" instead of "sacred tradition concerning law" or "the law books[3]" If this view be correct then a part at least of the *Smṛiti* literature was probably in existence in the days of Chandragupta. The *Indika* of Megasthenes, though largely based on personal observations of the famous ambassador, may have drawn upon texts of this type[4] as well as myths and legends some of which had probably a place in the folk literature of the day.

We have seen above that one of the occasions when the king came out of the palace was to offer sacrifice. This possibly implies that Chandragupta was known to the Greeks as a follower of the Brāhmaṇical religion. The celebrated Jaina author Hemachandra admits that the emperor patronised heretical (i.e., non-Jaina) teachers (*mithyādṛikpāshaṇḍimatabhāvitam*[5]). As has been noted above one of the king's ministers was a Jatilian or a follower of "a class of ascetics, so called on account of their matted hair[6]". Jaṭilakas figure in a list of "schools or corporate bodies of Wanderers, or of Hermits" mentioned in early Pali Canon[7]. We do not know what was exactly the attitude of Chandragupta towards the Buddhists. If the *Theragāthā* Commentary is to be believed he put into prison the father of an Elder (*Thera*) at the instigation of Chāṇakya[8].

1. Cf. the Bairat Edict and Pillar Edict VII. (EE. dhammāpadāne)
2. *Megasthenes and Arrian*, pp. 163, 206.
3. Monahan, *Early History of Bengal*, pp. 167 f.
4. Compare the statement of Strabo (McCrindle, *Ancient India as described by Megasthenes and Arrian.* p. 69) :
"They marry many wives, whom they buy from their parents, giving in exchange a yoke of oxen", with *Smṛiti* texts on *Ārsha* marriage (Gautama, IV. Baudhāyana, I. 11. 4. : Manu, III. 29). See also Monahan *op. cit*, p. 165.
5. *Pariśishṭaparvan.*, p. 232 (VIII. 415).
6. Malalasekera, *Dictionary of Pāli Proper Names*, Vol. I. p. 931.
7. Rhys Davids, *Buddhist India*, p. 145
8. Malalasekera *op. cit.* pp. 846. 860

But the person in question may have suffered for his political views or conduct. Jain tradition avers that towards the end of his life he became a convert to the religion of the Tīrthaṅkaras after the rival teachers had been discomfited in a synod[1]. It is also affirmed that when Magadha was confronted with a famine of twelve years Chandragupta abdicated in favour of a son named Siṁhasena and retired to Śravaṇa-Belgola in Mysore with the Saint (*Śruta-kevalin*) Bhadrabāhu. There he starved himself to death in the Jaina fashion[2]. Several inscriptions in Mysore dating from about 900 A.D. refer to the pair (*yugma*) Bhadrabāhu and Chandragupta[3].

Bindusāra

Chandragupta died after a reign of 24 years, probably some time after 301 B.C. But his work did not perish with him. This was no doubt due in large measure to the vigour and efficiency of the system of government which he had organised, and the wise policy he had followed. But the machinery of administration would by itself hardly have worked smoothly if it had not at its head a man who appreciated the ideals and methods of the dead king and did his best to preserve the traditions of the illustrious founder of his line. This is not the only title of Bindusāra, the son and successor of Chandragupta, to fame. If he sought to preserve unimpaired the heritage of his father, he also prepared in some respects the way for his great son. His reign is not merely a continuation of that of Chandragupta. It also presaged in some respects the glorious epoch of Dharmāśoka.

Little is known about the early life of the new king. If Jain tradition is to be believed the name of his mother was Durdharā. History does not record if he was one of the young

1. *Pariśishṭaparvan.* (Jacobi), 2nd ed., p. lxxix, VIII. 415 ff.

2. *Ibid.*, VIII. 444, *Samādhimaraṇaṁ prāpya Chandragupto divaṁ yayau* : *Rājavalīkathe I.A.* 1892, p. 157.

3. Rice, *Mysore and Coorg from Inscriptions*, pp. 3ff.
Fleet (*I.A.* 1892. pp. 156 ff : *J.R.A.S.*, 1909, p. 24n) regards the story as presented in the *Rājāvalīkathe* as "probably of quite modern invention". Even the legend in its earlier form "has not the slightest historical value as affecting Chandragupta, the grandfather of Aśoka".
Smith (*E.H.I.*, p. 154) however thinks "that the tradition probably is true in its main outline."

princes who, according to Aelian, amused themselves while fishing in the unruffled sheets of water within the palace grounds of the greatest of all the kings of India, and learning how to sail their boats. In later life he showed an aptitude for government and a taste for culture which in all possibility were acquired in boyhood. The name of Amitrochades (variants, Amitrachates and Allitrochades, the λ λ having arisen from a loosely formed cursive M)[1] by which he is known to the Greeks suggests not a weakling brought up amidst the pleasures of the harem, but a man of steel, fit to bear the weight of a great empire and defend it against all enemies. Fleet takes the Greek appellation as meaning "Amitrakhāda", 'devourer of enemies', which occurs as an epithet of Indra. Lassen and others prefer to equate it with the Sanskrit Amitraghāta, slayer of foes—a term that occurs in the *Mahābhāshya*[2] of Patañjali. *Amitrāṇāṁ hantā* is a well known title of royalty in the *Aitareya Brāhmaṇa* and *Amitraghātin* is frequently used in the *Mahābhārata* as an epithet of princes and warriors.[3]

As Chandragupta, according to the evidence of Plutarch and Justin, had not yet mounted the throne in 326—25 B.C. and is traditionally credited with a reign of 24 years, his successor could hardly have obtained the imperial crown before 301 B.C. The new monarch must have ceased to rule before 270—69 B.C. if the king Magas, mentioned in the rescripts of his son written not earlier than the twelfth regnal year, died in 258 B.C. Regarding the actual period of Bindusāra's rule the evidence is discrepant. The Purāṇas allot to him a period of 25 years. Burmese and Ceylonese chronicles raise the figure to 27 and 28 respectively.

Greek historians say little about the internal affairs of India in the days of Bindusāra. Our main reliance has to be placed on tradition. The accounts of the Buddhist and Jain writers of a late date suggest that the services of the most able and astute of Chandragupta's officials were retained by his son. Among these was Kauṭilya or Chāṇakya who is said to have had a rival

1. Fleet *J.R.A.S.*. 1909., p. 24,n.
2. III. 2. 2.
3. *Ait Br.* VIII. 17 : *Mbh.* II. 30. 19 ; 62. 8, VII. 22.16.

in Subandhu.[1] The post of chief minister (*agrāmātya*) eventually went to Khallāṭaka and later on to Rādhagupta[2]. The name of the principal queen was, according to the *Mahāvamśa Ṭikā*, Dhammā. The *Aśokāvadāna* calls her Subhadrāngī[3].

Bindusāra was fortunate in having in his sons, especially Aśoka, proconsuls of exceptional ability who did much to curb the impetuosity of some of his officials in the outlying provinces. With their help it was not difficult for him to maintain unimpaired the empire he had inherited from his father and even to extend its boundaries. The *Divyāvadana* tells the story of a revolt in Taxila, the citizens of which complained of the high-handedness of certain *amātyas*. That there was a substratum of truth in the complaint appears not improbable in view of certain words of Aśoka himself in the Kaliṅga edicts that refer to the measures adopted by that great emperor to check ministerial oppression in the provinces. When Bindusāra was confronted with a difficult situation in Taxila, he is said to have commissioned Aśoka with the task of restoring order. This the prince accomplished without much difficulty as the people "were not opposed to the *Kumāra* or even to king Bindusāra" and had grievance only against the "wicked officials" (*dushṭāmātyāh*). The Maurya prince is said to have pushed on to the Svaśa *rājya*, evidently a mislection for Khaśa *rājya*, the realm of the Khaśas, whose settlements extended, according to Stein, in a wide semicircle from Kastvar to the Vitasta (Jhelum) valley in the south and west of Kashmir.[4]

Some interesting details about the warlike activities of Bindusāra and his Chancellor, the Brāhmaṇ Chāṇakya, are recorded in the history of Tāranātha. We are told that they destroyed kings and nobles of about sixteen cities and reduced to submission all the territory between the eastern and the western seas. In view of the late date of the author it is difficult to say what

1. *Pariśishṭaparvan*, VIII. 446. ff. Cf. *Kathāsaritsāgra Kathapiṭhalambaka* 5th *Taranga*, Verse 115 ; Penzer's edition, I. p. 57.
2. *Divyāvadāna*, p. 372. *P.H.A.I.* 4th ed. ; pp. 243n, 248. The *Divyāvadāna*, p. 372 refers to a council of five hundred under Bindusāra.
3. R. L. Mitra, *Sanskrit Buddhist Literature of Nepal*, *p. 8*; Biganded II, p. 128.
4. *J.A.S.B.*, Extra No. 2, 1899 p. 69

element of truth is contained in his narrative. The vanquished monarches "between the eastern and the western oceans" have been taken to refer to the petty sovereigns of the Peninsula.[1] This is not a necessary inference as North India from Kāthiawar to Bengal may also be said to extend from sea to sea. Kaliṅga on the eastern coast of the Deccan is known to have retained its independence till the days of Aśoka. The statement of Tāranātha, if based on authentic tradition, need mean nothing more than the suppression of revolts of the type alluded to in the *Divyāvadāna* in the vast stretch of territory between Surāshṭra and the Gangetic delta. No Greek or Indian record of any early date connects the name of Bindusāra Amitraghāta with the conquest of any large tract of Peninsular India. Inscriptions of Kaliṅga and Mysore, which tell us so much about the Nandas, Chandragupta and Aśoka, are silent about the second Maurya.

Bindusāra seems to have been perfectly pacific abroad. He maintained the relations of friendship with the Hellenic world that had been established in the later days of his illustrious father. Diodorus testifies to the great love of the king of Palibothra (Pāṭaliputra), apparently an early Maurya monarch, for the Graecians. The policy was reciprocated by the Greek contemporaries of Bindusāra. Strabo refers to the sending of Deimachos to the court of "Allitrochades, son of Sandrokottos"[2]. We learn from Pliny that another envoy named Dionysius came from (Ptolemy II) Philadelphus, king of Egypt (285—47 B.C.)[3] The name of the monarch to whom he presented his credentials is not stated. The Egyptian king appears to have been a contemporary of both Bindusāra and Aśoka. The silence of Greek and Latin writers regarding Aśoka, when contrasted with repeated references to Chandragupta and Amitraghāta makes it probable that the monarch in question was Bindusāra, rather than his great son. Athenaeus, a Greek writer of the third century, tells us on the authority of Hegesander, that Amitrochates, king of the Indians, wrote to Antiochus (I of Syria) asking that monarch to buy and send him sweet wine, dried figs and a

1. *J.B.O.R.S.*, II, p. 79 ff.
2. II. 1.9. ; *Megasthenes and Arrian*, pp. 12, 19.
3. *Ibid.* pp. 13, 20 ; *Ancient India in classical Literature*, p. 108.

sophist. The Syrian king replied "we shall send you figs and the wine, but in Greece the laws forbid a sophist to be sold[1]".

The passage, brief as it is, is important in more respects than one. It reveals Bindusāra as a man who sought like his father to foster friendly contact with the outer world. The mention of sweet wine and figs coupled with the information vouchsafed by Phylarchus, Strabo and Appian, affords a glimpse of the kind of pacific intercourse between India and the west, diplomatic, social and commercial, that was ushered in by the treaty between Chandragupta and Seleucus. But the most significant fact noted by Hegesander is the demand for a Greek sophist. It affords proof not only of Bindusāra's taste for culture, but his special interest in philosophy. We may also take note of the story related by Diodorus of a Greek author Iambulous, who was hospitably received by the king of Palibothra who had a great love for Graecians. The name of the king is not given. But the tale admirably fits the correspondent of Antiochus. Nor was the interest of the king of Pāṭaliputra confined to Greeks alone. The *Divyāvadāna* has an interesting reference to an *Ājīva-parivrājaka* as a prominent figure in the court of the second Maurya[2]. Ājīvikas, it may be remembered, were special objects of the bounty of the later kings of the line like Aśoka and Daśaratha. The intensity of Aśoka's devotion to matters spiritual is better understood when we remember the kind of men his father loved to gather round himself. It is said in the Seventh Pillar edict that kings in times past also desired that "men might be made to progress by the promotion of Dhamma". Bindusāra might well claim a place among these past rulers. From him and some of the brilliant men who graced his court, Aśoka may well have imbibed ideas that fructified in later times, when he came into close touch with the Buddhist *Saṅgha*. The reign of Bindusāra may with plausibility be regarded as a prelude to that of his great son.

Certain unhappy incidents clouded, according to tradition, the last days of Bindusāra. He had doubtless many children, both sons and daughters, as we may infer from the Fifth Rock edict of Aśoka. If reliance can be placed on late chroniclers,

1. *Inv. Alex.*, p. 409n.
2. pp. 370ff ; *P.H.A.I*, 4th ed., p. 267n.

the relations among some of them were none too friendly. Aśoka, whom we have seen taking a prominent part in the affairs of the state during the life-time of his father, is represented as having seized the throne as the outcome of a fratricidal struggle. The story lacks confirmation from contemporary sources and its verification must await future discoveries. The incidents to which it refers, if they really took place, must have helped to deepen in the long run the religious conviction of Aśoka who sought to make amends for the misery he had inflicted on his fellow creatures in his unregenerate days.

CHAPTER V
MAURYAN POLITY

India attained political unity for the first time under the Mauryas ; it was the realization of age-long dreams associated with the names of many legendary heroes—Pṛithu, Bharata, Rāma and many other monarchs whose names occur in traditional lists of the performers of imperial sacrifices like the *Rājasūya* and *Aśvamedha*. In talking of the Mauryan empire, however, or indeed of any empire of ancient and mediaeval times, we should beware of importing notions of modern economic imperialism into the past. The Mauryan empire was indeed the first attempt in India to secure administrative centralization on an extended scale ; but it was nothing by the side of the ruthless concentration of policy achieved by modern empires, and the methodical and complete suppression of all local autonomy and initiative within their frontiers. Again, there was no belief then that the lord of the big battalions had a duty to impose the culture of his people on their weaker neighbours. Nothing can be farther from all this than the quiet tone in which Aśoka records the despatch of his missions to preach the *dharma* in alien lands and provide for the medical treatment of men and animals.

Sources

For the study of the political and administrative system of the Mauryan empire we are fortunately in possession of an abundance of authentic contemporary evidence such as we do not get for any other period of India's history until we reach the period of Mughal rule. Megasthenes, Kauṭilya and the Aśokan inscriptions, when correctly interpreted, supplement one another to a remarkable degree, and literary sources like *Divyāvadāna* and *Mudrārākshasa*, though they belong to much later times, appear to preserve a correct tradition in some parts and have their own contribution to make ; likewise the Girnār inscription of Rudradāman (A.D. 150) provides a welcome peep into the provincial administration of Gujarat under the Mauryas.

The real date and authenticity of the *Arthaśāstra* of Kauṭilya has been the subject of a long debate, which, while clearing up many issues, has led to no general consensus of opinion, though the balance is clearly in favour of the bulk of the work being accepted as a genuine picture of the conditions prevailing in the Mauryan epoch. In our view the book has stood the test of criticism and must now be accepted, with reservations, as the work of Kauṭilya, who shares with Chandragupta, the credit for the establishment of the empire and laying down the foundations of its administrative system. The position is set out in detail in an excursus at the end of this chapter.

The evidence of Greek and Latin authors and of the Aśoka inscriptions has been studied in some detail elsewhere in this volume, and will be adverted to only to the extent necessary for completing the sketch of polity attempted here.

Empire of Magadha

Magadha had already grown into a large imperial state under the Nandas, and the reports that reached Alexander's generals in the Punjab of the strength and efficiency of the army of the Prasii fixed them in their resolve not to hazard an encounter with a foe far more powerful than Porus, and thus compelled Alexander to abandon his dream of world conquest. The prestige of the empire of the Nandas, the failure of the tribal republics of the North-West in their hard-fought wars against the Greek invader, and subsequently the example of the empire of the Seleucids doubtless favoured the tendency already at work towards the formation of an all-India empire. The ideal of the *chakravartin* is for the first time brought down to earth from the cloud-land of religious myth and legend, and the *chakravartikshetram*, the sphere of the emperor's rule, is clearly defined in the *Arthaśāstra* as the whole of India extending from the Himalayas to the Indian Ocean and a thousand *yojanas* across.[1] The Mauryan epoch marks thus the definite triumph of the monarchical state against rival forms of political organization, particularly that of the tribal republic which became henceforth

1. *K.A.* IX. 1. I do not accept Dr. Raychaudhuri's limitation of the passage to Northern India, and I read *tiryak* and not *atiryak*. See *PHAI* 4., p. 220 n; also Jayaswal, *Hindu Polity*, Sect. 365; and *Rangaswami Comm. Vol.* p. 81.

much rarer than before and practically died out in the course of the next few centuries. There is reason to believe that Chandragupta and Kauṭilya were hostile to the non-monarchical states and that their policy was not averse to taking advantage of the weakened and impoverished condition in which these states found themselves after the ravages of the Greek war. The short section on policy towards *Saṅghas* (republics) in the *Arthaśāstra* (Bk. XI) gives a list of the names of important *saṅghas* still in existence, and describes numerous ways of sowing dissension among them and breaking them up that are open to a monarch who seeks to dominate them ; though, indeed, to preserve the character of a scientific treatise the section is concluded on a note of friendly advice to the *saṅghas* on how they could counteract the subtle assaults from ambitious monarchs on their unity and strength.

Republics

The names of republics actually mentioned by Kauṭilya fall into two groups ; one devoted to economic pursuits and to fighting with weapons like the Kambhojas, Surāshṭra, Kshatriya-śreṇi (Khathoi of the Greek writers) and others ; the others who used the title of *rājā*, apparently for marking the status of the members of the executive body of the republic, such as Licchivika, Vrijjika, Mallaka, Madraka, Kukura, Kuru, Pāñchāla and others. The Aśoka inscriptions mention Kambhojas and some other tribes. These republican states were apparently spread all over India at the beginning of the Mauryan empire, and many of them succeeded in retaining their individuality and surviving the Mauryan empire in spite of their hostile environment ; the use of the term *rājā* in many of them was perhaps a concession to a deep-rooted popular sentiment that favoured the name of the king.

Foreign Models

The age of the Mauryan empire was the age of the large monarchical state not only in India, but in all the lands that had formed the empire of Alexander for a brief period ; there was much similarity in the problems of political organization that had to be faced by the successors of Alexander and by Chandragupta Maurya. Considering the fairly steady contact maintained between the court of Pāṭaliputra and the Hellenistic monarchies, we may even suppose that Kauṭilya did not omit the study of foreign models in planning the administration of the newly established Indian empire and in the composition of his treatise on the *Arthaśāstra*. In fact he says expressly that he composed the work for the sake of his monarch after consulting all the *śāstras* then known and collecting information on the practices prevailing in states.[1] Without pressing the idea too far, we may find in it the explanation of the fairly close resemblances between the fiscal and bureaucratic arrangements in contemporary Egypt and Syria on the one side and the system of the *Arthaśāṣtra* on the other.

Royal Power

In an epoch of great monarchies, it was natural to exalt the power of the monarch. According to the general theory of Hindu Polity, the king was only the guardian of the law, not its maker ; laws depended for their validity on their intrinsic conformity to the standard of equity (*dharma*) and on the sanction of social usage ; and every decree of the king had to conform to both these sources of legal right.[2] With Kauṭilya, on the other hand, the royal decree has an independent validity of its own ; moreover, its validity is of so overriding a character that it must be taken to prevail against equity, private treaty or contract, and social usage.[3] This view of the supremacy of the royal decree is exceptional among Indian writers ; it comes in first with Kauṭilya, and is traced only in Nārada among subsequent texts. Kauṭilya also exalts reason (*nyāya*) above the prescription of texts (*śāstra*) in cases of conflict between the two, and boldly justifies the course on the plea that texts become corrupt with lapse of time. These statements placed by Kauṭilya at the head of the section on the administration of justice

1. End of *KA*. II. 10 *Śāsanādhikāra*, a chapter in which Stein sees evidence of a revision in the light of royal letters of the Early Roman Empire. *ZII*. Band 6, pp. 45—71.

2. Thus Kātyāyana :
nyāya-śāstrā-virodhena deśadrishṭes tathaiva cha I
yaṁ dharmaṁ sthāpayedrājā nyāyyam tad rājaśāsanam II
cited in *Parāśara-Mādhavīya, Vyāvahāra*, III. p. 13.

3. *KA*., III. 1 verses at end.

in the *Arthaśāstra*, clearly mark an attempt to evolve a new norm in civil law in the establishment of which the royal authority would be actively exerted both directly by the king himself, and indirectly by the judgements and rulings of the higher officials of state delivered in the name of the king. The same feature obtained in all the contemporary Hellenistic monarchies, and it is by no means unlikely that Kauṭilya was influenced by contemporary foreign practice when he put forward this new principle in his work.

Mauryan monarchy, however, was by no means a mere copy of foreign institutions any more than Mauryan art was an unthinking imitation of foreign models ; in either case specific features were borrowed but assimilated to the indigenous scheme so as to produce a harmonious whole ; that these efforts left no permanent results in Indian tradition is another matter.

The King

The king was primarily the wielder of the sceptre (*daṇḍa-dhara*), and his chief function was to maintain the social order by restraining the wrong-doers and ensuring the peace necessary for lawful men to pursue their avocations without hindrance.[1] Kings were described in this period as *devānāmpriya*, beloved of the Gods, and perhaps also as *priyadarśana*, of gracious appearance. The throne looked for support to the sacerdotal power and generally got it ; this becomes clear from the relation in which Kauṭilya stands to Chandragupta, from the place of the *purohita* in the state as the special adviser of the monarch with whom he conferred alone in a difficulty, and from the comprehensive statement in the *Arthaśāstra* which clinches the traditional view saying : "Royal power (*Kshatra*) triumphs (even) without arms and ever remains invincible when it is held up by the Brāhmaṇa, is sanctified by the counsels of ministers, and follows the precepts of the *śāstras*".[2] The king led a strenuous life and was ever intent on the promotion of the well-being of his subjects. His daily routine was prescribed by the text-books, and Kauṭilya also reproduces this model time-table ; but he adds wisely that the monarch is to adjust his programme of work

1. *KA.* I. 4.
2. *Ibid.* I. 9, final verse.

according to his capacity and inclination.[1] He should ever be prepared to deal with urgent matters with quick despatch and should not make himself inaccessible to persons who wished to meet him on business, as this would lead to grave political disaffection. Diligence is his first duty. Aśoka, we shall see, lived up to this exacting ideal ; we have no reason to believe that Chandragupta and Bindusāra did otherwise. The observations of Megasthenes on the arrangements in the royal palace and the precautions taken for ensuring the safety of the king's person are fully borne out in the chapters of the *Arthaśāstra*[2]. All personal services to the monarch were performed by women ; the risks of food poisoning, and intrigues in the harem were carefully guarded against ; and on the occasions when the king issued from the palace, his route was guarded by armed soldiers. The princes were trained carefully and employed in situations suited to their capacity and taste ; on this question, apt to be particularly vexatious owing to the prevalent polygamy of kings, Kauṭliya dismisses all the antiquated and ingenious views put forward in the works known to him, and lays down the course dictated alike by common sense, propriety and the public good ; he is very clear that in no case should an ill-disciplined prince, even if he happened to be the only son of the reigning monarch, be employed in the affairs of state or permitted to sit on the throne. Ill-natured princes were to be put under restraint and kept out of harm's way.

Ministers and Council

The king was assisted by a number of ministers, the *purohita* being in a separate and highly respected category by himself ; the ministers were generally men of proved ability and character. There was no hard and fast rule regarding their numbers at any time, and they often met in council for transacting public business, and in cases of difference in views decisions were taken by majority of votes. Ministers who were absent from the court were sometimes consulted by letter. The king considered himself free to consult a single minister, or a number of them, or

1. *Ibid.* I. 19.
2. *Ibid.* I. 20—21.

the whole council according to the requirements of the subject on hand.[1]

King not owner of land

The evidence of the Greek writers on the royal ownership of all land in the state has been noticed elsewhere. But the idea of the whole state being the property of the king was unknown to Indian tradition, and Kauṭilya does not assert such ownership for the king. It was admitted on all hands that the king had an interest in the land in as much as he was entitled to a sixth of its produce, the price of the protection he accorded to the people and their possessions ; by virtue of this eminent domain, the monarch controlled and regulated the use of land, and in the chapter on the superintendent of agriculture (*Sītādhyaksha*)[2] Kauṭilya is seen stretching this right of regulation to its utmost limits. The rules in this chapter, if enforced all round, would have made all agriculture a vast state-regulated enterprise ; the scheme of warehouses maintained by the state and controlled by a superintendent, *Koshṭhāgārādhyaksha*, set forth elsewhere in the *Arthaśāstra*, shows that this plan of regulation included extensive market operations on the part of the government. Thus without actually asserting the king's ownership of the soil, Kauṭilya advocated and doubtless introduced into the administration all the detailed supervision and control of agricultural and marketing operations that would have arisen from such ownership ; and Greek observers who saw them with Hellenistic eyes naturally thought that in India as elsewhere, as for example in Ptolemaic Egypt, the king was the owner of the soil, the cultivators being his tenants[3].

1. *Ibid.* I. 15.

2. *Ibid.* II. 24 ; also II. 2. The phrase *svabhūmau* in II. 24, 2 does not mean 'Royal domain' but 'land suited to the growth of particular produce', as Ganapati Sastri rightly glosses. Perhaps it is a mistake for *sva-sva bhūmau.*

3. The Hellenistic view is set forth thus by Rostovtzeff in his *Social and Economic History of the Hellenistic world*, p. 269. "Absolute rule meant, alike from the Egyptian and from the Macedonian point of view, the ownership of the State, of its soil and subsoil, and ultimately of the products of the soil and the subsoil. The state was the 'house' (*oikos*) of the king, and its territory his estate. So the King managed the state as a plain Macedonian or Greek would manage his own household'. This view of polity never obtained in India. So far as I know there is only one instance in Indian literature of the apparent assertion of royal ownership of all land and water, and that is in

Bureaucracy

In fact the great elaboration with which the machinery of central government is dealt with by Kauṭilya in the *Adhyaksha-prachāra* (Book II) is worthy of a modern Manual of Administration ; it contemplates a vast, numerous and all-pervading bureaucracy keeping itself in touch with all phases of the economic and social life of the country, and having at its command a mass of accurate and detailed information on the human and material resources of the entire country. The speedy and successful creation of an army of officials and the organisation of them into a well-ordered bureaucracy was by no means an easy task ; and the performance of this great task with reasonable efficiency is another point of resemblance between the Mauryan State and the Hellenistic monarchies. Both were aided here no doubt by models set by the empire of the Achaemenids ; for there is good reason to believe that the Persian administration had in its hands itineraries containing descriptions of the roads in the empire with a record of distances and stopping places, and that for purposes of taxation and preparation for war they maintained a fairly reliable census of the towns and villages, their inhabitants and resources. It is certain that the administrative machinery of Alexander and his successors was virtually a continuation of that of the Persian monarchs, and such continuity would not have been possible without the help of documents and information accumulated and preserved in the Persian archives.

Mauryan administration was a growing system subject to constant change under the stress of new situations and problems ; and the *Arthaśāstra*, though to a large extent based on contemporary practice, is still a *śāstra*, a normative plan rather than a description of existing conditions. Aśoka, as will be seen, introduced changes into the system, some of which he outlined in his inscriptions. Nevertheless, the central machinery of

the verse cited by Bhaṭṭasvâmi in his commentary—*KA*. II, 24 : *Rājā bhūmeḥ patirdṛshṭaḥ śāstrajñair udakasya cha, tābhyām anyat tu yad dravyaṁ tatra svāmyam kuṭumbinām*. But even here *pati* may indicate no more than the right of eminent domain, as is clearly the case with the expression '*bhūsvāmi*' in a closely argued passage of Kātyāyana which has not been always correctly understood in spite of the excellent gloss attached to it. See U. N. Ghoshal, *Beginnings of Indian Historiography etc.*, pp. 158—66.

administration envisaged in the *Arthaśāstra* may well be accepted as a representation of its condition towards the close of Chandragupta's reign, and Kauṭilya probably had no small share in building it up.

Central Offices

The business of supervising the collection of revenue from the whole kingdom was the work of the *Samāhartā* (Collector-general) ; he had to give his attention to all fortified towns, provinces, mines, gardens, forests, quadrupeds and trade-routes, which were the chief sources of income. Tolls, fines, fees for assaying weights and measures, police, currency, pass-ports, liquor, slaughter-houses, the manufacture of yarn, oil, ghee and sugar, goldsmiths, warehouses, prostitutes, gambling, buildings, guilds of carpenters and artisans, temples, and dues collected at the entrance (to towns) from troupes of performers (*bāhirikas*), formed the chief sources of revenue from towns. In the provinces the sources of income were land and agriculture, trade, ferries, traffic in rivers and roads, pastures and so on. The *Samāhartā* had the control of expenditure as well ; the chief items of expenditure were religious worship and gifts ; the royal family and the royal kitchen ; embassies, warehouses, armouries, factories and free labour, infantry, cavalry and elephant corps of the army ; cattle-farms and menageries, and storage of fodder and fire-wood. The *Sannidhātā* whose duties combined those of chamberlain and treasurer had charge of the construction of treasuries and warehouses of suitable strength and proportions wherever they were required, and was the custodian of the realised revenue in cash and kind. He cut counterfeit coins and received all articles only if they were of proper quality. He wa also made responsible for the construction of royal trading-houses, armoury, jails, courts of justice and offices of ministers and secretaries (*mahāmātriya*). All these buildings were to be equipped with wells, privies, bathrooms, fire-fighting appliances and other accessories. The accounts branch of the government had an elaborate organization, and the account year ran from *Āshāḍha* to *Āshāḍha* (July-August) as it does to this day in indigenous firms and banks ; expenditure was classified into current, recurrent, occasional and so on ; there were a number of prescribed registers calculated to facilitate checking, and detailed instructions laid down for the detection of embezzlement ; evasion of detection by clever officials was regarded as always possible, and frequent transfers advocated as a means of preventing them from eating into the substance of the state. The central accounts office was also the general record office (*akshapaṭala*).

The chapters of the *Arthaśāstra* dealing with the duties of superintendents (*adhyakshas*), of whom no fewer that twenty-six are mentioned in a regular series besides others incidentally referred to elsewhere, give a fair idea of the variety and range of the tasks attempted by the central executive of the empire. These superintendents were what we should now call heads of departments, functioning under the general control and supervision of a minister (*mantri*) who had charge of a group of allied departments. Their duties comprised the exploitation of crown property as well as the regulation and control of the economic and social life of the community. The names of the departments mentioned in the *Arthaśāstra*, are : Treasury, Mines, Metals, Mint, Salt, Gold, Storehouses, Trade, Forest produce, Armoury, Weights and Measures (capacity), Measurement of space and time, Tolls, Spinning and weaving, Agriculture, Intoxicating liquor, Slaughter houses, Courtesans, Shipping, Cattle, Horses, Elephants, Chariots, Infantry, Passports, Pastures, Elephant-forests, Spies, Religious Institutions, Gambling, Jails, and Ports. The duties of these superintendents are described in considerable detail and some of them at least were assisted in their work by boards[1] which seem to have caught the attention of Megasthenes rather more than the individual officers presiding over them. We need hardly enter here into all the administrative details found in the *Arthaśāstra* ; but only note that a government which undertook such delicate tasks as the medical inspection of or the regulation of the rates charged by courtesans, of the punishment of householders who turned ascetics without making adequate provision for their dependents, and of the control of the visits to villages of peripatetic parties of musicians, dancers and acrobats so as not to interfere with the

1. Such boards are expressly mentioned by Kauṭilya for the four main divisions of the army. *KA.* II. 4.

productive activity of the villagers[1] must have displayed an energy in administration altogether new in India. In other respects like the care of the sick and the destitute as well as of widows and orphans, the provision of work for the unemployed and regulation of wages and prices, the *Arthaśāstra* may be said to systematize and amplify administrative duties which had been accepted in principle by earlier Indian writers.

District and Town Administration

The revenue and general administration was carried on in the districts by *sthānikas* and *gopas*, with their own staffs of officials. The *gopa* had charge of five to ten villages in which he supervised the maintenance of boundaries, registered gifts, sales and mortgages, and kept an accurate census of the people and their material resources. The *sthānika* had similar duties in the district under his charge and the *gopas* necessarily functioned under him. The *sthānikas* were responsible to the *samāhartā* who commanded the services *pradeshṭṛs*,[2] doubtless identical with the *prādeśikas* of the Aśoka inscriptions, for the supervision of the details of local administration. Urban administration was organised on more or less similar lines under a *nāgaraka* (city magistrate) with *sthānikas* and *gopas* assisting him, the *gopa* having charge of the details of a fixed number of families in the city instead of a number of villages as in the rural areas.

Villages

The villages were, as ever in ancient India, semi-autonomous, enjoying a good deal of freedom in ordering their affairs; they regulated land and waterrights, cultivation and payment of revenue through the *grāmaṇi*, an official of the central goverenment ; the village-elders (*grāma-vṛiddhas*) are often mentiond in the *Arthaśāstra*[3] and they must have had a large share in guiding the people generally and in assisting the officials of the government in disposing of petty disputes arising in the village. Cultivable land was parcelled out in estates belonging to indivi-

1. *Ibid.* II. 1.
2. *Ibid.* II. 35.
3. *Ibid.* II. 1 ; III. 5, 9, 12.

duals, while pasture and forest lands were held in common. The check and control of the bureaucracy was provided not only by officials openly charged with such duties of inspection, audit and report like the *pradeshṭris*, but by the regular employment of spies and *agents provocateurs* ; the role of spies is no doubt greatly exaggerated in the scenes of the *Mudrārākshasa* which purports to dramatise the revolution by which the empire of the Nandas was overthrown and that of the Mauryas founded by Kauṭilya and Chandragupta ; but the constant use of secret means in administration, diplomacy and war was everywhere taken for granted and few modern governments could be said yet to have outgrown the practice.

Provinces

That the empire was divided into a number of provinces, each under a governor, and that princes of the blood royal were employed as governors whenever possible, becomes clear from the Aśoka inscriptions and Buddhist literature. The *avadānas* contain stories of oppression by wicked ministers in the outlying provinces like Gandhāra, and of the revolt of subjects against such oppression. But few definite facts bearing on the details of provincial administration are forthcoming, and we do not know exactly the relations of the governors to the central government on the one hand and the autonomous tribes and kingships comprised within their sphere of control on the other. We may guess that the provincial courts were smaller replicas of the imperial court at Pāṭaliputra, from which the emperor directly administered the home provinces. The distinction between rural and urban administration must have prevailed in the provinces also. There is a short and pithy reference in the Girnār inscription of Rudradāman (A.D. 150) to the construction of lake Sudarśana by the Rāshṭriya Vaiśya Pushyagupta in the reign of Maurya Chandragupta, and its extension and improvement by the addition of pipes, sluices and so on by the Yavanarāja Tushāspa acting on behalf of Aśoka[1] ; this is solid testimony to the continuous attention given by Mauryan emperors to large works of public utility,

1. *EI.* VIII. 43.

to the efficiency of their bureaucracy, and to the preservation of the memory of both through several centuries. Two records, the Sohgaura copper-plate from the U. P. and the Mahasthān inscription from Bengal, both fragmentary, are engraved in characters of the Mauryan epoch, and may well belong to that age ; but difficulties of interpretation detract much from their value to the historian. The Sohgaura plate seems to record an order of the Mahāmātras of Śrāvastī issued from their camp at a place called Mānāvasiti ; the order mentions the *koshṭhāgāras* of some places and the articles stored in them[1]. Store-houses also find a place in the Mahasthān record the import of which is still less certain.[2] Even these faint gleams should serve as warning against the facile characterisation of the vast administration of the Mauryan empire as 'no doubt more effective in theory than in practice.'

Finance

Of the revenue resources, public expenditure and the financial position of the Mauryan empire we can form only vague impressions as the data for quantitative estimates are totally lacking. Mention has already been made of the principal items of revenue in town and country listed by Kauṭilya in describing the duties of the *Samāhartā* (collector-general). Using modern expressions for easy comprehension, we may say that the main heads of revenue were : (1) a share of the produce of land, theoretically a sixth part, but in practice generally a higher proportion varying with local economic conditions ; (2) other dues and cesses laid on land including a water-rate which varied according to the nature of the land and crop, and tax on houses in towns ; (3) income from crown lands, from forests which must have been very much more extensive then than at present, and from mines and manufactures, some of them monopolies like salt, undertaken by government ; (4) customs at the frontiers, and octrois, tolls and ferry dues in the interior levied on merchandise in transport ; (5) profits of coinage and gains from trade operations carried on by the

1. *IA*. XXV. 261—6 ; *JRAS*. 1907, p. 501ff ; *ABORI*. XI. 32 ff ; *EI*. XXII. 1—3.
2. *EI*. XXI, 83 ff, *IHQ*. X, 57—66.

government ; (6) fees for licenses of various kinds to be taken out by artisans, craftsmen, professionals and traders ; (7) fines levied in law courts ; (8) miscellaneous receipts like presents, escheat of ownerless property and share in treasure-troves. In times of emergency 'benevolences' (*praṇaya*) were resorted to, and the rich were forced to pay considerable amounts to the state under one pretext or another. Patañjali mentions the fact that the Mauryas introduced images with a view to gain gold—*Mauryaīr hiraṇyārthibhir arcāḥ prakalpitāḥ* ; the exact method of thus replenishing the treasury is not clear. The practice had become established even in this early period of granting exemptions from payment of revenue—particularly land-revenue—in favour of Brahmins and religious institutions, and of making assignments of revenues, in whole or in part, in favour of state-officials, in lieu of or in addition to their salaries ; a careful register of such remissions and assignments was of course maintained, the village of Lumbini for instance was the recipient of a partial remission from Aśoka on the occasion of his visit to the place, it being required to pay only an eighth share of its produce to the royal fisc, instead of the usual fourth.

Under expenditure we should notice the maintenance of the monarch and his court and of the members of the royal family in due pomp and the salaries of ministers and other officials, high and low ; these salaries are defined in the *Arthaśāstra* (V. 3), but neither the unit of currency nor the period to which the figures relate is expressly stated. Public works including buildings, roads and irrigation works, the demands of the vast army in its various branches, the erection of forts and arsenals and their proper equipment, grants to religious institutions of various kinds, the maintenance of the families of soldiers and civil officials dying in state service, the care of the unemployed and the indigent are other heads that figure prominently in the *Arthaśāstra*. There must have been a considerable outlay on industrial, mining, and other enterprises worked by the state which recognized a special responsibility towards skilled artisans. Herdsmen and hunters were encouraged by allowances granted to them to keep the land clear of wild beasts and secure the safety of the roads. Aśoka spent large sums in establishing hospitals for men and animals and raising gardens of medicinal herbs within his vast empire and even outside it.

Justice

For the administration of justice, there were two sets of courts besides the village tribunals that dealt with petty cases under the guidance of the headman and elders ; these were styled the *Dharmasthīya* and *Kaṇṭakaśodhana*. At the top of the whole system was the king who could no longer make himself personally responsible for the entire administration of justice as in the smaller kingdoms of the earlier times reflected in the early *dharma-sūtras*, but was ever ready to hear matters on appeal and dispose of them without undue delay. The *dharmasthīya* courts were presided over by three *dharmasthas* learned in sacred law and three *amātyas*, and there were courts in all important cities and other convenient centres ; rules were laid down about circumstances which rendered agreements void, and about procedure in court—plea, counterplea and rejoinder. The main heads of civil law dealt with (1) marriage and dowry including divorce (*mokṣha*), (2) inheritance , (3) houses, house-sites and disputes regarding boundaries and water-rights, and trespass, (4) debt, (5) deposits, (6) serfs, (7) labour and contract, (8) sale, (9) violence, (10) abuse, (11) assault, (12) gaming and miscellanea. In many respects Kauṭilya is seen to lay down rules that alter and liberalise the precepts of the ancient texts, and in his hands the exposition of the whole subject is more rational and progressive than orthodox and conservative. In the absence of witnesses the ordeal was resorted to. Punishments were carefully graded and executed by royal authority ; they included fines, imprisonment, whipping and death with or without torture. There must have been in existence also caste *panchāyats* and guild courts which regulated the affairs of communities and professions and dealt with disputes among them in the first instance.

The *kaṇṭakaśodhana* (removal of thorns) courts were presided over by three *pradeshṭṛis* or three *amātyas*. The basis of the distinction between these courts and the *dharmasthīya* courts is nowhere clearly explained. The suggestion has been offered[1] that while the *dharma* courts dealt with disputes brought

1. Kane, *History of Dharmaśāstra* III. p. 257.

before them by the parties and strictly corresponded to our civil courts, in the *kaṇṭakaśodhana* courts the actions started on the initiative of the executive. This looks plausible in the light of modern juristic ideas, but it may well be doubted if the distinction between the two sets of courts was so simple and clear-cut. For instance, while assault and hurt were generally dealt with by the *dharma* courts, assault ending in manslaughter was reserved for the *kaṇṭakaśodhana*.[1] The truth seems to be that the *kaṇṭakaśodhana* courts were a new type introduced to meet the growing needs of an increasingly complex social economy, and to implement the decisions of a highly organized bureaucracy on all matters that were being brought under their control and regulation for the first time and were unknown to the old legal system. These courts were special tribunals which followed a more summary procedure than the regular *dharma* courts that dealt with *vyavahāra* as developed in the tradition of the *dharmaśāstras* ; their functions were only quasi-judicial, and their methods had more in common with those of a modern police force than of a judiciary. Their aim was to protect the state and people from baneful actions of anti-social persons, the thorns (*kaṇṭaka*) of society. They resorted to the use of spies for the detection of such activity and of torture for the extortion of confessions. The merchant who used short measure or false weights, the artisan who failed to keep his contract with his employer, the physician who caused the death of his patient by his lack of skill, the official who swindled the state or took bribes, and the conspirator who contemplated treason against the king—were all dealt with by these courts. Theft, murder, burglary, combinations to raise or depress prices, rape, defiant violation of caste rules and so on, are also among the offences brought before these courts. In these courts we may well recognize another innovation of Kauṭilya, based on foreign models and calculated to strengthen the power of the monarch and the position of the new bureaucracy. They represent an effort at once to safeguard government and society from the possible evils of the new order that was being introduced. Government control and regulation of activities of the people was

1. KA. III. 20. *vipattau kaṇṭakaśodhanāya niyeta*—Gaṇapati Śastri's reading. Also Kangle's, III 19, 15.

becoming more and more far-reaching and ubiquitous, and new offices carrying vast discretionary powers were coming into existence ; a mass of new regulations bearing on agriculture, trade and industry was being promulgated ; to secure the enforcement of these regulations and to see that they were not either employed by officials to tyrannize over the people or evaded by the people with the connivance of corrupt officials, there was required some machinery which would furnish the drive needed and provide the necessary checks and controls ; the *kaṇṭakaśodhana* courts were calculated to do all this. Later law books do indeed talk of *kaṇṭakaśodhana*[1]; but in them we miss the note of urgency that dominates the chapters of Kauṭilya on the subject, though the restraint of the wicked came generally to be accepted as part of the king's duty ancillary to the protection of the lawful citizens (*dushṭa nigraha śishṭa paripālana*).

Aśoka maintained the framework of polity as he found it though he created some new offices for the spread of Dharma and sought to impart by example and precept an earnest moral tone to the entire system of administration ; a detailed account of the emperor's work as administrator will be given in the chapter on his reign.

Foreign Policy

It is in the sphere of foreign policy that Kauṭilya's work seems to conform more to the tradition of his predecessors. That tradition was dominated more by a desire to make the *śāstra* complete by a systematic exposition of all possibilities than by an attempt to discuss real political situations. It is indeed often enough true that neighbouring states are seldom friendly to each other ; but the *maṇḍala* theory erects this into a principle, makes the unvarying assumption that the neighbour state is an enemy and the alternate one an ally, and works out the implications in tedious detail. We need not pursue this scheme here ; for the concepts of the *vijigīshu* (conqueror), the four *upāyas* (instruments of policy), the sixfold policy (*shāḍguṇya*) and so on are common to the treatises of polity of all ages in India, and had the least direct relation to political facts in the best days of the Mauryan empire when practically the whole of India acknowledged its

1. Manu IX. 252—3.

sway and there was little or no scope for the application of the precepts of the *maṇḍala* theory. Modern writers have often remarked on the unscrupulous and 'Machiavellian' nature of these precepts ; but one may well doubt whether the work of modern foreign and war offices described with a due regard, not to their professions, but to what they actually perform, will be seen to evince a better respect for morality. On the other hand the Indian text-books often developed extravagant theories having little relation to practice for the sake of the completeness of the *śāstra*. The ascertained facts bearing on the relations of the three great Mauryan emperors with the few independent states in India and the Hellenistic monarchies outside have been noticed in the accounts of the reigns of these monarchs.

Army

The Mauryan empire maintained a large standing army adequate to all its needs, internal and external. Pliny, doubtless basing his statement on Megasthenes, put the strength of Chandragupta's forces at 600,000 infantry, 30,000 cavalry and 9,000 elephants. He says nothing of chariots, but their number was placed at 2,000 by Diodorus and Curtius, and at 8,000 by Plutarch—all of them recording reports that reached Alexander about the number of chariots in the army of the King of the Prasii, that is, the Nanda predecessor of Chandragupta. The *Arthaśāstra* mentions different types of chariots—war chariots and chariots used for assaulting fortresses among them[1]. References to Mauryan war chariots seem to occur in some Tamil poems of a somewhat later date.[2] There were superintendents (*adhyakshas*) set over each of the four sections and they were charged with the duty of procuring the necessary supplies and keeping the men, animals and machines in proper trim. Stress is laid on the importance of the elephant corps and great attention devoted to the proper maintenance of elephant forests (*nāgavana*). Among the infantry Kauṭilya distinguishes different types—hereditary troops, doubtless the same as the fighting class (Kshatriyas) whom Megasthenes placed next to the cultivating classes in numbers and importance ; hired troops ; troops

1. KA. II. 33.
2. Chapter on South India and Ceylon.

maintained by guilds and available to the state at need ; and forest tribes who furnished troops to the king in times of war. The organization of the army in the field was an elaborate affair, and there are discussions of the value of different formations based on clear distinctions between vanguard, centre, rear, wings, reserves and so on, and between the requirements of march, attack and defence. The value and use of different types of weapons was also much canvassed, and among such weapons were a variety of stationary and mobile engines—one of them being known as the hundred-slayer. "The art of fortification was well understood and Indian forts of the time were strong and systematically designed with ditches, ramparts, battlements, covered ways, portcullises, and water-gates ; and in the assault the arts of mining, countermining, flooding mines were employed no less than the devices of diplomacy" (F. W. Thomas). Further details on the equipment of Indian troops and their mode of fighting preserved by Greek observers have been noticed elsewhere. The superintendents of the forces functioning either alone or with the assistance of boards must have been subject to the general control of the commander-in-chief (*Senāpati*) who was among the most important officers of the state. There were periodical inspections of all the troops by the commander-in-chief and the emperor ; according to Bāṇa, it was at one such military review that Pushyamitra contrived to do away with the last Mauryan ruler, the weak and shiftless Bṛihadratha. Kauṭilya mentions a *nāvadhyaksha,* superintendent of ships,—which might have included fighting units besides merchantmen.

Review

The polity of the Mauryan empire was thus in part a culmination of the development of an indigenous tradition of imperialism which had begun to take shape under the Nandas and in part comprised wise borrowings and adaptations from contemporary foreign models, immediately Hellenistic, but ult mately traceable to the Achaemenid empire of Persia ; the work of Kauṭilya which expounds the principles and describes the machinery of government was likewise based on the Indian tradition of the various schools of Arthaśāstra on the one side and on the known practice of foreign states on the other. Whatever was due to alien inspiration in Kauṭilya's system failed to take root ; the Mauryan system of administration like Mauryan art was in some of its essentials an exotic—a parenthesis that broke the course of normal indigenous development ; but both were splendid efforts marked by a considerable measure of success in their time. That Kauṭilya kept close to the fundamentals of Indian tradition is seen from his categorical statement that in order to be effective and successful, political power must command the support of the sacerdotal power besides having the sound advice of experienced statesmen at its disposal. He also gives to the welfare of the citizens the first place in all considerations of policy ; the good of the people and their sustained happiness are the main ends for the service of which he rears up the elaborate administrative system briefly described above. He does not by any means overlook the supreme importance of the presence of an able, energetic and good monarch for the proper functioning of that system ; that such rulers were not forthcoming after Aśoka was the tragedy of the Mauryan empire, as of all hereditary monarchies. Kauṭilya's ideal of good government is best seen from his exhortation to the king to place the happiness of the people above his own personal comfort, and feel that his happiness consists in their well-being.

prajā sukhe sukhaṁ rājñaḥ prajānāṁ ca hite hitaṁ I
nātmapriyaṁ hitaṁ rājñaḥ prajānāṁ tu priyaṁ hitaṁ II

"The happiness of the subjects is the happiness of the king ; their well-being, his. The king's welfare lies not in his own pleasure, but in that of his subjects."

Excursus on the Arthasastra

There is not, and probably there never will be, a general agreement about the date and authorship of the *Arthaśāstra* of Kauṭilya ; but doubts regarding the age and genuineness of the work have not been allowed to hinder the free use of the book in studies on Mauryan administration and society.

The volume of polemical literature that has grown round the work is too great to be reviewed here in its entirety. Prominent among those who have stood up for the genuineness of the work and a Mauryan date for it are : Shama Sastri who discovered the book and edited and translated it (1909—15) for the first time, Jacobi, V. A. Smith, Jayaswal, Ganapati Sastri—who issued a fresh edition of the text with an excellent commentary based on an earliar Malayalam-Tamil gloss and J. J. Meyer who translated the work into German, and more recently Breloer. On the other side we have Jolly, Keith, Winternitz, O. Stein, F. W. Thomas, E. H. Johnston. Other scholars like Hillebrandt hold that the present text contains a genuine core much overlaid with additions and emendations by later hands.

In the introductions to his edition of the *Arthaśāstra* and his English translation, Dr. Shama Sastri briefly set forth the evidence, internal and external, in favour of the work being accepted as a genuine production of Kauṭilya, the celebrated Chancellor of Chandragupta Maurya. That evidence is strong and remains unshaken in spite of everything that has been said to the contrary.

Some of the objections taken are trivial and due to misunderstanding of Indian literary practice or of the Sanskrit idiom. That Kauṭilya (Crooked) is not a name that a great minister of State would have borne, that if he was the author he would not cite himself as '*iti Kauṭilyaḥ*', much less refute himself, and that Daṇḍin refers to the work of *ācārya* Viṣṇugupta as recent, are examples. Other objections, vague and inconclusive, are of value only as indices to the prejudices of those that propose them : such are, for instance, the view that the Chancellor of the first Mauryan emperor had enough to do otherwise and could not have found time to write so systematic a treatise on politics and administration ; that the *Arthaśāstra* is so full of pedantry and schematic classifications that it could only have been written by a Pandit and no practical administrator or statesman ; that the polity of the *Arthaśāstra* is a small state and not an all-India empire like that of the Mauryas. The last statement appears a little more plausible than the rest only if we forget that the *Arthaśāstra* contains a specific reference to the whole of India being the *Cakravartikṣetram* (IX i), that Indian imperialism seldom resulted in the destruction of the polity of subject states, and that in the whole range of Indian political literature there is no other work with a better claim than the *Arthaśāstra* to be considered a manual of Imperial polity.

The KA., it has been argued, is too cyclopaedic a work to be considered the production of a single author, and in several technical sciences, civil and military, in architecture, metallurgy and so on, it represents a state of advancement which we can hardly ascribe to India of the fourth century B. C. This ignores Kauṭilya's express statement that he consulted *all* the *arthaśāstras* of his predecessors in the field (*yāvanti arthaśāstrāṇi pūrvācāryaiḥ prastāvitāni*), and *arthaśāstra* is a wide term which, as Winternitz has recognised, embraces technology, science, and all knowledge of practical arts besides politics. For the knowledge of agriculture, forestry, methods of elephant-lore, horse-training, mining and so on, the author may well have drawn upon such pre-existing works. And what right has any one to judge *a priori* the level of attainment in the practical arts that could legitimately be ascribed to India of the Mauryan epoch ? Let us not forget that the Aśoka pillars still exhibit a fine polish which time and neglect have not effaced, and of which the secret is yet to be discovered by the technicians of our own age. J. J. Meyer discusses these questions more fully in his introduction to his German translation of KA.

It has been said that no writer earlier than A.D. 300 is definitely known to allude to Kauṭilya ; but the Girnār inscription of Rudradāman (A.D. 150) knows of *praṇaya, vishṭi,* and other technical terms in the sense in which they are employed by him, and the *Tolkāppiyam* the earliest extant Tamil grammar, borrows the whole list of *Tantrayuktis* given at the end of the *Arthaśāstra* and adopts them with very minor and insignificant changes.

Kauṭilya deprecates the use of wood in fortifications and defences ; but that Pāṭaliputra was surrounded by a wooden palisade is evident from Greek writings and the results of excavations. But to assume that Kauṭilya must belong to a much later age is not by any means the only way in which this discrepancy could be explained. Other equally inconclusive evidences that have been cited as proof of a much later date for the *Arthaśāstra* than the Mauryan epoch are : the use of Sanskrit as the language of royal rescripts contemplated in the *Śāsanādhikāra* which is in striking contrast with the employment of Prākrit in the inscriptions for several centuries from the days of Asoka ; and the mention of Pārasamudra and Cīnabhūmi (II, ii) which remind us of Palasimundu of the Periplus and of the contact with the Chinese silk trade of a later epoch.

Several attempts have been made along different lines to arrive at a date for the *Arthaśāstra* later than the Mauryan epoch. Jolly has compared the *Arthaśāstra* with the *Dharmaśāstras* ; while he has succeeded in discovering many close parallels, it cannot be said that any clear conclusion can be drawn from them about the relative age of KA. Jolly has himself changed his mind ; in 1913[1] he was ready to concede that the text of Yājñavalkya as we know it did not exist when KA was written ; he said that while many neologisms are common between KA and the youngest smṛtis, there is little clue to decide which of them is earlier ; he was struck by many differences between KA and the smṛtis (torture, ordeals, divorce etc.) and accounted for them by assuming that they were due to deep-lying differences in standpoint known from the beginning between a code of custom and a text-book of politics. Finally he said that the kernel of KA belonged to about 300 B.C. and much of its contents was seen to be genuine by numerous early citations as shown by Zachariae, Hillebrandt, Hertel and Jacobi. The resemblances with the later smṛtis puzzled him and he left it an open question if the smṛtis revised the old law in the light of the KA or later ideas entered into KA and fused themselves inseparably with the text. Ten years later, in 1923 Jolly wrote : 'One cannot help arriving at the conclusion that Kauṭilya must have been acquainted with the whole body of Dharmaśāstra literature much as we now have it, from the earliest Dharmaśāstras down to the most recent metrical smṛtis and smṛti fragments'. Even the great authority of Jolly cannot gain assent for so extravagant a conclusion in preference to the hesitant tone that marked his expressions a decade earlier, especially when we find him adding as an afterthought : 'It is true that some facts seem to point the other way, so that Yājñavalkya instead of Kauṭilya would have to be regarded as the borrower, either directly or indirectly through the medium of a common source.'

1. *ZDMG.* 1913, pp. 49-96.
2. Introd. pp. 17-18.

Jolly employs a more general argument. 'Generally speaking', he says, 'the Dharmaśāstra or science of duty and religion has far better claims to a high antiquity than the Arthaśāstra or science of gain which in its turn is older than the Kāmaśāstra or science of love, the three sciences based on Trivarga having followed each other in point of time as well as in rank and value'.[1] One may well doubt this ; for even the earliest *dharmasūtras* known contain a core of rājanīti, the subject-matter of Arthaśāstra. Even granting the correctness of this sequence in the evolution of the sciences, we can get no decision from it about the age of any single work in view of the long tradition each of the sciences lays claim to. A plausible *a priori* case can be made out for the view that early Indo-Aryan life was gayer and more materialist in its outlook, that the sciences of gain and love had a better chance of coming up in that period than in a later time when Indians became more and more intent on the other world and began to lay greater stress on dharma and conceived of mokṣa as the *summum bonum* of life. In truth, we know as yet too little of the growth of the concept of *puruṣārthas* to be in a position to affirm or deny the truth of Jolly's proposition regarding the sequence of the sciences. But the Indian writers are seen to have recognised in their works the interdependence of the different ends of human endeavour, and no work is purely a work of dharma or artha to the exclusion of the other. And one of the best summaries of general dharma is found in the pages of the *Carakasamhitā*, a work of medicine. It is not much use laying stress on the open recognition in KA of 'reprehensible practices such as the murder of distinguished officers, the levying of highly oppressive taxes, the corrupt system of espionage', and seek to draw any inference from it either about the age of the work or on the character of administration in the age which produced the work. The author of the *Kāmasūtra* gives the clue which has not received the attention that it merits. He says :

na śāstram-astītyetena prayogo hi samīkṣyate |
śāstrārthān vyāpino vidyāt prayogāmstv-ekadeśikān ||

Science is all-embracing thought ; practice is quite another affair. The relentless logic with which the implications of

1. *Ib.* p. 20.

state policy are worked out in the KA is an example of the perfection of scientific thought such as it was, and is no index to everyday practice.

The *Kāmasūtra* of Vātsyāyana borrows from KA its plan and scope, and many peculiar terms as well as entire paragraphs. Hence, says Jolly, 'no long interval of time can have passed between the composition of two such cognate productions.[1]' Jacobi, as Jolly knows, did not think so, and in truth there can be no rule governing the interval necessary between an original and its imitation. The same consideration applies to the similarity of textual structure and of tantrayuktis between KA and the *Suśruta* to which attention has been drawn.[2] J. J. Meyer has also studied the relation between KA and the smṛtis with a view to determine the place of KA ; though his conclusion on the age of KA puts it in the Mauryan age, his views regarding the relative ages of the other smṛtis have not gained general acceptance and it seems unlikely that they ever will[3].

The comparison of the KA with the epics has also led to no better results. Following up a line of thought suggested by Jacobi in the first instance, Charpentier compared the legendary examples cited by KA with the corresponding episodes in the *Mahābhārata,* and he reached the conclusion that the current text of the epic must have come into existence sometime between the date of the KA and that of the *Kāmandakīya Nītisāra*[4]. He also pointed out that KA (1, 5) defines *itihāsa* in a manner that shows that K. was not thinking of our epic. On the other hand Hillebrandt and Meyer point out that the *Mahābhārata* knows all the predecessors of K. mentioned by him, but not K. himself ; and that the *kaccit* chapters in the *Rāmāyaṇa* (II 100) and the *Mahābhārata* (II 5) which agree with one another closely contain phrases which recall whole chapters of KA to the mind[5]. Hillebrandt shows further that the *Rāmāyaṇa* is fully acquainted with the detailed terminology of the *Arthaśāstra* and apparently draws several verses from older systematic treatises on the science.

1. *Introd.* pp. 21-24.
2. *IC.* IV. pp. 439-40.
3. *Uber das Wesen* and *IHQ*. IV. (1928) pp. 570-92.
4. *WZKM*. 28. (1914). pp. 211—40.
5. Meyer : *Das Arthasastra* Intr. pp. xxxvii ff. Also Hilleberandt : *Altindische-Politik*. pp. 6-16.

Clearly there is no hope of reaching along this line any precise chronological indications regarding the date of KA.

Another inconclusive effort to place KA about A. D. 250 is that made by E. H. Johnston[1]. He argues that Kauṭilya's work must have come into existence after the time of Aśvaghoṣa, but not very long after ; Aśvaghoṣa does not use the term *vijigiṣu* though he knows the forms *jigiṣat* and *jigiṣu*, and he remains well within the limits of Dharma in his references to politics; hence he must have preceded Kauṭilya. Yet, the common use of neologisms by the two writers (of which examples are cited) shows that no long interval separated the two writers. And the fact that Āryaśūra (A. D. 434) unlike Aśvaghoṣa parades his knowledge of Arthaśāstra in the *Jātakamālā*, and refers to Kauṭilya, shows clearly that he came later than Kauṭilya. But the only certainty that emerges from Johnston's arguments is that Kauṭilya wrote earlier than Āryaśūra's time. For Aśvaghoṣa was under no compulsion to accept Kauṭilya's outlook and vocabulary if he had the work before him ; many later writers are known to have declined to do so like Daṇḍin and Bāṇa, and to have condemned his doctrines and methods.

O. Stein's attempt to demonstrate that Megasthenes and Kauṭilya could not have belonged to the same period cannot be held a success. The detailed comparison of the fragments of Megasthenes with corresponding passages from the *Arthaśāstra* is valuable so far as it goes ; but as Breloer has pointed out the method followed is too superficial and mechanical. On important subjects like the ownership of the soil, slavery, social organisation, legal procedure, and administrative arrangements it is quite possible, as we have seen, to explain the apparent differences and discover much closer similarity than Stein has found between the statements of the Hellenistic ambassador and of the Brahmin Chancellor of the first Mauryan emperor. And Stein apparently fails to note that some of his results e.g. the difference between the two writers on milestones point logically to the conclusion that Megasthenes must have written after Kauṭilya. But we may not follow Breloer the whole length[2]. For we see little reason to accept his view that the

1. *JRAS.* 1929, pp. 77-89
2. Cf. *IHQ.* XI (1935). pp. 328-50.

theory of State-landlordism was introduced into India for the first time in the Mauryan epoch and borrowed from Ptolemaic Egypt ; as a matter of fact, as Breloer admits, there is no clear statement of this theory in the whole of Kauṭilya's work. According to Egyptian notions, the State was the 'house' of the king and its territory his estate[1]. Such an idea was not accepted in India even by extreme advocates of State-landlordism who only made the king *adhipati* suzerain or major partner, whose rights were strictly limited by law and custom. Much less are we persuaded that the Kauṭilyan polity was a completely planned economy after the Nazi model as Breloer seeks to make out in the latest and most comprehensive of his Kauṭilya-studies. The principle of local and sectional autonomy was too deeply rooted in Indian cultural tradition for even the all-powerful bureaucratic control and regulation of the Mauryan empire to extinguish it or even to curtail its operation to any very considerable extent ; witness the multiplicity of *metayage* arrangements in ch. II 14 on *sītādhyakṣa* which finds parallels in several other sections of the work. In the war years German scholarship turned, possibly had to turn, to Nazi propaganda which no one should take seriously[2].

The great value of the Kauṭilya studies of Breloer cannot be gainsaid. They offer several convincing interpretations by which the apparent conflicts between Megasthenes and Kauṭilya are resolved ; and they have done well to stress the fact that after Alexander's astonishing career, the world was no longer the same as before[3]. The great economic and political revolutions initiated by the establishment and the early break up of Alexander's empire, the increase in trade due to the multiplication of armed camps in the wars of 'the successors' and the divisions of the empire, the accumulation of large fortunes by some and the coming up of a proletariate, the dispersion of the large gold treasures of Persia and the quickening transition from a rural to a money economy, and the rise of several large territorial states under absolute monarchs were the chief features

1. Rostovtzeff, *Soc. and Ec. His. of the Hellenistic world* (1941) p. 269
2. Cf. Hauer, *Glaubengeschite der Indo-Germanen* i where Hitler is compared to Śrī Krishna.
3. KS. i. 108 ff.

of the new epoch. India was drawn more and more into this welter, and Chandragupta and his teacher grew up in this atmosphere of rapid change and new formations. War, trade, diplomacy and travel, opened up numerous channels of increasing contacts with the outer world, and it should be no wonder if the unique character of the *Arthaśāstra* is partly due to the stress of foreign ideas and influences pressing their way into the political and administrative system of the newly founded empire of the Mauryas. There is much force in Rostovtzeff's observation that 'if one believes in the historical character and the early date of the kernel of the *Arthaśāstra* of Kauṭilya and in the radical centralization of Indian government effected by Chandragupta on Hellenistic lines, one may say that Chandragupta did more to Hellenize India than Demetrius and Menander.'[1] It is, however, not merely a question of Hellenic influence; for we know with certainty that the administrative system of the Hellenistic monarchies in Asia and Africa 'was practically a continuation of that of the Persian kings and it is equally certain that no such continuation would have been possible without the help of the documents and information assembled in the Persian archives'[2]. In the natural reaction against Spooner's pompous announcement of a 'Zoroastrian period' in Indian history, there is a danger of Persian influences on Indian life being either altogether denied or considerably under-estimated. The mass and variety of detailed statistical information which the *Arthaśāstra* requires the officials of the State to collect and arrange for ready reference (e.g. in II 35 on *samāhartā* and 36 on *nāgaraka*) is something unique in all Indian political literature ; we are tempted to suppose that the model for Kauṭilya and the Hellenistic states was furnished by the practice of Persian kings and satraps maintaining lists of inhabited centres of eachs atrapy, together with approximate estimates of their population and material resources, lists which they employed alike for purposes of taxation and preparation for war[3]. Kauṭilya's categorical statement in III (i) that a royal edict (*rājaśāsana*) overrides *dharma*, *vyavahāra* and *caritra* is somewhat exceptional in the political

1. *Op. cit.* pp. 550-1.
2. *Ib.* p. 1034.
3. *Ib.* p. 1033.

literature of India though *Nāradasmṛti* follows the *Arthaśāstra* on this point ; the more usual rule is to require the king to frame his edicts in conformity to Dharma, and some writers even go the length of implying that if this condition was not satisfied the royal order was invalid. Kauṭilya's exaltation of the royal edict above canon and custom deserves to be compared with the growing dominance of royal legislation and jurisdiction, and the active exercise of royal authority in the sphere of civil law that were characteristic of the Persian empire and the Hellenistic monarchies[1].

Sylvain Lévi has argued that the mention of coral from Alexandria (*pravālam Alakandakam* II, 11, 41) shows that the *Arthaśāstra* must be later than the first century A.D. when the coral trade shifted to India according to Pliny and the Periplus[2]. But there are numerous references to *pravāla* (coral) in the earliest strata of the *Mahābhārata* not to speak of the occurrence of the word in the *gaṇapāṭha* where we cannot be sure of the sense of the term. There is little reason to doubt that the coral was known in India much earlier than the first century A.D., and we know that coral was a valued article of trade in the Hellenistic world.

It has been pointed out[3], lastly, that while Kauṭilya prescribes at II 6 the recording of the year, month, *pakṣa* and the day in specifying dates, the inscriptions of Aśoka nowhere follow this system while an approach to it is seen in the Kuṣāṇa records which give the regnal year, season and day, and the exact adoption of the rule of Kauṭilya is found for the first time in the Girnar inscription of Rudradāman. Rudradāman's inscription also employs the terms *praṇaya* and *viṣṭi* in the same senses as those known to KA. But this only shows that the composer of the Girnar praśasti may have known the KA, and means little for the date of that work. The Kuṣāṇa inscriptions do not follow the system of KA and may be left on one side ; Aśoka gives only the year from his coronation in his records and no other detail, evidently following the Persian models which he

1. *Ib.* pp. 1067-8.
2. *IHQ.* 12 (1936). pp. 120-33.
3. *IC.* IV. p. 442.

consciously followed. The Persian monarchs knew of a system of dating quite like that of the KA, but they did not employ it on all occasions, and the chronology of Darius's inscriptions is rather vague. Let us not forget also that the prescription in the KA regarding the manner of dating occurs in the chapter on revenue collection, and obviously bears a close relation to the form of accounts and is not connected with the issue of proclamations or edicts.

The author of the *Arthaśāstra* has been hailed on the one hand as the Indian Bismarck and a Realpolitiker, and dismissed on the other as a Pandit, a schematic theoretician whose logical categories had no relation to realities. An open-minded study of the entire work will reveal that there is some support from the work for either view; while the author does not shrink from pursuing traditional theories relentlessly to their logical conclusion as e.g. in the *maṇḍala* theory, still there are other sections of the work particularly the *adhyakṣa pracāra* which, like modern administrative manuals, deal with details of day to day work in public offices. And we should not omit to notice that in its concern for details of practical administration the *Arthaśāstra* is unique in the whole range of the Artha literature of ancient India. And some of its administrative terms like *puruṣa*, *yukta*, *mahāmātra* and so on re-appear in the edicts of Aśoka.

Considering its age and its technical character, we have reason to think that the text tradition of the KA has been quite good. Its length is indicated as 6,000 *ślokas* in the text itself and by Daṇḍin ; and our text, according to Dr. Shama Sastri 'is of about the same extent.'[1] But scribal errors, particularly in the transcription of unfamiliar geographical names about which Bühler has uttered a clear warning, and occasional interpolations or even rehandlings of parts of the text are not altogether ruled out of the range of probability. In a very useful and penetrating analysis of the *Śāsanādhikāra* (II 10)[2], Stein has sought to establish that this chapter as it stands bears a composite appearance and shows signs of having been remodelled in the light of Roman Imperial letters of a later time. But in

1. p. VII of the English translation.
2. *ZII.* VI (1928) pp. 45-71.

the opinion of the present writer the *Arthaśāstra* has stood the test of very vigorous criticism for so long that its genuineness must now be recognised to have been placed beyond doubt and that, with minor reservations, the work may properly be looked upon as the authentic production of the scholar and statesman who took a hand in the foundation of the Mauryan empire.

CHAPTER VI

AŚOKA AND HIS SUCCESSORS

The reign of Aśoka forms the brightest page in the history of India. The ruler himself takes rank easily among the master-minds of the world, and under his leadership India came to occupy the foremost place among the civilized nations of the time. Inheritor of an extensive and highly organised empire, Aśoka proved fully worthy of his heritage ; he was a man of unbounded energy and he gave himself without stint to the tasks of perfecting the administration of his empire and ensuring the happiness of his subjects. The range of his sympathies was wide, and he was by no means unwilling to adapt foreign models of administration and art to the growing needs and tastes of his country.

His own inscriptions clearly reveal to us the chief stages in the history of his reign and the motives underlying his activities. For more than a century these famous records have been the subject of patient and critical study by generations of scholars, and as a result of this study there has emerged a general agreement about the meaning of all inscriptions, though a few expressions still remain obscure. But the inscriptions are by no means evenly spread over the reign ; most of them fall into two large groups, one about the thirteenth and fourteenth years after the king's coronation, and another in the twenty-seventh and twenty-eighth years. Though they do mention a few events with the time of their occurrence, they are far from being a full record of the reign. In this respect they constitute a complete contrast to the difficult Hāthīgumphā inscription of Khāravela, and the much later *praśastis* of the various mediaeval dynasties.

Sources

Legend has cast a halo of glory around Aśoka as around all such heroes of nations ; and the legend of one age often derives its colour from the history of its predecessor. The cycle of Aśokan legends has come down to us in two versions. The southern recension, found in the two Pali chronicles of Ceylon

—*Dīpavamsa* and *Mahāvamsa*, in its present form, dates from the fourth and fifth centuries A.D., but rests on material of much earlier origin. The northern account in the *avadānas* presents the same features with variations. Some indication of the age of the *avadānas* we get from the fact that they are illustrated in the sculptures on the gateways of Sāñchī. Both versions contain amplifications, under the influence of local conditions, of a more primitive legend that had grown up among the Buddhist communities in the neighbourghood of Pāṭaliputra. Kauśāmbī and Mathurā might have been the centres where the peculiarities of the Southern and Northern recensions were developed round about 150-50 B.C[1]. The legends were primarily meant for the religious edification of the faithful ; the more valuable on that account to the historian are the historical details which they have preserved and which fit in with the data from the inscriptions. For the rest we must accept as fact whatever is not intrinsically improbable, though we have no means of deciding between contradictions in the rival versions. Was Aśoka in his youth viceroy at Ujjayinī (*Mahāvamsa*) or at Takṣaśilā (*Avadāna*) ? Was Tissa Moggaliputta or Upagupta the spiritual guide of Aśoka ? Both are placed by legend in the same relation to Buddha by a chain of four intervening patri archs. Or did Aśoka, as seems not improbable, follow his own bent and the redactors of legend invent the relation between the emperor and the patriarchs each after his own fashion ? To such questions no definite answers can be given.

'The extent of Aśoka's empire may be guessed already', says Hultzsch[2], 'from the distribution of his rock-edicts, which it seems were engraved along the very confines of his territories. In the west they are found at Girnar on the Kathiawar Peninsula and at Sopara on the Bombay coast ; in the south in the Raichur district of the Nizam's dominions and in the Chitaldroog district of the Mysore State ; and in the east at Dhauli and Jaugaḍa in the Purī and Ganjam districts. The north-eastern boundary line is marked by the rock edicts at Shāhbazgarhī and Mānsehrā in the Peshāvār and Hazāra districts and at

1. Przyluski—*La Legende*, ch. v. Also Marshall and Foucher—*Monuments of Sāñchī.*

2. *Inscriptions of Aśoka*, pp. xxxvi—vii.

Kālsī in the Dehrā Dūn district, and it is continued by the Nigālī Sāgar and Rummindeī pillars in the Nepalese Tarāī and by the Rāmpurvā pillar in the Champarān district'. The discovery in 1929 of a fresh set of the Fourteen Rock-Edicts and a minor Rock Edict at Yerraguḍi (near Gooty) in the Kurnool district, of fragments of Rock and Pillar edicts in Aramaic script in Laghman[1] and of a bilingual Greek and Aramaic version of a Minor Rock Edict at Kandahar in 1958 do not materially alter our estimate of the extent of the empire as borne out by the spread of the inscriptions. But one may legitimately doubt the surmise that the rock-edicts were engraved 'along the very confines' of Aśoka's territories; for tradition and probability alike suggest that the empire extended in some directions particularly in the north, north-west and the south well beyond the extent so defined.

The Greek and Aramaic inscription of Kandahar, issued in the eleventh year of the reign and anticipating in some ways the Minor Rock Edicts, is in a separate class by itself. The other inscriptions of Aśoka fall into the following classes which are set forth in the order in which they were issued in the course of the reign:

(1) Two Barābar cave inscriptions recording gifts of caves to Ājīvakas when the king had been anointed twelve years.

(2) The Minor Rock Edicts found in slightly different versions in several places—Bairāt (Rājasthān); Ahraura, Mirzapur district, (U.P.); Sahasram (Bihar), and Rūpnath (M.P.) and Gujarra in Northern India; Maski, Pālkiguṇḍu and Gāvīmaṭh (Andhra Pradesh); Brahmagiri, Siddāpura and Jatinga Rāmeśvara in Mysore, Yerraguḍi and Rajula Mandagiri (Kurnool) district) in the South. The Mysore and Yerraguḍi versions have a closer agreement among themselves, and they contain an addition to the edict of which the Yerraguḍi version is the fullest. These were issued in the thirteenth year afer Aśoka's coronation, along with.

(3) The unique Bhābrā edict, designated the Calcutta-Bairāṭ rock inscription by Hultzsch, and addressed to the Buddhist Saṅgha.

1. *BSOS*. xiii, p. 80

(4) The Fourteen Rock Edicts found in seven more or less complete versions at Girnār, Kālsī, Shahbāzgarhī, Mānsehrā, Dhauli, Jaugaḍa and Yerraguḍi, not to speak of the small fragment of the eighth rock edict found in Sopāra and others in Laghman. These were issued about the fourteenth year after the coronation.

(4a) The two Kalinga edicts, 'separate rock-edicts' as they are sometimes called, meant only for Kalinga ; at Dhauli and Jaugaḍa they take the place of the eleventh to the thirteenth edicts in the other collections, and they must have been issued along with (4) or very soon after.

(1a) The third Barābar cave inscription, the king having been anointed nineteen years.

(5) The Rummindeī and Nigālī Sāgar pillar inscriptions dated twenty years after the Coronation.

(6) The Seven Pillar Edicts dated 26 and 27 years after the coronation and found in six places ; the seventh edict, the longest and in some ways most important, is found only once with the others on the Delhi-Topra pillar. The Delhi-Mirath, Lauriya-Ararāj, Lauriya Nandangarh, Rāmpurvā, and the Allahabad-Kośām pillars contain only the first six edicts ; the last has in addition two short inscriptions, the unique record, called 'Queen's edict', and 'Kauśāmbī edict' on *Saṅghabheda* which falls into another class.

(5a) The minor Pillar edicts found in Sāñcī and Sārnāth besides Kauśāmbī, the Sārnāth version being the best preserved. This must have been issued towards the end of the reign sometime after the Seven Pillar Edicts.

There are thus about thirty-five Aśoka inscriptions of varying length and importance, many of them available in different versions. The language of the inscriptions is generally Māgadhī, the official language of the royal chancery at Pāṭaliputra; only some versions, particularly those of Girnār and Shābazgarhī, exhibit certain not very important indications of the influence of local dialectical variations.[1] The inscriptions in Shābazgarhī and Mānsehrā are in the Kharoṣṭhī alphabet written from right to left; a bowl of grey schist stone apparently from the Gandhāra

1. Senart in *IA*. xxi, p. 174.

region and now in the Prince of Wales Museum Bombay is found bearing the seventh Rock Edict in Kharoṣṭhī characters;[1] at the end of the inscriptions in the Mysore state the word *lipikareṇa* is also found written in Kharoṣṭhī ; otherwise all the Aśoka inscriptions except the Laghman fragments and the Kandahara record are written in one variety or other of the Brāhmī script. At Yerraguḍi, the Minor Rock Edict is found written partly in the boustrophedon style, that is alternately from left to right and vice-versa[2].

There are two lines of evidence bearing on the chronology of Aśoka's reign, in fact, of the history of the Mauryan empire ; neither of them leads to a precise conclusion, though both together may be taken to point approximately to the truth.

One is the reckoning in the era of the *pari-nirvāṇa* of the Buddha, preserved in the *Dīpavamsa,* which dates Aśoka's accession in 214 A.B. and his coronation in 218[3]. These precise indications unfortunately lose much of their value owing to the uncertainty of the date of the *nirvāṇa.* The choice seems to lie between 543 B.C. and 483 ; with the first date as the starting point, 218 A.B. would bring us to 325 B.C., a date more suited to the beginning of the Mauryan empire and of Chandragupta's reign than that of Aśoka. And the suggestion has been offered that in the chronicles of Ceylon, the epoch of the beginning of the Mauryan empire was mixed up with that of the Coronation of Aśoka which was the event they really cared for[4]. Ingenious as this reconciliation is, it is not easy to accept it in view of the fact the Buddha-varsha of 543 B.C. is a comparatively modern fabrication, whereas 483 B.C. has much better claims to be considered the true date of the Buddha era.,[5] With this as starting point, we get 265 B.C. for the coronation of Aśoka, 269 B.C. for his accession, 297 for that of Bindusāra and 321 for the accession cf Chandragupta, a scheme which has intrinsically much in its favour[6]. Some writers would,

1. Letter from the Museum dated 1-10-1963.
2. *ASI.* 1928-9 p. 164.
3. Obviously the *Divayāvadāna* (p. 368) and other northern works giving 100 years as the interval between the *pari-nirvāṇa* and Aśoka are confusing two Aśokas—Geiger tr. MV. p. lx.
4. *JBORS.* i. 97.
5. See Geiger's tr. of MV. Intr. Sectt. 5 and 6.
6. Hultzsch doubts the value of the figure 218—p. xxxiii.

however, prefer the date 486 B.C. for the death of the Buddha, on the strength of the Chinese 'dotted record[1].'

This scheme gains in strength from the confirmation it receives from the second line of evidence furnished by Rock-Edict XIII which gives the names of five contemporary Hellenistic monarchs : 'the Yona king Antiyoka, and beyond him four kings, viz., Turumaya, Antekina, Maka and Alikasudara'. The same monarchs are mentioned more summarily in the second Rock-Edict as : 'the Yona king Antiyoka and the kings who are the neighbours of this Antiyoka'. These kings are now identified respectively with Antiochus II Theos of Syria (261-46 B.C.), Ptolemy II Philadelphus of Egypt (285-247), Antigonus Gonatas of Macedonia (276—239), Magas of Cyrene (c. 300-250) and Alexander of Corinth (252-c.244). The date of the edict, thirteen years after the *abhisheka* would fall therefore between 252 and 250 B.C.[2], the period when all the kings mentioned were living, and the year of Aśoka's coronation must therefore lie between 265 and 263, and of his accession between 269 and 267 B.C. It is seen thus that these two lines of reasoning confirm and corroborate each other.

Some writers prefer to think of Alexander of Epirus who died about B.C. 255 in the place of the less known Alexander of Corinth, and thus fix the date of R. E. XIII at about that date[3].

It is now settled that the figure 256 at the end of the first Minor Rock inscription, whatever its exact significance may be, has no reference to a date in the Buddha era, and that far from being one of the latest inscriptions of the reign, it is most probably one of the earliest inscriptions of Aśoka.

Fleet drew attention to the references to the Tishya day in the Aśoka inscriptions ; and assuming that Aśoka held his *abhisheka* on such a day, and taking October 13, 483 B.C. as the day of Buddha's nirvāṇa, he calculated that April 25, 264 B.C. was the day of Aśoka's *abhisheka*[4]. But such precise calculations rest on too many unproved assumptions and will by no means command easy assent.

1. *JRAS* 1905, p. 51.

2. The limits would differ if Alexander of Epirus (272—c. 255) is thought of. See also discussion of chrnology under Chandragupta by H. C. Raychaudhuri.

3. *Acta Orientalia,* 1940 pt. *ii.*

4. *JRAS* 1909 pp. 26 and 28-34.

Name

The name Aśoka (sorrow-free) occurs but twice in the inscriptions, once in the Maski record which begins *devānāṁpiyasa Asokasa* and again in the Gujarra record; but this fact, first found in 1915, has confirmed the identity of Piyadasi of the inscriptions with Aśoka of the Buddhist sources and Aśokavardhana of the Purāṇas which had so long been a matter of inference. Aśoka the Maurya is mentioned in the Girnār inscription of Rudradāman (A.D. 150). In the Calcutta-Bairāṭ inscription Aśoka refers to himself as 'Piyadasi lājā māgadhe', Piyadasi, the king of Magadha. The more usual formula is 'devānaṁpiya piyadasi lājā'. The compound word devānāṁpiya, meaning 'dear to the gods', was in Aśoka's time and until much later, an honorofic term, sometimes used also as a synonym of rājan, though by some obscure transition it came to mean 'fool' in relatively recent times[1]. Piyadasi and the slightly altered form Piyadassana occur repeatedly in the *Dipavamsa* as equivalents of Aśoka; and the same epithet is often applied by Vālmīki to the hero of the *Rāmāyaṇa*[2]; and was adopted by the Sātavāhanas and some rulers of Central Asia; it is applied to Chandragupta Maurya in the *Mudrārākṣasa*; the expression means both 'of amiable appearance' and 'who sees with affection'. Whether piyadasi was the proper name and Aśoka the *biruda* as has been thought, or the other way round, this great king will ever be known to history as Aśoka.

Early life.

Of the birth and early life of Aśoka we hear very little even from tradition. According to *Divyāvadāna*, his mother was Janapadakalyāṇī (Subhadrāṅgī in other versions), the lovely daughter of a Brahman of Champā, who was kept out of her rights for some time by the intrigues of the other queens of Bindusāra, but succeeded ultimately in winning the king's favour and bearing him two sons, Aśoka and Vigatāśoka. Some modern scholars would make Aśoka the son of the Greek princess, the

1. Hultzsch xxix—xxx ; also *Nāgari Pracāriṇī Patrikā* 46.2 pp. 135—46. Bāṇa (*HC.* pp. 28, 268 : tr. 20, 239) knows the use of the phrase in the good sense while the great advaita teacher Śankara is seen using it in an ironical sense (*BS*, I. 2.8) to indicate a ritualist. I see no irony in Patañjali on Pāṇini II, 4, 56 *pace* Kielhorn and Hultzsch.

2. In the very first chapter Vālmīki asks Nārada : 'Kaścaika-priya-darśanaḥ'. (I. 1, 3,). Also Valle-Poussain, *L'Inde aux temps des Mauryas*, pp. 79-80.

daughter of Seleucus who became the wife of Bindusāra according to the terms of peace between the founder of the Mauryan empire and the Hellenistic ruler of Western Asia[1]. True, a mixed descent for Aśoka might not have evoked such violent disapproval in his time as in later days ; and it may be taken to explain Aśoka's adoption and propagation of Buddhism and his close relations with Hellenistic rulers and even the disputes at the accession of Aśoka to the throne ; but there is no clear evidence in favour of it.

Tradition associates Aśoka with the viceroyalties of Takshaśilā and Ujjayinī, and we know from the inscriptions[2] that these were held by princes of the royal family. The beginning of young Aśoka's viceroyalty of Ujjayinī was marked by romance ; when he halted at Vidiśā on his way to the provincial capital, he fell in love with Devī, the beautiful daughter of a merchant, and made her his wife; the two children born out of this marriage, a son and a daughter, were Mahinda and Saṅghamittā, who having renounced the world attained celebrity as the authors of the conversion of Ceylon to Buddhism[3]. It is possible that Aśoka founded a Saṅghārāma and erected the stūpa at Sāñchī because of the pleasant associations he had with the birthplace of his beautiful Devī.

When Bindusāra fell ill and was near his end, Aśoka left Ujjayinī and went over to Pushpapura (Pāṭaliputra) and took charge of the administration of the empire. Legend[4] implies that

1. K. H. Dhruva—*JBORS* XVI (1930) p. 35 n. 28 ; Tarn, *The Greeks in Bactria and India*, p. 152.

2. Separate RE. I. AA—BB.

3. MV. XIII 8—11 ; DV. VI 15—17. As Mahinda was twenty years of age in the sixth year after his father's coronation (DV. VI 21—2 ; VII 21—2 and 24), his birth would fall ten years before Aśoka's accession, and this gives us some idea of the duration of Aśoka's political apprenticeship under his father. Smith (*Aśoka*, pp. 48, 50) accepts Hiuen Tsang's statement that Mahendra was a brother, not son, of Aśoka, and follows Oldenberg in doubting the real existence of Saṅghamitrā.

4. Ceylon legends contain two different statements—one that Aśoka killed ninety-nine brothers born of different mothers before becoming sovereign (MV. V 20 ; DV. VI 21—2) and the other that after his father's death he caused his eldest brother to be slain before seizing the sovereignty of Pushpapura, (MV. V. 40). The *Divyāvadāna* says that when Bindusāra, lying in his deathbed, wanted to anoint his son Susīma, his ministers substituted Aśoka in his place : and when the dying monarch discovered the trick and became angry, Aśoka established his right by successfully calling upon the gods to give him the diadem if it was his by right. (p. 372—3). But elsewhere in the same work Aśoka speaks of his attaining sovereignty by killing his enemies (pp. 387, 400).

this was done against the wish of Bindusāra who had other ideas regarding succession, and there was an interval of four years between the end of Bindusāra's rule and the formal *abhisheka* of Aśoka from which event his regnal years are counted in the inscriptions. It seems probable that Aśoka's accession was not uncontested, but stories of wholesale destruction of all his brothers are given the lie direct by the inscriptions of the reign.

Adoption of Buddhism

Like his father Bindusāra, Aśoka was an adherent of the Vedic religion at the commencement of his reign. According to the *Dīpavamsa*, Aśoka entered upon a religious quest and began 'searching where truth and where falsehood was' among the sects; he sent for the exponents of all the various doctrines, offered them presents, and propounded questions. None of the answers he got satisfied him until one day standing at the window of his palace he saw the Samaṇa Nigrodha going along the road for alms and felt attracted to him. Nigrodha was the posthumous son of the elder brother of Aśoka, Sumana, whom Aśoka had slain to clear his way to the throne. Aśoka adopted Buddhism as his religion as the result of Nigrodha's sermon to him. This was in the fourth year after the king's coronation[1].

In truth, the conversion of Aśoka is connected with the first historical event of the reign of which the inscriptions speak, the conquest of Kalinga, and this is given out by Aśoka himself in the thirteenth Rock Edict. He says that he effected the conquest of Kalinga eight years after his anointment; he deplores the slaughter, death and deportation of people involved in the conquest of an unconquered country, and affirms that 150,000 men were deported, 100,000 were slain in battle, and

1. MV. v. 34—8 and 62—72 abridges and slightly alters DV. vi 25—99. The later account omits the religious quest part of the story and lays stress on the 'want of self-control' of the Brāhmaṇas at the distribution of food, which led the king to send for the other sects. The *Divyāvadāna* (xxvi) gives quite another account of Aśoka's conversion. It describes a prison which the king established in Pāṭaliputra under the control of Girika and the tortures to which persons who entered it were subjected; Samudra, a merchant prince of Śrāvastī, turned monk, entered the prison and by his miraculous powers, escaped the usual fate of persons who went in there. Aśoka heard of this, and witnessed more miracles performed by the *Bhikshu* and was converted (pp. 374—82) See also Watters, ii 88—91. Senart's remarks at IA xx p. 235 seek to account plausibly for the earlier date for the conversion given by the Sinhalese chronicles.

many times that number died ; he lays stress on the injury to the beloved ones of the virtuous Brāhmaṇas and Śramaṇas ; out of repentance (*anuśochana*) for these evils of conquest, he began to study Dhamma with zeal, to love Dhamma and to devote himself to the instruction of people in Dhamma. The stages of Aśoka's spiritual progress we may infer from the hints scattered in other inscriptions[1]. In the opening sections of the Minor Rock Inscription he says that for over a year after he had openly proclaimed himself a Buddha-Śākya (Maski) he was not very zealous ; then he visited the Sangha and by the time he issued this inscription he had been exerting himself with zeal for over a year in the realisation of Dhamma. The total period between the original conversion and this record is given as two years and a half. The visit to Sambodhi at the end of ten years after the *abhisheka* (eighth Rock Edict) may well have signalised the initial conversion of the emperor to Buddhism.

Thus Aśoka effected the conquest of Kalinga in the ninth and tenth years after the *abhisheka* (c. 256-5 B.C.) ; in the eleventh year, on account of his remorse at the thought of the incidents of the Kalinga war, he adopted Buddhism as his creed, undertook the pilgrimage to Gayā (Sambodhi) became an *upāsaka* and gave up the time-honoured practice of going out on hunting and pleasure tours.[2] Not much happened for one year after that ; then he paid a visit to the Sangha, derived instruction, became more zealous in the cause of Dhamma, and began to live apart as a celibate ; after 256 nights spent in this manner[3], he caused a record of his experiences to be made along with an exhortation to all to exert themselves likewise in the good cause (Minor Rock Edict.). About the same time (253 B.C.) he declared his mind to the Sangha in a letter which was engraved on a rock in Bairāṭ (Rajaputana). In this letter Aśoka says that his faith in the Buddha, Dhamma and Sangha is well known to the monks and proceeds to pick out and name

1. These have been discussed by Hultzsch p. xlvi ; also Senart IA xx pp. 229—31.

2. RE. VIII C—Hultzsch p. 15 and n. cf. also MV. xi 34.

3. Fleet's suggestion (JRAS. 1910 p. 1308) that 256 represents the number of years after the *nirvāṇa* may yet hold, if we relate it not to the *parinirvāṇa* of Buddha, but to his enlightenment—which seems not unlikely considering that Aśoka signifies his conversion at the outset by a journey to the spot where the Buddha attained knowledge.

seven texts from the scriptures[1] which he desires the monks and nuns should hear frequently expounded and should meditate upon ; this, in his opinion, is calculated to secure the long duration of the true Dhamma. At the same time he presented to the Ājīvaka monks two caves with polished interiors in the Khalatika mountain, now known as Barābar hills, in South Bihar. Seven years later Aśoka presented a third cave-dwelling in the same hills, but the inscription does not say to whom.[2]

Rock Edicts

The thirteenth and fourteenth years (252—1 B. C.) after the coronation were marked by the issue of the most important set of proclamations for the whole reign, the Fourteen Rock Edicts, and the two Kalinga Edicts which, in Kalinga, take the place of Nos. 11-13 in the series, and concern themselves particularly with the administration of the newly conquered country. In the Rock-Edicts which were engraved at different places all over the empire, Aśoka sets forth the principles of Dhamma which he wishes to inculcate on his officials and on the people over whom they were set to rule, and the steps he took to secure the observance of these principles within his empire and to propagate them in foreign lands. These we shall consider later in some detail.

Pilgrimage

In the fifteenth year (250 B. C.) he enlarged the stūpa of Koṇakamana at Nigālī Sāgar in the Nepalese Tarāī to double its original size ; six years later he came himself to the spot for worship and set up a pillar bearing an inscription briefly recording both the facts. Koṇakamana, also called Koṇāgamana and

1. For the identification of these texts see IA xli (1912) pp. 37—40 and JRAS 1913 p. 387 ; also Smith's *Aśoka* 3 pp. 156—7 and Hultzsch, p. 174 n2. The texts are (1) Vinaya Samukasa—Buddha's first sermon at Benares (*Udāna* V. 3) (2) Aliya Vasāni—*Anguttara* ii. p. 27 (3) Anāgata-bhayāni—*Anguttara* iii p. 103, sutta 78 (4) Muni-gāthā—*Sūtta-nipāta* i. 12. p. 36 (5) Moneya-sute—*ib*. iii. ii pp. 131—4 (6) Upatisa-pasine—*ib*. iv. 16, pp. 76—9 (7) Laghulovāde—*Majjhima Nik*. ii, 2, 1 Vol. i. p. 414 (references to PTS editions.) See also Winternitz, *Hist. of Ind. Liter*. Calcutta, 1933 ii, App. iii. pp. 606—9. See also the Chapter on 'Religion' *post*.

2. The Ājīvakas might have been *ekadaṇḍi* worshippers of Śiva earlier than Gosala whose disciples they are generally represented to be. Charpentier in JRAS 1913 pp. 669—74.

Kanakamuni, is the name of one of the legendary Buddhas that preceded the historical Buddha Śākyamuni, and Hiuen Tsang records that in the course of his travels he saw the stūpa containing the relics of Kanakamuni Buddha, and in front of it an inscribed pillar about 20 feet high and surmounted by a lion ; he heard that the pillar was erected by Aśoka.

Aśoka's pilgrimage (244 B.C.) must have extended to other sacred spots as well. The short Rummindeī pillar inscription states that he visited Lumbinivana and worshipped the spot where the Buddha Śākyamuni was born, caused a memorial pillar to be set up on the spot to show 'that the Blessed One was born here', and declared the village of Lumbini to be thenceforth free of taxes (*ubalika*) and liable to only an eighth of its produce (*aṭhabhāgiye*) in land assessment instead of the higher rate usually taken. The *Divyāvadāna* preserves the memory of Aśoka's pilgrimage to the sacred places under the guidance of Upagupta to whom Aśoka declares his desire to go and worship all the spots hallowed by the presence of the Buddha and to leave marks there for the benefit of future generations of men. Lumbinivana is placed first among the places to which Upagupta guided Aśoka[1].

Other edicts

In 238 B. C. Aśoka began the issue of the Pillar Edicts which together with the Fourteen Rock Edicts form the most important records of the reign. The first six Pillar Edicts which were issued in the first instance contained further elaboration of the principles of Dhamma and the administrative measures calculated to secure their voluntary observance by the people, and their enforcement, where necessary, by the officials of the imperial government. A year later in 237, another edict, the longest in this series, was added ; and this inscription, found only on one pillar, constitutes a more or less systematic review of all

1. Div. pp. 389-96, Upagupta is said to have made Aśoka worship at the stūpas of the apostles of Buddhism also. He made large gifts at each of the spots visited, except in the stūpa of Vakkula where he gave a *kākanī* for the reason that Vakkula did not do so much good to his fellow-creatures as others. Cf. *hida Budhe jate Sakyamuni* and *hida Bhagavān jateti* of the Rummindei inscr. with Upagupta's words to Aśoka : *asmin mahārāja pradeśe Bhagavān jātaḥ*. (*Div.* p. 389).

the steps taken by Aśoka so far for the promotion of Dhamma and the motives which actuated them ; incidentally it gives some idea of the results obtained by the action of the monarch and of his hopes for the future.

Aśoka continued to reign for ten years after he issued the seventh Pillar edict, and the closing decade of the reign is nearly as poor in its epigraphy as the first. We have only two inscriptions, both undated but most certainly belonging to this period. One of them is the order of the king issued to his *mahāmātras* that the monk or nun who causes schism in the Sangha should be punished by expulsion, being required to wear white robes and live outside the *vihāra* in a place not fit for the members of the Sangha to live in ; this order was to be properly circulated among the monks and nuns and lay worshippers; officials and lay worshippers were to assist in carrying out this instruction by attending service on every *uposatha* day. In the other record the king gives effect to the request of his second queen, Kāluvāki, the mother of Tivala, and orders all his *mahāmātras* to register in her name all the gifts made by her, mango-groves, gardens, alms houses or anything else.

Tradition : Third Council

Tradition helps us to eke out these meagre references to the doings of the great king in his long reign, though it is often characterised by grotesque exaggeration, and some of it is doubtless pure invention[1]. The *Dīpavamsa* contains the earliest

1. Some stories from the Aśoka cycle have been touched upon already, particularly in the notes. The execution by the king's own hand of five hundred ministers for their refusing to carry out the order to cut down all fruit trees and flower plants and look after the thorny trees ; and the burning alive of five hundred women of the harem for their having denuded an Aśoka tree to spite the king who bore its name (*Divyāvadāna* p. 373-4) are just edifying invention meant to stress the good effects of the conversion on Aśoka ; the number 500 gives the show away. The construction of 84,000 stūpas and the distribution of Buddha relics among them (*Divy*. 380-1), the number representing the sections of Dharma according tot he Ceylonese books(DV. vi, 86-99), and Queen Padmāvatī bringing forth Kuṇāla on the day on which the stūpas were completed (*Divy*. p. 405) can hardly be accepted at face value. The story of Vītāśoka, the brother of Aśoka, (Div. xxviii pp. 419-29) may also be only edifying legend with no historical basis. The brother is at first devoted to the Tīrthyas and accuses the Bauddha monks of being pleasure-lovers ; to teach him a lesson, Aśoka gets his ministers to entice Vītāśoka into assuming the insignia of royalty, condemns him to death as a traitor, and then grants him a seven days' respite, during which all the amenities of royalty are permitted to him ; fear of death made all enjoyment impossible to him during

account we possess of the third Buddhist council held in the reign of Aśoka[1]. That monarch's patronage of Buddhism resulted in the enrichment of the Sangha and the relative impoverishment of other faiths; many adherents of the neglected creeds, 'Ājīvakas and sectarians of different descriptions' to the number of sixty thousands, began to wear the yellow robe and dwell together with the *bhikshus* in the Aśokārāma for the sake of the revenue; they proclaimed their own heresies as the doctrines of the Buddha and caused much confusion by their unruly behaviour. This went on for a period of seven years during which 'the *uposatha* ceremonies were performed by incomplete congregations', 'saintly, clever and modest men' not making their appearance at them. At last, Aśoka summoned to his aid the venerable Moggaliputta Tissa who was living at that time in solitary retreat to escape the confusion prevailing in Aśokārāma; under Tissa's presidency a council was held at which all the adherents of the false doctrine who had stealthily attached themselves to the Sangha were unfrocked, compelled to put on white robes and expelled, the Theravāda was firmly established and the great *thera* Tissa 'set forth the treatise belonging to the Abhidhamma, which is called *Kathāvatthu*'.

the period, and then, being convinced that Bauddha monks who meditated on the death of hundreds of beings could not be pleasure seekers, he became one of them himself. Later, Aśoka ordered all the *nirgranthas* (also called Ājīvakas *Div.* p. 427) of Puṇḍravardhana to be beheaded, offering reward to those who did so, because they had painted the Buddha as prostrating before a *nirgrantha* image: Vītāśoka also fell a victim to this persecution as he was mistaken for a *nirgrantha*: in his grief at this occurrence, Aśoka allowed himself to be persuaded to declare immunity from fear for all creatures in his realms. This story is clearly a clumsy invention meant to account for the well-known fact that Aśoka promoted *ahimsā*. The celebrated story of Kuṇāla losing his eyes by the machination of his step-mother Tishyarakshitā whose illicit passion for him he failed to reciprocate, and his miraculous recovery, is also a legend: the revenge of 'women whose love is scorned' is a popular *motif* (Penzer, *Ocean of Story*, ii. p. 120) and the name of the woman 'Protected by Tiṣya' is suspicious, for Tiṣya we have good reason to think was the asterism of Aśoka's birth or *ahisheka* (JRAS 1909 pp. 28—34). If this is accepted, Tiṣyarakṣitā's jealously of the bodhi tree, her attempted destruction of it and its effects on the king, and the revival of both would also be mythical though some of the scenes are known to be representated in sculpture on the *toraṇas* of Sāñchī. (*Monuments of Sāñchī*, Marshall and Foucher pp. 212—3). Aśoka's gift of everything he had including the whole earth to the Sangha to make up the 100 crores he had promised, the concern of Sampadi, the heir-apparent, and the ministers at this extravagance, and the steps they took to stop the effects of Aśoka's dotage, and his last gift of half a myrobalan which was all that was left to him to the Kukuṭārāma—are likewise legends of pious fame.

1. DV. 7. 34-59; MV. 5. 288—82; *Samantapāsādika* in Oldenberg Vin. Pit. iii pp. 282 ff. esp. p. 312 for white robes given to degraded monks.

The Council comprised one thousand of the best Arhats, was held under the King's protection, and lasted nine months.

This Council was held according to tradition at the end of 236 years after the Buddha's death (*Dīpavamsa*) and in the seventeenth year of the reign of Aśoka (*Mahāvamsa*). But there is no mention of the Council in the Seventh Pillar Edict ; this has led some scholars to discredit the entire story of the third Council. This, however, is not easy in the face of the edict against schism (*saṅghabheda*) which strikingly corroborates the account of the Council ; and judging by the position of its Kauśāmbī version on the Allahabad pillar, it was issued some time after the Seventh Pillar Edict and fell towards the end of the reign ; the Council must have been held about the same time.

Buddhist Missions

At the conclusion of the Council Moggaliputta Tissa sent *theras* to different countries to preach and establish the Dhamma in those lands. The names of the missionaries and the countries to which they were sent are as follows[1] :

Majjhantika	Kaśmīra and Gāndhāra
Mahādeva	Mahiṣamaṇḍala (Mysore)
Rakkhita	Vanavāsi (N. Kanara Dt.)
Yona Dhammarakkhita	Aparantaka (Northern half of Bombay Coast).
Mahadhammarakkhita	Maharaṭṭha
Maharakkhita	Yona (Greek settlements in the N. W. of India)
Majjhima	Himalaya country
Sona and Uttara	Suvaṇṇabhūmi
Mahinda (Mahendra) and four others.	Laṅkā.

The *Dīpavamsa* mentions that besides Majjhima, the mission to the Himalayas included Kassapagotta, Dundubhissara, Sahadeva and Mūlakadeva. Some of these names figure in inscriptions on relic caskets from Sāñchī and its neighbourhood. But Mogaliputa of these inscriptions could not be Moggaliputa Tissa ,as was thought at one time, because he was the pupil of

1. DV. viii, MV. xii. Thomas accepts Waddel's identification of M. Tissa with Upagupta (CHI. i. p. 506) : but see Przyluski ; *La Legende* Pt. I ch. 2.

Gotīputa, the heir of Dundubhisara who may well be identical with the missionary of the Himalayan region just mentioned. The names Kassapagotta and Majjhima are also found on the caskets, and the former is styled 'Sava-Hemavata-ācāriya'; there was a Hemavata school among the Theravādins, and it might have had its origin in the Himalayan region converted by Kassapagotta, whose name is placed first in *Dīpavaṃsa* in the list of missionaries to the Yakkhas of Himavanta. The inscriptions are clearly later than the age of Aśoka, but this may be due to a redistribution of the relics undertaken some time subsequent to the death of the *theras*[1]. It is worthy of note that the name of a Yona (foreigner, Greek or Persian) *thera* is included among these early missionaries of the faith.

This account of the missions given by the Ceylonese chronicles may be accepted as evidence that in the later years of his reign Aśoka continued to strive for the spread of Buddhism with the same zeal as before. The action taken earlier in the reign had resulted in the establishment of a net-work of missions within the empire and outside. In the Thirteenth Rock Edict Aśoka forswears war as a means of conquest, declares that the true conquest is conquest of Dhamma (Dhammavijaya) and then records :

'And this (conquest) has been won repeatedly by Devānāmpriya both here and among all (his) borderers, even as far as at (the distance of) six hundred *yojanas*, where the Yona king named (Antiyoka) (is ruling), and beyond this Antiyoka (where) four kings (are ruling), (viz., the king) named Turumaya, (the king) named Antikini, (the king) named Maka, (and the king) named Alikasudara, (and) towards the south, (where) the Choḍas and Pāṇḍyas (are ruling) as far as Tāmraparṇī.

'Likewise here in the king's territory, among the Yonas and Kambojas, among the Nābhākas and Nābhitis (Nabhapamtis), among the Bhojas and Pitinikas, and the Andhras and Palidas, everywhere (people) are conforming to Devānāmpriya's instruction in morality.

'Even those to whom the envoys of Devānāmpriya do not go, having heard of the duties of morality, the ordinances, (and)

1. *Monuments of Sāñchi* i. pp. 291-4.

the instruction in morality of Devānāmpriya, are conforming to morality and will conform to (it)'.

No tangible evidence is forthcoming to enable us to estimate the measure of success that attended the missions to foreign lands; some stones bearing the obviously Buddhist symbols of the wheel and trident have been found in Egypt, but in the absence of any inscriptions on them, their age must remain uncertain, and they may have nothing to do with the missions of Aśoka. But the discovery at Memphis of some of Indian figures made in moulds about 200B.C. may be more to the point[1]. The conversion of Ceylon has been treated with epic fulness in the Ceylonese chronicles; but even here the details of the story are open to doubt. Devānāmpriya Tissa was the contemporary of Aśoka in Ceylon, and the two monarchs were friends 'though they had never seen each other'. Soon after his accession Tissa sent an embassy to Aśoka; it was led by his nephew Ariṭṭha and carried valuable presents to Aśoka; the mission took a week for the journey by sea from Jambukola to Tāmralipti and another week from there to reach Pāṭliputra. It was received with great honours, spent five weeks in the Mauryan capital, and then returned to Ceylon bringing as a return present 'all that was needful for consecrating a king' and the gift of the true doctrine in the form of a message telling Tissa that Aśoka had become a lay disciple in the religion of the Buddha and exhorting him to do likewise. Tissa consecrated himself a second time thereafter; Mahinda came one month later, says the *Dīpavamsa*. Some time later Ariṭṭha was despatched once more to Pāṭaliputra to fetch Saṅghamittā for the ordination of Queen Anulā and her companions, and a

1. Aryan woman of the Punjab, seated figure in Indian attitude with the scarf over the left shoulder. 'These are the first remains of Indians known on the Mediterranean. Hitherto there have been no material evidences for that connection which is stated to have existed, both by embassies from Egypt and Syria to India and by the great Buddhist mission sent by Aśoka as far west as Greece and Cyrene. We seem now to have touched the Indian colony in Memphis, and we may hope for more light on that connection which seems to have been so momentous for Western thought'. Petrie in *Man* VIII (1908) No. 71; See also Petrie—*Seventy years in Archaelogy* p. 213 and *British School of Archaelogy in Egypt and Egyptian research Account—Fourteenth year*, 1908—*Memphis* by Petrie (1908) ch. VIII. I owe these references to Prof. T. Balakrishna Nayar of Presidency College, Madras. For the Ptolemaic grave-stone with Buddhist symbols, wheel and *triratna*, see JRAS 1898, p. 875.

branch of the Bodhi-tree for being planted in Ceylon[1]. Some modern writers are inclined to discredit the whole account, but there is nothing intrinsically improbable here, and Aśoka's reference to Taṁbapaṇṇi twice in his inscriptions shows that once more the chronicles are only embellishing historical occurrences.

After his conquest of Kalinga, the empire of Aśoka extended practically over the whole of India with the exception of the extreme south of the peninsula which according to the second Rock Edict was occupied by the independent states of Choḷa, Pāṇḍya, Satiyaputa and Keraḷaputa. Hiuen Tsang notices the existence of numerous stūpas ascribed to Aśoka all over India ; this does not always help us to determine the limits of the empire. Towards the north and north-west the empire clearly reached much farther than the frontier of British India. The territory gained by treaty from Seleucus continued in the Mauryan empire, and Aśoka refers to Antiochus of Syria in a manner that implies that their territories were contiguous ; thus the southern half of Afghanistan up to the Hindu Kush, and practically the whole of British Baluchistan was included in the empire which thus held the 'scientific frontier' which eluded the grasp of British rulers of India in the nineteenth century. Tradition is strong that Kashmir was under Aśoka's rule. Following earlier authorities, Kalhaṇa, the historian of Kashmir, records[2] that Aśoka built the town of Śrīnagarī besides a large number of stūpas and some shrines to Śiva, two of which were called Aśokeśvara after the king. Aśoka is said to have been followed in this region by his son Jalauka who expelled the *mlecchas* that had overrun the land and then continued the policy of his father and introduced wholesome administrative reforms. Pandrethan, a small village three miles above the modern city of Śrīnagar, is supposed to represent Kalhaṇa's Purāṇādhishṭhāna (ancient capital), a name used even in Hiuen Tsang's time for Aśoka's city. Kashmir

1. DV. XI 25—40 : XII 1—7 ; xv 74—95 ; XVI 1—7, 38—41 and XVII 81-87. The account of MV is much better arranged. XI 18-42, XVIII and XIX. I have omitted from my account all reference to the part of Sumana, the son of Saṅghamittā.

2. I 101—23. ed. Stein. Watters, Yuan Chwang i, 158—70 ; Beal. *Life* ch. 2 ; Albirūni (Sachau) i. 207.

was a stronghold of Śaivism in later historical times, and to this, rather than to any real leanings to Śaivism on the part of Aśoka, must be traced the notion that he built important Śiva temples in Kashmir. We have noted already that Kashmir and Gandhāra received one of the missions sent out for the spread of the Dhamma, and Hiuen Tsang, who saw four Aśoka stūpas in Kashmir, records several edifying legends of local import.

Khotan

In Khotan also legend connects the foundation of the kingdom with Kunāla and Taxila, the seat of his viceroyalty. The story takes different forms in the pages of Hiuen Tsang and his biographer, and in Tibetan books of later date[1]. Miracles apart, all forms of the legend agree in tracing the origin of Khotan to two settlements one of Indians from Taxila and the other of Chinese, the former led by Kunāḷa or the officials of Taxila who were banished for their share in his blinding, the latter bya Chinese prince ; the two settlements which were founded at the same time and in the same neighbourhood started by quarrelling, and their differences were composed by divine intervention. We may not now hope to discover the actual facts that gave rise to this tradition ; but we may note the facts in the ethnic and cultural history of Khotan as now known which have a bearing on the historicity of these traditions. The earliest documents from Khotan so far known belong to about the middle of the third century A.D. ; they are numerous, and relate to secular affairs of public administration or ordinary private life ; they are written in Kharoshṭhī, a script used for some centuries before and after the Christian era in the region round Taxila, the traditional home of the Indian colonists of Khotan ; the language of the records likewise is 'beyond all doubt an Indian language closely allied to the old Prākṛits of North-Western India' (Stein). Buddhism by itself cannot account for these features ; for the language of Northern Buddhism was Sanskrit and its script Brāhmī. On the ethnic side a general resemblance between the features of the Khotanese and Kashmiris has been noted by

1. Rockhill : *Life of the Buddha* ch. viii ; Beal—*Buddhist Records* i. pp. 143 ff. ii. pp. 309 ff : *Life*, p. 203 : Watters ii. pp. 295-305. Stein, *Ancient Khotan* (Oxford, 1907) i. pp. 156-66, and 368. Konow, *Khotan Studies* JRAS 1914, pp. 344 ff.

Stein, and in the early sculpture and painting of Khotan quasi-Mongolian facial features appear in the midst of art forms otherwise entirely Indian in character. Thus the cultural milieu of the antiquities of Ancient Khotan can be adequately explained by the postulate of an early connection between Khotan and the Taxila region, and there is nothing against our assuming that it began in Aśoka's reign.

Nepal

The Tibetan historian Tāranāth mentions a tradition that Aśoka reduced a rising of the Nepālas and Khāśyas, tribes of Himalayan mountaineers, during his father's reign[1]. Aśoka's pilgrimage to the birth-place of the Buddha and his inscribed pillars at Rummindeī and Nigālī Sāgar attest the inclusion of the Nepalese Tarāī in the empire. Nepalese tradition further affirms that the pilgrimage of Aśoka under the guidance of Upagupta was continued into Nepal where he founded the city of Patan (two miles S. E. of Khatmandu) and built five *chaityas*, one at the centre of the new city and the rest at the cardinal points on its perimeter ; the latter subsist to this day and conform in shape to the Sāñchī and Gandhāra types. Many stūpas marked the route of Aśoka from and to Pāṭaliputra. The king is said to have been accompanied by his daughter Cārumatī for whom a husband was found among the Kshatriyas of Nepal, by name Devapāla. Both Cārumatī and Devapāla resolved to spend their days in Nepal, and the city of Deopatan, one of the oldest cities of Nepal, is said to have been founded by him. In her old age Cārumatī built a *vihāra* named after her (now Chabahil) to the north of Deopatan, and she lived there a recluse till her death. The celebrated shrine of Svayambhunāth in Western Nepal, consecrated to the primordial Buddha, is also connected by tradition with the memory of the great emperor Aśoka.

Assam and Bengal

Aśoka's empire did not extend to Kāmarūpa. No Aśoka monuments have been discovered there, and Hiuen Tsang did

1. Schiefner p. 27 : S. Levi—*Le Nepal* Index s. v. Aśoka.

not notice any in his time ; in fact he asserts that there had never been a Buddhist monastery in the land. The Brahmaputrā must have been the frontier of the empire on this side. The discovery in 1931 of the Mahasthān inscription written in Brāhmī characters clearly of the Mauryan epoch makes it certain that Bengal was included within the empire of Aśoka ; Hiuen Tsang saw Aśoka stūpas in Samataṭa (E. Bengal) and in Tāmralipti, which figures as a port of considerable importance in the events of Aśoka's reign as recorded in the Ceylonese chronicles. The southern limit of the empire may be taken to be indicated by the Aśoka stūpas mentioned by Hiuen Tsang in the neighbourhood of Kāñchīpuram in the Dravida country (about 12° N. L.) ; the stūpa near the capital (Madura ?) of Malakūṭa (Pāṇḍya) was built, according to him, not by Aśoka, but by his brother Mahendra.

Tribes

In the inscriptions we find the names of a number of tribes, and not all of them can be identified with certainty. There is also some room for doubt about their political relation to the empire. Rock Edict V (J) mentions the Yonas, Kambojas, Gāndhāras, Raṭhikas, Peteṇikas and other Western borderers, and says that all the religious sects among these tribes were looked after by the new officials of the empire, the *dharmamahāmātras*. Rock Edict XIII(R) speaks of the tribes 'here in the king's territory' (*iha rājavishye*), viz., 'the Yonas and Kambojas, the Nābhakas and Nābhapaṅktis (Nābhiti-Shab.), the Bhojas and Pitinikas, the Andhras and Pārindas'. Clearly the Yonas and Kāmbojas of the lists are identical, and the 'western borderers' must be taken to have lived within the empire, 'in the king's territory.'[1] The Yonas in this period obviously means Greeks, and they seem to have formed a small state ruled over by Greek princes in the north-west frontier[2]. The Kāmbojas are to be located in the region of the Pāmirs, to the north of Kashmir[3].

1. *Contra* Hultzsch p. xxxviii. *Aṁta* is a dubious term which may describe a 'borderer' inside or outside the boundary, and the interpretation must depend on the context.
2. Hultzsch p. xxxix and Tarn, *Greeks in Bactria and India* p. 101.
3. Hultzsch says Kabul region. I prefer on this point to follow Jayachandra Vidyālankara, *Proc. Sixth All-India Or. Conference*, pp. 102—9.

The Gāndhāras lived round about Peshawar, the ancient Purushapura, now included in the North-West Frontier province. We are less certain of the location of the other tribes named. The Raṭhikas may be the people of Kathiawad, if the name stands for Rāshṭṛika ; the governor of this region was known as Rashṭriya in Chandragupta's reign[1]. The Peteṇikas or Pitinikas who are coupled with the Bhojas in Rock Edict XIII must also be looked for in the west ; but Peteṇika is not Pratishṭhāna as the identification is 'phonetically impossible', and the Bhojas could not be located in Berar. The Nābhakas and Nābhapaṅktis have been plausibly assigned to the Nepalese frontier, and the Andhras and Pārindas were in Eastern Deccan[2].

Administration

From other geographical references in the inscriptions we may form some idea of the scheme of Aśoka's administration of the empire. Pāṭaliputra (Patna) was the capital, as in the days of Aśoka's grandfather Chandragupta[3]. Kośāmbī (Kosam on the Jamna about 28 miles above Allahabad), Ujjeni, Takshaśilā (Taxila), Suvarṇagiri (perhaps modern Zonnagiri in the neighbourhood of Yerraguḍi[4]). with Isila (Siddhāpura) as a subordinate division, and Tosali (Dhauli) and Sāmapā (near Jaugaḍa) in the Kalinga country are important centres of provincial administration that are expressly mentioned. There might have been others. Thus in an inscription of A.D. 150 the Yavanarāja Tushaspa is said to have represented Aśoka's authority in Kathiawad. The Viceroys of Tosali and Ujjeni are called Kumāra in the Kalinga edicts ; and Āyaputa (Āryaputra) is the term by which the viceroy of Suvarṇagiri is described in the Mysore (Brahmagiri-Siddhāpura) edicts, and they were obviously princes of the imperial royal family. The more generic term for provincial officers is *Mahāmātra*. The two

1. Junāgadh Rock Inscr. of Rudradāman EI. viii p. 46, n. 7.

2. Hultzsch p. xxxix. The Purāṇas, however know of a land of the Pāradas in Eastern India watered by the Ganges and noted for its horses, Br. II 18, 50 : 31, 83, : Mats. 121, 45.

3. Hultzsch p. xxx.

4. NIA i pp 596—7. *Contra* Hultzsch who suggests Kanakagiri in the Nizam's dominions.

Kumāras were probably sons of the king. Rock-Edict V (M) mentions the harems of the king's brothers, of his sisters and other relatives both in the capital and in all the outlying towns, a clear indication that the king availed himself freely of the assistance of his relatives in carrying on the administration of the empire.

Officers of different grades are mentioned, and the highest rank seems to have been held by the Rājūkas and Mahāmātras. The word Rājūka is held by some to be connected with *rājā* ; but the better view seems to be that of Bühler who considers it an abbreviation of Rajjugrāhaka (rope-holder) of the Jātakas. This class of officer "originally 'held the rope' in order to measure the fields of the ryots and to assess the land-tax", and revenue administration must have been among their chief duties. Aśoka says that he appointed the Rājūkas for the welfare and happiness of the country people (*janapadasa hitasukhāye* PE IV, I). The *Arthaśāstra* knows, however, *rajjū* and *chora-rajjū* as sources of revenue in the *rāshṭra* (*janapada*), and *chora-rajjuka* as a rural officer ; and Megasthenes has described a class of highly-placed rural officers, *agronomoi*, whose duties are very similar to those of the *rājūkas* of the inscriptions. We must assume therefore that Aśoka did not create a new office, but reorganised and improved the existing arrangements for rural administration. The Rājūkas each held sway over 'many hundred thousands of men', and 'either rewards or punishments were left to their discretion' in order that they should perform their duties confidently and fearlessly. Aśoka desires that the care of these officers for the people should resemble that of an intelligent nurse for the child in her charge. The Rājūkas had the power of life and death ; but to secure that no mistakes should occur and opportunity may be found by Rājūkas either on their own initiative or as a result of persuasion by the relatives of the condemned man to revise the order, and in order to enable the prisoner to prepare adequately by fasts, prayer and gifts, to meet his end, a respite of three days was required to be granted in all cases of capital punishment. And they were particularly enjoined to be impartial in the investigation of disputes and the award of punishments. This was not all. The Rājūkas were kept in constant touch with the king by his agents, *purushas* (*pulisā*) who knew the king's mind and were constantly on the move. (PE. IV). They were also to take a hand in the propagation of Dhamma among the people (PE. VII, N). and direct the Jānapadas and rāṭhikas employed under them to be active in this work (MRE, Yerraguḍi).

The term Mahāmātra indicated a certain definite high rank in the hierarchy of officials ; the duties that devolved on each were implied by more specific titles. Thus there were the Dhamma-mahāmātras whose offices were newly created by Aśoka thirteen years after his abhisheka as he states in Rock-Edict V which sets forth their duties in some detail. They were to establish and promote dhamma among all the sects in the land and promote the happiness of people devoted to dhamma among the Yonas, Kambhojas and Gāndhāras and other tribes on the western border. They were to help in all difficulties experienced by servants and masters, by Brahmins and Vaiśyas, and by the destitute and the aged ; they reviewed all sentences awarded by courts and mitigated or remitted them after taking into account the particular circumstances of each case such as motive, the presence of children, instigation, and advanced age[1] ; in Pāṭaliputra and in all outlying towns, they had duties in harems and households of the king's relatives, brothers and sisters, and generally they regulated morality and charity throughout the empire. The Seventh Pillar-Edict throws further light on their work ; after a general statement that their activity was fraught with benefit for ascetics and householders of all sects, Aśoka makes the following declaration : 'Some were ordered by me to busy themselves with the affairs of the Saṅgha ; likewise others were ordered by me to busy themselves also with the Brāhmaṇas and Ājīvakas ; others were ordered by me to busy themselves also with the Nirgranthas ; others were ordered by me to busy themselves also with various other sects[2]'.

Then there were the *mahāmātras* who were *nagara-vyavahārakas* at Tosali and Sāmapā in Kalinga, and perhaps in other large cities elsewhere. They were obviously the same as the

1. I have followed Jayaswal and Smith in the interpretation of this difficult section as Hultzsch's translation seems to me wholly inadequate.

2. PE. VII, X-AA I treat as one section dealing with Dhamma-mahāmātras Cf. Smith, *Aśoka* 3 p. 210 vi ; *contra* Hultzsch p. 136, n. 5.

Pauravyavahārikas of Kauṭilya. They administered justice in the cities[1], as the *rājūkas* did in the rural areas, and were, like the *rājūkas*, required to be strictly impartial in the discharge of their duties[2], and strive to overcome defects of personal character that might hamper them in attaining this end[3]. There were the *aṁta-mahāmātras*, officers of the borders, who were engaged in civilizing and preaching dhamma among the wild tribes on the borders and elsewhere ; these tribes were not full members of the empire and retained something of their primitive independence, and the king's policy towards them was one of benevolent paternalism.[4] Lastly there were the *strī-adhyaksha-mahāmātras*, whose name indicates that they had control of women, but of whose exact duties no details are forthcoming; they may be taken to correspond to the Gaṇikādhyaksha, 'the overseer of courtesans' of the *Arthaśāstra*[5].

Yuktas

The *mahāmātras* met periodically in Councils and discussed matters of common interest in the administration of their respective charges. They had control over the *Yuktas* of the Accounts Department (Gaṇanā) and issued instructions to them to secure moderation in the expenditure of public funds and in the accumulation of treasury balances[6]. In the sixth Rock-Edict Aśoka makes a statement which provides a glimpse into some details of administrative practice. 'And if in the Council (of mahāmātras) a dispute arises, or an amendment is moved, in connection with any donation or proclamation which I myself am ordering verbally, or (in connection with) an emergent matter which has been delegated to the *mahāmātras*, it must be reported to me immediately, anywhere, (and) at any time.'

1. Hultzsch p. 95, n. 2.
2. Cf. Sep. Ed. I, J-L and PE. IV, K-N.
3. Sep. Ed. I M-Q.
4. Sep. Ed. II F-M (Dhauli) and PE. I.F.
5. RE. xii M. Hultzsch p. 22 n 4.
6. RE. III E. Here I follow D. R. Bhandarkar and Smith in preference to Lüders and Hultzsch. True this rendering looks like the abrupt introduction of a new idea : but sharp transitions are not uncommon in the Edicts : and the preceding sentence having commended to individuals the merit of moderation in expenditure and in possessions. the statement that the same principle was observed in the administration of public finance is not a serious break in the sequence of thought.

The issue of oral orders by the king to be recorded and executed by ministers and other officials was an abiding feature of Indian polity ; the continuous interest in the execution of such orders evinced by Aśoka was peculiar to him. The *parishā* (Council) of the Edicts is clearly the *mantri-parishad* of the *Arthaśāstra*[1] ; but neither from the Edicts nor from the *Arthaśāstra* do we get a complete picture of its composition and duties.

The higher officials were required to go on tours of inspection (*anusamyāna*) generally once in five years, but once in three years in the provinces of Ujjayinī and Takshaśilā. Among these officials were Yuktas, Rājūkas and Prādeśikas. The term *Yukta* is general, and known also to the *Arthaśāstra* ; in the second Kalinga edict, Aśoka says that in all the divisions (*deśa*) of the province he will maintain officers (*āyuktikas*) for the carrying out of his policy. Prādeśika may well be the *pradeshṭṛ* of the *Arthaśāstra* ; he has been taken to correspond to the District officer (Collector) of modern times and his rank may have been that of a *mahāmātra*, though of this we have no certainty. The officers going on tour were, at least some of them, specially selected for their personal qualities of moderation and gentleness, and they had other duties, particularly to supervise the judicial administration[2].

The *purushas* (agents) were other officers who were organised under three different grades, and those who, as already noted, served as liaison officers between the Rājūkas and the king, must have belonged to the highest grade ; they are said to be occupied with many people, like the Rājūkas. A similar class of officers newly created by Aśoka were the *prativedakas* (reporters) who were posted everywhere, as he says, 'in order to report to me the affairs of the people at any time, while I am eating, in the harem, in the inner apartment, even at the cowpen, in the palanquin, and in the parks'. There were *purushas* of middling and lower rank also ; but we have no knowledge of the exact nature of the work entrusted to them[3].

1. Hultzsch p. 5 n. 7.
2. RE. III C: Sep. E. Dhauli Z. CC: Jaugaḍa II L. Hultzsch p.5.n.3. Thomas (IA. 1915 pp. 97—112) derives *prādeśika* from *pradeśa* meaning report and compares *tena pradeśena* of KA ch. 39 with *etena vyañjanena* of the edicts.
3. Purushas PE. I. E. : IV G : VII M. Prativedakas RE. VI B. Also Hultzsch p. xli.

Other officers mentioned in the edicts are—*Vacabhūmikas*, controllers of cow-pens, whose duties must have been similar to those of the go-adhyaksha of the *Arthaśāstra*, and other groups (*nikāya*) of officials whose names and duties are not specified[1]. The Seventh Pillar-Edict also mentions many chief officials, or departments according to Thomas, occupied with the delivery of gifts made by the king, his queen, his children, and the sons of other royal princesses (devīkumāras) both in the capital city and in the provinces[2]. Obviously there are many gaps in our knowledge of the details, and the inscriptions are by no means a complete manual of administration.

Aśoka's part

But they leave us in no doubt about the supreme importance of the part taken by Aśoka himself in the daily work of the State, and of the tone imparted to it by the king's precept and example. The monarch spared neither himself nor his officers in the continuous and active promotion of the well-being of the people. His devotion to duty was keen and he displayed unwonted energy in discharging it. He affirmed that no duty was more important than promoting the welfare of all people. He valued glory and fame only in so far as they enabled him to promote morality, good will and happiness among men. He attached great importance to his personal contact with the different parts of his vast empire and the different sections among his subjects. 'And whatever effort I am making', he declares, 'is made in order that I may discharge the debt which I owe to living beings' ; and this time-honoured doctrine of *ṛṇa* (debt) is recalled repeatedly by Aśoka, and his officers are exhorted by him to discharge to the full the debt they owed to the monarch for the proper care of subjects placed under their charge. Firmly convinced as Aśoka was that persuasion was better than force as the means of moral reform, he had sufficient discernment to realise that in practice he could not altogether dispense with the police power of the state, or even the use of the army. He declares expressly that he will even put up with wrong-doing

1. RE. XII M.
2. PE. VII CC—DD.

within limits and forgive whatever can be forgiven ; and he exhorts people not to do the things that would compel him to exercise the power of punishment, for that would cause him pain and remorse, though he would not, on that account, shrink from the performance of his duty as king. The annual release of prisoners which Aśoka regularly ordered shows that he was ready to uphold traditional forms where they coincided with his inclination to be merciful and considerate to all. After once witnessing the horrors of war in the campaign against Kalinga, he was struck with remorse, renounced war as an instrument of policy, and not only abjured fresh conquests for himself but recorded his wish that his descendants should follow him in this regard ; but he is by no means sure that his advice would be followed by them and takes care to add that if conquest should still have its attractions for them, they should be gentle and merciful in the pursuit of their plans, and never loose sight of the ideal of true conquest which is not conquest by force, but conquest by moral superiority (dhamma-vijaya)——another proof that Aśoka was no visionary who had lost touch with realities, but a practical statesman who had a shrewd knowledge of human nature and was not prepared to risk the possible improvements in society and administration in the uncompromising pursuit of impossible ideals. And he records with legitimate satisfaction that his example has borne fruit in his lifetime. 'Whatever good deeds have been performed by me', he says in the Seventh Pillar-Edict, 'these the people have imitated, and to those they are conforming'.[1]

Religious policy

So far we have viewed Aśoka as ruler, administrator and statesman. We must now turn to a consideration of the evidence of the inscriptions on his attitude to Buddhism and its

1. PE. VII GG. For the energy of the king RE. VI H-K, N : his view of glory and fame RE. X A-C, PE . VI F : ṛṇa doctrine as applied to the king himself RE. VI L, Kalinga E. II H : to his officers Kalinga edict I, Q. U, II L : forbearance RE. XIII L-N : twenty-five jail deliveries are mentioned in the twenty-sixth year PE. V L. and Hultzsch's n 8 at p. 128 : renunciation of arms RE. xiii O-AA (Shāhbazgarhī) : value of the king's example PE. VII GG. Aśoka's view of Dhammavijaya has been discussed in some detail by the present writer in *The Calcutta Review* Feb. 1943 pp. 114—23.

consequences to the people, the state, and to Buddhism itself. At the time of Aśoka's accession when he was still a votary of the orthodox Brahmanical faith, Buddhism was doubtless the most important among the various sects that flourished outside its pale and competed with one another for popular acceptance and royal patronage. The Saṅgha was from the beginning an organised brotherhood with a well-established tradition of its own already fixed by the authority of two General Councils ; the bulk of the canon had come into existence in some form and was awaiting the finishing touch that Tissa gave it under Aśoka's patronage by the composition of the *Kathāvatthu*. The erection of stūpas and the worship of the Buddhas who had preceded Gautama had come into vogue. Senart first pointed out the striking parallelism between the ethical ideas of the Aśokan edicts and those of the *Dhammapada* and demonstrated that it extended to the terms and phrases employed by both in similar contexts ; they may both be taken therefore to mark one stage in the development of Bauddha doctrine and ethics. Hultzsch has argued, however, that as Aśoka's inscriptions do not yet know anything of Nirvāṇa, they must be taken to reflect an earlier stage in the development of Buddhist theology or metaphysics than the *Dhammapada*[1]. But it is highly improbable that the conception of *nirvāṇa* which occurs in the earliest strata of the canon was unknown to Buddhism in the days of Aśoka and was developed later. The truth is that Aśoka refrained studiously from introducing into his edicts any of the fundamental tenets of the Buddhist faith—such as the Four Sacred Truths, the Chain of Causality, and the Noble Eight-fold Path, besides the Nirvāṇa, all conceptions which must have been fully developed long before the time of Aśoka. This omission, together with the repeated references to the doctrine of *ṛṇa* (debt), to *svarga* and to happiness in the other world as the reward of good deeds done here, has misled some to assert that Aśoka never accepted Buddhism as his personal faith, but continued to remain all through his life what he was at its beginning—a follower of the Vedic religion. Others have hailed Aśoka for this very reason as a reformer of Buddhism who, being determined

1. p. liii. See also Bagch on the development of the Canon in the Chapter on Religion *post*.

on propagating it not only in his own empire but beyond its borders, set about adapting it to suit the new requirements. On this view Buddha's religion was in its earlier phase too restricted and monastic in its outlook, too puritanical and too cold in its reasoning and its individualism ; by simplifying it, by virtually inaugurating the cult of the stūpa, and the worship of relics, Aśoka introduced a more catholic spirit into the church ; indeed these were elements alien to the creed of the Founder, but they enabled the church to cast its net wider among all races and all classes of society ; and the simple principle of sound behaviour repeated often in the edicts, the Dharma of the inscriptions, is purely ethical in its content and universal in its appeal . Aśoka turned Buddhism from a dry academic-pursuit of the path of knowledge to a colourful and emotional religion of devotion with a wide popular appeal. Such a view of Aśoka's work errs by attributing much too conscious a purpose to the great emperor, and by seeking to focus into his reign the entire development of Mahāyāna Buddhism on the one side and the transition on the other from Jñānamārga to Bhaktimārga, which after all had perhaps no place as such in the history of early Buddhist development ; it also exaggerates the academic and doctrinal side of primitive Buddhism and overlooks its strongly ethical character.

After all, the inscriptions themselves are the best guide to Aśoka's attitude to Buddhism ; and a study of these documents shows decisively that Aśoka's approach to Buddhism was that of a profound humanist ; it was practical, pragmatic, and intensely ethical. The tragic war against Kalinga stirred his humanity to its depths ; he felt drawn to the creed already well known for its ethical and humanitarian character. Progress in the new way of life was slow at first, but soon Aśoka developed a greater zeal ; he visited the Saṅgha and gained instruction in the Faith ; he went on a pilgrimage, in due course, to the spots hallowed by the Master's presence, and commemorated his visits by gifts, monuments, foundations, inscriptions. The worship of Buddhas and of their relics, enshrined in stūpas was already known and practised ; when the great Mauryan emperor accepted the Buddha's faith as his own, the vast material resources of an extensive empire were pressed into the service of that creed, and there ensued an enormous increase in the numbers of stūpas and vihāras, because the emperor naturally did all he could to spread the symbols of his faith all over his empire, and his example was followed by others who were near to him and naturally accepted his lead. But of any attempt on Aśoka's part to secure converts to Buddhism as such or to reform that faith by introducing fresh features into it in order to render it more acceptable to the populace, there is no sign whatever. In fact Aśoka is at some pains to mark off his innovations from the rest of his work where he was only following the established tradition (*porāṇā pakiti*), breathing fresh life into it and adapting it to his wider aims for the moral upliftment of the people. The greatest of Aśoka's innovations, that for which he seems to claim the most credit, is that he rescued the ideal of Dharma from the relative neglect into which it had fallen and placed it in the forefront of national life, making it the touchstone of the whole of his life's work. This ideal was more ethical and social, than religious ; though the energy with which Aśoka pursued its propagation was the direct result of his having accepted Buddhism as his personal religion, the ideal itself was the common ground on which all Indian creeds met. Aśoka himself says in the Seventh Rock-Edict : 'All sects desire both self-control and purity of mind'. In the sphere of formal religion, Aśoka makes it clear that he did not mind what a man's particular creed was ; but he did require that all should cultivate mutual respect, should live in peace and friendliness, and should cultivate habits of social good conduct. Aśoka bent the entire maehinery of the state towards the practical realization of the ideal of good life among men within his empire, and to the extent possible even beyond its borders ; and his chief claim to statesmanship lies in his strenuous endeavour to discover the widest possible basis of agreement attainable among all the sections of his subjects and to build his policy on that basis. Aśoka was the one ruler before Akbar who faced the problem of Indian national unity, and he came much nearer success than Akbar because he had a better understanding of human nature, and instead of seeking to invent a new common faith or compel everybody to adopt the faith he had accepted as his own, he took the established order for granted and struck the road along which there was the best chance of healthy and ordered development. He never departed from his rule of tolerance, and the only two instances where he appears to have done so—the prohibition of animal sacrifice and the deprecation of tiresome rituals—are really particular cases of the general promotion of *ahimsā* which commanded widespread assent.

Let us now turn to details and consider the content of Aśoka's Dharma and the means he employed for its propagation. The method of publishing and popularising administrative orders and royal proclamations by having them engraved on rock-faces was well known to the imperial administration of Persia under the Achaemenids, and Aśoka's adoption of the same method for the propagation of Dharma—he calls his inscriptions Dharma-lipis—was doubtless inspired by familiarity with that practice. The preamble of many of Aśoka's edicts, often repeated in the body of edicts themselves to introduce important statements, viz. 'Thus speaks king Devānāmpriya Priyadarśin', and the abrupt changes in the style of address from the third person to the first, are strongly reminiscent of the Achaemenid inscriptions ; the words *dipi* and *nipishṭa* of Aśoka's edicts are evidently taken over from the Ancient Persian language ; Tushāspa who, as we learn from an inscription of Rudradāman, was Aśoka's governor of Girnār, was doubtless a Persian, and might be, there were several other Persian officials like him in Aśoka's service particularly in the North-West which had been under Persian occupation for a considerable time before the coming of Alexander. The Kharoshṭhī alphabet and the Persepolitan capital of the Aśoka columns also came from Persia[1].

The fourteen Rock-Edicts together with the two Kalinga edicts, and Seven Pillar Edicts are mostly given to descriptions of the different aspects of Dharma in accordance with the programme Aśoka placed before himself when he issued the Minor Rock-Edict (Rūpnāth). In that edict, the first record of the reign issued very soon after the king began to be zealous in the practice of Buddhism and the propagation of Dharma, Aśoka claims that good results had already attended his efforts, and gods had begun to mingle with men in Jambudvīpa as they had

1. Hultzsch p. xlii.

never done before—a statement which remains something of an enigma. Two interpretations have been suggested : one by Smith—that the practice of Dharma raises men to the level of the gods ; the other, which seems better, by Hultzsch who explains the statement in the light of the fourth Rock-Edict which mentions 'religious shows at which Aśoka had exhibited to his subjects *in effigie* the gods whose abodes they would be able to reach by the zealous practice of Dharma'[1]. Aśoka then proceeds to say that his success has been the fruit of zeal (*prakrama*) and exhorts all persons of whatever rank, high or low, to practise the like zeal and attain heaven in due course ; he records his resolution to increase Dharma greatly, and to avail himself of rock faces and stone pillars for engraving his message of Dharma on them ; finally he orders his provincial officers to despatch men everywhere within their charges for preaching the Dharma. The two series of Rock and Pillar Edicts that followed comprised an elaboration and steady execution of the programme thus briefly sketched at the outset, and Aśoka states expressly more than once in these Edicts that this was a new departure introduced by him to make up for the apathy of centuries in which the moral well-being and progress of the people, though vaguely recognised by monarchs as desirable, had seldom been actively promoted by them[2].

Aśoka's Dharma

Aśoka's Dharma is primarily ethical social conduct and it includes even the animal kingdom within the scope of its all-embracing benevolence. We read at the end of the Minor Rock-Edict (Yerraguḍi) 'Obedience must be rendered to mother and father, likewise to elders ; compassion should be shown towards men ; the truth must be spoken ; these moral virtues (*dhamma-guṇā*) must be practised.... Pupils should respect their teachers in accordance with the ancient rule (*porāṇā pakiti*)'[3]. Again in the third Rock Edict : 'Meritorious (*sādhu*) is obedience to mother and father. Liberality (*dānam*) to friends, acquaintances, and relatives, to Brāhmaṇas and Śramaṇas is meritorious.

1. *ib.* p. 168 *n* 3.
2. RE. IV A : PE. VII B-E.
3 ASI. 1928—29 pp. 165—7. cf. Brahmagiri N—P (Hultzsch p. 178).

Abstention from killing animals is meritorious. Moderation in expenditure and moderation in possessions are meritorious[1]'. Emphasis is laid on qualities of mind (*bhāva śuddhi*) in the Seventh Rock-Edict : 'But even one who practises great liberality but does not possess self-control, purity of mind, gratitude, and firm devotion, is very mean[2].' Proper treatment of serfs (*dāsa*) and servants (*bhataka*) is particularly mentioned in the eleventh and thirteenth Rock Edicts[3]. The Second Pillar-Edict contains this striking and comprehensive statement of the emperor on Dharma : 'To practise morality is meritorious ; but what does morality include ? It includes few sins, many virtuous deeds, compassion, liberality, truthfulness and purity. The gift of spiritual insight (*cakkhu-dāna*) also has been bestowed by me in many ways[4].'

The promotion of toleration and harmony among different religious sects and of kindness towards animal life were two particular aspects of Dharma to which Aśoka gave very special attention. The twelfth Rock-Edict sets forth the principles of religious toleration in very clear terms and constitutes one of the noblest documents of human history and we are justified in citing the edict in full[5].

"King Devānāmpriya Priyadarśin is honouring all sects (*pāshaṇḍas*) : both ascetics and householders ; both with gifts and with honours of various kinds he is honouring them. But Devānāmpriya does not value either gifts or honours so highly as this viz., that a promotion of the essentials of all sects (*sāra-vṛddhi*) should take place. But a promotion of the essentials is possible in many ways. But the root is this, viz., guarding one's speech (*vaco-gupti*), i.e. that neither praising one's own sect nor blaming other sects should take place on improper occasions, or that it should be moderate in every case. But other sects ought to be duly honoured in every case.

"If one is acting thus, he is both promoting his own sect and benefiting other sects. If one is acting otherwise than thus,

1. Hultzsch p. 5 RE. III D. cf. RE IV C.
2. *ib.* p. 14 VII E.
3. *ib.* p. 19 XI C : p. 47, XIII G.
4. *ib.* p. 121, PE II B-D cf. PE VII EE, which with following HH forms a fairly complete account of Dharma.
5. *ib.* p. 21.

he is both hurting his own sect and wronging other sects as well. For whosoever praises his own sect or blames other sects—all this out of devotion to his own sect, (i.e.) with the view of glorifying his own sect,—if he is acting thus, he rather injures his own sect very severely.

"Therefore concord alone is meritorious, (i.e.), that they should both hear and obey each other's morals (Dharma). For this is the desire of Devānāmpriya, (viz.) that all sects should be full of learning (*bahuśrutāḥ*), and should be pure in doctrine (*kalyāṇāgamāḥ*).

"And those who are attached to their respective sects ought to be spoken to as follows : Devānāmpriya does not value either gifts or honours so highly as this, (viz.) that a promotion of the essentials (*sārvṛddhi*) of all sects should take place. And many officers are occupied for this purpose, (viz.) the Mahāmātras of morality, the Mahāmātras controlling wcmen, the inspectors of cowpens, and other classes of officials. And this is the fruit of it, (viz.) that both the promotion of one's own sect takes place, and the glorification of Morality (*Dharmasya ca dīpanā*)."

The universality of Aśoka's toleration, and his realisation of the limits set by common human nature to the success of his policy are best seen in his words in the seventh Rock-Edict[1] : 'King Devānāmpriya Priyadarśin desires that all sects may reside everywhere. For all these desire both self-control and purity of mind. But men possess various desires and various passions. Either they will fulfil the whole or they will fulfil only a portion (of their duties)'. Some more details regarding the particular sects and the attention given to them by Aśoka's officials are vouchafed by the Seventh Pillar-Edict, and these have been noticed already in connection with the duties of the various classes of Mahāmātras[2].

In the ninth Rock-Edict Aśoka deprecates the observance of vulgar and useless (*kshudra* and *nirarthaka*) ceremonies, particularly by women on sundry occasions as during illness, at marriage or child-birth, when setting out on a journey and so on. He wants such fruitless *mangalas* to be reduced to a mini-

1. *ib*. p. 14 VII A-D. cf. PE. VI D-E. *ib*. p. 129 :
2. *Ante* p. 225 and n. 2.

mum and that people should devote themselves more and more to the real *mangala* which is the practice of Dharma[1].

That men should treat animals kindly and not inflict pain on them unnecessarily was as much the concern of Aśoka as that they should preserve concord among themselves. He became a wholehearted adherent of the doctrine of *ahimsā*, and devised several regulations for the encouragement of its practice and the prevention of cruelty to animals. In the first Rock-Edict Aśoka forbids the slaughter and sacrifice of animals in his territory and the holding of all *samājas* (festive gatherings) except those considered meritorious by him. He also states that whereas formerly hundreds of thousands of animals were killed every day in the royal kitchen for the sake of curry (*sūpārthāya*), only three animals were slaughtered at the time the edict was being issued, viz., two peacocks and one deer, but even the deer not regularly, and that in future even these animals would not be killed[2]. Aśoka, it will be noticed, does not impose any restrictions on others which he does not put upon himself, and in this edict we seem to find what was perhaps the most decisive step in the acceptance of vegetarianism by considerable sections of the Indian population outside the Jaina community. The prohibition of animal sacrifice has been viewed by some writers as a measure of intolerance directed against Brahmanism ; doubtless Vedic sacrifices involving the killing of live animals fell under the prohibition, and to that extent it must count as virtually a hindrance to the practice of Vedic religion ; but its importance is easily exaggerated. The primacy of Vedic religion in all India was by no means as well assured in Aśoka's time as it became since; the followers of Vedic religion were themselves debating if the time had not come for a change in sacrificial practice giving up the immolation of live victims ; and in any case the number of such sacrifices would never have been very great as the smallest *paśuyāga* is a costly business, and the practical inconvenience caused by the prohibition would have been very little ; lastly, for every victim in a brahminical sacrifice, there would have been hundreds

1. Hultzsch pp. 38—9. Jayaswal shows that Mangalas often involved sacrifices of birds and beasts (JBORS. iv pp. 144—7).

2. Hultzsch p. 2.

of victims sacrificed in the worship of lesser godlings by the mass of the populace who were still largely addicted to relatively primitive types of worship, and the prohibition affected them much more than the upper strata of society and religion. Likewise the *samājas* that were prohibited were occasions for the slaughter of numerous animals for feeding the large numbers that gathered together and made merry on such occasions ; there was another type of *samājas* approved of Aśoka where semi-religious theatrical and other shows like representations of aerial chariots, of elephants, of *agniskandhas* and other divine figures, instructed and edified the assemblies, and these were actively encouraged[1]. All the prohibitions of the First Rock-Edict had therefore no other object in view than to minimise the destruction of animal life.

The second Rock-Edict details the arrangements made by Aśoka within his empire and beyond its borders for the convenience of man and beast ; they consisted primarily in the provision of medical treatment (*cikitsā*) and gardens of medicinal herbs (*oshadhīni*) beneficial to both. This provision was made in the words of the Edict, 'everywhere in the dominions of King Devānāmpriya Priyadarśin, and likewise among his borderers such as the Choḍas, the Pāṇḍyas, the Satiyaputa, the Ketala puta, even Tāmraparṇī, the Yona king Antiyoka, and also the kings who are the neighbours of this Antiyoka.' The location of Satiyaputa was till recently matter for much speculation. Recently, however, it has been identified with the Kingdom of the Adigamāns round about Dharmapuri in Salem district on good philological grounds.[2] And Ketalaputa, for which we have Keralaputra in Mānsehrā, is doubtless the Malabar country. Besides medical aid being made available everywhere, wells with flights of steps leading to the water were caused to be dug at intervals of eight *kos* (nine miles) along the roads, and banyan trees and mango groves planted for the use of cattle and men; and numerous drinking-places (*āpāna*) were also established in addition[3].

1. Cf. Smith, *Aśoka* (3) p. 159 and RE. IV B, Hultzsch p. 7.

2. Smith's latest surmise on Satiyaputa viz., that 'in all probability it is represented by the Satyamangalam Taluk or sub-division of the Coimbatore district', and the reasons urged by him in favour of it (*Aśoka* 3 p. 161) can hardly be accepted. D. R. Bhandarkar's reference to the current Maratha surname Sātpute sounds more convincing, but Aśoka's Satiyaputa was a kingdom definitely somewhere in South India, and so far as I can see nowhere in or near Mahārāshṭra. Cf. Hultzsch p. 3 n. 7 See also 'South India and Ceylon' *post.*

3. RE. II D (p. 4) : PE VII R-T (pp. 134—5) and II E, (p. 121).

Aśoka suppressed the time-honoured institution of the Royal Hunt[1] of which we get a detailed account from Megasthenes. The final development of Aśoka's policy of *ahimsā* took the shape of a very elaborate code of regulation and restriction of the slaughter and mutilation of birds and animals. This code, which is set forth in the fifth Pillar-Edict ends by mentioning the twenty-five annual releases of prisoners that had already taken place. In both respects, Aśoka seems to have amplified the traditional practices known to the *Arthaśāstra* and mentioned there particularly in the chapters on the Superintendent of slaughter-houses and on the pacification of newly conquered territory[2]. Aśoka's code begins with the absolute prohibition of the slaughter of a long list of birds and animals which among others includes parrots, bulls set at liberty[3], and she-goats, ewes and sows either with young or in milk, and their young ones which are less than six months old. It continues; 'Cocks must not be caponed. Husks containing living animals must not be burnt. Forests must not be burnt either uselessly or in order to destroy living beings. Living animals must not be fed with other living animals.' After this catalogue of total prohibitions, there follow restrictions to be observed on specified holy days making up a good fraction of the year : 'Fish are inviolable, and must not be sold, on the three Cāturmāsis and on the Tiṣya full-moon during three days, (viz.) the fourteenth, the fifteenth and the first *tithi*, and invariably on every fast day. And during these same days also no other classes of animals which are in the elephant-park (*nāga-vana*) and in the preserves of the fisherman (*kaivarta-bhoga*), must be killed.' Lastly the castration of bulls, he-goats, rams and boar was forbidden on all holy days, and so too the branding of horses and bullocks, practices which Aśoka did not consider it practicable to prohibit

1. RE. VII A-D, Hultzsch p. 37.
2. Hultzsch pp. 127—8 and n. 8 on p. 128. Also *Arthaśāstra* II 26, and XIII 5.
3. Evidently other bulls and cows are not included in the protected list : all cows and bulls are so included in the *Arthaśāstra* which lays down : *Vatso vṛṣo dhenuścaiṣām avadhyāh ghnataḥ pañcāśatko daṇḍaḥ, klishṭaghātam ghātayayataśca* i.e. calves, bulls and cows shall not be slaughtered. Whoever kills them or causes them to be killed with torture shall be fined fifty Paṇas'. Opinion on beef-eating was apparently in a fluid state in the Mauryan epoch, and while the *Arthaśāstra* forbids it, Aśoka's edict does not appear to do so. See also Hultzsch p. 127, n. 8, and Smith's *Aśoka* 3 pp. 206—7.

altogether. Though based on ancient tradition, this code bears on it the impress of Aśoka's mind, and it app ied to the whole of his empire. Its strict enforcement in all its details must have been found difficult; but, though no sanctions are stated in the Code, as in the *Arthaśāstra*, it was certainly much more than the expression of pious wishes on the part of the emperor, and must have gone far towards the realisation of the practical objects Aśoka had in view; the rules were only elaborations of practices already well known in the land, and they could not have been felt as a vexatious interference with the details of daily life.

The Dharma of Aśoka was thus a practical code of social ethics, and had little to do with religion or theology as such; and the emperor showed in many ways that he attached the greatest importance to the practice of the virtues he commended to his subjects. He lays stress on *śila* (conduct); points out how easy it is to fall into evil ways and how difficut it is, particularly for the highly placed, to be always well-behaved. He deprecates evil passions like fierceness, cruelty, anger, pride, envy, and warns all against being led to commit evil deeds by the force of such passions. He praises *dharmadāna* (the gift of morality) as the highest of gifts, and exhorts friends and relations, even neighbours, to practise mutual help by telling one another as occasion demanded : 'This is meritorious, this ought to be done.' He recognises the immensity of the task of the moral regeneration of a whole nation, and says in the epilogue to the fourteen Rock-Edicts : 'My dominions are wide, and much has been written, and I shall cause still more to be written. And some of this has been stated again and again because of the charm of certain topics and in order that men should act accordingly'. And he recognises the superiority of conversion due to moral education to administrative regulation as a means of moral upliftment, and avers his faith in the Seventh Pillar-Edict : 'Now this progress of morality among men has been promoted by me only in two ways, viz. by moral restrictions (*dhammaniyama*) and conversion (*nijhati*). But among these two, those moral restrictions are of little consequence ; by conversion, however, morality is promoted more considerably'. Above all he reinforced his exhortations by his untiring personal example ; he gave up the traditional pleasure tours (*vihārayātras*) in which royal hunt was included, and substitued *dharmayātras* (tours of morality) in their place, and explained their object thus : 'On these tours the following takes place, (viz.) visiting Brāhmaṇas and Śramaṇas and making gifts to them, visiting the aged and supporting them with gold, visiting the people of the country, instructing them in morality, and questioning them about morality'[1]. And he repeatedly expresses the hope that his sons and grandsons will follow his steps in promoting morality among men.

Aśoka, then, was a great monarch whose reign constitutes one of those 'rare and lightning epochs' in the annals of nations when a people is vouchsafed a glimpse of happiness, perceived, if not possessed. His greatness lay in his early and clear realisation of the values of human life, and in his endeavouring strenuously throughout his life to rouse India to listen to the call of moral life she received through him. He did much for Buddhism, and his memory has been kept green through the ages in all the vast lands where Buddhist tradition has prevailed to this day ; towards the close of the thirteenth century A. D., the Burmese recognised an old Caitya in Bodh Gayā as one of the 84,000 caityas built by Siri Dhammāśoka when 218 years of the era of the Lord Buddha had passed away[2].

But was Aśoka monk and monarch at the same time ? Did he accept the position and exercise the duties of the Head of the Buddhist Church ? Is it correct to describe his activity as 'not so much that of a pious Emperor as of an archbishop possessed of exceptional temporal power' ?[3] Such statements derive little support except from false analogies and wrong interpretations of the inscriptions of the reign. Aśoka's edicts, great as is their

1. For emphasis on śila RE. IV H, F : difficulty of practising virtue RE. V B-C, PE I C ; for the high in particular RE. X E-F. Easy to sin RE. V G : evil due to passions PE. III F ; Dharmadāna praised RE. IX J-L ; B, D., E. epilogue RE. xiv : restriction vs. conversion PE. VII JJ-NN : Dharmayātras RE. VIII A-D. Sons and grandsons RE iv F, V E, VI M. Further the following passages are also of interest : PE. VI B stating that engraving of Dhammalipis began in thirteenth year after *abhisheka* : *ib.* C. on king's attention to his relatives ; PE VII J-L and P on active preaching of morality among the people.

2. Ep. Ind. xi. p. 119.

3. Smith, *Aśoka* (3) pp. 35-6 : Eliot, *Hinduism and Buddhism* i. p. 265.

value, are not concerned with public affairs, but only with one aspect, though indeed a very important one, of Aśoka's work as ruler—the promotion of Dharma. They are in fact what he calls them, Dharma-lipis. And this Dharma, though inspired by Aśoka's conversion to Buddhism and coloured by the practical ethics so characteristic of that faith, was hardly more distinctive of Buddhism than of any other Indian faith. Again, a church in the strict sense of the term, organised on hierarchical lines, and owning allegiance to a central authority, the Buddhist Saṅgha was not ; there was no room for the Head of the Church in an organisation which comprised an infinite number of independent *vihāras* which were united in their professing a common faith in the *triratna* (Buddha, Dhamma and Saṅgha), but regulated themselves each according to their own views of Dhamma and Vinaya. Aśoka's letter to the Saṅgha (the Calcutta-Bairat inscription or Bhābrū edict as it is called) commending seven scriptural passages to them, far from asserting royal authority, is couched in the most respectful terms and ends with the statement : 'I desire, sirs, that many groups of monks and many nuns may repeatedly listen to these expositions of Dhamma and may reflect on them. In the same way both laymen and laywomen should act. For the following purpose, Sirs, am I causing this, to be written, (viz.) in order that they may know my intention'[1]. Surely this expression of opinion on the part of the great king, coming from him at the conclusion of his study of Dhamma, with the aid of the Saṅgha and the reflection that followed upon it, would have been received with all the respect it merited ; but this is hardly an instance of the use of authority of any kind, royal or ecclesiastical. The edict on Saṅghabheda can with better justice be regarded as use of royal authority, for in plain terms it orders the officials of the civil administration to see that within their respective jurisdictions all schismatic monks are expelled from the Saṅgha, compelled to wear white robes, and driven to live in places not suited for the residence of monks (*avāsa*)[2]. But here the authority of the king was obviously invoked by the Saṅgha which had recently experienced great difficulty by the

1. Hultzsch p. 174.
2. *ib.* pp. 163—4 and Corrigenda.

intrusion of undesirable elements within its fold ; a Council had been held and a fresh settlement of the affairs reached ; not feeling equal to the task of securing its proper observance without the aid of the secular arm, the Saṅgha appealed to the State for aid, and got it ; the assistance which Aśoka gave to the Saṅgha in such circumstances, he would have given to any other corporate body which suffered similarly at the hands of assailants from outside. Lastly the evidence for Aśoka's taking orders is very meagre. The phrase *Saṅgham-upa-ī* in the Minor Rock-Edict is too vague to convey the precise idea of ordination (*pabbajjā*) which must have been well established by Aśoka's time. And the situation of a king turning monk while retaining the life and prerogatives of royalty is incompatible with all our notions of ancient monachism. And the *Mahāvamsa* says that in his message to the king of Ceylon Aśoka said that he had become 'lay-disciple in the religion of the Śākya son'[1]. And barring the vague phrase in the Minor Rock-Edict there is no other evidence in favour of Aśoka's ordination than that centuries afterwards I-tsing records his having seen an image of the emperor in monastic robes. This image may be satisfactorily explained in one of two ways : either Aśoka may have worn the robes of a monk whenever he visited the Saṅgha for listening to the exposition of Dhamma, an act of courtesy to the members of the Saṅgha which was commemorated by such an image ; or towards the end of his life, Aśoka renounced the empire and turned monk as a prophecy attributed to the Buddha himself in the Aśokavardhanāvadāna (XI) of the *Divyāvadāna*[2] may lead us to suppose.

The successors of Aśoka

An impenetrable obscurity settles on the Mauryan empire after the reign of Aśoka. The only certainty is that the great empire founded by Chandragupta and extended and maintained in all its splendour by his son and grandson, did not long survive in its itegrity. Tīvara, the only son of Aśoka named in his inscriptions, is not heard of again, and must be presumed to have predeceased his father. The Purāṇas, the Avadānas,

1. MV. xi. 34. Also Hultzsch pp. xliv—xlv.
2. Div. pp. 140—1.

and the Jaina accounts have different tales to tell, and later writers like Kalhaṇa of Kashmir and Tāranāth of Tibet give their own versions of what happened. There is no means of reconciling these divergent accounts except to assume that the empire was in some manner divided among the surviving sons of Aśoka, and that each of our sources preserves the story of that part of the empire with which it was concerned. A continuous history of the Mauryan empire after Aśoka is, in the present state of knowledge, out of the question ; all we can do is to reproduce the lists of monarchs with the periods of their rule found in the authorities, and note what we know of them.[1]

The Purāṇas		*Divyāvadāna*
1. Kunāla—	8 years.	1. Kunāla (did not reign)
2. Bandhupālita, son (1)	8 years	2. Sampadi—son of (1)
[2]3. Indrapālita, dāyāda (brother?) of (2)—	10 years	3. Bṛhaspati—son of (2)
4. Daśona, naptā (grandson) of (2)—	7 years	4. Vṛshasena—son of (3)
5. Daśaratha, son of (4)—	8 years	5. Pushyadharman—son of (4)
6. Samprati, son of (5)—	9 years	6. Pushyamitra—son of (5)
7. Śāliśūka—	13 years	*Tāranātha.*
8. Devadharman—	7 years	1. Kunāla
9. Śatadhanus, son of (8)—	8 years	2. Vigatāśoka
10. Bṛhadratha—	7 years	3. Vīrasena

Though the Purāṇas generally agree in stating that altogether nine Mauryas ruled for a period of 137 years, none of the lists gives details corresponding to these total figures which refer presumably to Magadha and the eastern half of the empire. The only name in these lists confirmed by epigraphy is that of Daśaratha who is ignored in the Buddhist and Jain accounts ; he is known by three short dedicatory inscriptions bestowing on the Ājīvakas caves in the Nāgārjuni hills immediately after his

1. For Purāṇa Texts—Pargiter, *Dynasties of the Kali Age*, pp. 27—30 ; Div. ed. Cowell and Neil (1886) p. 430 ; Tāranāth, *History of Buddhism*, trans. Schiefner pp. 48 ff.

2. Mentioned only in some lists.

abhisheka (coronation) ; the script and the style of these records closely resemble those of the similar inscriptions of Aśoka in the neighbouring Barābar hills[1]. For the rest we have only tradition ; though it is possible that tradition preserves the memory of what has been lost to history, perhaps for ever.

Sampadi or Samprati is well known both in Buddhist and Jaina literature. According to the *Divyāvadāna* he was the son of Kunāla and was established on the throne of Magadha by the ministers of state under strange circumstances ; Aśoka had promised a hundred crores to the Saṅgha of which he had paid only ninety-six crores by the end of his reign ; so he handed the kingdom over to them in lieu of the balance of four crores. The ministers managed to raise this money, pay it to the Saṅgha, and thus redeem the kingdom over which they set Samprati[2]. The Jaina accounts also make Samprati the immediate successor of Aśoka, and say that after his conversion to Jainism by Suhastin he did for Jainism nearly everything that Aśoka did for Buddhism, such as building temples and endowing them liberally and spreading the faith even in non-Aryan lands. Though Pāṭaliputra is mentioned as the seat of his government in some accounts, others, with greater probability, make him ruler of Ujjain[3]. If Samprati was a grandson of Aśoka ruling from from Ujjain, Daśaratha was perhaps another who held sway at Pāṭaliputra. Whether Bandhupālita (Vāyu) and Vigatāśoka (Tāranāth) were alternative names of Samprati, or those of his brothers, is not easily ascertained.

Kalhaṇa, the historian of Kashmir, as we have seen[4], reproduces from earlier accounts the story of Jalauka, a son of Aśoka, and his successor in Kashmir ; Jalauka is said to have freed his country from an invasion of *mlecchas* (Greeks?) and extended his dominions as far as Kanauj ; he was also a great patron of Śaivism.

Śāliśūka is a name attested not only by the Vāyu and Vishṇu Purāṇas but by the 'Yugapurāṇa' section of the *Gārgī Samhitā*

1. IA. 1891 pp. 361 ff.
2. Div. *ibid* ; earlier in the same story, we are told that Samprati and his ministers took steps to prevent Aśoka fulfilling his promise to the Saṅgha to the detriment of his kingdom and his subjects.
3. Bom. Gaz. I. i. pp. 14-5.
4. *Ante*, p. 219.

where he is said to have done much to further the cause of Jainism even by the use of force.

Tāranātha's Vīrasena, said to have been ruling in Gandhāra, must have been related to Subhāgasena with whom Antiochus the Great of Syria renewed his friendship about 206 B. C. Polybius says of Antiochus[1] : 'Crossing the Caucasus he descended into India and renewed his alliance with Sophagasenus the Indian king. Here he procured more elephants, so that his total force of them amounted now to hundred-and-fifty, and after a further distribution of corn to his troops, set out himself with his army, leaving Androsthenes of Cyzicus to collect the treasure which the king had agreed to pay.' Clearly this was a renewal of the friendly relations that had prevailed between the Seleucids and the Mauryas since the days of the founders of both lines ; as usual the Greek monarch asked for and obtained some elephants for his army from the Indian ruler. Subhāgasena may well have been a Maurya[2].

The *Divyāvadāna* is clearly wrong in including Pushyamitra among the Mauryas. By all other accounts, he was the first of the Śuṅgas who rose to power first as the commander-in-chief of the forces of Bṛhadratha, the last of the successors of Aśoka. In his *Harsha-charitra*, Bāṇa finds occasion to introduce a calendar of treacherous assassinations, and there occurs the statement : 'The wicked generalissimo Pushpamitra crushed his master, the Mauryan Bṛhadratha, who had little sense, and to whom the general pretended to show the whole army in a review'. Likewise, the *Vishṇu Purāṇa* says : 'Pushyamitra the commander-in-chief will uproot Bṛhadratha and will rule the kingdom as king 36 years'[3]. The fall of Bṛhadratha must be taken to mark the end of the Mauryan empire as such; it occurred about 185 B. C.

Pushyamitra was doubtless a Brahmin ; the Chetas of Kalinga and the Sātavāhanas who succeeded the Mauryas in other

1. *Histories*, xi. 39, Vol. IV p. 303 (Loeb classical library Tr. by W. R. Paton).

2. Cf. H. C. Raychaudhuri *Political History* (4) pp. 300-1 ; Tarn, *The Greeks in Bactria and India* pp. 130 and 154.

3. The reading 'Pratijñādurbalam' for 'prajñā-durbalam' in Bāṇa's sentence, (H.C. Bombay N. S. Press 1897, pp. 198-9) and the far-reaching theories based on it (See Smith EHI (4) p. 208 n. 1) seem to me altogether unwarranted. For V. P. see Pargiter *op. cit.* pp. 31 and 70.

portions of the empire are also held to have been Brahmins[1]. The argument has been advanced that the fall of the Mauryan empire was largely the result of a Brahminical reaction against the pro-Buddhist policy of Aśoka, and possibly the pro-Jaina policy of some of his successors. Our account of Aśoka's reign has shown that far from being narrowly Buddhist in its character, that emperor's religious policy deliberately aimed at universal tolerance and amity among all the religious sects ; the Brāhmaṇas were, if anything, selected for being honoured equally with the Śramaṇas, and there is no reason to believe that Aśoka was animated by an anti-Brahmanical bias to any degree. In fact we have little definite knowledge of what actually happened after the close of Aśoka's rule, and Pushyamitra, the Chetas and the Sātavāhanas are too far removed from the reign of Aśoka for them to lend support to the idea of a Brahmin reaction against Aśoka's religious policy. The oppressive conduct of imperial officials in the provinces of the empire and Aśoka's pacificism have been adduced as other causes for the decline and fall of the Mauryan empire. The casual references to wicked officials (*dushṭa amātyaś*) in the legends of the *Divyāvadāna* can give no secure foundation for postulating the general prevalence of oppression throughout the empire ; and there is nothing in the separate Kalinga edicts that goes to prove, as has been urged, that such oppression was a reality. Aśoka's pacificism, his abandonment of war as an instrument of policy, and his exhortation to his successors to follow him in this respect, had nothing doctrinaire about it, and was kept within limits by a wise awareness of the complexity of human situations and motives. There is no evidence that he diminished the strength of the army or weakened the defences of the empire.

Dynastic empires depend for their continued existence on the supply of able monarchs in the line ; Aśoka was great in every way ; he was not only the greatest of the Mauryas, but one of the few truly great rulers of the world. There was evidently none among his children equal to the task of maintaining the unity of the vast empire, and the division which, according to

1. Smith EHI (4) p. 204 and n. 2 *contra* H. C. Raychaudhuri, *Pol. His 4.* pp. 294 ff. where the arguments of Haraprasada Śāstri who first propounded this view are examined at length.

legend, threatened the empire even at the accession of Aśoka, actually overtook it after the close of his reign. But in India the rise and fall of empires, important though they are as landmarks, do not touch the cultural life of the nation as deeply as in other lands. Indian imperialism was never a fully centralised form of administration ; without exception an Indian empire was more or less a loose confederation of nearly independent units, kingdoms, cities, tribes and so on, held together by loyalty to the person of the emperor when he had the strength to dominate them ; but under the strongest emperor, the local rulers and institutions continued as before ; and the disruption of an empire or its division did not raise those difficult problems of reorganisation which would have come up with the decadence of a more centralized system. In the day of its prosperity an empire did enhance the glory of the race and its achievements in the various spheres of national life did excel greatly those of the smaller kingdoms which usually filled the political map of the country ; but the disappearance of an empire led by no means to a relapse into chaos or barbarism. India's ancient culture was the achievement of Indian society, not of the Indian state ; an empire led to the efflorescence of that culture.

Scions of the Mauryan family are heard of centuries after the fall of the Mauryan empire, and in remote parts of the country. In Magadha itself a certain Pūrṇavarman is mentioned by Hiuen Tsang as a descendant of Aśoka ; and Śankara, the great philospher of Advaita, might have had him in mind when he said : there have been no world emperors (*sārvabhauma*) after Pūrṇavarman ! The Mauryas of Konkan had their capital at Purī, a flourishing emporium on the Elephanta island near Bombay, and they became subject to the Chālukyas of Bādāmi in the sixth century A. D. A certain Dhavaḷa is heard of in the Kanaswa inscription (A. D. 738-9) in the Kotah state, Rajputana. And a Maurya chief Govindarāja is mentioned in an eleventh century inscription from Khandesh as a subordinate of the Yādava Seuṇachandra II[1]. The memory of Mauryan rule persisted in Kuntala for a long time and it is alluded to in Kannaḍa inscriptions of the eleventh century from Karṇāṭaka.

1. Watters II p. 115 ; Śankara B.S. II. 1. 18; BG. I ii pp. 282-4. For the location of Purī, *Imp. Inscrr.* from the *Baroda State* by A. S. Gadre (1943) pp. 44-5.

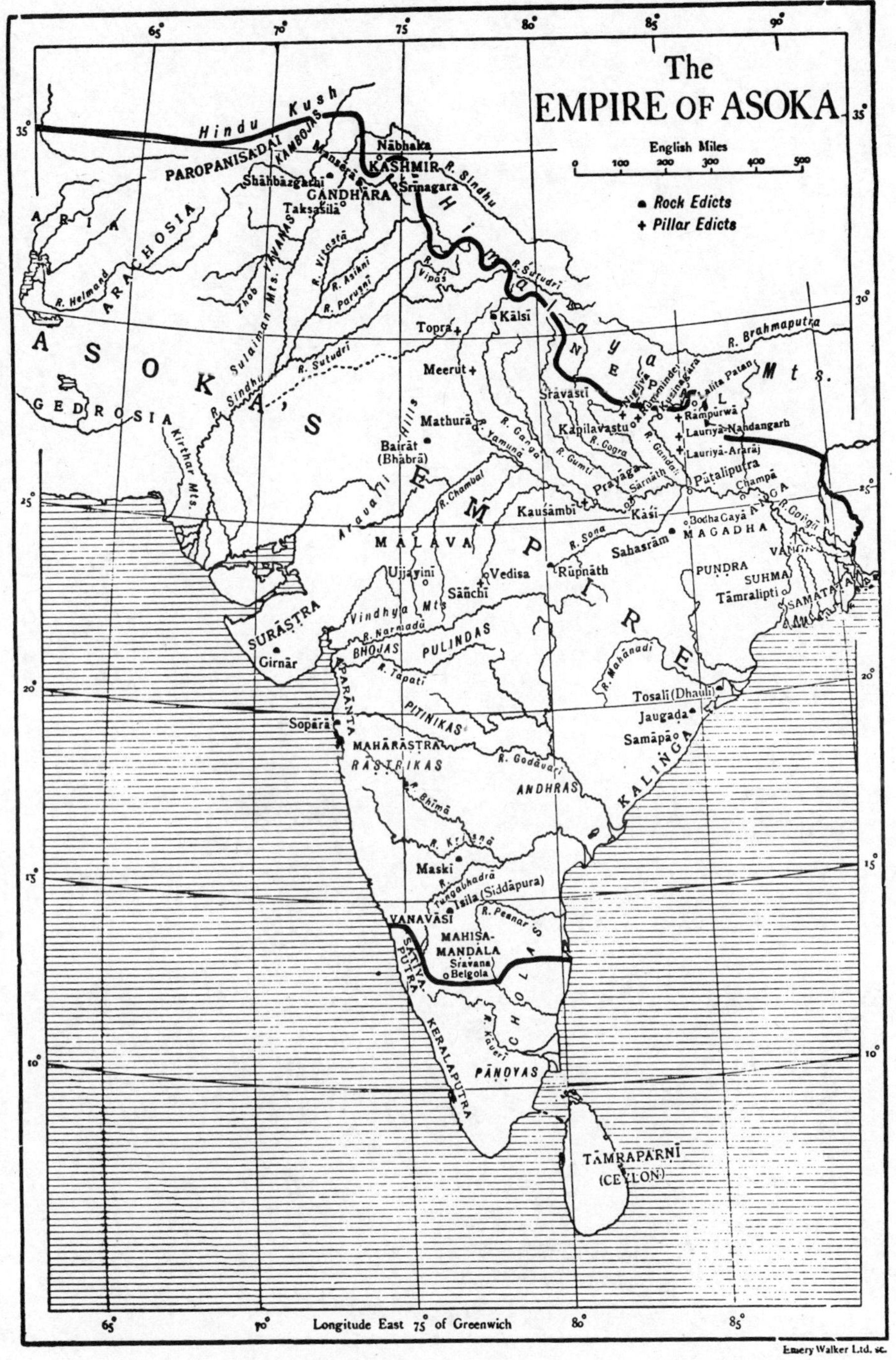
The
EMPIRE OF ASOKA
English Miles
0 100 200 300 400 500
Rock Edicts
Pillar Edicts
65° 70° 75° 80° 85° 90°
35° 30° 25° 20° 15° 10°
Hindu Kush
PAROPANISADAI
KAMBOJAS
Mansērā
Nābhaka
KASHMIR
Srinagara
R. Sindhu
Shāhbāzgarhi
GANDHĀRA
Taksasilā
ARIA
ARACHOSIA
YAVANAS
R. Vitastā
R. Asikni
R. Parusnī
R. Vipās
R. Sutudri
R. Helmand
Zhob
Sulaiman Mts.
HIMALAYA
Kālsī
Topra
Meerut
R. Brahmaputra
NEPAL
Mts.
Lalita Patan
Nigliva
Rummindei
Kusinagara
Srāvastī
Rāmpurwā
Lauriyā-Nandangarh
Lauriyā-Ararāj
Kapilavastu
R. Gogra
R. Gandak
R. Gumti
Prayāga
Sārnāth
Pātaliputra
Champā
ANGA
R. Ganga
R. Yamuna
Mathurā
Bairāt
(Bhābrā)
ASOKA'S EMPIRE
GEDROSIA
R. Sindhu
R. Sutudri
Kirthar Mts.
Aravalli Hills
R. Chambal
Kausāmbi
Kāsī
Bodha Gayā
MAGADHA
R. Sona
Sahasrām
MĀLAVA
Ujjayinī
Vedisa
Sānchī
Rūpnāth
PUNDRA
SUHMA
VANGA
Tāmralipti
SAMATATA
Vindhya Mts.
R. Narmadā
SURĀSTRA
Girnār
BHOJAS
PULINDAS
R. Tapatī
APARĀNTA
R. Mahānadī
Tosali (Dhauli)
Jaugada
Samāpā
Sopārā
PITINIKAS
MAHĀRĀSTRA
RĀSTRIKAS
R. Godāvarī
ANDHRAS
KALINGA
R. Bhīmā
R. Krsnā
Maski
R. Tungabhadrā
Isila (Siddāpura)
VANAVĀSI
R. Peanar
MAHISA-
MANDALA
Sravana
Belgola
SATIYA-
PUTRA
CHOLAS
KERALAPUTRA
R. Kāverī
PĀNDYAS
TĀMRAPARNĪ
(CEYLON)
Longitude East 75° of Greenwich
Emery Walker Ltd. sc.

CHAPTER VII

SOUTH INDIA AND CEYLON

The inscriptions of Aśoka at Brahmagiri and Siddhāpura in Mysore mark clearly the southern limit of the Mauryan empire which might have extended even a little further south to the latitude of the modern city of Madras. Kannaḍa inscriptions from Mysore and Bombay Karnāṭak of the tenth and eleventh centuries A. D. preserve faint memories of the rule of Nandas in those parts, but there is little tangible confirmation of this tradition, unless it be that the punch-marked *purāṇa* coins found all over Deccan, South India and Ceylon are to be accepted as witnesses of ancient contacts between the North and South of which the details are now lost beyond recovery. Then there is the Jaina legend, late, multiform, and oft-discussed, of the migration of Chandragupta to Śravaṇa Beḷgoḷa when Bhadrabāhu, the Jain patriarch, foretold a famine of twelve years' duration. Chandragupta is said to have lived several years as a Jain monk in Sravaṇa Beḷgoḷa until his death by the rite of Sallèkhana. The legend is improbable in itself and the identity of the Chandragupta it relates to is not above doubt. A late Pallava charter mentions an Aśōkavarmā among the earliest rulers of Kāñchī, and one may wonder if this is a reference to the Mauryan emperor.

The most direct clues to the condition of South India and Ceylon in the Mauryan epoch are furnished by the references to the Southern kingdoms in Megasthenes, in the edicts of Aśoka, and in the short Brāhmī inscriptions in natural caverns with rock-cut beds scattered all over South India and found in somewhat larger numbers in the Madura and Tinnevelly districts, and much more on the island of Ceylon. The oldest strata of extant Tamil literature cannot lay claim to equal antiquity, but they contain references to Nandas and Mauryas, and it will be necessary to review them in their contexts, particularly because they have been made the basis of far-reaching theories regarding a Mauryan invasion of South India by some writers, while others have seen in them a reference to the Mauryas of Koṅkān.

Lastly, the *Mahāvaṁsa* has conserved the story of Ceylonese affairs in much detail, and as the chronicle is obviously worked up from more ancient records, and some of its details find confirmation in the rock-cut Brāhmī inscriptions above mentioned, we come to know a little more of Ceylon in this period than of the mainland of South India.

The second and thirteenth Rock-Edicts of Aśoka mention the Southern kingdoms and Ceylon ; the list in the second edict is fuller and comprises the names of Cōḍa, Pāṇḍya, Satiyaputa, Keralaputa and Tāmbapaṇṇi. All these lands lay outside the empire of Aśoka, but he was on such friendly terms with them that he could arrange for the medical treatment of men and animals in all these lands, and for the importation and planting of useful medicinal herbs and roots wherever they were needed ; he also sent missionaries for the preaching of the Dhamma among the people of these countries—thus evincing his interest in the physical and mental well-being of his neighbouring states. Now the merest mention of such facts raises the presumption of a certain level of culture and progress in the arts of life. The Tamils and the Sinhalese had a settled polity and lived in well-ordered states, and some decades before the date of the Aśoka inscriptions, Megasthenes had heard somewhat of the trade of the Sinhalese and of the polity of the Pāṇḍyan kingdom[1]. He knows that Ceylon is an island more productive than India of gold and large pearls ; a good part of the island was forest inhabited by wild beasts, a large breed of elephants among them. His quaint account of the Pāṇḍyan kingdom seems to be an idealised mixture of fact and fable. He says that Heracles had a daughter Pandaea to whom he assigned the southernmost portion of India; the people in this country comprised 365 villages which brought by turns their tribute to the royal treasury every day of the year ; what is called tribute here seems to have been the supply of the provisions needed for a day for the royal household ; in the *Śilappadikāram*, a work of eight or nine centuries later than the time of Megasthenes, we hear of households of shepherds in the capital city of Madura supplying ghee by turns to the palace[2].

1. K. A. N. Sastri, *Foreign Notices*, p. 41.
2. xvii, l.7.

Much discussion has taken place on the name Satiyaputa. And good reason has been shown recently for equating Satiyaputa with Adigamān.[1] After the three well-known Tamil kingdoms, Pāṇḍya, Chōḷa and Chera (Kēraḷa), the Adigamān chieftains of Tagaḍūr (Dharmapuri in Salem District) may be said to occupy a considerable place in the literature of the Śaṅgam period, and it seems highly probable that they should find a place in the earlist enumeration of the political divisions of the Tamil country.

The impression of a fairly developed cultural *milieu* in the Tamil land derived from the references in Megasthenes and the Aśoka inscriptions is confirmed by other lines of evidence. Kauṭilya notes that the Pāṇḍya-kavāṭa, a pearl fishery on the coast of the mainland on the gulf of Mannar, was noted for the quality of the pearls it exported, and that Madhurā, the capital of the Pāṇḍyas, lent its name to some of the finest cotton fabrics of all India[2]. The Brāhmī inscriptions in rock caverns in hills have many features in common with the similar records of Ceylon, and these are among the earliest monuments of the Tamil country to which we may assign a date with some confidence. The script employed has much in common with the brief inscriptions from Bhaṭṭiprōlu, and some of them may well be assigned to the second century B.C. while others may be as late as the second or third century A.D. Though these inscriptions have not yet been fully elucidated, enough is known to say that they are mostly either brief donative records or simply the names of monks who once occupied the beds or caverns. The close resemblance between these monuments and inscriptions and others of the same age in Ceylon and the name Kaḷugumalai, Tamil for Gṛdhrakūṭa, of one of the places where such inscribed caves are found, have been held to establish an exclusively Buddhist origin for these monuments ; it is, however, premature to formulate any views conclusively on such questions. New caverns and inscriptions are still being discovered one by one—witness the inscribed natural cavern at Mālakoṇḍa in the Nellore district.[3] and another at Ariccalūr in Coimbatore district. And tradition is strong that Jainism came into South India about the same time as Buddhism if not earlier.

1. BSOAS. XII (1948), pp. 136-7 and 146-7. See ante p. 238 and n. 2.
2. KA. II. 11.
3. ARE. 1937-8 II. 1, *Silver Jubilee Volume Archaeological Society of South India*, 1952.

While it is thus not possible to decide if these monuments are Jain or Buddhist or both in their origin, the study of the inscriptions made so far[1] suggests that though the script employed in them was Brāhmī of the southern variety, the language was Tamil still in its formative stages. The script was alphabetic, and already included signs for peculiarly Dravidian sounds like *ṛ*, *ḻ*, *ḷ*, and *ṉ*; other peculiarities are that vocalic consonants were represented by two symbols first the sign for the consonant and then the complete vowel signs—thus *yu* was written as *y* (a) *u*. These developments and other peculiarities, not detailed here, must have come as the result of a pretty long process of trial and error extending over several generations.

The exact contents of the inscriptions still remain obscure, but a few facts emerge from tentative studies of them. A husbandman (*kuṭumbika*) of Ceylon (Īḷa) figures as a donor; and a woman, members of the Karaṇi caste, and merchants (*vaṇikan*) figure in other inscriptions in a like capacity. These brief inscriptions are thus seen already to bear testimony to the support commanded from all classes of the laity by the ascetics who were engaged in the pursuit of the life divine in the solitudes of mountains and forests.

We must now turn to a consideration of the references to the Nandas and Mauryas in early Tamil literature. They occur in five poems, three of which are by one writer, Māmūlanār whose statements are the clearest, and one each by two other poets. The relative chronology of the Śaṅgam poets is by no means settled, and the whole body of Śaṅgam literature can only be dated within broad limits in the first three centuries A. D. Thus the mention of Nandas and Mauryas in these poems is by no means a reference to contemporary facts, but to events preserved in the memory of people or in other ways of which we have no knowledge now. It may even be doubted if two poets whose references are not half as intelligible as those of Māmūlanār were really referring to the Mauryas of history or some aspects of an obscure mythology; that they both refer to the same fact or myt his clear beyond doubt; the expressions used are identical, though one of them Kaḷḷil Āttiraiyanār[2],

1. *Proc. Third Oriental Conference.* pp. 275 ff.
2. Puṟam 175.

gives more details than the other—Paraṅgorranār.[1] The fuller account refers to the Mōriyar, their victorious lance, their sky-scraping umbrella, and their chariots bearing banners ; it then states that their strong bright-rayed wheel cut across a mountain at the end of the earth and rolled past it and past the broad disc of the sun fixed near the pass so made. The commentator ekes out the sense by some additions of his own ; he says that the Mōriyar ruled the whole world, and that the mountain cut across by their discus was the silver-mountain which separated this earth from another world, and that the sun's disc was fixed near the pass by the gods. He also adds that the Mōriyar were the Chakravāla emperors or Vidyādharas and Nāgas, an interpretation which would suit the alternative reading 'Ōriyar' much better than the Mōriyar, the Mauryas of history. But stress need not be laid on the alternative reading, because, the cutting of the hill and the rolling of the wheel are features that, as we shall see, recur in the unmistakable references of Māmūlanār to the Mauryan emperors. It is clear at any rate, that if these two other poets were also thinking of the Mauryas, they had but vague notions about them and their achievements, and classed them with the superhuman beings whose deeds fill the annals of universal history for many aeons after the dawn of creation according to the Purāṇic lore of India.

Māmūlanār had a better knowledge of the Nandas and the Mauryas, and his statements are much more precise and credible though he too retains the quasi-legendary feature which is all that the two other poets recorded about the Mauryas. He mentions the Nandas and the enormous treasure accumulated by them in a telling context. 'What is it', asks a love-lorn lady, 'that has attracted my lover better than my charms?' ; and among the alternatives postulated occurs this[2] : 'Is it the treasure accumulated in the prosperous Pāṭaliputra and hidden in the waters of the Ganges by the Nandas of great renown, victorious in war?' Here is much that we know of the Nandas from other sources, and one fact that is new—the manner in which they kept the treasure hidden under the waters of the Ganges, which reminds one of a similar practice attributed to the Mahārājas

1. Aham 69.
2. Aham 265.

of Zabag by Arab travellers of the eighth century A. D. Māmūlanār's mention of the Mauryas is accompanied by equally clear and precise indications of historical events. There are two passages for consideration, both from the *Ahanānūṛu*. One[1] starts by saying that the lover would not stay behind even if he got the wealth of the Nanda for doing so—a second reference to this topic by this poet ; it then proceeds to say that Kōśar of the victorious banner started operations against their foes and gained victories against several ; but as Mōhūr did not submit to them, the Mōriyas who had a large army led an expedition ; and it adds that the Mōriyar's chariots rolled across a cutting made in the mountain for that purpose. Here is perhaps some indication that the Mauryan imperial power was so friendly to the Kōśar as to be ready to go to their help in their wars against their enemies; this active intervention in the politics of the Tamil country brings to our view a phase of Mauryan imperialism that has so far escaped notice. The last reference in Māmūlanār[2] adds some more particulars; it says that when the Mōriyar turned to the south, the war-like Vaḍugar preceded them as their van, and the mountain which was cut to make a way for the chariots on this occasion is described as the large snow-mountain reaching up to the skies—obviously the Himālayas. This last detail betrays that Māmūlanār too is by no means free from the legendary notion about Mauryas that was the entire stock-in-trade of the two other poets; only he manages to convey to us some facts besides the legend. Vaḍugar is a rather vague term in Tamil literature ; it means literally northerners, and was generally applied to the Kannaḍa-Ṭelugu peoples of Southern and Eastern Deccan together. These peoples were included in the Mauryan empire, and it is probable that in a move further south they were called upon to take the lead.

One last reference to the Nandas is simple and clear ; it occurs in *Kuṛundogai*[3] and refers to the abundance of gold in Pāṭaliputra besides mentioning elephants bathing in the Son river.

1. Aham 251.
2. *ib.* 281.
3. Poem no. 75.

These Tamil texts, separated from the age of the Mauryas by about five centuries, thus indicate to us that the Tamil states were within the sphere of Mauryan influence, if we may use a convenient modern expression for the relation, and that at least on one occasion the Mauryas went to the assistance of the Kōśar to enable them to subdue the rebellious chieftain of Mōhūr ; the Vaḍugar took a hand in this expedition.

And now one word on the legendary feature of the mountain being cut to make way for the wheel to roll across. This is obviously an echo of the mythology centring round the concept of the Chakravartin, the universal emperor, one of whose paraphernalia (*ratnas*) is the *chakra* (discus) ; this *chakra* leads the way in his *digvijaya* and has many mysterious properties, and Aśoka was counted as one of such emperors as the *Mahāvamsa* and other Buddhist books show. It is significant that in most of the references to the wheel cited above, it is not clear if the wheel of the war-chariots or the symbol of empire is meant, though once Māmūlanār definitely says it was the former. This feature in any event cannot be treated as history.

Ceylon, like South India, steps into the light of history with its notice by Megasthenes and by the Aśoka inscriptions—both under the name Tāmbapaṇṇi which becomes Taprabane with the Greek writer. The opening chapters of the *Mahāvamsa* contain much edifying legend about the Buddha's visits to the island, the arrival of Vijaya, and his encounter with Kuvaṇṇā (Kuveṇi in other accounts), and his marriage with a princess from the Pāṇḍya country. Modern research has shown that the primitive population of the island were the Vaeddas, who were hunters living in forests and natural rock-dwellings ; the first immigrants into the island were probably people from the Malabar coasts who called themselves Nāgas and gave the name Nāgadvīpa to the northern section of the island, the ancestors of the modern Nāyars of Malabar—Nāya being but the Prākṛit form of the word Nāga. The Vijaya legend, the Sinhalese language, and the Brāhmī script of the earliest inscriptions, are clear proofs of the advent of North Indian influences directly by sea, and the story of the marriage of Vijaya with a Pāṇḍyan princess represents perhaps the growth of contact between Ceylon and South India after they had both been Aryanized, each in its own way. Sinhalese memory goes back to a time prior to the advent of Vijaya when trading vessels coming in search of local products like ivory, wax, incense, pearls and gems, were sometimes wrecked on the shores of Ceylon. Much of this pre-history is necessarily speculative, and there can be no certainty about details. By the beginning of the Mauryan period in India, however, we may be certain that important settlements had been established in different parts of Ceylon and a fairly high degree of culture attained. The northern plain where was located Anurādhapura, the capital city, Rōhaṇa in the South-east, and Kalyāṇi in the South-west were perhaps the most notable divisions in this period, and they might have started as independent colonies established by separate groups of settlers from the different parts of the mainland, being the first fruits, as it were, of the overflow beyond the limits of India proper and across the sea of the great movement of Aryan expansion begun in Vedic times. Agriculture was practised and rice grown in considerable quantity to meet the necessities of a growing population ; artificial irrigation by means of dams thrown across rivers and canals taking off from them had come into vogue ; and the art of building with large-sized burnt bricks was known.

According to the *Mahāvamsa*, the period covered by this volume comprised in the history of Ceylon the reigns of Paṇḍukābhaya (B.C. 377-307), Muṭasiva (307-247), Devānampiya Tissa (247-207) and Uttiya (207-197). The chronology of the first two reigns is suspect, as there is good reason to believe that their duration has been unduly lengthened in order to make Vijaya and the Buddha contemporaries[1]. The account of Paṇḍukābhaya's reign in the *Mahāvamsa*[2] is much of it palpable legend ; but from it we may conclude generally that the king had to fight some of his collateral relations ruling in different parts of the island to impose his authority on those areas, that he made Anurādhapura the capital of the newly united kingdom, and that his reign witnessed decided advancement in the evolution of Sinhalese culture by the blending of the indigenous

1. Geiger MV. (Tr.) p. xxi.
2. *ib.* ch. x.

Vaeda (Yakkha) elements with the Indo-Aryan elements which had entered the island with Vijaya and his followers. The capital city was well laid out with tanks, parks, and separate quarters for the different elements in the population including yōnas, and among the recipients of the king's benefactions were Nirgranthas, Ājivakas and Brāhmaṇas, besides various other heretical sects. Of the reign of Muṭasiva the chronicle has nothing to say except that he laid out the beautiful garden called mahāmegha-vana and that he ruled the fair land of Laṅkā from the splendid city of Anurādhapura. He had ten sons 'each thoughtful of the others' welfare' and two daughters. The second son Devānaṁpiya Tissa was foremost among the brothers in virtue and intelligence, and succeeded his father. His friendly relations with the Mauryan emperor Aśoka, the exchanges of embassies and presents between them, the introduction of Buddhism into Ceylon by Mahinda and the fetching of a branch of the bōdhi-tree have been narrated in our account of Aśoka's reign. For the rest, there is good reason to believe that the development of culture by the reconciliation of the indigenous and exotic elements, by the growth of cities and the laying out of roads and extension of cultivation was going on apace. The Brāhmī inscriptions found by the score in practically all the caverns on every hill in the island and clearly belonging to the short period between the middle of the third century B. C. and the beginning of the first, attest the large numbers of Buddhist monks, votaries of the new sect introduced by Mahinda, and their peaceful occupation of these dwellings : but the primitive religious practices of the Vaeḍas seem to have been kept up side by side with other forms of worship. It is quite probable that some of the dagōbas and vihāras now in ruins, particularly those in Anurādhapura, may in their origin date back to the age of Tissa[1] and his successors, and that the style of these structures was borrowed from India along with Buddhism. The greeting of Mahinda by queen Anulā and five hundred (i.e. many) other women[2], and their subsequent ordination after the arrival of

1. MV. ch. xx.
2. *ib.* xv 18.

Saṅghamittā[1], as also some references to women in the cave inscriptions show that women enjoyed a considerable amount of freedom and influence in this early Sinhalese society. The earliest coins of Ceylon were like those of India, *purāṇas* or *śalākas*, pieces of silver or copper of varying shapes, generally circular or oblong with a corner or corners chipped in some specimens and bearing punch marks on one side. Silver and copper are not products of Ceylon, and the metals, if not the coins themselves, must have been imported from India. A fragment of an admirably engraved thin cornelian showingthe figure of a king sitting upon an ornamental chair 'which can be no other than a royal throne' was found in 1884 among the debris left round the Yaṭṭhāla dagoba at Tissa ; and this is considered by Parker a specimen of early North Indian work under strong Greek influence affording proof of the intercourse between Tissa and Aśoka recorded in the *Mahāvamsa* ; he even suggests that the seated figure on the cornelian may be Aśoka himself[2].

Tissa had no son and was succeeded by his brother Uttiya. During his reign Mahinda and Saṅghamittā attained nirvāṇa and their remains were disposed of with all honours, and stūpas erected in their memory.

1. *ib.* xix 65.
2. *Anc. Ceylon*, pp. 494-8.

CHAPTER VIII

INDUSTRY, TRADE, AND CURRENCY

Introductory

The outstanding achievement of Mahāpadma Nanda, the founder of the Nanda dynasty, was the completion of the political unity of Northern India, excluding the Indus basin, but including the Malwa tableland, the Kaliṅga seaboard and probably also a good part of the Deccan. Probably because of his low birth, he was led to make a clean sweep of the principal Kshatriya ruling families of his time and make himself, in the expressive language of the Purāṇas, 'the sole ruler of the earth.' The consequence of this absorption of the petty States of Northern India into a large empire could not but have been highly beneficial to the cause of material progress. Northern India, by virtue of its fertile soil and favourable climate, its magnificent waterways and its extensive coastline must have from the first enjoyed exceptional opportunities provided by nature for economic prosperity. Under the strong and centralised administration of the Nandas, trade and industry could not but advance greatly. In particular, the needs of their exceptionally wealthy court, to which later traditions bear witness[1] and their organised administration heralding that of the Mauryas must have given a great impetus to industrial and commercial effort. The direct interest of the Nandas in commercial development is perhaps indicated by their invention of a new standard measure referred to in the *Kāśikā* commentary[2] as well as their standardisation of the old silver coinage to be described later on.

Beyond the limits of the Nanda dominions lay the Indus basin conquered long before by the Achaemenids, but divided at this period into a group of small kingdoms and republics. Politically as disorganised as was Madhyadeśa at the time of the Buddha more than a century earlier, it stood now at a high level

1. Cf. *Mudrā-rākshasa* Act iii, v. 37 referring to the Nandas as *navanavati-śata-dravyakoṭiśvarāḥ*.

2. On Pāṇini ii. 4. 21.

of economic prosperity. The accounts of Alexander's officers inform us not only of numbers of rich and populous cities located in the land of the Five Rivers, but also of the wealth of the royal courts and republics. The devastating effects of Alexander's invasion could not but have affected disastrously the economic condition of the territories subdued by his arms and none of his measures for laying the foundation of an extensive commerce between India and the Hellenistic world took root immediately.

The liberation of North-western India by Chandragupta Maurya, preceded or followed in a short time by his deposition of the last king of the Nanda line, and the series of his subsequent victories laid the foundation of an empire extending from the Bay of Bengal to the Afghan highlands and from the Himalayas to the Narmadā and beyond. The military successes of Bindusāra and Aśoka helped not only to complete and consolidate the newly built empire, but extended its limits till it abutted on the Tamil Kingdoms of the far south. For three generations from the time of the founder the strong arm of the Mauryas ensured internal security and immunity from foreign aggression. Aśoka's vigorous propaganda further paved the way for the spread of Indian culture to distant Ceylon and the Hellenistic states almost to their furthest limits. It is not unreasonable to suppose that these favourable conditions were attended with a phenomenal development of industry as well as inland and foreign trade of the empire under Maurya rule.

Industry

The enormous advance of Indian industries which has just been postulated for the Nanda and Maurya times was rendered possible by the abundance of India's agricultural and mineral resources to which the Greek writers allude with evident admiration. 'India,' says Diodorus (ii. 35-7) quoting from Megasthenes, 'has many huge mountains which abound in fruit trees of every kind and many vast plains of great fertility—more or less beautiful, but all alike intersected by a multitude of rivers ....And while the soil bears on its surface all kinds of fruits, it has also underground numerous veins of all sorts of metals, for it contains much gold and silver and copper and iron in no small quantity and even tin and other metals.....India again possesses many rivers both large and navigable[1].' A no less important factor of economic progress noted likewise by the observant Greeks was the extraordinary skill of the Indian craftsman which has been his heritage down to our own times. Thus, to continue the quotation from Diodorus given above, 'The inhabitants are found to be well skilled in the arts.' Concrete instances of the skill of the Indian craftsmen are found in the *Geography* of Strabo (xv. 1.67) from information supplied by Nearchus[2].

One of the oldest Indian industries is that of textile manufacture. The technical terms for warp (*tantu*) and woof (*otu*) are found in the *Ṛigveda* and *Atharva-veda*, while the shuttle (*tasara*) and the loom (*veman*) are mentioned in the *Yajus-saṁhitā* and other texts[3]. Among the textile industries, that of cotton manufacture held the first place. It found an excellent market at home in the habits of the people whose immemorial dress consisting of a pair of cotton garments is referred to alike in the early Buddhist texts and in the writings of the Greek observers[4]. No wonder then that among the presents offered by the Mālavas and their allies to the victorious Alexander was included a large quantity of cotton cloth. While the cotton industry evidently was spread over the whole land, certain centres had early become famous for the excellence of their fabrics. The early Buddhist texts speak with high praise of Benares cloth (*Kāsikuttama* or *Kāsika-vattha*) as well as the cloth of the Śivi country (*Siveyyaka* or *Sīveyyaka*)[5]. We have a fuller list in Kauṭilya's *Arthaśāstra* (ii. 11) where Madhurā (capital of the Pāṇḍya country), Aparānta (Konkan on the western coast), Kāśi, Vaṅga, Vatsa (Kauśāmbī region), and Mahiṣa are said to produce the best

1. According to the above account, gold, silver, copper and iron to a large extent along with tin and other metals to a much less degree were mined from India itself. Among the five sources of gold and five of silver specified in the *Arthaśāstra* (ii. 13), however, Gauḍa alone can be definitely identified as belonging to India.

2. Thus we are told that Indian craftsmen, seeing sponges used for the first time by the Macedonians, immediately manufactured imitations of them with fine thread and wool. They also quickly learnt to make Greek articles such as the scrapers and oil flasks used by the athletes.

3. See *Vedic Index, s.v.*

4. See *P. T. S. Dictionary*, s. v. *kappāsa*, and Arrian's *Indica*, ch. xvi.

5. Cf. *Aṅguttara Nikāya* i. 248 : *Vinaya Piṭaka* i. 278, 280 : *Jātakas* iv. 401 : vi. 51 etc.

cotton fabrics (*kārpāsika*). In the same context, the *Arthaśāstra* specifically mentions three varieties of *dukūla* (an unidentified species of fibrous fabric) distinguished by their place of origin and their colour. These were the products of Vaṅga (East Bengal), Puṇḍra (North Bengal) and Suvarṇakuḍya (in Kāmarūpa). They were respectively white, dark and coloured like the rising sun. In the same connection, the *Arthaśāstra* mentions linen fabrics (*kshauma*) of Kāśi as well as Puṇḍra. Kauṭilya also refers to the fabrics produced in Magadha, Puṇḍra and Suvarṇakuḍya. Linen fabrics (*khoma*) are also referred to in the early Buddhist literature[1].

It will be noticed from the above that Bengal, Kāmarūpa and Benares were the regions noted thus early as centres of the textile industry. The technical perfection of the industry is well illustrated by the fact that the *Arthaśāstra* distinguishes varieties of *dukūla* and *kshauma* according to their colour and process of manufacture, while those of *patrorṇā* are distinguished according to their material and colour.

Coming to costlier textiles, we find references to silk cloth (*koseya* and *koseyya-pāvāra*) in the Pāli canonical works and the *Jātakas*[2]. Kauṭilya (ii. 11) also mentions *kauśeya* along with *chīna-paṭṭa chīna-bhūmija* (Chinese fabric of Chinese manufacture). This last passage points to the fact that silks of Chinese origin competed at this time with the home-made product.

On the other hand, the manufacture of wool was an old and indigenous industry. The fame of the fine wool of Gandhāri goes back to the *Ṛigveda* which also knows a woollen garment called *śāmulya*[3]. The woollen fabrics of Gandhāra along with those of Koṭumbara or Koḍumbara—a region connected by Jean Przyluski[4] with the Audumbaras of the Punjab—are mentioned with high praise in the *Jātakas*[5]. Kauṭilya, while silent about Gandhāra, mentions by name (ii. 11) the woollen goods of Nepal called *bhiṅgisī* or *apasāraka*. These are said to be formed of eight pieces, dark in colour and rain-proof. What advance

1. See *P. T. S. Dict.*, s. v. *khoma*.
2. *Ibid.*, s.v.
3. See *Vedic Index*, s.v., for references.
4. *Un ancien people de Penjab* ; *Les Udumbara* in *J. As.*, 1926, pp. 25-36.
5. See *Jat.* vi. 500.

the manufacture of this material had attained during the period of the *Arthaśāstra* is proved by the fact that Kauṭilya specifies three varieties of fabrics of sheep's wool distinguished by colour, four varieties distinguished by their manufacturing process, and no less than ten varieties distinguished by their use for human beings and for animals. The qualities of the best wool are carefully noted by the author in the same connection. The *Arthaśāstra* also distinguishes in the same context six kinds of fabrics manufactured from the hair of wild animals, and differing in their uses and qualities.

Before closing the subject of textile manufacture, we may mention a few of its finer forms known at that period. The use of embroidered cloth (*pesas*) is as old as the *Ṛigveda*, its manufacture according to a *Yajus Saṁhitā* text being normally carried on by women[1]. The *Jātakas* refer to golden turbans used by kings and golden trappings for the use of State elephants[2]. In the times of the Nandas and the Mauryas, gold-embroidered garments were worn by Indians evidently of the richer class. This is borne out by the testimony of Strabo, who says (xv. 1.54). 'They (the Indians) wear apparel embroidered with gold and use ornaments set with precious stones and gay-coloured linen garments[3].' These gorgeous dresses were specially displayed during festive occasions. Describing the festive processions of the Indians, Strabo (xv.1. 69) mentions not only the train of elephants adorned with gold and silver, but also the attendants wearing 'garments embroidered and inter-woven with gold.' Curtius, again, in the course of his description of the Indian king's public appearance, says that the king is 'robed in fine muslin embroidered with purple and gold.'

Wood-work is a very old Indian industry. Reference to the carpenter (*takshan* or *tashṭṛi*) and his tools may be traced back to the *Ṛigveda*[4]. The art of the carpenter had attained a high skill by the time of the Pāli canonical and other texts. There

1. See *Vedic Index*, s.v. *peśas*.

2. *Jāt.* iv 404 : v. 322.

3. Somewhat different is McCrindle's translation which is as follows ; (*Ancient India as described by Megasthenes and Arrian*, Calcutta ed., p. 69) :— 'Their robes are worked in gold and ornamented with precious stones and they wear also flowered garments made of the finest muslin.'

4. See *Vedic Index*, s.v.

we find the *vaḍḍhaki* engaged in all kinds of wood-work including ship-building, the making of carts and chariots, the manufacture of machines and house-building[1]. To the absolute perfection of the craft in Maurya times we have a surviving testimony in the shape of the mysterious wooden platforms that have been recently dug up in the vicinity of Patna[2]. The excellent sculpture of Aśoka's time is admittedly modelled upon the much older art of the indigenous craftsmen in wood and ivory.

Reference has just been made to the Indian ivory-worker. The Indians have excelled in ivory-work from early times down to the present. Specially, in the *Jātakas* we are introduced to various ornamental and useful articles prepared from this costly material[3]. The use of ivory ear-rings is noted by Arrian (*Indica* xvi) as a characteristic of very wealthy Indians.

Another industry in which Indians have distinguished themselves in ancient and mediaeval as in modern times is stone-cutting. In the *Jātakas* the stone-cutter (*pāsāṇa-koṭṭaka*) is found engaged in building houses with the materials of a ruined village, in hollowing a cavity in a block of the purest crystal and so forth[4]. The wonderful stone pillars of Aśoka's reign are standing examples of the unsurpassed skill of the stone-cutters of the age. 'The art of polishing hard stone,' as Vincent Smith observes[5], 'was carried to such perfection that it is said to have become a lost art beyond modern powers.' The 'Mauryan polish' is seen at its best in the walls of the Barabar caves of the hardest gneiss rock, which are burnished like glass mirrors.

The use of deer and goat skins for clothing is as old as the *Ṛigveda*[6]. The leather-worker and his handiwork of various kinds are referred to in the early Buddhist literature[7]. Kauṭilya's

1. See *P. T. S. Dict.*, s.v. *vaḍḍhaki*. : also cf. *Jāt.* ii. 18 (for house-building) : v. 159 : vi. 427 (for ship-building) : iv. 207 (for carts and chariots) : v. 242 (for machines).

2. *Ann. Rep. Arch. Surv. Ind.*, 1912-13, pp. 53 ff.

3. See *P. T. S Dict.*, s.v. *danta* cf. *Jāt.* v. 302 (for ivory handle of a glass mirror) : vi. 223 (for an ivory chariot).

4. *Jāt*, I, 470.

5. *Oxford History of India*, Part I, 2nd ed., p. 113.

6. See *Vedic Index*, s.v. *ajina*.

7. See *P. T S Dict.*, s.v. *upāhānā* and *chamma* : cf. also *Jāt.* ii. 153 (for traps of leather) : iii. 79 (for single soled shoes) : iii. 116 and vi. 431 (for leather sacks) : vi. 454 (for leather shield). etc.

Arthaśāstra (ii. 11) shows knowledge of a wide variety of skins (*charma*) distinguished by their place of origin as well as colour and size. It is interesting to observe that the principal varieties are said to be products of various Himalayan regions. In the description of the Indian dress by Arrian (*Indica* xvi), to which we have referred above, we have an incidental allusion to the skill of the Indian leather-worker. 'The Indians,' we are told, 'wear shoes made of white leather and these are elaborately trimmed, while the soles are variegated.'

India has always been famous for its trees producing fragrant wood. Several varieties such as *chandana*, *agalu* and *ṭagara* are mentioned in the Pāli canonical texts and the *Jātakas*[1]. Kauṭilya (ii. 11) mentions five kinds of fragrant wood, *viz.*, *chandana aguru*, *taila-parṇika*, *bhadraśri*, and *kāleyaka*. These are further distinguished according to their place of origin, colour, fragrance and so forth. To judge from the commentator's identification, many of these varieties came from Kāmarūpa, while other kinds came from Ceylon, the Himalayan region and the like.

The use of metals may be traced back to the Indus people of pre-historic times. The Vedic Indians were acquainted with a large variety of metals, *viz.* gold (*chandra*, *jātarūpa*, *hiraṇya*, *suvarṇa*, *harita*), silver (*rajata*), iron (*krishṇāyasa*, *śyāma*), copper (*lohitāyasa*, *loha*), lead (*sīsa*) and tin (*trapu*). Mention is also made of gold and silver ornaments as well as ordinary metalware[2]. The *Jātakas* refer not only to numerous metals including brass and bronze, but also to the manufacture of ornaments from precious metals and that of domestic and agricultural implements from baser ones[3]. Kauṭilya (ii. 12) specifics the characteristics of various metallic ores including gold, silver, copper, lead, tin, iron and *vaikṛintaka* (unidentified). What is more, he refers to technical sciences dealing with veins of ore and metals, to the art of smelting metals and so forth[4]. In this connection, reference is made to the manufacture of copper, lead, tin, bronze,

1. See *P. T. S. Dict.*, s.v.

2. See *Vedic Index*. s.v., and *ibid*, English index, s.v. *metals and ornaments* for references.

3. See *Jāt.* i. 351 : iv. 60, 85, 296 etc.

4. *Sulba-dhātuśāstra-rasa-pāka-maṇirāga* in the original, rendered as above by Meyer. The translation of Shamasastry is inaccurate.

brass, iron and other wares. In the following chapters (ii. 13 and 14), Kauṭilya deals with the characteristic qualities of several varieties of gold and silver together with the methods of their testing and purification, as well as the technical processes of their manufacture. These striking references may be taken effectually to dispose of the strange verdict of a Greek writer who, while describing the richness of the country in gold and silver mines, observes : 'Nevertheless the Indians, inexperienced in the art of mining and smelting, do not even know their own resources, but set about their business in too primitive a way[1].'

As regards the period of the Nandas and the Mauryas, we have positive evidence testifying to the skill of the Indian metal worker. From this standpoint the bare observation of Diodorus (ii. 36) based no doubt on Megasthenes, *viz.* that the Indians employed their rich store of metals in manufacturing articles of use and ornaments is not of much moment. More significant is the fact that among the presents offered to Alexander by the Mālavas and their allies were included a hundred talents of 'white iron' (*ferrum candidum*). This has been generally taken to mean steel, although Cunningham[2] identified it with nickel. Of the copper work of the Maurya times, an excellent specimen has survived in the shape of a solid copper bolt which was found in the Aśokan pillar at Rampurva and was evidently used for fixing the colossal lion-capital to the pillar itself[3]. The Greek contemporary accounts also testify to the precious metal-work used in the royal court. In Strabo's description (xv. 1.69) of the Indian festive processions to which we have referred above, we read how the great host of royal attendants carried 'vessels of gold such as large basins and goblets six feet in breadth,' as well as 'drinking cups and lavers all made of Indian copper and set many of them with precious stones,—emeralds, beryls, and Indian garnets.' Similarly Curtius, in describing the king's public appearance, states how the royal attendants 'carry in their hands silver censers', while

1. Strabo xv. 1.31.

2. *Num. Chron.*, xiii (1873), pp. 188 ff.

3. For a description of the copper-bolt with an accompanying photograph, see Panchanan Neogi, *Copper in Ancient India*. pp. 18-20.

the king himself 'lolls in a golden palanquin furnished with pearls which dangle all around it.'

The use of jewellery may be traced back to the Indus peoples of prehistoric times. The profession of a jeweller (*maṇikara*) is referred to in the *Vājasaneyi-Samhitā* and the *Taittirīya Brāhmaṇa*[1]. Coming to post-Vedic times, we find the *Jātakas* referring to pearls, crystals and jewels as well as the art of cutting and polishing gems for ornaments[2]. Kauṭilya (ii. 11) shows acquaintance with pearls (*muktika*), jewels (*maṇi*), diamonds (*vajra*) and corals (*pravāla*) of Indian as well as foreign origin. What is more, he carefully notes the characteristics of good and bad pearls as well as the different colours and qualities of rubies, beryls, sapphires, crystals, diamonds and corals. The skill of the manufacturing jeweller is indicated by the fact that Kauṭilya mentions no less that five varieties of pearl necklaces (*yashṭi*) which are sub-divided into other classes. In a postscript, he adds that the same varieties apply to the ornaments for the head, arms, feet and waist. Coming definitely to the Nanda-Maurya times we find that the Indian love of ornaments is pointedly referred to by a Greek writer[3].

We have not space enough to describe the other industries to which the *Jātakas* and other records of this period bear witness, such as the manufacture of dyes, gums, drugs and perfumes, as well as that of pottery. But a word may be said about the manufacture of implements and weapons of war. Offensive and defensive weapons like the bow and the arrow, the sword and the spear, the helmet and the coat of mail are known from Vedic times[4]. Later in the *Arthaśāstra* (ii. 18), we find mention of bows and arrows made of different materials along with different kinds of swords, axes, spears and the like. The *Arthaśāstra* also refers to two classes of war machines, viz. immovable (*sthitayantrāṇi*) and movable (*chala-yantrāṇi*), the first consisting of ten and the second of seventeen named varieties. The Greek accounts relating specifically to the Nanda-Maurya

1. See *Vedic Index*. s.v.
2. Cf. *Jāt.* i. 351, 479 : ii. 6 : iv. 60, 85, 296 : vi. 117-20, 279.
3. See Strabo xv, 1.
4. See *Vedic Index*, English index, s.v. *war* for references.

times bear out these observations. According to Arrian (*Indica* xvi), the Indian foot-soldiers were armed with bows and javelins as well as broad-bladed swords, while the horsemen carried two lances. In the list of presents offered by the Mālavas and their allies to Alexander were included 1050 (or, according to another account, 500) four-horsed chariots and 1000 bucklers.

Trade

By the time of the early Buddhist literature the Indians had developed an extensive system of inland trade which was borne along well-known trade-routes. These routes were marked by convenient stages and served to link up the most distant parts of the country with one another. Among them we may mention specifically the following :—

1. East to west. This most important route ran principally along the great rivers. From Champā boats plied up to Benares, the great industrial and trading centre of those times. From Benares they led up the Ganges as far as Sahajāti and up the Jumna as far as Kauśāmbī. Further west the route led by land-tracts to Sindhu, famous for its breed of horses and Sauvīra ('Sophir' or 'Ophir' of the Old Testament ?).
2. North to south-west. This route extended from Śrāvastī, the famous capital of Kosala, to Pratishṭhāna on the Godāvarī and the stations lying on it in the reverse direction included Ujjayinī, Vidiśā and Kauśāmbī.
3. North to south-east. Along this route which ran from Śrāvastī to Rājagṛiha lay a number of stations including Kapilavastu, Vaiśālī, Pāṭaliputra and Nālandā.
4. North-west route, also referred to by Pāṇini[1]. It stretched along the land of the Five Rivers to the great highways of Central and Western Asia.

We also hear of merchants travelling from Kashmir and Gandhāra to Videha, from Benares to Ujjayinī, from Magadha to Sauvīra and so forth[2]. What vast wealth accrued from this system of inland trade is illustrated by references to merchant

1. V. 1.17 :—*Uttarapathenāhṛtaṁ ca.*
2. Cf. *Jāt.* ii. 248 : iii. 365 : *Vimānavatthu* commentary 370 etc.

princes like Anāthapiṇḍika of Śrāvastī whose trading connections extended to Rājagṛiha on the one side and Kāśī on the other. Nevertheless, the path of the trader was anything but easy. Not only were the roads (specially through the forests) infested by robbers against whom the merchants protected themselves by hiring the services of forest-guards, but the deserts had to be crossed at night with the help of land-pilots (*thala-niyāmaka*) guiding the caravan by the stars. Associated with the wilderness was a host of real and imaginary dangers viz., drought, famine, wild beasts, robbers and demons. Some of the roads were already distinguished as 'royal' or 'great' roads (*rājapatha* or *mahāmagga*) unlike the ordinary bye-paths (*upapatha*). But the rivers were not bridged and had to be crossed by ferries. The overland as well as oversea trade likewise attracted the attention of Indian merchants. The Pāli canonical texts speak of voyages lasting six months in ships (*nāvā*) which could be drawn up on shore in the winter[1]. The *Jātakas*, above all, have preserved memories of voyages of daring Indian merchants beyond the seas and lands to distant countries of the east and west. References are made in these works to merchants voyaging from Champā or even Benares to the mysterious land of Suvarṇabhūmi which has been proved to be a generic title in those days for Burma, the Malay Peninsula and the Malay Archipelago. We hear even of merchants voyaging from the great western seaport Bharukachchha to the same destination, obviously *via* a Ceylonese port. Indeed, Ceylon (Tambapaṇṇi) at that time was 'another bourne of oversea commerce'. We also learn how another body of merchants travelled from Benares to Bāveru (Babylon)[2]. An interesting sidelight is thrown upon the methods of Indian navigation by the reference to the direction-giving crows (*disā-kāka*) showing the navigators as they flew towards the land, in what direction lay the coast[3]. This practice, as has been remarked[4], was also known to the sea-faring Babylonians and Phoenicians of early times.

The references in Kauṭilya's *Arthaśāstra*, scattered and incidental as they are, register some advance in the conditions of

1. Cf. *Saṁ. N. III* p. 155 : *Ibid.* v p. 51 : *Aṅg. N.* iv. p. 127.
2. Cf. *Jāt.* iv. 15-7 : vi. 34 : iii. 126 ff.
3. Cf. *Jāt.* iii. 126-7, 267 etc.
4. See Fick. *op. cit.*, Eng. tr. p. 269.

trade above described. Active encouragement of trade on the part of the State is proved by the care with which Kauṭilya provides for the construction and security of trade-routes and the foundations of market-towns in his scheme of State colonisation of the country-part. Elsewhere (ii. 4), the largest scale of width—eight *daṇḍas* as compared with the usual four *daṇḍas*—is prescribed for roads leading to the market-towns (*saṁyānīya patha*). Intelligent appreciation of the importance of trade-routes is shown by the discussion in *Arthaśāstra* circles (vii. 12) of the relative advantages of different types of trade-routes from the standpoint of their conduciveness to commerce. Such are the pairs: land and water-routes, water-routes along the coast and through mid-water, the Himalayan and the southern land-routes. In comparing the last pair, the *Arthaśāstra* authors give us a valuable, though far from exhaustive, list of the imports borne along both routes evidently to the Ganges valley. According to an un-named teacher quoted by Kauṭilya, the costlier merchandise consisting of elephants, horses, fragrant products, tusks, skins, gold and silver were more plentiful in the Himalayas. In Kauṭilya's opinion, on the other hand, the merchandise other than blankets, skins and horses, and consisting of conch-shells, diamonds, jewels, pearls and gold, was more plentiful in the South. For the rest, the remarkable lists of agricultural, manufacturing and other products of different lands which Kauṭilya mentions (ii. 11-12) testify to the extent as well as the objects of India's internal and foreign trade. Among these products are found textiles of Bengal, Assam, Benares, the Konkan and Pāṇḍya, the silks of China, the woollens of Nepal, the skins of the Himalayan regions, the fragrant wood of Assam, Ceylon (?) and the Himalayas, the gems of Ceylon (?), Alakanda and Vivarna (unidentified) and the like[1].

All indications point to the fact that the rise of the Nandas and the Mauryas helped greatly to improve India's inland and foreign trade. The liberation of the Indus valley, and still more the repulse of Seleucus, gave Chandragupta Maurya complete

1. It is interesting to recall Pāṇini's *sūtra* vi. 2.13 referring to the practice of merchants being named from the countries which they visited. The late *Kāśikā* commentary gives the following illustrations of the above :—

Madra-vāṇija, Kaśmīra-vāṇija and *Gandhāra-vāṇija.*

control over the coveted north-western route to which we have referred above. With the conquest of the Deccan by Chandragupta Maurya or Bindusāra, the possession of the equally, or still more, valuable western and southern routes was ensured to the Mauryas. The conquest of Kaliṅga by Aśoka destroyed the only possible rival for the mastery of the eastern trade. While the Mauryas thus brought all the great inland trade-routes under the control of a highly centralised and efficient administration, their rule was helpful for the growth of trade in other ways. That the Mauryas had a special department for the construction of roads is proved by Megasthenes' reference (quoted, Strabo xv.1.50) to the duties of officers called *Agoranomoi* ('market commissioners'). They had, among other duties, to 'construct roads and at every ten *stadia* set up a pillar to show the bye-roads and distances.' The most renowned of the imperial roads of these times was 'the Royal Road' connecting the North-West Frontier with Pāṭaliputra and leading thence to the mouths of the Ganges. The stages of this first Indian Grand Trunk Road together with their distances have been recorded by the Roman writer Pliny in his encyclopaedic work called *Natural History* (vi. 21). His somewhat confused account may be summed up in the following table[1] :—

	Roman miles
From Peucelaotis (Pushkarāvatī) to the Indus	60
Thence to the Hydaspes (Jhelum) ..	60
Thence to the Hyphasis (Beas)	270
From the Hyphasis to the Hesidrus (Sutlej)	168
From the Hesidrus to the Jomanes (Jumna)	168 (*sic*)
From the Jomanes to the Ganges ..	112
From the Ganges to Rhodopha (unidentified)	119
From Rhodopha to Kalinipaxa (unidentified)	167 (or 265)
From Kalinipaxa to the confluence of the Jomanes and the Ganges	625 (*sic*)

1. For a useful summary of the discussion relating to Pliny's account see McCrindle, *Ancient India as described by Megasthenes and Arrian*, Calcutta ed., pp. 130-34. Arrian (*Indica*, ch. iii) quotes Eratosthenes to say that the Royal Road was measured by *schoeni*. According to Pliny, (Arrian's *Indica*, E. J. Chinnock's tr. p. 401*n*) the *schoenus* was reckoned by Erastothenes at 40 *stadia* (about five miles). Strabo (*Geography* xv. 1.11) mentions measurement of the Royal Road 'with necessary lines', which by a slight emendation of the text may be taken to mean 'in terms of the *schoenus*' (Loeb's Classical Library ed., Vol. viii. p. 17*n*).

From the confluence to Palibothra .. 425 (*sic*)
From Palibothra to the mouths of the Ganges 638

We have reasons to believe that the ancient foreign trade of India, like its inland trade, benefited by the strong and efficient administration of the Mauryas. The wise policy of friendship with the Hellenistic powers started by Chandragupta Maurya after the repulse of Seleucus and maintained by his son and grandson, must have favoured the expansion of the Indian trade with West Asia and Egypt. It is interesting to learn from Greek classical sources that the main commerce between the early Seleucid Empire and India was borne partly by the land-route (the northern one passing through Bactria and the southern through Gedrosia and Carmania, Persis and Susiana) and partly by the sea-route (through Gerrha on the west coast of the Persian Gulf). Like the Indian route to Egypt stretching along the east shore of the Red Sea, the route through the Persian Gulf was controlled by powerful Arab tribes engaged in a highly developed trade[1]. How valuable was this western trade to India will appear from the list of her exports into Egypt, which, according to Greek classical sources, consisted of ivory, tortoise-shell, pearls, pigments and dyes (specially indigo), nard, costum, malabathron and rare woods[2]. It is probably in the light of this extensive commerce with western lands that we have to understand Aśoka's ambitious attempt to extend the benefits of his religious and humanitarian propaganda to the Hellenistic kingdoms almost to their furthest limits. To the mutual knowledge and understanding derived from long-continued commercial intercourse, again, we may probably attribute the success which

1. For references see Rostovtzeff, *The Social and Economic Histoty of the Hellenistic World*, p. 457.

2. Rostovtzeff, *op. cit.*, pp. 386-7. We have an interesting reminiscence of Indians sharing in this western trade in a story narrated by Posidonius and quoted by Strabo in his *Geography* (ii. 3.4). According to this story while Euergetes II (145-116 B.C.) was reigning in Egypt, an Indian being stranded on the shore of the Arabian Sea was brought to Alexandria and having learnt Greek gave the Court information of the sea-route to India. Then the king sent out an expedition under Eudoxus of Cyzicus. The expedition set out probably in the last years of Euergetes II and returned heavily laden with goods. Equal success attended a second expedition sent out under the same captain in the following reign. It has been recently suggested on good grounds that the discovery of the monsoon attributed to Hippalus in the literary records was made by Eudoxus himself who probably derived his information from the stranded Indian merchant and undertook his first expedition with his help. On the whole subject, see Rostovtzeff, *op. cit.* pp. 926, 927, 929.

attended Aśoka's mission to Ceylon and, if this can be taken to be authentic, the mission of Soṇa and Uttara to Suvaṇṇabhūmī (Further India).

The Organisation of Industry and Trade

The organisation of crafts and trades in some forms of association was known from early times. In so far as the crafts are concerned, we find in the *Jātakas* that sons ordinarily, if not invariably, followed the occupations of their father, while the industries used to be localised in towns and villages, and the separate crafts had frequently a *pamukha* (president) or *jeṭṭha* (alderman) presiding over them. These three features, as Fick observed long ago[1], point to an organisation similar to that of the craft-guilds in mediaeval Europe. The *Jātakas* in fact refer to eighteen *seṇis* (guilds), mentioning four by name, viz., those of woodcutters, smiths, leather dressers and painters[2]. As regards the organisation of trade, the *Jātakas* refer to *satthavāhas* whose directions were obeyed by the caravans along the trade-routes as well as to *pamukhas* and *jeṭṭhas* of the separate trades. We also hear of disputes between guilds being decided by a *mahāseṭṭhi* who acted practically as 'chief alderman over the aldermen of the guilds[3].' The early *Dharmaśāstras* and the *Arthaśāstra* register a somewhat advanced stage of development. From an oft-quoted passage (xi 1) of Gautama's *Dharmasūtra* supposed to be the oldest of the existing *Dharmasūtras*, we learn that traders and artisans along with others had the authority to lay down rules for their respective classes. Of the *Saṅghas* ('corporations') described by Kauṭilya (xi. 1), who were ruled by *mukhyas* ('executive officers'), one class consisted of certain specified and unspecified groups living by *vārtā* (agriculture, cattle-breeding and trade) as well as by *śastra* (fighting). Elsewhere (ii. 7, iii. 1 , viii. 4 etc.) Kauṭilya refers to *śreṇis* (guilds) organised under *mukhyas*, which were thought to be sufficiently important for their customs to be recorded in official registers and were otherwise a factor to be reckoned with in the working of the State administration.

1. *The Social Organisation in North-east India in Buddha's time* (Eng. tr. of *Die Social Gliederung in Nordostlichen Indian zu Buddhas zeit*), pp. 177-183.
2. Cf. *Jāt.* i. 267, 314 : iii. 281 : iv. 411 : vi 22.
3. Cf. Rhys Davids, *Buddhist India*, p. 97.

The industrial and commercial *śreṇis* and *saṅghas* we have described above represent the type of guild organisation under which there could be little scope for a separate class of wage-earners as distinguished from producers. But already in these times we hear of another type of organisation involving the employment of hiredl abourers by the capitalists. The *Jātakas* make frequent references to free labourers working for hire (*kammakara* and *bhatakas*) often along with slaves (*dāsas*) ands ervants (*pessas*)[1]. Kauṭilya (iii. 13-14) not only refers to free labourers (*karmakaras* and *bhṛitakas*) along with slaves (*dāsas*), but gives a whole body of laws for regulating their work and wages. That the free labourers along with slaves formed an important element of the population in Maurya times is proved by Aśoka including the kind treatment of *dāsas* and *bhatakas* among the constituent qualities of his *dhamma* (R. E. ix, xi etc.)

State Industrial and Commercial Policy

No account of the economic conditions of the Nanda-Maurya times will be complete without some reference to the policy pursued by the State in relation to industry and trade. We may begin by noticing some features of the traditional policy in these respects as reflected in the *Arthaśāstra*. That the active encouragement of industry and commerce was contemplated as a duty of the State is illustrated by the measures included in Kauṭilya's scheme of State colonisation of rural areas (ii. 1) : they include the working of mines and forests, the construction and security of trade-routes and the foundation of market-towns. In this connection the king is enjoined to secure trade-routes from obstruction by his favourities (*vallabhas*), officers (*kārmikas*) and frontier guards (*anta-pālas*) as well as by thieves and animal herds—a list sufficiently instructive as putting the danger from the King's officers on a level with that caused by thieves and animals. How fully the industrial and commercial classes were associated with the royal court and capital is proved by the immediately following rules (ii. 4) relating to the planned settlement of the fortified capital (*durga*). According to this description which, by the way, illustrates the relative social status of

1. See *P. T. S. Dict.*, s.v. Also cf. Fick, *op. cit.* pp. 303-4.

different groups of artisans and traders in the times concerned, the dealers in scents, garlands, paddy etc. and the chief artisans should live along with Kshatriyas to the east of the royal palace. The dealers in cooked food, liquors and flesh should live along with Vaiśyas to the south. The manufacturers of woollen and cotton goods, the armour-makers etc. should live along with Śūdras on the west. The manufacturers of base metals and precious stones should live along with Brāhmaṇas on the north.

Not only did the State associate itself closely with the trading and industrial classes, but it also undertook manufactures and trading on its own account[1]. What is more, the rules of the *Arthaśāstra* repeatedly show how thoroughly the agricultural, mineral and other resources of the State were understood to be the sources of its strength. Thus among the qualities of a good country are included (vi. 1) the possession of agricultural tracts, mines, forests of various kinds, land and waterways and the like. Very characteristic again, is the general rule of foreign policy (vii. 1) stating that the king should follow that one of the six-fold forms by which he can exploit his own mines and forests and obstruct those of his enemy. No wonder, then, that the nice balancing of the advantages of working tracts rich in mines and in food grains, of working mines yielding a precious but small output and those producing inferior but large output, of working trade-routes by land and water and so forth, formed the subject of keen discussion in *Arthaśāstra* circles dealing with questions of foreign policy (vii. 11-12).

Another aspect of State industrial policy in these times is that relating to the strict control of artisans and traders. We have in the *Arthaśāstra* a whole Section (Section iv) significantly called '*Removal of Thorns*' (*kaṇṭaka śodhanam*), which describes successively the measures to be taken by the king for securing the people against artisans and merchants, against natural calamities, against persons living by clandestine means and so forth. In thorough accord with this attitude is the fact that elsewhere

1. For examples see *Contributions to the History of the Hindu Revenue System*, pp. 73, 77, 90-1, 106 8. In the chapter (v. 3) describing what may be called the expenses of the king's establishment, we have the following rates of pay :—

Carpenters—2,000 *paṇas*.
Skilled and unskilled craftsmen—120 *paṇas*.

(iv. 1), Kauṭilya characterises merchants, artisans and some other specified classes as thieves in fact, though not in name. In the class of artisans just mentioned, are included weavers, washermen, goldsmiths, workers in copper and other metals, physicians, actors, minstrels and beggars. How drastically paternal the State regulations for protection of the public against these classes sometimes might be, is proved by a number of examples. Not only is a differential scale of wages fixed for weaving different kinds of cloth, but fines and other penalties are prescribed for reduction in their weight and measures. Fines are also prescribed for washermen washing clothes elsewhere than on wooden planks or on smooth stone, for wearing clothes other than those marked with a cudgel, for selling, mortgaging or hiring clothes of others, and even for delay in returning the clothes. Wages at varying rates are laid down for dyeing different qualities of cloth. A scale of penalties is laid down for physicians failing in or neglecting the treatment of diseases.

The measures for public security (iv. 2) against traders partake of the same character. We read that such old wares as are of proved ownership should be sold or mortgaged at the market-place (*paṇya-saṁsthā*) under supervision of the market-superintendent (*saṁsthādhyaksha*). A graduated scale of fines is prescribed for deficiency in weights and measures. There is a similar scale of fines for exceeding the profit-limit of five per cent permitted on home-grown merchandise and of ten per cent allowed on foreign merchandise. In a later chapter of the same section (iv. 4) dealing with lost and stolen property, we are pointedly told that the sale or mortgage of old wares should not be carried out without informing the market-superintendent. It is characteristic of Kauṭilya's attitude towards traders (*vaidehaka*) that unlike an unnamed *Arthaśāstra* authority whom he quotes, he thinks (viii. 4) the oppression from traders to be worse even than that caused by the Guardian of the Frontier (*antapāla*).

On the other hand it is only fair to add that the State in these times also took special steps to protect the artisans and merchants. For theft of small articles belonging to artisans and craftsmen, Kauṭilya prescribes (iv. 10) fines as high as 100 *paṇas*. Elsewhere (iv. 13) he lays down elaborate rules for compensating merchants (*sārthika*) for theft or robbery of their merchandise during their journeys.

The Mauryas followed the traditional State policy in relation to industry and trade at least in some important respects. We have already seen what care they bestowed upon the construction of roads through a special class of officers called *Agoranomoi* by Megasthenes. That they established State manufactures on their own account is proved by Megasthenes' reference to his fourth Indian caste, viz. that of artisans. Speaking of this class, Diodorus (ii. 41) says that they were not only exempted from paying taxes, but even received maintenance from the Royal exchequer. More guardedly Arrian (*Indica* Ch. xii) states that while handicraftsmen and retail dealers pay tribute, an exception is made in favour of makers of weapons of war, ship-builders and sailors, who even draw pay from the State. Evidently, the artisans maintained by the State were employed on government service. What strict control was maintained by the Maurya government over the artisans and merchants alike of the country-side and of the capital is proved by other statements of Megasthenes. We learn that the *Agoranomoi* had among other duties, to superintend crafts connected with land such as those of the wood-cutters, carpenters, blacksmiths and miners. Again, the officers known as *Astynomoi* ('city commissioners') were divided into six boards. Of these the fourth 'is that which has to do with sales and barter, and these look after the measure, and the fruits of the season, that the latter may be sold by stamp': the fifth 'is that of those who have charge of the works made by artisans and sell these by stamps, the new apart from the old'[1]. We have elsewhere[2] given reasons for identifying Megasthenes' officers in charge of measures with Kauṭilya's *pautavādhyaksha* ('superintendent of weights and measures') and *saṁsthādhyaksha* ('market superintendent'), while connecting 'the stamp' mentioned by the Greek writer with the *abhijñāna-mudrā*, which according to *Arthaśāstra* (ii. 27) was given by the *antapāla* to incoming traders. We have finally to mention in the present place another reference suggesting that the person of the artisans

1. Strabo. xv. 1.50-51, tr. the Loeb Classical Library, Vol. vii, pp. 83-4.
2. *Contributions to the History of the Hindu Revenue System*, p. 117.

was protected by a special law unlike the general rule of law known to the *Arthaśāstra*. According to Strabo (xv. 1.54), if a person caused the loss of a hand or an eye to a craftsman, he was put to death. This is a severe departure from the milder rule of law in the *Arthaśāstra* (iii. 19) imposing fines alone for the same offences.

Currency

Long before the rise of the Nandas and the Mauryas India had evolved her own monetary system based on the indigenous standards. The Vedic *nishka, śatamāna* and *suvarṇa* may have been ingots of gold of definite weights. Of these *nishka* was probably a gold coin even in the Vedic age as it was later in the time of *Manusmriti.*[1] Māna of *Śatamāna*, is generally taken to stand for *Ratti* or *Krishṇala* and on this basis, the weight of this coin is taken to be 100 Rattīs. But later Authorities, Pāṇini, Manu and Yājñavalkya refer to it, as a silver money, weighing, according to the two latter sources, 320 *Krishṇalas*. But, the early Vedic literature appears to be acquainted with the manās of gold. And if they are to be associated with *mina*, a definite Babylonian weight, the Vedic *manā* will not be considered as an indigenous weight or coin. Probably *Śatamāna* of the later periods has nothing to do with Vedic *manā*. *Śatamāna* in early periods was possibly a gold coin, but in the 6th Cent. B.C. it appears as a silver coin weighing about 175 grains or 100 *rattīs*. V.S. Agrawala and Altekar identify the known bent bar coins with the literary *Śatamāna* and recognise various denominations. *Suvarṇa* was another type of gold coin weighing about 140 grains. But as actual gold specimens of the *nishka*, *Śatamāna*, and *Suvarṇa* are wanting, nothing can be said about them with certainty. But in later works such as the *Jātakas*, the grammar of Pāṇini and the *Arthaśāstra* of Kauṭilya, we have definite references to gold coins called *nishka* and *suvarṇa*, (actual specimens of which are not found),' silver coins called *kārshāpaṇas*, or *dharaṇas* and copper coins also called *kārshāpaṇas*, along with their multiples and sub-divisions. The Vedic *śatamāna*, as its name implies, was based on the *māna* unit, a weight known to the *Ṛigveda*. In later times the *māna*

1. ASA, *JNSI* XV, 1, 12
2. A. K. Narain *JNSI*, XIX, II, pp. 181-183.

was changed for the lighter unit called *krishṇala* or *rati*, the seed of the *guñja*-berry. The weight of the gold *suvarṇa* in the *Arthaśāstra* as well as in Manu and Yājñavalkya is given as 80 *guñjas* or *ratis*, the copper *kārshāpaṇa* according to Manu and Yājñavalkya also weighing 80 *ratis*. The weight of the silver *dharaṇas* in the *Arthaśāstra*, however, amounts very nearly to 80 *ratis*, while in Manu and Yājñavalkya it is only 32 *ratis*.[1] According to A.K. Narain *Karsha* is a unit of weight mentioned in the inscriptions of the Achaemanid kings of Iran. One *Karsha* was equal to 10 shekels equal to 83·3 grammes. In India it became popular under the Achaemenid kings and came to be prefixed to *paṇa*. "It is true that the weight of the Achaemenid *Karsha* is very heavy compared to the average weight of the punch-marked coins but so also there is much difference in their weight compared to the theoretical weights given in Manu for no silver punch marked coin weighs 146 grains."[2] But this difference may as well be due to local numismatic traditions. As Professor Rapson has well observed[3], the silver and copper coinages in Ancient India were often independent of each other, with different areas of circulation. In the *Arthaśāstra*, however, the silver *paṇa* with its sub-divisions is evidently recognised as the standard coin, while the copper *māshaka* with its divisions ranks as a token currency. Apparently copper was linked up with silver in such a way that the *māshaka* was one-sixteenth in value of the silver *paṇa*, its weight varying with the ratio between the two metals[4].

The punch-marked silver coins that have been found in large numbers all over India have been identified on all hands with

1. On the antiquity of the Indian coinage and its evolution, see D. R. Bhandarkar, *Ancient Indian Numismatics*, Lecture ii : S. K. Chakravorty, *Ancien Indian Numismatics*, Chs. ii. and iv. On the origin of the 32 *rati* standard fo silver coins, see Bhandarkar *op. cit.*, pp. 93—4 and specially Chakravorty *op. cit.*, pp. 43 ff. Cf. also Altekar, On origin and Antiquity of coinage in ancient India, *JNSI* XV, I, pp. 1-26; Agrawala, Ancient Coins as known to Paṇini, *JNSI*, XV, I, pp. 27-41; Sircar. The Satamana, JNSI XV 11, pp. 136-150; Sircar, Kauṭilya and Indian Numismatics, *JNSI*, XIV, I, pp. 128-143; Gupta, P.L., Numismatic data in Arthaśāstra of Kautilya, *JNSI*, XXII, pp. 13-37; Agrawala, V.S., Coin data in the Mahābhārata, *JNSI* XVIII, II, pp. 143-156.'

3. *Catalogue of Indian Coins in the British Museum*, p. clxxix.

4. Chakravorty, *op. cit.*, 56-8.

the silver *kārshāpaṇas*, *dharaṇas* or *purāṇas* of the Smṛitis and the *Arthaśāstra*. Some classes of these coins have been traced back to pre-Mauryan times. Thus a distinctive class of such coins, which was found some years ago in a deposit at Paila in the Kheri district of the Uttar Pradesh, has been generally identified as the local currency of the independent Kosala kingdom before its absorption by Magadha. These coins bear four obverse marks instead of the usual five, among which is included the four-spoked wheel in place of the usual five-spoked one. They are of the reduced standard of 24 to 30 *ratis* in place of the theoretical 32 *ratis*[1]. Recently attempts have been made by P.L. Gupta to distinguish the coinages of the *Mahājanapadas* and the *Janapadas*. To him the local varieties of punch-marked silver coins are found generally "confined to a particular locality and mostly consist of exclusive types and fabric. They are not generally found together with any other variety of punch-marked coins. Their association with the imperial punch-market coins is also very limited." He further thinks that this currency of the local states of 6th century B.C. "was discontinued, as soon as the territory of their origin merged into the Magadhan empire". The only exceptions to this, however, were the bent bar coins of Gandhāra. Among such local coinages, he lists, besides those of Paila and Gandhāra, the cup-shaped coins of Kāśī. His saucer-like coins from Bhabhua, might well be the issues of the kingdom of Magadha in the 6th Cent. B.C. (P.L. Gupta, JNSI, XXIV, pp. 134-6).' Of the punch-marked silver coins bearing the usual number of five obverse marks, two distinct classes assignable to as many distinct periods have been recovered from recent excavations on the site of Taxila. The Older Class is dated *circa* 317 B.C. by the presence in its midst of gold coins of Alexander and his half-brother Philip Arrhidaeus 'in mint condition,' while the date of the Later Class is fixed at *circa* 248 B.C. by the occurrence of a coin of Diodotus in the same deposit. The two classes are distinguished from each other by their fabric

1. On the above see Durga Prasad, *Num. Supp*. xlvii. p. 77 ; Walsh. *JNSI*., No. ii. p. 15-26 : *JRAS*. 1937, pp. 300-303. Walsh gives the average weight of the Paila hoard as 25 *ratis*, but see D. D. Kosambi, *NIA*. iv. p. 56.

as well as symbols, though equally approximating to the standard of 32 *ratis*. The Older (pre-Maurya) Class consists of large thin pieces unlike the small thick coins of the Later (Maurya) Class. The obverse marks of the Older Class are conspicuously lacking in the distinctive Maurya symbols ('hill and crescent' as well as 'peacock'). Punch marked coins of the older class containing animal symbols as the third mark, in the symbol group, are considered by P.L. Gupta "as the pre-imperial issues, issued by local rulers, dynastic or tribal" and those bearing hill symbol on the same place as the issues of the Nanda Dynasty".[1] Archaeologically, however, both the hoards from Taxila have been regarded as post-Mauryan deposits by Dani and Narain, and hence the evidence from Taxila should no longer be used to prove the pre-Mauryan character of some of the punch marked coins[2] although "the possibility of Mauryan or pre-Mauryan currency of the punch-marked coinage" need not be denied[3]. P.L. Gupta classifies the punch-marked coinage into five chronological periods. The coins of Period I, are pre Mauryan, of Periods II and III Mauryan, and the remaining pieces belonging to the Periods IV and V as post-Mauryan.[4] It seems to be generally agreed that some coins of the Older Class go back to the 4th or even the 5th century B.C[5]. On the other hand, it must be admitted that the symbolism and metrology of the silver punch-marked coins are still an unsolved problem[6]

1. *JNSI*, XII, II, 136-50; Cf. also *JNSI*, XI, II. pp. 114-145.

2. Dani, A.H., *JNSI*, XVII, II, pp. 27-32; cf. also in *JNSI*, XIX, II, pp. 180-181; P.L. Gupta, *JNSI*, XIX, I, pp. 1-8: Narain, *JNSI*, XIX, II, pp. 29-106.

3. *JNSI*, XXI, I, pp. 1-8; Ibid XXI, II, pp. 114-119; *JNSI*, XXI, II, pp. 120-128.

4. P.L. Gupta, *Punch-marked coins in the Andhra Pradesh Govt. Museum*, (1961).

5 Thus Durga Prasad, *Num. Supp.* xlv. Pl. viii and *ibid*, xlvii, pp. 78—9, takes some early silver punch-marked coins to go back to the kingdom of Magadha shortly after Buddha's time. According to Walsh (*JBORS.* 1937, pp. 303-4), some very old coins of the Taxila Hoard which were re-stamped for circulation may go back to 200 years or more before the date of the deposit, viz., c. 317 B.C. More recently D. D. Kosambi (*op. cit.*, pp. 60-6) premising that the early coins of Taxila were imported from the east, assigns some select types on the basis of his interpretation of the obverse marks to Śaiśunāga and Nanda kings. See also some of the articles of P.L. Gupta etc. mentioned above.

6. On different interpretations of the obverse marks, see Durga Prasad, *JASB.*, N. S. XXX(1934), pp. 17 ff. : Walsh, *Punch-marked Coins from Taxila*, pp. 18-25 : D.D. Kosambi, *op. cit.*, pp. 2 ff. Regarding metrology A. S. Hemmy (*JRAS*, 1937, pp. 1-26) concluded after an elaborate examination that the

In circulation with the Older Class of silver coins just described, though probably dating from much earlier times, was a class of coins consisting of thick slightly bent bars of silver with 'the six-armed symbol' on the obverse and a blank reverse. Weighing from 165.8 to 173 grains, these *śalākā* coins, as they have been called, have been sometimes identified[1] with the *śatamāna* of 100 *ratis*. Specimens of this coinage have been found in denominations of one-half, one-fourth, one-eighth and one-sixteenth pieces. This identification of the bent bars with *Śatamāna* and the determinination of its multiples from amongst the available punched silver coins is purely conjectural. Other classes of coins of the same early type comprising (as they have been called) single and double *kārshāpaṇas* or only half *kārshāpaṇas* have been found in deposits from western India and an unrecorded provenance in northern India[2].

To the same period as the Older Class of silver punch-marked coins as well as the bent bar coins belongs, if we are to judge from their simultaneous occurrence in the same Taxila deposit of *c.* 317 B.C., a group of minute silver coins with a single obverse mark and a blank reverse[3]. They have been found not only on the site of Taxila, but also at Thathari in the Madhya Pradesh[4].

silver punch-marked coins conform to the weight-standard of 54 grains, which is exactly one-quarter of the principal weight of the revised Indus system of weights, and nominally represents Manu's standard of 32 *ratis* (58.56 grains). Criticising this view, D. D. Kosambi concludes (*op. cit.* pp. 58-9) that the system of Mohenjodaro weights was applied for the earlier Taxilan hoard, while in the Maurya period although the average remained the same, the variance increased enormously thus pointing to a far cruder system than before.

1. See Durga Prasad, *Num. Supp.* xlvii, pp. 86-7. This view is contradicted by D. D. Kosambi, *op. cit.*, p. 19. On the other hand, Mr. Charan Das Chatterji in his paper *Numismatic data in Pali literature* (*Buddhistic Studies*, p. 426 *n*) suggests that the bent bar coins were struck on the *karsha* of 100 *ratis* known to Yājñavalkya unlike the usual *karsha* of 80 *ratis*. See also V.S. Agrawala, op. cit., and Altekar, op. cit.; J.A. Decourdemanches (J. A., 1912, pp. 117-32) held that the punch-marked coinage was merely an Indian variety of the Achaemenian coinage, issued side by side with their *Siglois*. He thinks the bent bars were meant for a double *Sigloi*. His views are not tenable, see Altekar, op. cit., p. 6-7.

2. See Allan *Catalogue of the Indian Coins in the British Museum* (*Ancient India*), pp. xvii—xix : clxi—clxii. 4-10.

3. According to Walsh (*Punch-marked coins from Taxila*, pp. 3-4), these coins weighing from 2.3 to 2.86 grains were the silver *paṇas* or *māshas* of two *ratis*. This view is criticised by D. D. Kosambi who provisionally calls them one-twentieh *kārāshāpaṇa* (See Kosambi, *op. cit.*, p. 19). Cf. also V.S. Agrawala on this point, JNSI, XIII, II, PP. 160-168; P.L. Gupta, Ibid, 168-171.'

4. See Allan. *op. cit.*, pp. lxix and Pl. xlvi.

We have an interesting glimpse of the condition of the currency in north-western India at the time of Alexander's invasion in the casual observation of a classical writer. We are told by Quintus Curtius that among the presents offered by the king of Taxila to Alexander were included thirty talents of *signatum argentum* ('coined silver'). These pieces might not have been actual coins in circulation. Possibly they are comparable with the gigantic gold and silver pieces of 2000 *tolas* mentioned by Abul-fazl and Jehangir, meant, according to Manucci, especially to be given as presents to ladies and others whom the Moghuls liked. But otherwise we may identify these coins either with the Older Class of punch-marked coins or with the class of bent bar coins above described. The reference to silver coins in this connection, as R. B. Whitehead[1] justly observes, probably signifies that silver was employed as the standard metal at that time. Of the currency conditions of the Maurya empire in Aśoka's last years, we have probably a valuable record in the shape of the Taxila hoard of punch-marked coins of the Later Class of *circa* 248 B.C. as above mentioned. These coins contain a considerable alloy of copper (75.3 p.c.) as compared with silver (40.3 p.c.) and in many cases are more than 54 grains in weight.

Turning to the subsidiary copper coinage of these times, we may mention that the class of square or rectangular cast coins bearing the characteristic symbols of 'the hill and crescent', the hollow cross and the like has been held to have been issued by the Mauryas[2]. This too is purely speculative. To the same period has probably to be assigned a class of punch marked copper coins with Maurya obverse marks, of which a hoard was found at Bhagalpur in 1925[3]. (the term Maurya marks' for certain symbols is hypothetical). With the Mauryas again we may probably connect numerous specimens of the remarkable copper coinage of Taxila which extends over several centuries and is mostly un-

1. *The Pre-Mohammedan Coinage of North-Western India*, p. 42.

2. On a hoard of such coins, excavated at Bulandibagh (near Patna) from the Mauryan level of 15 to 18 feet below ground-level and on two such pieces dug out from below the Aśokan level near the Aśokan monolith at Sārnāth, see Durga Prasad, *Num. Suppl.*, xlvii, pp. 62-6. Previously, Allan (*op. cit.*, p. lxxvii) had cautiously suggested the 3rd-2nd century B. C. as the date of the cast copper coins.

3. See Allan, *op. cit.*, lxxix.

inscribed and die-struck[1]. In a fragmentary stone-plaque inscription of *circa* third century B.C., which was discovered some years ago at Mahasthan in the Bogra district of Bengal[2], reference is made to 'a coin of the value of four cowries' called *gaṇḍaka*[3].

The downfall of the Maurya empire was not followed by the withdrawal of the imperial currency from circulation. From the finds of Indo-Greek coins in the same deposits at various sites, we may safely conclude that the punch-marked silver coins were in circulation down at least to the 2nd and 1st centuries B.C[4]. That their circulation was continued even down to the Kushān times is proved by a Mathurā stone-pillar inscription of the twentieth year of Huvishka mentioning an endowment of 11,000 *purāṇas*.[5] However, on the basis of literary evidence one may agree that the punch-marked coins were not only in circulation, but were even manufactured, at least, down to the times of the Guptas.[6]

1. According to Allan (*op. cit.*, cxxxix) the copper coinage of Taxila began late in the 3rd century B.C. when Taxila was under Maurya governors and ended with the Greek conquest before the middle of the 2nd century B.C. On independent grounds Vincent Smith (*Cat. of cions in the Ind. Mus.*, p. 147) had previously held that the single die-struck pieces of Taxila began not later than 350 B. C., while the double-die coins were prior to the coins of Agathocles and Pantaleon, *c.* 190-180 B. C.

2. See *Ep. Ind.* xxi, pp. 83-91.

3. It may be added that on a number of inscribed coins which had been read differently by previous scholars, K. P. Jayaswal (*JBORS.* xx. pp. 279-308) claimed to have read the names of the Maurya kings Bṛhaspatimitra, Śātadharman, Daśaratha, Samprati, Devadharman and Śāliśūra. Many of the said readings of Jayaswal were based on incorrect decipherment and others appear to be the coins of homonymous local kings. See Jai Prakash, *JNSI*, XXIII, pp. 242-244; and Hari Kishore Prasad, *JNSI*, XVII, 1 pp. 24-35.

4. For references cf. the Bajaur hoard of 1942 described by H. L. Haughton in *JNSI*, iv. part i, and the hoard at Bairat described by Daya Ram Sahni in *Archaeological Remains and Excavations at Bairat* (not dated.)

5. *Ep. Ind.* xxi. pp. 60 ff.

6. See D.C. Sircar, *JNSI*, XIII, II, 183-191; Ibid, XXIII, pp. 297-302.

CHAPTER IX

RELIGION

Literary Background

There are unfortunately no definitely dated literary records of the Nanda-Maurya period. The epigraphic records that only date from the time of Aśoka give a one-sided picture of the religion of the people. The Śrauta and Gṛhya Sūtras which possibly belong to this period do not give a picture of the religion in practice but attempt at a systematisation of the orthodox Brahmanical traditions both social and ritualistic. They show Brahmanism on the defensive trying to safeguard its rights and privileges against the newly started religious movements such as Buddhism and Jainism. The now famous *Arthaśāstra* of Kauṭilya is of suspected authenticity and may be used only as a source of secondary importance. The *Aṣṭādhyāyī* of Pāṇini is a compilation of this period and contains some important references to the religious institutions of the times. What is more important, it mentions the *Mahābhārata*. But it is not known which Mahābhārata it was. It was certainly not the epic in its present developed form. Supposing it was the old Pāṇḍu story, it does not throw any light on the age of the present epic. The epic therefore cannot be used as a source of information for the religious history of the Nanda-Maurya period.

The early Buddhist texts, in spite of the ecclesiastical violence of different ages, seem to have preserved some authentic traditions of the pre-Aśokan times. They contain, to a limited extent, the picture of the religion as practised in those days and also of the struggle that was going on between Buddhism and the opposing sects. But this does not mean that the entire Buddhist canon in its present form can be used as a source of information for the period in question. The Buddhist traditions would have us believe that the first two collections of the Buddhist Tripiṭaka namely the Sūtrapiṭaka with its five *nikāyas* and the Vinayapiṭaka were brought together in the council of Rājagṛha, held immediately after the death of Buddha and that the third collection, the Abhidharmapiṭaka assumed its final form in the time of Aśoka, in the third council held at Pāṭaliputra. But this claim has been proved to be too exaggerated to be naively accepted. The Aśokan edicts show that the Buddhist canon was then in the making and not a full-fledged Tripiṭaka. In the Bhabru edict, Aśoka specially recommends to the Saṅgha a number of religious texts with the following instruction : 'I desire that many groups of monks and nuns may repeatedly listen to these expositions of the Dharma (*dhamma-paliyāyāni*) and reflect on them. In the same way both laymen and laywomen (should act)'.

The seven expositions of Dharma recommended by Aśoka were the following :

1. Vinaya-samukase (Vinaya-samutkarṣa).
2. Aliyavasāni (Āryavaṁśāni)
3. Anāgatabhayāni
4. Munigāthā
5. Moneyasute (Moneyyasūtra)
6. Upatisapasine (Upatissapraśna)
7. Lāghulovāde (Rāhulavāda)

It is generally assumed that these Sūtras were selections from the extensive Buddhist canon, which according to the tradition, had been constituted already before the time of Aśoka. Under this assumption, all the texts except the first have been identified. Accordingly Aliyavasāni has been identified with Aṅguttara II, 27, Anāgatabhayāni with Aṅguttara III, 103, Munigāthā with Munisutta of the Suttanipāta, Moneyasute with Nālaka-sutta of the same text, Upatisa-pasine with the Rathavinīta-sutta of the Majjhima (I, 146-51) and the Lāghulovāde with the Rāhulavāda-sutta of the Majjhima (I. 414).

Aśoka clearly says that these texts had been spoken by the Buddha himself (*bhagavatā buddhena bhāsite*). They are called Dhamma-paliyāya or Dharmaparyāya which regularly means a Buddhist religious text according to the old tradition of the north. But their identification is doubtful as there is no clue in the inscription to their contents excepting in the case of Lāghulovāde. It is said that this text concerned falsehood (*musāvādam adhigicya*) and in fact the Rāhulavāda-sūtra as preserved in the Pāli Majjhimanikāya and the northern Madhyamāgama contains a warning to Rāhula against falsehood.

But in which form was the text known to Aśoka ? It was certainly not known in its present amplified form. It is probable that the Aśokan text consisted of the gāthā portions which contain the essentials of the Sūtra.

Then again the language in which they were known to Aśoka was neither Sanskrit nor Pāli. The titles of texts which Aśoka mentions in his edict have marked Māgadhī characteristics (cf. *aliya* for Pāli *ariya*, *Lāghulo* for *Rāhula*, the termination *e* as in *-sute, samukase*, for Pāli *o*). Admitting that Aśoka was quoting the exact titles of the texts known to him, the conclusion is inevitable that the form in which he knew them was Māgadhī. This pre-Aśokan Māgadhī canon was not yet a well-constituted Tripiṭaka, as the Pāli tradition would have us believe, but a literature still in the making. It should be remembered that although there was occasion for it, Aśoka does not mention either the *piṭaka* or the *nikāya*, words which occur on the Buddhist monuments within a century from Aśoka's time. It is therefore almost clear that the literature was not yet available in the time of Aśoka in a tangible form and that the community was not yet much given to the scripture. But a lead had already been given in this direction either by Aśoka on his own initiative or by Magadhan church and the old traditions had begun to be collected. Hence arose the necessity of encouraging the monks as well as the laymen to study them. Under these circumstances it is permitted to take some of the traditions embodied in the Buddhist canon as old and genuine.

But the same thing cannot be said about the Jaina canon. The first systematic collection of the canon was made only in the 6th centuary A.D. apparently from old manuscripts but also from the mouths of the monks who could still recite them from memory. But the form in which the Aṅgas have come down to us is admittedly later than that of the Pāli canon which itself is post-Aśokan. Then again an important section of the Jaina community, the Digambaras, disown this canon and dispute its authenticity as true utterances of Mahāvīra. Under these circumstances, although the assumption that it contains some very old traditions of the Jaina church may not be wholly unjustified, our scope of discrimination in using them is extremely limited.

The contemporary Greek records, specially the fragments of the lost account of Megasthenes, contain some valuable references to the religious life of the Maurya age and confirm to some extent the information available from the Buddhist texts.

A study of these sources shows that in the Nanda-Maurya period, Brahmanism was still mainly an aristocratic religion of which the principal supporters were the kings, the nobles, and the rich Brahmin householders. The real custodians of the religious lore were the priests who occupied the highest rank in the social hierarchy. There was also an ascetic class among the Brahmins which consisted of teachers advocating somewhat new ways of religious thoughts and practices which may be traced to Upanishadic origin. Those teachers had a more direct appeal to the common people and attracted people from other classes of society too to a life of renunciation. It was probably at the hands of this ascetic class that new theistic movements originated in the Maurya period. Closely allied to this ascetic class but with definitely distinctive features were the two religious movements, Buddhism and Jainism, which began to play a very important part in the religious life of the country from the Maurya period.

Brahmanism

The Vedic and domestic ritual certainly occupied the most important place in the Brahmanical religion of this period. The account of Megasthenes bears clear testimony to it. Megasthenes tells us (Frag. I. B : Diod. III, 63) that the philosophers, by which he means the priestly class, although inferior in number, were prominent over all the classes in point of dignity and that they were engaged by private persons to offer sacrifices. Aśoka's reference to the Deva-worshippers relates to this class of priests who were engaged in sacrifices and not to the popular religious movements which do not seem to have as yet gained any considerable importance.

The references to the Vedic lore and ritualism in the canonical Buddhist texts clearly bring out their importance in the Nanda-Maurya period. The Vedic Ṛṣis such as Aṭṭhaka, Vāmaka, Vāmadeva, Vessāmitta, Yamataggi, Aṅgirasa, Bhāradvāja, Vāseṭṭha, Kassapa and Bhagu were popularly claimed to be the ancestors of the Brahmins and the seers of the Vedic mantras (*mantānām kattā*). Some of these Ṛṣis were actually composers of the hymns. Vāmadeva was the composer of the hymns of the fourth Maṇḍala of the *Ṛgveda*, Bhāradvāja of the sixth maṇḍala, and Vāseṭṭha (Vasiṣṭha) of the hymns of the seventh maṇḍala. The sage Aṭṭhaka (Aṣṭaka) is mentioned in the *Aitareya Brāhmaṇa* (VII, 17) and the *Śāṅkhāyana Śrauta Sūtra* (XV, 26) as one of the sons of Viśvāmitra. Vāmaka and Bhagu (Bhṛgu) appear as teachers and sages in the *Śatapatha Brāhmaṇa* (X. 6. 5. 9 ; VII, 2, 1, 11). Yamataggi (Jamadagni) was a rival of the famous sage Vasiṣṭha. Āṅgirasa is mentioned as a famous teacher in the *Taittirīya-saṁhitā* (III, 1. 7. 3 ; VII, 1.4.1). It is further said in the Buddhist texts that the Brahmins of the period not only claimed descent from those ancient teachers but also were capable of reciting the ancient *mantras*. They were serious students and teachers of the sacrificial literature and were proficient in the three Vedas. Those who were engaged for the performance of sacrifices were famous for their knowledge of the Vedic lore and purity of origin. Purity implied purity in descent up to the seventh generation both on the father's and the mother's side, and proficiency in the Vedic lore not only meant proficiency in the three Vedas but also in the Nighaṇḍu (etymology), the Keṭubha (ritual), Itihāsa, Veyyākaraṇa (grammar), Lokāyata etc. (*Vedānaṁ pāragū sanighaṇḍu-keṭubhānaṁ sākkharappabhadānaṁ itihāsa-pañcamānaṁ padako veyyākaraṇo lokāyata-mahāpurisalakkhaṇesu anavayo*—Majjhima II, p. 210 ; Digha I, p. 128.)

The Buddhist texts mention a class of Brahmins named Brāhmaṇa-mahāśālas who used to receive revenues of lands granted to them by the king of the country. These Brahmins were rich and capable of undertaking for themselves the most expensive sacrifices. They also used to entertain a large number of students, sometimes 300 to 500, coming to them from different parts of the country and to impart to them the knowledge of the Vedic lore. These Brahmins were the most respected and are described as not only pure in descent but also as possessing a divine colour (*brahmavaṇṇi*), a divine radiance (*brahmavaccasi*) and of agreeable speech and language (*kalyāṇavāco*, *kalyāṇavākkaraṇo*). The names of some of these Brahmins are given in the Buddhist texts : Caṅki, Tārukkha, Pokkharasāti, Jānussoni, Todeyya, Kuṭadanta etc.

The Buddhist literature also knows the names of the various Vedas and the number of their *śākhās*. Thus in the Pāli texts (Digha I, 237) there is mention of the Addharīya, the Tittiriya, the Chandokā and the Bavharija (Bahvṛca). The Sanskrit Buddhist texts know more of the Vedic lore. In the Śārdūlakarṇāvadāna (Divyāva. xxxiii) there is a detailed description of the Vedic literature. Besides, it mentions the 21 *śākhās* of the Ṛigveda, 100 of the Yajurveda and 8000 (*sic.* 1000) of the Sāmaveda. The tradition is old as it is also recorded in the *Mahābhāṣya* of Patañjali (xv, 10, 11 : *ekaśatam adhvaryuśākhāḥ sahasravartmā sāmavedaḥ ekaviṁśatidhāḥ bahvṛcyaṁ*). The principal Vedic *śākhās* are also mentioned by names in the same text.

The Pāli canon mentions some of the Vedic sacrifices by names such as : Aśvamedha, Naramedha, Sammāpāsa, Vājapeyya and Niraggalam (Samyutta, p. 299). The same are mentioned in the Sanskrit Buddhist texts as Vājapeya, Aśvamedha, Puruṣamedha, Śamyāprāsa, Nirargadam and Samāprābharaṁ. It is not clear which sacrifices were meant by the Śamyāprāsa, Nirargadam and Samāprābharam. They were no doubt Śrauta rituals as there is question of gains by the priests from those sacrifices. No big gain could be expected from the Gṛhya rituals. As they are mentioned along with the important Soma sacrifices such as Aśvamedha, Vājapeya and Puruṣamedha, they seem to have been also Soma sacrifices which entailed large expenditure.

But this ritual had also a darker side. The huge gains offered by them must have increased the greed of at least some of the priests. The large sacrifices required the immolation of a large number of animals of the herds and the felling of big trees possessed by the villagers. These meant a further taxation of the poor people by the nobles who were the real performers of the sacrifices. It is therefore impossible not to believe in some of the charges levelled against ritualism in the Buddhist texts. The Buddhist attitude is well presented in the Brāhmaṇa-dhammikasutta (Sutta-nipāta p. 50).

'The ancient Ṛṣis were ascetics (tapassino) and practised self-control and avoided the five pleasures of the sense. Their riches consisted not of cattle, gold or grains but of learning and purity. They lived on food left at the door by the faithful and used the bed and clothes offered to them reverentially by the rich people. They were never harmed nor dominated, protected as they were by the dhamma, and their access to any house was never barred. They spent 48 years of their life as brahmacārins in quest of knowledge and good conduct. Even after their marriage they lived a life of restraint. They held austerity, rectitude, tenderness, love and forbearance in high esteem. They performed sacrifices with rice, beds, clothes, ghee or oil, which they could collect by begging and never killed cows in sacrifices.

'They possessed a noble stature and a tender and bright mien and remained always engaged in their own pursuits. In course of time, however, they began to covet a king's riches and splendour and objects of pleasure such as women with ornaments, chariots yoked with stately horses. With an eye to these gains they approached king Okkāku (Ikṣvāku), persuaded him to celebrate aśvamedha, puruṣamedha, śamyāprāsa and vājapeyya and received as fees from him wealth, women and chariots, horses and cows, beds and clothes. Coveting more and more they again persuaded him to celebrate sacrifices by the offering of cows, which they said, constituted also the wealth of men as are land, gold or grains, and such were equally fit objects for offering. The slaughter of cows enraged the gods Brahma, Indra and even the Asuras and Rākṣasas and multiplied the diseases which were originally three, viz. desires, hunger and decrepitude, to ninety-eight and further caused to appear discord among the people and within the household, and acts improper and impious among the various classes of men.'

In the *Majjhimanikāya* (I, pp. 342-44) there is the true picture of how sacrifices used to be performed. It is in way of explaining that kind of puggala (individual) which practises self-mortification, and for self-chastisement sacrifices animals and causes sufferings to other beings. 'This kind of puggala', the text says, 'includes the king or the kṣatriya noble whose head has been anointed (muddhāvasitto) as well as the wealthy Brahmins (Brāhmaṇo mahāsālo). He gets a sacrificial shed (santhāgāra) built outside the town, shaves his hair and beard, puts on deer skin, lubricates his body with mustard oil and enters the sacrificial shed, accompanied by his chief queen and his Brahmin priest, rubbing his body with an antelope horn. He then prepares his own bed on the bare ground and lives on cow's milk. The queen and the priest also live on milk. A part of the milk goes to the sacrificial fire and the rest goes to the calves. He then orders : kill so many bulls for the sacrifice, kill so many he-calves, so many she-calves, so many goats, so many rams, all for the sacrifice ; fell so many trees for the yūpa, pluck so much kuśa grass for the barhis. His servants, messengers, workers, all make the preparation either with tears in their eyes or weeping for fear of punishment or chastisement.' The confirmation of this account is found in the Śrauta manuals. They clearly show that the Pāli description is a true and objective picture of the Śrauta ritual as practised in those days.

But this aspect of the Vedic religion was confined, as we have already said, to aristocratic classes, the nobles and the wealthy Brahmins. The intellectual aspect of the Vedic religion was also not without its force. The Upanishadic ideal of life still moved the hearts of many people and they lived up to it.

The life of the forest-dwelling Brahmin philosophers has been described by the contemporary Greek writers. It was, we are told, a life of great simplicity and hardship. The philosophers had their cottages in front of the city within an enclosed space. They lived in simple style, used beds of rushes and deer skins and abstained from animal food and sexual pleasures. They passed their time in listening to serious discourses and in imparting their knowledge to those who would follow them. In the story of Mandanis, as told by Megasthenes, we get the true picture of a Brahmanical sage of those times. The story runs that Alexander while in India was attracted by the reputation of a sage named Mandanis and sent a messenger inviting him and promising him great reward. But Mandanis, although threatened with death, refused to accept his invitation and sent the following reply :

'God, the supreme king, is never the author of insolent wrong, but is the creator of light, of peace, of life, of water, of the body of man, and of souls and these he receives when death sets them free, being in no way subject to evil desire. He alone is the god of my homage, who abhors slaughters and instigates no wars....Know this, however, that what Alexander offers me and the gifts he promises, are all things to me utterly useless ; but the things I prize, and of real use and worth, are these leaves which are my house, these blooming plants which supply me with dainty food, and the water which is my drink, while all other possessions and things which are amassed with anxious care, are wont to prove ruinous to those who amass them, and cause only sorrow and vexation, with which every poor mortal is fully fraught. But as for me, I lie upon the forest leaves, and having nothing which requires guarding, close my eyes in tranquil slumber ; whereas had I gold to guard, that would banish sleep ....Should Alexander cut off my head, he cannot also destroy my soul. My head alone, now silent, will remain but the soul will go away to its Master, leaving the body like a torn garment upon the earth, whence also it was taken. I then, becoming spirit, shall ascend to my God.' (cf. Megasthenes, Frag. LV ; also Frags. xli, xliv, xlv.).

The account doubtless had a real basis as we come across such types of Brahmanical sages not infrequently in the Buddhist texts. The true Brahmins are distinguished from the false ones by Buddha and are well spoken of by him. Such Brahmins were expected to observe the five dhammas : truthfulness (saccam), austerity (tapam), continence (brahmacariyam), study (ajjhenam) and gifts (cāgam). These alone could conduce to the attainment of the Brahma-sahavyatā or the attainment of the world of Brahman (Majjhima ii, 199 ; Sutta Nipāta, p. 79).

This makes it clear that in the Nanda-Maurya period both the Vedic ritual and Upanishadic thought were active forces in the religious life of the country. There were the kings, nobles and wealthy Brahmins who believed in the efficacy of sacrifices and used to perform them with the help of hired priests. These priests who formed a class by themselves were the custodians of the Vedic lore. Many of them were attracted by the fees for officiating at the sacrifices and had become almost professional. But there were others too who saw no attractions in such gains and lived a simple life of austerities, far away from the inhabited localities, in the forests, striving hard to realise the Brahman through tapasyā or asceticism.

The ascetic movement

The ascetics were known under the general name of Śramaṇa. Although the Buddhists alone appropriated this title to themselves in later times, the order of the Śramaṇas originated in the Brahmanical fold. It assumed a distinct shape in the Nanda-Maurya period. Already in the Upanishads there are references to the Brahmacārins and the Yatis besides the sacrificers and the hermits. For the first time in the law books there is mention of a full-fledged order called either Vaikhānasa or Vānaprastha (Gautama, III, 2 ; Āpastamba, III, 9, 21, 1 ; Vasiṣṭha, VII, 2). This is the third among the four orders (*āśrama*) in which a householder in his ripe old age is required to retire to the forest after leaving the family duties to his son. In this stage he lives like an anchorite, wears the bark of trees, eats fruits and passes his days in higher thoughts. The origin of the Śramaṇas goes back to this order of the Vaikhānasas.

The Greek writers also give the same account of the Śramaṇas whom they call either Sarmanes or Sramnai. The most respected among them were the Hylobioi (υλοβιος), 'the forest-dwellers'. It has been said about them : 'They live in woods, where they subsist on leaves of trees and wild fruits, and wear garments made from the bark of trees' (Megasthenes, Frag. XLI, 60). They observed the vow of chastity and abstained from drinking wine. They were so much esteemed that even the kings communicated with them through messengers in order to ascertain the causes of things and to get divine favour. These forest-dwellers were the same as those included in the Vaikhānasa order.

Besides the Vānaprasthas, the *Vasiṣṭha Dharmasūtra* (loc. cit.) mentions another order of ascetics called Parivrājaka. In the Buddhist texts they are depicted as wandering teachers who had specialised in ethics, philosophy, nature-lore and mysticism. Their only difference with other forest-dwellers probably consisted in their travelling from place to place and in enlightening the people on various matters concerning religion and philosophy. In the early Buddhist texts there are frequent references to them and to special houses called *paribbājaka-ārāma* provided for them near the towns. The villagers and town-folk also provided them with meeting places called *kotuhalasālās* (Digha, III, pp. 36, ff., Divyāvadāna, p. 143).

The Greek writers seem to have included them within the class of Sarmanes and philosophers. Speaking of some of the philosophers in one place Megasthenes says : 'To the people of India at large they render great benefits ; when gathered together at the beginning of the year, they forewarn the assembled multitudes about droughts and wet weather, and also about propitious winds, diseases, and other topics capable of profiting the hearers' (Frag. I, 40). The physicians also belonged to the Śramaṇa class. Megasthenes tells us that they were engaged in the study of the nature of man and that they were simple in their habits. They had as their food either rice or barley meal which they would get either by begging or from those who entertained them as guests. They like other Śramaṇas practised asceticism.

The Greek accounts as well as the Buddhist texts tell us that among the Śramaṇas there were also the diviners, sorcerers, and adepts in the rites and customs relating to the dead. They lived on begging in the villages and towns. Megasthenes informs us that there were also female ascetics in some classes of the Śramaṇas. Such female ascetics are mentioned in the Buddhist texts too. They are referred to as paribbājikā and a special class of them as *molibaddhā* paribbājikā who used to go about in the company of male ascetics (Megasthenes Frag. XLI, 60; Majjhima, I, p. 305 ; Samyutta, III. pp. 238-240).

There is no doubt that the order of the Śramaṇas and Parivrājakas was open to the people of all castes but there is no clear evidence as to whether they used to give up their caste distinctions and obligations after joining that order. Buddha is once decried by a Brahmin not so much for becoming a Śramaṇa but for giving up his caste distinctions and thus becoming a vṛṣala (Vasalasutta, Sutta Nipāta, p. 21). In the Buddhist texts four kinds of Śramaṇas are spoken of according to their religious conduct. They were : Maggajino—those who had reached the end of the way and attained Nirvāṇa, Maggadesako—

those who show the way to the highest goal, Magge Jīvati—those who live according to the way, and Maggadusī—those who are vain, talkative, devoid of self-restraint and although wearing the dress of religious men destroy the good name of the line of their own teachers (Cundasutta, Sutta Nipāta, p. 16).

Closely allied to the general order of the Śramaṇas and Parivrājakas, there were some communities of religious men which claimed their origin from some well-known teachers contemporaneous with Buddha and followed some distinct religious beliefs. They were the sophists or Tīrthikas (vādasīlā titthiyā), the Ājivikas and the Nigaṇṭhas (cf. Dhammikasutta, Sutta Nipāta, v. 381). The famous Tīrthika teachers in the time of Buddha were Pūraṇa Kassapa, Pakudha Kaccāyana, Ajita Keśa-Kambala, Sañjaya Belaṭṭhiputta, Makkhali Gosāla and Nigaṇṭha Nātaputta. Of the religious orders founded by them only those of the last two teachers had lived up to the Nanda-Maurya period ; the followers of the first four teachers had probably merged into the general Śramaṇa order for want of strong leaders. The religious order of Makkhali Gosāla was the Ājīvika and that of Nigaṇṭha Nātaputta, the Nigaṇṭha (Nirgrantha).

The Ajīvika and Nirgrantha movements

Although the origin of these two religious movements goes back to the times of Buddha, nothing precisely is known about their progress before the Maurya period. The word Makkhali which is used as a part of the name of Gosāla, the founder of the Ājīvika order, was probably the name of the order. It corresponds to the Sanskrit word Maskarin. Pāṇini in one of his Sūtras (VI, 1, 154) refers to the Maskarin as a class of parivrājakas who carried a bamboo-staff (maskara) in their hands. They were also styled for this reason Ekadaṇḍin. While commenting on the Sūtra, Patañjali in his *Mahābhāṣya*, refers to their fatalistic belief. The Buddhist and Jain texts too ascribe to them a fatalistic creed and say that they held that there is no cause either ultimate or remote, no reward or retribution, no such thing as power or energy and that all 'are bent this way or that by their fate, by the necessary conditions of the class to which they belong, by their individual nature' (Sāmaññaphalasutta, Dialogues of Buddha II, p. 71 where all the references to the principal Buddhist and Jaina texts have been collected).

The Ājīvikas appear to have attained some importance in the time of Aśoka as the latter mentions them side by side with the Buddhists and Nirgranthas and says that his Mahāmātras had been asked to look after their welfare and progress as well (Pillar edict VII). In the 12th year of his reign, Aśoka made gifts of two caves in the Barābar hills to the Ājīvikas. The order seems to have maintained its importance throughout the Maurya period as one of the grandsons of Aśoka, Daśaratha, is also known to have dedicated some caves in the Nāgārjuni hills to the Ājīvika order.

The Ājīvikas, as we have already seen, belonged to the Śramaṇa class. Their order had assumed a distinct shape in later times but they must have inherited many of the Śramaṇa traditions. As such they had among them both Brahmin and non-Brahmin recluses but there is no evidence of their having two different orders, Brahminical and non-Brahmanical.

The Nirgrantha was also a Śramaṇa order closely connected with the Ājīvika. The later Jainism which claims descent from this ancient order has foisted many traditions on it but in spite of them, the ancient Nirgrantha order does not seem to have been a religious movement of any considerable importance in the Nanda-Maurya period. We learn from the Buddhist texts that the founder of the Nirgrantha order was Mahāvīra otherwise known as Nātaputta (Jñātṛkaputra) who was called a Nirgrantha because he belonged to that order of Śramaṇas. The name of the order meant 'those who have destroyed the worldly ties' and also 'those who have given up their clothes.' In the first sense they were pravrajita or the houseless ascetics and in the second sense, the naked ascetics. They were thus the same as the *acelakas* who are often mentioned in the Buddhist texts. In fact a slightly doubtful fragment of the account of Megasthenes, speaks of a sect of philosophers who used to go naked throughout their life and to say that the body had been given by God as a covering of the soul. They abstained from animal food and all food cooked by fire, being content to live on fruits picked up when they had dropped to the ground (Fragm. LIV). These few points of their doctrines have a good deal of similarity with the doctrines ascribed to the Nigaṇṭhas in the Buddhist texts. They believed in the existence of soul and desisted from killing animals and destroying even plants which according to them were endowed with life. They were besides naked ascetics. We may therefore consider the naked ascetics referred to in the account of Megasthenes as identical with the Nirgranthas. Megasthenes, however, calls them Brahmin and not Śramaṇa. This might have been due to their standing near to the Brahmin philosophers in point of purity of conduct and religious beliefs and distinguishing themselves from the peripatetic monks who were also recruited from the lower classes.

Except in the Buddhist texts there are not many references to the Nirgranthas in the contemporary literature. In the seventh pillar edict, Aśoka mentions them along with the Ājīvikas and the Buddhists to state that his Mahāmātras were also occupied with their welfare.

The tradition as embodied in the late Jain books, has, however, a more connected history of the church to present. The Nirgrantha community was confined in the 4th century B. C. to Magadha and the heads of the church were in chronological order Sayambhava, Yaśobhadra, Sambhūtivijaya and Bhadrabāhu. Bhadrabāhu was a contemporary of Chandragupta Maurya and had converted the latter to the Nirgrantha religion. While Bhadrabāhu was the head of the church, a terrible famine broke out in Magadha and it became difficult for the monks to get alms. Bhadrabāhu then decided to leave the country with a part of the community. Accordingly Sthūlabhadra who was the son of Śakaḍāla, the minister of the Nanda king, was appcinted head of the Magadhan community. Bhadrabāhu took a part of the community with him to the South where they settled down at Śravaṇa Beḷgoḷa in Mysore. It is further said that Chandragupta also abdicated the throne at this time and followed his teacher to Śravaṇa Beḷgoḷa where he died of voluntary starvation, as prescribed by the Nirgrantha religion. Sthūlabhadra for fear that the ancient traditions might be lost convoked a council of the monks at Pāṭaliputra in which the sacred literature consisting of the 11 Aṅgas and 14 Pūrvas was recited and fixed. Bhadrabāhu returned to Magadha after twelve years, when the famine had passed away, with a section of his followers. He found that the sacred texts collected in the Council of Pāṭaliputra did not contain the authentic traditions of the church and so he turned them down as spurious. The Magadhan monks had in the meantime begun to put on clothes and this practice was also declared by him as contrary to the original teachings of Mahāvīra. This denunciation however did not lead to an immediate schism in the church. The successor of Sthūlabhadra in the Magadhan church was Mahāgiri. He remained in power till the end of the Maurya period. It was in his time that Samprati, the grandson and successor of Aśoka, became a convert to the Nirgrantha faith and tried to imitate his grandfather in the matter of the propagation of the faith which he professed.

The *Kalpasūtra* (translation, S.B.E. XXII, pp. 288 ff.) gives a list of the Gaṇas and Śākhās that originated in the 4th and 3rd centuries B.C. within the Nirgrantha community. According to it, one of the disciples of Bhadrabāhu, named Godāsa founded the Godāsa-gaṇa which divided itself into four Śākhās namely : Tāmraliptika, Koṭivarṣīya, Puṇḍravardhanīya and Dāsīkharbaṭika. The first three are well known names of places in Bengal. The tradition would thus have us believe that the Nirgrantha religion, in the beginning of the 3rd century B.C., had spread to Bengal to such an extent as to lead to the formation of local subsects. The *Kalpasūtra* further says that Mahāgiri had eight disciples, two of whom, Uttara and Balissaha, founded a Gaṇa named Uttarabalissaha. This Gaṇa also divided itself into four Śākhās namely : Kauśāmbīkā, Sautaptikā, Kauṭumbinī and Candanāgarī.

Another tradition recorded in the *Niryukti* of the *Āvaśyakasūtra* speaks of a certain number of schisms in the Church. The leaders of the schismatic monks are said to have maintained philosophical views different from those taught by Mahāvīra. Three such schisms occurred in the 4th and 3rd centuries B.C. The first of these was led by one Āṣādhasena who, we are told, carried the doctrine of *syādvāda* to an impossible extreme and also maintained that there was no difference between accomplished ascetics and gods. The second was led by Aśvamitra who refused to admit the doctrine of *kṣaṇika*, and the third by Gaṅga who admitted the perception of two sensations simultaneously.

Confirmation of these traditions is however lacking. Two inscriptions of Śravaṇa Beḷgoḷa, of course, refer to Bhadrabāhu and Chandragupta but they belong only to the 10th century A. D. Aśoka does not take any special interest in the religion of his grandfather except ordering his officials to look after them as after the Ājīvikas and other religious communities. It should also be remembered that although Aśoka and his grandson make gifts of cave dwellings to the Ājīvikas they do not do anything of the kind to the Nirgranthas. As to the spread of the Nirgrantha religion to Bengal, the *Divyāvadāna* speaks of their presence in Puṇḍravardhana (North Bengal) in the time of Aśoka but only as parivrājakas and not as members of an organised church. As to the schisms, it may be noted that the established Jaina philosophy does not bear the stamp of the new philosophical doctrines which their leaders are said to have introduced. Besides the doctrine of *kṣaṇika*, which Aśvamitra is said to have opposed, was not a Jaina doctrine but belonged to Buddhism. Under these circumstances it is impossible to accept the traditional story as historical.

It therefore appears that the two religious orders, the Ājīvika and Nirgrantha, were still small local communities of Magadha, not powerful enough to demand that protection from the state which Buddhism enjoyed. The Nirgrantha order was even less important than the Ājīvika but it managed to survive the latter up to later times and to rise into greater importance.

Buddhism

Although originally a Śramaṇa movement, Buddhism had emerged out of it in the 4th century B.C. as a distinct and powerful religion endowed with great potentiality for expansion. But the extent of this expansion before the time of the Emperor Aśoka is still a matter of conjecture. Its activity in pre-Aśokan times seems to have been confined to Kosala and Magadha but small communities of brethren had probably come into existence in the west in Mathurā and Ujjayinī. The traditional account of the second Buddhist council which is said to have taken place 100 years after the Nirvāṇa of Buddha at Vaiśālī, refers to invitations sent to the *pātheyya* monks and to the communities in such distant places as Avanti, Kauśāmbī, Sāṅkāśya and Kanauj. Pātheyya meant the western monks including probably the community of Mathurā. The Aśokan legends attach great importance to the monastery of Naṭabhaṭa on the Urumuṇḍa hill at Mathurā, as Upagupta, the spiritual guide of the Emperor, and Śāṇavāsa, the teacher of Upagupta, both belonged to that institution. The legends at least show that Mathurā had attained some importance in the Buddhist church already before the time of Aśoka.

The most outstanding events in the history of the church in this period were the two councils, the second and the third. The second council was held, according to all traditions, one hundred years after the Nirvāṇa, at Vaiśālī. It is said to have originated on account of some difference in points of monastic discipline. The monks of Vaiśālī had declared as admissible ten new points viz. : 1. storing of salt in a horn, 2. the taking of the midday meal when the sun's shadow shows two finger-breadths after noon, 3. the going to some village and there eating fresh food, 4. residing in the same parish and yet holding the uposatha separately, 5. sanction of a solemn act in an incomplete chapter, 6. (unconditional) following of a precedent, 7. the partaking of unchurned milk, 8. the use of unfermented toddy, 9. the use of a mat without fringes (not conforming with the model prescribed), 10 the acceptance of gold and silver

This action was not however approved by other monks and hence a council was called at Vaiśālī. This council after a long deliberation appointed a committee cf eight elders, four of them hailed from the east and the other four from the west. Among the former was Sabbakāmi, thera of Vaiśālī who, it is said, had received his ordination 120 years earlier and among the latter was Sambhūta Śāṇavāsa of Mathurā who was probably the same as the teacher of Upagupta. The ten points of the monks of Vaiśālī were declared to be against the rules. In a plenary session of the council, the Vinaya was rehearsed. The Bhikṣus who were excommunicated are also said to have convened another meeting which was a great council (Mahāsaṅgīti). Henceforth the followers of the wrong views who were then most probably more numerous came to be known as the Mahāsāṅghika.

So far, the story seems to be generally reliable but the difficulty arises when the question of chronology comes in. The tradition says that the council was held in the time of Aśoka, or Kālāśoka, the son of Śiśunāga. But history does not know of any such king. Attempts have been made to identify Kālāśoka with Kākavarṇa who is mentioned in the Puranic lists as the son of Śiśunāga but the identification is based on unconvincing grounds. The Pāli as well as Sanskrit Buddhist sources say that Aśoka flourished one hundred years after the Nirvāṇa and that until he embraced the Buddhist faith he was living a life of black and sinful deeds. He was then a Caṇḍāśoka or a Kāmāśoka but after his conversion he became a Dharmāśoka. It is this Aśoka then who is contemplated in the traditional account of the second council. Some of the monks who took a leading part in the conference seem to have been contemporaneous with the Maurya emperor whereas others belonged to one generation earlier.

Although the story of the second council in its present form is a garbled version and does not give a faithful picture of the event, it, however, seems that it had a historical basis. A Vinaya council had certainly been held at Vaiśālī and its session might have been necessitated by the arbitrary conduct of the local monks, but the time when it was held cannot be fixed with any amount of certainty. It is not impossible that it was held during the earlier part of the reign of Aśoka. This council led to the first schism in the church and the foundation of the Mahāsāṅghika school.

The account of the third council which was held at Pāṭaliputra is still more confused. It was not a general council but a party meeting of the Elders—the Theravādins. The Ceylonese tradition says that it was held 18 years after the coronation of Aśoka but there is no confirmation of this fact in the edicts of the emperor. As it was a meeting of the Theravādins, the Mahāsāṅghikas were excluded from it. The Ceylonese account of the council runs as follows :

'When 236 years had elapsed after Nirvāṇa, sixty thousand monks dwelt in the Aśokārāma. Sectarians of different descriptions, all of them wearing the kaṣāya, ruined the Doctrine of the Jina. It was then that Tissa Moggaliputta convoked a council, attended by 1000 monks. Having destroyed the false doctrines and subdued many shameless people, he restored the true faith, and propounded the Abhidhamma treatise *Kathāvatthu*. It was from him that Mahendra, the future apostle of Buddha, learnt the 5 nikāyas, the 7 books of the Abhidhamma and the whole Vinaya.'

The account, as may be seen, has a pronounced sectarian tendency and tries to prove the originality and superiority of the Theravāda or the Vibhajyavāda school. This clearly shows that it was a party meeting of which the historicity may not be disputed, but the story of the compilation of the *Kathāvatthu*, which again presupposes the existence of the entire Pāli canon consisting of the Vinaya, the 5 nikāyas and six other Abhidhamma works must be made an exception.

The history of the Buddhist church in this period was not in all appearance an undistrubed one. The church was gradually losing its unity on account of its expansion and for want of regular communication between the various distant communities. Local influences were slowly affecting their conduct and shaping them in different ways. These tendencies ultimately gave rise to different Buddhist schools. The community of Vaiśālī, as we have already seen, formed itself into a school either before the time of Aśoka or in a period when Aśoka had not yet taken up the cause of Buddhism. Under Aśoka's patronage, the Buddhist community of Pāṭaliputra, which pretended to be more loyal to the teachings of Buddha, reorganised itself and tried to check the schismatic tendency in the church . It is probably under their influence that Aśoka advised his officials to see that nobody might destroy the unity of the Saṅgha. The Sārnāth Pillar edict contains the following order of the emperor to his officers at Pāṭaliputra :

'. . . .the Saṅgha cannot be divided by any one. But indeed the monk or nun who shall break up the Saṅgha should be caused to put on white robes and to reside in non-residence.'

The same instruction was also issued by the emperor to the Mahāmātras of Kauśāmbī. In the Sāñchī version of the edict, the instruction is given in a slightly different form : 'The Saṅgha of both monks and nuns is made united as long as (my) sons and great-grandsons (shall reign) and as long as the moon and the sun (shall shine).'

The compelling of a monk or a nun to put on white robes and to reside in non-residence meant expulsion from the community, a punishment prescribed in the Vinayas for the offence of Saṅghabheda. Aśoka certainly did not issue the edict to give publicity to the already existing Vinaya rule concerning Saṅghabheda. The church must have shown serious symptoms of disintegration and this was a special measure to safeguard its unity. The tradition confirms that Aśoka's fears were justified. It is said that during the third century of the Nirvāṇa, a number of schools such as Sarvāstivāda, Mahiśāsaka, Dharmaguptaka etc. made their appearance within the orthodox section of the church (Theravāda). The Mahāsāṅghika school which had long separated from it was also split up into a number of schools.

The greatest event in the history of Buddhism in this period was the conversion of Aśoka. The legendary accounts, although marred by many exaggerated claims of the community, enable us to give a connected picture of Aśoka as a Buddhist. The traditions are confirmed by the inscriptions and both have been reviewed in the account of the reign of Aśoka given above.

Aśoka's patronage must have contributed to the spread of Buddhism not only within the empire but also to distant lands even in his lifetime. We learn from the edicts that he himself had given a lead in this direction. Throughout his empire he had circulated instructions on the Dhamma, and caused them to be inscribed on rocks and pillars overlooking the highroads so that they could attract the notice of his subjects. We have seen that he had specially advised his officials to afford facilities to his subjects and to encourage them so that they might follow the Dhamma. When he says that he had achieved the conquest by law (dhamma-vijaya) both within his empire and outside, he probably means that he had entrusted his officers with this mission within his own empire and deputed missionaries to the foreign countries.

The credit of the initiative in this direction is attributed by the Ceyloness chronicles to Tissa Moggaliputta. In the inscriptions Aśoka speaks of the missions as his own. To whomsoever the initiative might have been due, either to Tissa Moggaliputta, as the tradition claims, or to Aśoka himself under the inspiration of the Saṅgha, it is quite conceivable that after the reorganisation of the Magadhan church in the third council and with the co-operation of the emperor himself, efforts were made to carry Buddhism to distant countries. The success of the first missionary activity might not have been very large so far as the foreign countries were concerned but within the Maurya empire they must have been crowned with immense success. The epigraphic records and Buddhist monuments of the post-Aśokan times bear clear testimony to it.

Theistic Movements

The rise of some of the new theistic movements which later on became the religion of the people may be placed in this period. The absence of any noteworthy references to such movements in the early Buddhist texts probably shows that they were far from being established religions in this age. The Brahmanism represented in the texts was a Vedic cult. Hence it seems probable that the theistic movements were started only when Buddhism had become an established religion of the country. Buddhism was on the way to becoming a religion of Bhakti. Buddha had been made the object of profound devotion and his relics and symbols had begun to be worshipped. In this form the Buddhist faith had a direct appeal to the common people who had so long been only the uninterested spectators of the occasional sacrifices performed by the nobles and the unwilling workers for them.

The first trace of the existence of such a movement is found in the grammar of Pāṇini. In his Sūtra iv. 3. 98 Pāṇini states that 'The affix *vun* is affixed to the name of Vāsudeva and Arjuna in the sense of the worshipful one' (*Vāsudevārjunābhyāṁ vun*). Thus the derivative forms, Vāsudevaka and Ārjunaka mean respectively : 'the devotee of Vāsudeva' and 'the devotee of Arjuna'. While commenting on this aphorism Patañjali points out that in this case the names are probably not to be taken as the names of the Kshatriya heroes but as the designation of the *tatrabhavat*—'the adorable one.'

It is therefore almost certain that the cult of Vāsudeva and Arjuna were current at least in the Punjab in the age of Pāṇini. It is now recognised that Pāṇini was acquainted with the Mahābhārata story, as he refers not only to the heroes depicted in the story but also to the epic itself. This epic was the Pāṇḍu story. The two heroes, Vāsudeva and Arjuna, must have been deified in it.

Vāsudeva or Kṛishṇa is mentioned by the Greek writers under the name Heracles. Megasthenes (Frag. XLI) tells us : 'Heracles was worshipped by the inhabitants of the plains, especially by the Sourasenai, an Indian tribe possessed of two cities, Methora (Mathurā) and Kleisobora (Krishṇapura ?) and who had a large navigable river, the Jobares (Jumna) flowing through their territories.' Curtius informs us that 'an image of Heracles was carried in front of the army of Porus as he advanced against Alexander.'

The epigraphic records of the second century B.C. amply confirm that the cult of Vāsudeva was being widely followed not only by the people of the country but also by some foreign settlers. The famous Besnagar inscription records that Heliodorus, the ambassador of a Greek king named Antialcidas, was raising a Garuḍa pillar at Vidiśā in honour of Vāsudeva, 'the god of gods'. Almost in the same period and in the same place, another devotee of Vāsudeva named Gautamīputra erected a Garuḍa column in front of the temple of the Bhagvat. The Ghasundi inscription speaks of a *pūjā* stone wall for the worship of Bhagavat Saṁkarṣana and Vāsudeva. Saṁkarṣana and Vāsudeva are also mentioned in the Nānāghāt cave inscription among the objects of adoration.

It is therefore permissible to think that the cult of Vāsudeva must have originated at least a century earlier in order to enable its followers to carry the faith to distant parts of the country. Vāsudeva was no longer a hero-god like Arjuna, as he seems to have been in the time of Pāṇini, but the greatest god, the god of gods, as Heliodorus would have us believe. This evolution in the conception of the god must have taken a fairly long time.

As to the cult of Saṁkarṣana, it is difficult to say whether it had originated in the earlier period along with the cult of Vāsudeva. Saṁkarṣana was the elder brother of Vāsudeva and a member of the Vṛshṇi race. But he does not play the same important role in the Great Epic as his younger brother. He appears as a hero, endowed with great power which he seldom exercises, his sole concern being wine. In the *Arthaśāstra* there is mention of the votaries of Saṁkarṣaṇa. It is said : 'Spies disguised as ascetics with shaved head or braided hair and pretending to be worshippers of god Saṁkarṣaṇa, may mix their sacrificial beverage with the juice of *madana* plant (and give to the cowherds) and carry off the cattle' (translation, p. 485). This might arouse a suspicion that the cult of Saṁkarṣaṇa was in vogue among the cowherds or the Ābhīras but the inscriptions of the second century B.C. already referred to do not allow any such suspicion as Saṁkarṣana is ranked there with Vāsudeva and is an object of adoration even with the higher classes.

The contemporary Greek writers speak of a god named Dionysus along with Heracles. Megasthenes tells us that the Oxydrakai claimed descent from Dionysus, 'because the vine grew in their country, and their processions were conducted with great pomp, and their kings on going forth to war and on other occasions marched in Bacchic fashion with drums beating' (Frag, XLVI). Megasthenes also informs us that the worshippers of Dionysus lived on mountains and observed certain customs which were Bacchanalian. They dressed in muslin, wore turbans, used perfumes and arrayed themselves in garments dyed of bright colours (Frag. XLI). The cult of Dionysus with its Bacchanalian features reminds us of the cult of Saṁkarṣaṇa.

Aśoka refers to *pāshaṁḍas* in the sense of religious sects. They include the Brāhmaṇas, Śramaṇas as well as other sects but it is not clear if they included the followers of these new cults as well. In the ninth Rock edict, Aśoka speaks of the various *maṁgalas* or auspicious rites performed by the people in sickness, marriage, birth of offspring and at the time of undertaking a journey. These *maṁgalas* were evidently domestic rites and no religious cults are meant by them. Aśoka, we have seen, had introduced certain edifying shows for the instruction of the people in the Buddhist law. It is probable that similar other shows for the edification of the non-Buddhist popular cults were also known in the country. We have already discussed the reference made by Curtius to the image of Heracles being carried in the front of the army of Porus. A curious passage of the *Mahābhāṣya* of Patañjali mentions the images of gods (*arccā*) set up by the Mauryas to obtain gold. All this shows that images of gods and their cults were known in the country in the Maurya period but on a very limited scale and among the common people. They were still looked down on by the aristocratic followers of the Vedic cult.

CHAPTER XI

LANGUAGE AND LITERATURE

LANGUAGE

By 600 B.C., a little before Buddha, the Aryan speech would appear to have spread from Gandhāra to Videha and Campā in Eastern India, and to have been the common language of Indian Aryandom of the times that embraced the Mahājanapadas. The hill and forest tracts of Central India just to the south of the tracts watered by the Ganges were unquestionably Austric and Dravidian in speech ; also Bengal and Assam and Orissa ; and within the Ar yandom of the upper Gangetic area and the Punjab, particularly within the former, there were still large areas, or small pockets, of non-aryan speech which were fast becoming smaller and smaller. In the Jātakas for instance, we read of Caṇḍāla villages where they spoke the the Caṇḍāla speech, and we are told of an incident in which a Caṇḍāla masquerading as a Brahmin was discovered when he unconsciously cried out *giligili* in the Caṇḍāla language when he put some very hot rice-milk within his mouth in a Brahman feast which he had joined.

For the linguistic situation in India during the Nanda and Mauryan periods, we have literary evidence only for the Nanda period, and both literary and epigraphical for the Mauryan period. The Brāhmaṇas, Āraṇyakas and Upanishads, the dates of which cannot be satisfactorily determined, cover at least 600 years, from 800 B.C. to 200 B C. ; and the Buddhist and Jaina canonical literatures also, in their substance, refer to the period immediately before the Nandas ; and conditions during the Nanda age not being very different from those obtaining a few centuries earlier, the evidence from the Brāhmaṇas and other works mentioned above can be regarded as equally applicable to it. The Brahmanical Sūtras, Yāska, Pāṇini, Kātyāyana, Patañjali, Kauṭilya, Vātsyāyana, probably Bharata, and above all, the *Mahābhārata* and the *Rāmāyaṇa*—all these belong either wholly or partly (as in the case of the two epics) to the Nanda and Mauryan periods. On the epigraphic side, we have to take note of the earliest Brāhmī inscriptions which are few and very small, and Brāhmī legends on the early coins and seals, some of which may be pre-Maurya ; and the inscriptions of Aśoka and his successors. Post-Maurya inscriptions for a couple of centuries after the extinction of the Maurya dynasty also have some value for these periods.

The Aryan speech during the Nanda and Maurya periods would appear to have been current, in its various local or dialectal forms, as the language of the land, from the Punjab to the eastern boundary of Bihar, which thus became the true home of the Aryan speech in India, the land of the great Aryan states : and from this area, where Brahmanism was developing as the result of a synthesis of the worlds of the Aryan and the non-Aryan, the Aryan speech was spreading south, mainly along the west, through Rajputana and Malwa and Sindh ; and it had already been established in Gujarat ; and colonies of Aryan speakers would seem to have been formed in what is now northern Mahārāshṭra, as far down as the Godāvarī. The belt of forest land in the east, corresponding to present day Eastern Madhya Pradesh and Chota Nagpur, harboured rather backward groups of Non-Aryan tribes, the ancestors of the present day Kol (Munda) peoples and of Dravidian tribes like the Gonds, the Oraons and the Maler, and effectively checked, though only for a time, the penetration of the Aryan language into these tracts. Although the conquest of Kalinga (corresponding to Orissa of the present day) by Aśoka in the third century B.C. opened up this area to the Aryan language, it was some time before the latter could establish itself in Eastern India—in Bengal proper, and then (by a double current from Bengal and from Kosala or Eastern U. P. through Mahākosala or Eastern Madhya Pradesh) into Orissa. The main line of North Indian Aryan linguistic expansion into South India thus from the second half of the first millennium B.C. has always been along the west—from the Midland through Rajputana and Malwa ; and subsequently North Indian Muslim expansion into the Deccan carrying with it the Hindi speech followed the same route, in both pre-Mogul and Mogul times.

From the Brāhmaṇas we find that probably a century or two before Buddha, North Indian Aryandom included the following ten states—Gandhāra, Kekaya, Madra, Uśīnara, Matsya, Kuru, Pañcāla, Kāśi, Kosala and Videha. These included practically the entire Aryan-speaking world of say 700 B.C., and these states fell under three groups—*Udīcya* or Northern (including Gandhāra or the northern part of the present N. W. Frontier province and probably also the continuous parts of Eastern Afghanistan, Kekaya or North-Western Punjab east of the Gandhāra country including part of the Sind Sagar Doab, and the Jeep and Rechna Doabs and Madra in two groups—the Uttara or Northern Madras probably in Kashmir and the Dakshiṇa or Southern Madras in North Central Punjab consisting of part of the Rechna and Bari Doabs), *Madhyadeśīya* or the Midland (comprising Uśīnara in the west and north, corresponding to N. E. Punjab and N. W. Uttar Pradesh, Matsya or N. E. Rajputana, and Kuru and Pañcāla or Western U. P.) and *Prācya* or the Eastern (Kosala or Oudh, Kāśī or Eastern U. P., and Videha or Northern Bihar). Other States within this Aryan tract also came to be established quickly enough, Śālva, connected with Matsya, and Magadha and Anga in Bihar to the South of the Ganges. It would appear that the division of Aryan India into these three tracts, *Udīcya*, *Madhyadeśa* and *Prācya*, had some basis in dialectal differences. They correspond roughly to the three-fold division of the Indus valley and the upper Gangetic valley which is still prevalent—*Punjab*, *Pachāhā*, and *Pūrab*, corresponding roughly to the Hindki or Lahnda or Western Punjabi and Eastern Punjabi tracts, to the Western Hindi area, and to the tract of the country in the east where Kosali or Eastern Hindi and the Bihari speeches are spoken. Northern, or North-Western, Midland or Central, and Eastern—these formed the three dialect areas of the Aryan tract by 500 B. C., and to these three we shall have probably to add a fourth—the *Dākshiṇātya* or Southern, which at this ancient period was probably not much different from the dialect area of the Midland from where the Aryan language was spreading through Rajputana and Malwa into Gujarat and the trans-Vindhyan tracts.

About the speech of the Udīcya tract, the popular opinion in the Midland in the age of Brāhmaṇas has been thus expressed in the ***Kaushītakī Brāhmaṇa*** (vii 6): ***tasmād udīcyām prajñā-***

tatarā vag udyate : *udañcau eva yanti vācam śikshitum* ; *yo vā tata āgacchati, tasya vā śuśrūshante* 'therefore speech is uttered in the North with mere discernment ; they go to the northern lands to learn speech ; and people like to listen to him who comes from there.' Thus the people of the other tracts acknowledged the Aryan language as spoken in the north-west as being the best and purest form of it. About Prācya or the east some stray and rather obscure references in the Brāhmaṇas would suggest that the Aryan speech was becoming altered or debased there : it was the land inhabited by the Vrātyas, who did not follow the Vedic religion—they were *adīkshitas* or uninitiated people, but spoke the language of those who were *dīkshitas* or followers of Vedic rites and customs, and at the same time declared words or sentences not articulated with difficulty as being articulated with difficulty (*a-durukta-vākyam duruktam āhuḥ, a-dīkshitā dīkshita-vācam vadanti*). This statement about the speech of the Vrātyas of the East would appear to suggest the presence already of Middle Indo-Aryan or Prākṛitic habits of speech, which found the characteristic consonant combinations of the old Aryan speech difficult, and brought in consonant assimilation and cerebralisation on a large scale. In the Brāhmaṇas there is no hint about a Dākshiṇātya or southern land as being largely inhabited by Aryan speakers, and nothing about any dialectal or linguistic speciality there.

The assumption is quite allowable that by the time of the Buddha, the spoken Aryan language had deviated considerably from the Old Indo-Aryan norm as presented by the speech of the Rigveda, and had developed at least three distinct dialects—a Northern or North-Western, a Central, and an Eastern. This last was already fairly in the Middle Indo-Aryan or Prākṛit stage ; but the North-Western was conservative, and was regarded as the purest form of the Aryan speech, the well of Aryan undefiled—and it was exceedingly likely that in the Udīcya as the *nidus* of the Aryan people in India there was the largest settled Aryan population, and consequently the language was better preserved ; the more Aryan speakers were penetrating further into the East, among masses of non-Aryans, the more they were getting to be smaller in numbers compared with the surrounding non-Aryans, and the Aryan language, in a non-Aryan environment that was growing stronger and stronger, was susceptible to a more rapid change and to change along new lines than in the North-west.

Epigraphical records of the 4th-3rd centuries B.C. bear out the occurrence of the situation as deduced from literary references—only some new developments had in the meanwhile taken place. The oldest Brāhmī inscriptions including of course those of Aśoka give us a sufficiently clear idea as to the linguistic conditions for Aryan India ; Aśoka's inscriptions, giving the same texts in as many as three distinct local dialects have been aptly described as the first 'Linguistic Survey of India'. In the Aśokan documents, we have : (i) a Prākṛit or Aryan speech of the North-West, as in the edicts at Mansehra and Shahbazgarhi. This is based on the Udīcya dialect of the earlier period, and its phonetics even in the 3rd century B.C. shows that it had deviated the least from the Old Indo-Aryan norm, and it thus bears out the encomium of the earlier author of the Brāhmaṇas that speech here was *prajñāta-tarā*, more discerning. Northern and North-Western Punjab thus showed a great deal of conservatism in its language, even as late as the 3rd century B.C. We may even say that it was still in the Old Aryan stage (at least in its phonetics, retaining as it did a good many conjunct consonants, and the three sibilants *ś*, *ṣ*, *s*), while the speech of the East had deviated most. (ii) There is a Prākṛit of the East, found in Eastern inscriptions of Aśoka and elsewhere. This form of Indo-Aryan speech has deviated exceedingly from Old Indo-Aryan norm, and besides it shows phonetic peculiarities (e.g. use of only *l* and no *r*) and some forms (e.g. *-e* from *-aḥ* rather than *-o* in the case of masculine nouns ending in *-a*) which are not found in the other dialectal areas. It is exceedingly likely that this Prākṛit of the East was the language of Aśoka's court at Pāṭaliputra, and the edicts of Aśoka were first written at Pāṭaliputra in this dialect, and sent to the provinces for publication by being engraved on stone at prominent places. Where the local dialect differed so appreciably from this court speech as to make the latter not easy to follow locally, as for example in the North-West (Mansehra and

Shahbazgarhi) and in the South-West (Girnār), the edicts were rendered in the local dialect ; but this rendering was not very careful, but rather haphazard as a good many forms and expressions from the court dialect were allowed to find a place in the versions in the North-western and South-western dialects. Where the local dialect did not differ so much as to make the Prācya court dialect unintelligible, it would appear that the latter was employed, as much as in the home districts in Eastern India. Thus in Rajputana, in Western U. P., in North-western U. P. (Kalsi), and in Central U. P. (Allahabad), the Eastern dialect is employed as much as in Eastern U. P., Benares (Sarnath) and Bihar (Lauriya, Rummindei, Barabar caves). A few special characteristics may occasionally be noted, e.g., at Kalsi ; the exact reason for this is not known. It would appear that the use of Eastern Prākṛit, the Court dialect of Bihar and Benares, was like that of the use of Hindi (a form of Western Hindi of Western U. P.) in Eastern U. P. and Bihar. Generally it has been the language of the Midland that has prevailed in the East, but in the Aśoka inscriptions, owing to the political importance of Magadha as the home province of the empire, for the first and last time we have an Eastern speech established as the official language in the Midland.

In tracts far away from Arya-land, where Dravidian and also probably Kol (Munda) languages were spoken, the edicts were published in this Eastern official speech, e.g. at Dhauli and Jaugaḍa in the Kalinga country, which was both Dravidian (old Telugu, old Kannada) and Kol in speech, and at Siddhapur, Maski and Yeṛṛaguḍi where the language was equally Dravidian (Old Kannada).

This Eastern speech was unquestionably the same for the upper classes in Kosala, Kāśī, Videha and Magadha ; it was the language of the Buddha, who called himself a Kshatriya of Kosala (Kosala Khaṭṭiya), and of Mahāvīra also ; it was the language of Aśoka and also of Chandragupta and the Nandas. The oldest Buddhist canon, as Sylvain Lévi and Heinrich Lüders amply demonstrated, was composed in this Eastern Prākṛit, and not in Pāli. The Pāli canon appears not yet to have been known—at least, sufficiently known, in Magadha. Aśoka, when he quoted from the Buddhist texts, quotes from a version in this Eastern dialect, and not from the Pāli.

Epigraphical evidence from the 4th century B.C. shows that in Magadha had appeared a local form of this Eastern Prākṛit which deviated in two of its sounds from what may be called the standard Prācya or Eastern Prākṛit ; it had palatal *ś* for the dental *s* of the latter (<*ś*, *sh*, *s* of old Indo-Aryan), and probably it had developed a palatalised *ky* from *k* after a palatal vowel. This specialised Magadhan form of Prācya was in all likelihood current among the masses of the people, of less exalted ranks, and the *ś* pronounciation was evidently looked upon as something vulgar and uneducated, judging from the fact than in later times in the Sanskrit drama the *ś* dialect was relegated to the least exalted characters.

(iii) The third dialect of Aśoka is that of the South-west as in Surāshṭra or peninsular Gujarat (Girnār). This is well-established there, and if the Gujarat speech of the 3rd century B.C. is derived from that of the Midland, then in Aśoka's Girnār edict we can see a form of the Midland speech, slightly modified perhaps from the genuine Midland dialect of the Mathurā area, given a recognition far away from its own home district—for, as we have just seen, in the Midland proper the Eastern official language was used in inscriptions.

This roughly is the situation for the spoken dialects of Aryan India during the Nanda and Maurya periods. Aśoka employed them in his inscriptions as already the Eastern speech appears to have attained a certain literary position through the Buddhist and Jaina canons being redacted in it ; and the use of the North-Western and South-Western speeches was just a concession to two distant and important dialects the speakers of which would find difficulty in following the Pāṭaliputra court speech. We know that the Greeks when they first came to India were confined to the area of the Udīcya or North-Western dialect, a dialect which Aśoka's officials employed in the inscriptions at Mansehra and Shahbazgarhi. That this North-Western dialect retained some archaic or old Indo-Aryan characters is borne out not only by the evidence from the Brāhmaṇas and from the inscriptions of Aśoka, but also from the Greek transcriptions of Indian names heard from speakers of this dialect. Thus names like Sandrakottos, Sandraphagos, Prasioi, Eronnaboas, Brachmanes, Ottorakorrhas, Amitrokhatés or Amitrokhadés and Palibothra are Greek renderings of *Chandrakupta (a genuine North-Western form for Candragupta, with *-k-* for *-g-* characterising the Darada or Piśāca Prākṛit of the North-West), Candrabhāgā, Prācya, Hiraṇyavāha, Brāhmaṇa, Uttarakuru, Amitraghāta and *Pāllibutra for *Pad'liputra = Pāṭaliputra as heard in the north-west, where, as partially indicated by the Mansehra and Shahbazgarhi and later North-western inscriptions, groups like *pr*, *tr*, *kr*, *br*, *dr*, *gr*, did not assimilate the *r*.

The relationship between the Aśokan dialects and the later forms of Indo-Aryan can be tentatively indicated as follows :

1. The North-Western dialect—from this originated Hindi, Lahnda, or Western Punjabi, Eastern Punjabi (the latter strongly influenced by the Midlands peech) and Sindhi. This N. W. dialect was taken by Indian settlers to Chinese Turkistan where it was in use for some centuries as an official speech, in the southern part of the country.

2. The Midland dialect : Not represented in the Aśoka inscriptions, but the Girnār dialect is probably a form of Midland. From this originated the Western Hindi dialect (partially influenced by the North-Western dialect), and Rajasthāni-Gujarāti.

We do not know anything about an Aryan speech being current in the Deccan, but evidently from Mālava and Gujarat and Varad (h)ā-taṭa (Varhāḍ or Berar) Aryan dialects, mostly from the Śauraseni area, were spreading into Mahārāshṭra.

3. The Eastern dialect. The standard form of it, at first current all over Eastern U. P. (Oudh etc.) and Bihar, differentiated into Eastern Prācya (Māgadhi) and Western Prācya (Ardha-Māgadhi). The latter came strongly under Midland influence, and became finally transformed into the Kosali or Eastern Hindi dialects (Awadhi, Bagheli, Chattisgarhi). The former, Māgadhi, spread into Bengal and Assam and Orissa, and it is the source of Bhojpuri, Magahi-Maithili, Bengali-Assamese and Oriya.

There is no evidence from the Nanda and Maurya documents about the spread of the Aryan tongue into the Himalayan regions. Probably the Dardic speaking Aryans (Khasas and other tribes) were penetrating into the Central Himalayan areas (the present

Western Pahari and Eastern Pahari regions), and their Dardic Khasa speech was later overlaid by Indo-Aryan from the Midland.

As for literary Indo-Aryan of the Nanda and Maurya periods we have to reckon first with classical Sanskrit, which became fully established as the language of Brahmanism and Brahman organisation before the Nanda regime. It was at first confined to the Brahman schools, and as a language, in the 5th century B. C. when Pāṇini flourished in the Udīcya *region*, it was sufficiently near to the spoken dialect of Pāṇini's home districts as to merit from him the name Laukika i.e. 'popular or current' as differentiated from the elder Vedic dialect which he called Chāndasa or Chandas i.e., 'poetic speech' which was tantamount to 'archaic speech'. Classical Sanskrit was not the creation of the Udīcya people only ; just as the modern literary forms of the Hindi or Hindustani language of Delhi, viz. High Hindi and Urdu, are the creation not only of High Hindi and Urdu writers of Delhi and Agra and Meerut, but also of Lahore and Lucknow and Haidarabad and Mathurā and Allahabad and Benares. The *śishṭas* or learned men, i.e. Brahmans, in the Midland, in the Prācya, and also in the Dākshiṇātya, also helped to build it up ; and it came to be closely connected with the Midland as here the Brahman synthesis of Aryan and non-Aryan cultures into Hindu culture and religion seems to have started. Because of its archaic character and the clarity of its forms, it obtained the homage of the Buddhists and the Jains as well, just from the end of the Maurya period.

The Eastern Prākṛit became an important vehicle of religious culture when the message of Buddha and Mahāvīra was delivered in it in the 6th-5th centuries B.C. and although it was a very much advanced or degenerate speech from Old Indo-Aryan standards, it obtained some pre-eminence in the Nanda Maurya periods both as the language of the Buddhist and Jaina faiths and official language of the court or of the empire. But this pre-eminence seems to have died out with the passing away of the Mauryan empire.

Pāli as a literary language associated with the Theravāda school of Hīnayāna Buddhism appears not to have been prominent during the Nanda and Maurya periods, if it had come into existence at all. Buddha gave a great charter to all the languages of mankind when he declared that people were to study his message in their own languages : and we may presume that as a result of this great pronouncement, translations into different dialects were encouraged. There is evidence that the teachings of Buddha were first written in the Eastern Prākṛit. But this form of Aryan speech, in spite of its being the official language of the empire was not a central dialect, but belonged to the easternmost extremity of the empire, and it was most deviated from the norm of the rest of Aryandom. As such it was not much intelligible to the rest of India. The Midland forming the real heart of Āryāvarta, had a dialect which could be understood by the Udīcya people, as well as by the Prācyas and the Dākshiṇātyas. It was the precursor of the Śaurasenī apabrahmśa of late medieaval times (c. 600-1200 A.D.) and of Brajbhākhā (c. 1500-1700) and the Khariboli Hindi or Hindustani of the present day. Buddha's discourses were rendered into the Midland dialect, as current in Mathurā (and extended from Mathurā into Ujjain and Malwa) : after the death of the master, some of his disciples who were from Mathurā had a hand in redacting the canon—at least one version of it ; just as they were rendered into the North-western Prākṛit, as fragments in this dialect recovered from Central Asia show. The same process was repeated in later times : Kabir (15th century A.D.) spoke and composed in the Bhojpuri dialect current in his native city of Benares, and yet his writings are found in a mixed variety of Western Hindi, Brajbhākhā and Khariboli of Delhi with plenty of Awadhi (Eastern Hindi) forms and a few Bhojpuri forms occurring as palimpsests. Mahendra, the son of Aśoka born and brought up in his mother's city of Ujjain, according to the Ceylonese tradition, took the Pāli canon to Ceylon. It is likely that Mahendra studied his Buddhist texts not in the Eastern version as his father evidently did, but in the Midland one (which was Pāli) as it was current in Ujjain.

Pāli does not at all agree with the Māgadhi and Ardha-Māgadhi dialects, later variants of the Prācya speech—it agrees rather with Śauraseni, which is the Midland speech as we find it in its later Prākrit form. Pāli can only be looked upon linguistically as a literary form of the Midland speech as it was current in the centuries immediately before Christ. The Midland speech in its literary form thus was taken to Ceylon by Mahendra from Ujjain via Pāṭaliputra and Tāmralipti and from there brought back again into North India with the Theravāda doctrine by Buddhaghosha. In the meanwhile, it was coming into prominence from about the time of Christ, as an important and the best cultured form of a Middle Indo-Aryan speech, as Śauraseni Prākṛit, the earliest use of which we find in the drama fragment from Aśvaghosha discovered in Central Asia, and possibly also in Śūdraka's *Mṛicchakaṭikā* , a Prākṛit which Bharata noted some time during the early centuries after Christ and which Rājaśekhara lauded as the most elegant form of speech in the 8th century A.D.

The Aryan speech was taken out of India by Indian missionaries or military adventurers who went out of India during the time of the Nandas and Mauryas. In Sin-Kiang, the city of Khotan (*Ku-stana* in Sanskrit) was colonised by Indians from Taxila in the 3rd century B.C., and the Indian community in the Khotan territory became quite numerous and strong, and although they lost their separate existence among the surrounding Iranian and Tibeto-Burmese speaking peoples, the Indian North-Western Prākṛit taken by them continued to be used (in a form much influenced by the local languages) as an official language in all state documents. Indian troops were found in the armies of the Achaemenian emperors and in Xerxes' army there were Indian troops. At the battle of Gaugamela or Arbela where Alexander finally overthrew Darius, the last Achaemenian emperor, Indian troops fought very stubbornly. The Indians came in touch with the Greeks through the Persian empire, and this must have taken place by 500 B.C., when the old form of the word *Iones* (Ionians, the Greeks of Asia Minor who came to be best known in the East) viz., *Iawones* or *Iavones* came to India as *Yavana*. Indian elephants with Indian *mahouts* were in the army of Pyrrhus when he fought the Romans in the 3rd century B.C. and in the Carthagenian army led by Hasdrubal and Hannibal in Italy, Indian elephant drivers also came into prominence. Indian philosophers and learned men, and later Buddhist missionaries sent by Aśoka, found their way into Greece, and we have mention in Greek records of at least one Indian philosopher who came to Athens and with whom Socrates had a conversation (before 400 B.C.). There was a good deal of intellectual and cultural intermixture both through the Achaemenian empire and the Greek empire of Alexander and his successors, and the Indian languages (including the newly formed literary speech, classical Sanskrit) came to acquire a number of Iranian (Persian) and Greek words (e.g. *mudrā*, *dipi* or *lipi*, *nipista*. 'written', *asavāri*, *kshatrapa*, *kārshā* in *kārshā paṇa*, *tashta-tast*, *pusta* etc., and *dramma* from Greek *drakhmé*, *suranga* from *surinks* or *syrinx*, *samidā* from *semidalis*, *khalīna*, and astronomical terms which came in later). The languages of the West, Greek specially, similarly obtained a number of Indian words. Connection with China though commerce may have commenced from the 4th century B.C. by way of Assam and South-West China (Yun-nan), and probably before Christ a few Chinese words came to be admitted into Indian languages (e. g. the name *Chīna*—China, *kīchaka*—'a kind of bamboo', *musāra*—'a kind of precious stone'.) There were persons in India speaking Iranian dialects and Greek, and the Persian official language as in the cuneiform inscriptions appears to have exerted some influence on the style of the inscriptions of Aśoka. The presence of different languages side by side in India, Indo-Aryan, Dravidian, Austric and the foreign Persian and Greek, gave rise to what I have called 'Translation compounds' in Indo-Aryan, in which words of same or similar meaning from two languages are combined to give a single word in Indo-Aryan (e.g. Iranian *Karṣa* 'a monetary unit' and Indo-Aryan *paṇa* of non-Aryan Austric origin-'computation on the basis of four' gave *kārshāpaṇa* in Sanskrit, *kahāpaṇa* in Pāli, meaning 'a coin'; Austric *sāta*, *sāda*>*śāli* 'horse' and non-Aryan of unknown origin **ghutra*, **hotra* whence we have *ghoṭa* 'horse' gave Sanskrit *śāli-hōtra* 'horse' etc.)

The *rapprochement* between the Indo-Aryan and the Dravidian and Austric speeches was going on intensely during this period when the fusion of the diverse elements of the population into a common Hindu people under the intellectual domination of the Brahmans was in full swing. The Aryan language was being transformed from its purer Indo-European character into something different under the impact on Non-Aryan, through a larger and larger number of non-Aryan speakers turning into speakers of Indo-Aryan. In Middle Indo-Aryan, the Old Indo-Aryan accent had changed from a free pitch to a fixed stress. Vowel length became dependent more on speech rhythm than on etymology, a tendency towards an open rather than closed pronunciation of syllables became established (this led to widespread assimilation of conjunct consonants 'ushering in the Middle Indo-Aryan stage e.g. *dhar-ma*, *sah-ya*, *bhak-ta*, of earlier Old Indo-Aryan became *dha-rma*, *sa-hya*, *bha-kta*, etc. which were soon assimilated to *dhamma*, *sajjha*, *bhatta*), and there was an increase in the cerebralisation of *t*, *th*, *d*, *dh*, *n*, to *ṭ*, *ṭh*, *ḍ*, *ḍh*, *ṇ* and of *l* to *ḷ* ; also the voicing of the intervocal unvoiced stops and aspirates started by which *loka* became *loga*, *atavī* became *aḍavi* and *aḷavī* etc., and in morphology we note a tendency towards reducing all declensions and conjugations of Old Indo-Aryan to a single type, and the commencement of the use of post-positional help words after case inflexions of the noun ; besides, the inflected tenses and moods of the verb were reduced, and there was a larger use of participial adjectives, present, past and future, to express the time idea of the finite verb ; further, the conjunctive participle or gerund in the *-tvā* (*-tvī*) and *-ya* became an exceedingly popular form. The vocabulary changed its character : a great many Old Aryans words were dropped, and their places were taken either by new Indo-Aryan formations, or by borrowings from the non-Aryan languages which entered the Aryan language through the back-door (i.e. without scholars admitting that they were non-Aryan words) and by the score. The entire spirit of Indo-Aryan was during the second half of the first millennium B. C. being changed fundamentally, and Aryan was more and more approximating the spirit of Dravidian and Kol (Austric).

Probably a good deal of the masses, in the Northern Indian plains, particularly among the lower classes, were bilingual, but the fast disappearing non-Aryan was not getting anybody's sympathy. The situation is like what one still sees in certain parts of India like Chota Nagpur and Assam, where the non-Aryan speeches are being steadily pushed out by Aryan.

In the Deccan and South India, except possibly in the Western Deccan right down to the early course of Godāvarī where Aryan settlements were taking place, the non-Aryan languages were reigning supreme. Vidarbha or Varad(h)ā-taṭa (present day Varhād or Berar), and Aśmaka on the Godā-varī, were Aryan states in the Deccan prior to 400 B.C. The *Aitareya Brāhmaṇa,* anterior to Buddha, mentions the Andhras, the Śavaras, the Pulindas and the Mutibas as *dasyu* or non-Aryan (probably Dravidian) tribes in the Deccan (of these the Śavaras, probably also the Pulindas were Kol tribes), and North Indian Aryans before the Buddha do not seem to have known much about the Southern Dravidian states. Sindh, from the evidence of the *Baudhāyana Dharma-sūtra,* was, like Bengal, still outside the Aryan pale during the closing centuries before the Christian era; Sindh was probably still Dravidian, a language allied to Brahui being current in it : and the Greeks say that a tribe named Arabitai lived in south Sindh. But there cannot be any doubt that throughout the whole of southern and eastern Deccan and South India, the ancestors of the Telugus, the Kannaḍas and the Tamil-Malayalis were flourishing as independent states with their distinctive South Indian or Dravidian culture which is best represented in the ancient Tamil literature ascribed to the centuries immediately after Christ. But unfortunately no authentic specimen of a Dravidian language is available before the early centuries of the Christian era.

The Dravidian language-family is now confined to India: but if the original Dravidian speakers were a Mediterranean people, then Dravidian must be relegated to a common stock with the language of the ancient Aegean and Asia Minor peoples who were living in Greece and the Islands and Asia Minor before the Indo-European Hellenes came to Greece. I have suggested that a tribal name of this people was **Dr(a)mil-* or **Dr(a)miẓ,* which is found in one branch of them in the Island of Crete in the Hellenised spelling as *Termilai,* and in another branch of it in Lycia in Southern Asia minor as *Trm̃mili.* Various tribes with their different names naturally made up these Mediterranean invaders of India, and *Dramiẓ was evidently one of them. This name was Aryanised as *Dramiḍa* or *Dramiḷa* and then as *Draviḍa,* certainly earlier than the Christian era. Round about the time of Christ, the name became **Damiẓ* in the mouth of the people who bore the name, and they had by this time been fully settled and had built their culture and founded their states in the extreme south of India. The ancient Sinhalese Aryan-speaking settlers from Gujarat and Sindh, heard this name and wrote it in Pāli and Sinhalese as *Damiḷa* ; and Greek and Egyptian traders similarly heard the name as **Damir* and called the country the native name of which was obviously **Damiẓakam* *Damirikē* in Greek. Then certain wide-spread phonetic changes swept the language of the **Dramiẓ-Damiẓ* (and probably also of the Kannaḍiga) people, among which was the unvoicing of the voiced stops *g j ḍ d b* to *k c ṭ t p* ; and in a few centuries after Christ, the language entered a phase which we find in the oldest Tamil texts now found (the Śangam texts), and the name became *Tamiẓ* or *Tamiḻ* which is the form still obtaining in the Tamil language.

Although both Dravidian and Kol influenced the evolution of the Aryan language in the North—this influencing was at its height during the second half of the first millennium B.C. during the Nanda-Maurya period—and although culturally and politically highly advanced Dravidian states were flourishing in South India, states which had relations with Aśoka Maurya, it is curious and almost inexplicable why any of the Dravidian speeches did not manifest a literary life during the period under review. The finished character of the old Tamil *poruḷ* or *artha* i.e. matter of poetry, and of old Tamil literary ideas and ideals (dividing, for instance, poetic subjects into two categories of *aham* and *puṟam*, roughly corresponding to love and war, subjective and objective), took some centuries to develop, and it can be reasonably expected that during the Nanda and Maurya periods, the cultivated South Indian languages, particularly old Tamil and old Kannaḍa were essaying their first footsteps in the direction of sophisticated or advanced poetic composition, as opposed to purely popular poetry about love and war which we find orally among all peoples in the earlier stages of their history.

The advancement of a language is not possible without writing, and the Aryan speech came to be written down in all likelihood at a time when it made it possible for the Veda books to be compiled ; and this may well have taken place during the 10th century B.C., which is the date of the Mahābhārata battle and of Vyāsa, according to F. E. Pargiter and Hemchandra Raychaudhuri. The discovery of the Mohen-jo-Daro and Harappa script, with characters seemingly the pictorial prototypes of the Brāhmī letters of the 4th-3rd centuries B.C., now enables us to discard the theory of the Phoenician origin of the ancient Indian alphabet. The Brāhmī script in its oldest form—the proto-Brāhmī of the 10th century B.C. showing but an intermediate stage between the Mohen-jo-Daro script of *c* 2500 B. C. and the finished Brāhmī of 300 B.C.—could not be, as is natural in a similar situation, the finished alphabet with a scientific and etymologically sound orthography which we see in the Maurya and post-Maurya times. It was at the best a makeshift script, acting rather as a mnemonical writing than a proper and a complete alphabet. The orthography of Brāhmī as used for Prākrit in the 3rd century B.C. is not yet complete ; thus, e.g. certain consonant combinations are cumbrously made, and double consonants are not indicated at all (*vassa* being written as *văsa* or as *vāsa*). It was still a rather stumbling medium for the Prākrit dialects ; it was much more so for Sanskrit. The Kharoshṭhī script current in the Udīcya country during the period 400 B.C.—A.D.400 is admittedly of Semitic origin, a legacy of the Syrian scribes in the employment of the Achaemenian *sirkar* in India ; and its existence in India was an isolated episode, as isolated as the phenomenon of Gandhāra art. The name would appear to be a folk-etymology in India (whether *khara+oshṭha* or 'ass-lip' character as advocated by Sten Konow, or *Khara-ushṭra* or 'ass-and-camel country' character, as sought to be established by Sylvain Lévi, it is not necessary to take sides) of a Semitic word for 'writing' which we find in Hebrew as Xarošeθ (Kharosheth). The discovery of an inscription of the 4th-3rd century B.C. in Aramaic (Syriac) at Taxila, which has been read by Herzfeld, giving the name of 'our Lord Priyadarśi' (*mr'n prydrś*) is a direct proof of the contact of India with Aramaic writing, and helps us to envisage the origin of Kharoshṭhī.

The Indian Brāhmī alphabet is in all likelihood a derivative of the Mohen-jo-Daro script. But it is strange that a knowledge of writing should have been obtained by the later Dravidians from the North Indian Aryan speakers round about the time of Christ, if the Mohen-jo-Daro people were really the ancestors of the Dravidians. It is likely that the Mohen-jo-Daro script of *c*. 2500 and later was a very complicated thing, and when the Aryan alphabet was evolved out of it as a simpler system of writing after the Mohen-jo-Daro civilization had become moribund through Aryan impact as well as internal decay, and the people probably scattered, the simpler alphabet associated with a new and a vigorous people of a composite origin such as the ancient Hindus, descendants of both Aryans and non-Aryans, won the day,—making the more complicated, syllabic script of early Mohen-jo-Daro obsolete ; and this alphabet, as well as the Aryan language of which it was the vehicle, became a conquering force in the South—the old script being no longer current among a probably dispersed people—during the closing centuries of the first millennium B.C.

II. LEARNING, LITERATURE AND POPULAR LIFE

Brahmanical Learning

Though Buddhism gained the support of royalty and captured the hearts of sections of the people, Brahmanism continued in this period to be a great force in society. Neither the output of Brahmanical literature nor the patronage of Brahmanical scholars was impaired in any great degree. It is significant that the notices of the Greek writers of the times contain no mention of the Buddha or the popularity of his new faith, except the solitary reference of Clemens of Alexandria to philosophers who followed the precepts of Boutta[1]. Even the edicts of Aśoka call upon people to honour Brahmans. The *Āryamañjuśrīmūlakalpa* records that Nanda was a great patron of Brahman Tārkikas, proud of their learning, to whom he gave large sums of money[2]; the tirade of the same text against Chāṇakya shows the extensive patronage enjoyed by Brahmanism and Brahmanic learning under Chandragupta and Bindusāra, and Kauṭilya on his part does not conceal his animosity towards Buddhism and Jainism and levies a fine of a hundred pieces on

1. McCrindle-*Ancient India as described in classical literature*, p. 67 *n*.
2. K. P. Jayaswal—*Imperial History of India*, p. 31, Sanskrit text.

one who deceitfully brings to a dinner in honour of the gods and manes any of the śūdra ascetics of the Śākya or Ājīvaka sects[1]. In fact every page of Kauṭilya's work confirms the thoroughly Brahmanical mode of life dominating these times ; Kauṭilya speaks of the minister as one qualified in the Vedas and their six *aṅgas* (auxiliaries), mentions the Vedic sacraments and sacrifices, and prescribes Vedic rites and rituals to ward off every kind of evil and to procure success and prosperity to the people and the king ; he refers to free Brahmadeya lands given to Ritvigs, Ācāryas, Purohitas and Śrotriyas (II, i; III, 10) ; the work is also replete with references to *tāpasas* and *tapovanas* ; so much so that it would hardly be an exaggeration to say that, far from affecting adversely the hold of the Vedic way of life, the rise of Buddhism and Jainism had given only a fillip to Brahmanical activity in the various departments of life and literature.

Sanskrit Language

Though the nascent faiths of the Buddha and Mahāvīra had attempted to by-pass the Sanskrit language and contact the masses through the vernacular tongues, Sanskrit did not lose the position as a spoken language or the medium in which subjects of theoretical and practical value were cultivated by the Brahmanas in the several centres of learning. Among such centres Taxila in the north-west and the Mauryan capital Pāṭaliputra itself in the east were the most renowned. The *Bṛhatkathā* and the Buddhistic tradition make Pāṇini, connected with Śālātura in the north-west, a friend of a Magadhan Nanda, and bring Chāṇakya of the Taxila college to Pāṭaliputra in quest of a scholarly disputation ; and Brahmanical tradition recorded by Rājaśekhara speaks of a court of learning at Pāṭaliputra where Upavarsha and Varsha, Pāṇini and Piṅgala, Vyāḍi, Vararuchi and Patañjali attained fame by passing their tests in Śāstras.

The appellation Bhāshā which Pāṇini gives to his language and many of the rules laid down by him are not intelligible except as having reference to a spoken language. Such evidences of Sanskrit being a spoken tongue do not grow less

1. III. 20

in Kātyāyana or Patañjali, both of whom mention local and other variations and popular corruptions. That Kātyāyana was a southerner, that southerners delighted in using derivative forms (Taddhita) and that in the South, a big lake or *saras* was referred to as *sarasī* are statements of Patañjali showing the inclusion of the southern regions in the provenance of Sanskrit speech. The well-known dialogue in Patañjali (under Pāṇini II. 4. 56) between the grammarian and the charioteer, *sūta*, involving a grammatical subtlety bears out the fact that Sanskrit speech was not confined to either the academic circles or the learned classes of society. The use of Sanskrit in literature was so securely established that even Buddhism and Jainism which began with using the Prākrits had to line up early with Sanskrit literary tradition.

In this period the abundant variety of the Vedic morphology had got simplified considerably on both the declensional and conjugational sides and this process of simplification could be seen in progress through the Brāhmaṇas and the older Upanishads. It is such a Bhāshā which Pāṇini codified in order to render it more handy. Even after him a certain amount of fluidity persisted, as evidenced by the necessity for the work of the many Vārttikakāras, but at the close of the period of our study, Patañjali's work finally fixed the language as the unchanging Samskṛta. The language had become sufficiently distant from that of the Vedas to be characterised as classic Sanskrit, through its employment all this time in a growing body of epic and poetic literature. The Vedic accent had changed and the free use of verbal forms had given place to what may be called the nominal style characterised by participles; a small loss of vocabulary is to be seen, as also some amount of semantic change; a few new word forms were also added to the language in this period.

Sanskrit Grammar

The legends in the Sanskrit versions of the *Bṛhatkathā* introduce Pāṇini and Vararuchi as contemporaries of the Nandas; the *Āryamañjuśrīmūlakalpa* also refers to Pāṇini as a friend of the Nanda. On the basis of the *Bṛhatkathā* legends it was held by Max Müller, Weber and others that Pāṇini flourished about

315 B.C.; but as has been proved by several writers from Goldstücker onwards, Pāṇini and Kātyāyana could not have been contemporaries in view of the changes that the language had undergone in the days of the latter, and Pāṇini could at the latest be assigned only to 500 B.C., and in this respect, Tāranāth whose account puts Pāṇini a generation earlier than Kātyāyana is less faulty. In the period of the Nandas and Mauryas, there was indeed a great deal of grammatical activity. The Prātiśākhyas are to be referred to the post-Pāṇinian age, and between Pāṇini and Patañjali, there appeared a number of Vārttikakāras who appended their *vārttikas* or *addenda et corrigenda* (*uktā-'nukta-durukta-chintana*) to Pāṇini's aphorisms.

The foremost of the post-Pāṇinian grammarians is Vyāḍi, a descendant of Pāṇini himself removed from him by at least two generations, as we learn from his matronymic Dākshāyaṇa derived from Dākshī, the gotronymic of Pāṇini's own mother. Vyāḍi followed his ancestor's system and produced the grand work (*śobhana* as Patañjali describes it) called *Samgraha* in 100,000 verses. Patañjali held Vyāḍi in as much respect as he held Pāṇini himself. In fact, Bhartṛhari says at the end of the second book of his *Vākyapadīya* that the *Mahābhāshya* is based on the *Samgraha*. Vyāḍi's view that *vyakti* or *dravya* constituted *padārtha*, as expounded in his *Samgraha* is cited by Kātyāyana, Patañjali (I. ii. 64), Bhartṛhari and others. A grammatical tradition noted in the *Laghu-paribhāshāvṛtti* ascribes the Paribhāshās or the rules for interpreting Pāṇini's Sūtras to Vyāḍi, and some manuscripts, *Vyāḍiparibhāshā* and *Vyāḍiparibhāshāvṛtti*[1], support the tradition. Besides these a lexicon named *Utpalinī*, containing a reference to Buddhism, is also remembered as a work of Vyāḍi. As other grammarians of this time like Kātya and Kātyāyana Vararuchi are also quoted in the lexicons, we have to suppose that besides writing grammatical treatises, the authors compiled, somewhat after the manner of the older Nighaṇṭu, lists of words as accessories to their grammatical treatises. The story in the initial book of the several versions of the *Bṛhatkathā* would make Vyāḍi and Vararuchi class-fellows and friends ; Vyāḍi is however, as we have

1. Aufrecht, *Catalogus Catalogorum* I. p. 618b.

seen, one of the authorities quoted by Kātyāyana (I. ii.64).

The mention in these *Bṛhatkathā* legends of an Indradatta in a group of which the two others, Vyāḍi and Vararuchi, are grammarians may lead us to surmise that he too might have been a grammarian, not necessarily a contemporary, and though there is no evidence, it may be suggested that the Aindra grammar mentioned in the traditional accounts as having been superseded by the Pāṇinian and as being the basis of the Tamil system of the *Tolkāppiyam* and of the Sanskrit *Kālāpa*, may in reality be a work of this Indradatta.

The Vārttikakāras of grammar belonging to this age are headed by one whom Patañjali refers to with reverence as Bhagavān Kātya (III. ii. 3) and correspondingly his *vārttikas* are known as Mahāvārttikas in contrast not only to the other miscellaneous *vārttikas* but to those of Kātyāyana Vararuchi himself. In his Bhāshya (IV. ii. 65), Patañjali gives the illustration 'Māhāvārttika' meaning 'one who has studied the Mahāvārttika' and in the encyclopaedic *Śṛṅgāra Prakāśa* of king Bhoja we actually get quotations of two *vārttikas* from the Mahāvārttikas under Pāṇini II. i. 51 and I. iv. 21. Kātya like Vyāḍi added a lexicon to his grammatical contribution.

As distinct as the Mahāvārttikas, are the metrical dicta of a Vārttika character quoted by Patañjali, which, as can be made out from Bhartṛhari, Kaiyaṭa and Nāgoji, formed part of a work called the *Ślokavārttika*. Coming chronologically after Vyāḍi were the followers of the grammar of Gautama (VI. 2. 36). The other Vārttikas referred to by Patañjali are Bhāradvājīya, Saunāga, Kroshṭīya, Saura Bhagavad and those of Kuṇi Vāḍava or Kuṇaravāḍava, all of these being later than the *vārttikas* of Kātyāyana on which they have bearing. It is not known if the *Māthurī Vṛtti* mentioned by Patañjali under IV. iii 101 is another Vārttika.

The most important of these Vārttikakāras is the one known generally as the Vārttikakāra of grammar, viz., Kātyāyana alias Vararuchi. From the literary traditions referred to, we may take him to be a contemporary of the Nandas. He is also the author of the *Vājasaneyiprātiśākhya*, where he deals with the language and the gramm ar ofthe *Vājasaneyisamhitā*, and the

Kathāsaritsāgara story too makes mention of his proficiency in the Prātiśākhya taught by Vyāḍi (I. 2. 38). In this Prātiśākhya, Kātyāyana gives a number of criticisms of the relevant sūtras of Pāṇini. In his Vārttikas which number about 4,000, he subjects about 1,500 sūtras of Pāṇini to his critical observations, these comprehending on the whole about 10,000 grammatical points. Kātyāyana was neither hostile to Pāṇini nor rash in his criticism as one might be led to believe from the way Patañjali handles him ; the natural phenomena of linguistic change necessitated the compilation of Kātyāyana's corrections and additions. Besides the dicta, Kātyāyana sometimes made his grammatical observations in verses which Patañjali quotes as *bhrājāḥ ślokāḥ* and Kaiyaṭa identifies as Kātyāyana's. As noticed already Patañjali speaks of him as a southerner fond of Taddhita forms, while the *Bṛhatkathā* story makes him a native of Kauśāmbi, an all-round scholar, sometime minister of Nanda at Pāṭaliputra and an incarnation of a Śivagaṇa known as Pushpadanta. The Buddhistic *Mañjuśrīmūlakalpa* too mentions him as a minister under Nanda.

The Prātiśākhyas are a class of works designed to preserve Vedic texts correctly, as handed down in their several *śākhās* or groups of *śākhās* (Prati-śākhā) ; and these treatises may generally be assigned to the period between Pāṇini and Patañjali according to Goldstücker, say between 600 B.C. and 200 B.C. Mention has already been made of the *Vājasaneyi Prātiśākhya* of the Vārttikakāra Kātyāyana. As Vyāḍi is several times quoted in the *Rigveda Prātiśākhya* ascribed to Śaunaka, we may assign that Prātiśākhya too to our period. To Vyāḍi himself is ascribed a treatise on *Veda lakshaṇa*[1].

Classical Sanskrit Literature and Fine Arts

The Sanskrit versions of the *Bṛhatkathā*, the Jaina *Bṛhatkathā Kośa* of Harisheṇa and the Buddhistic *Mañjuśrīmūlakalpa* speak of a Subandhu as a Brahman minister of Nanda, Chandragupta and Bindusāra. In Abhinavagupta's commentary on the Nāṭya Śāstra, *Abhinavabhāratī*, there is more than one reference to a Subandhu as a Mahākavi who composed a unique variety

1. Aufrecht, *Catalogus Catalogorum* III part.

of dramatic composition, emboxing one act within another, and making the characters of each preceding act the spectators of its successor ; the work was called the *Vāsavadattā Nāṭya-dhārā* or the dramatic series of Vāsavadattā[1]. This Vāsavadattā is the Ujjain princess figuring in Udayana's story[2], with which Subandhu wove one of Bindusāra himself. It is this drama of Subandhu that Vāmana quotes in his *Kāvyālaṅkārasūtravṛtti*, where we have the suggestion of Chandragupta's son having difficulties and being helped by wise ministers like Subandhu, a circumstance which is confirmed by the *Mañjuśrīmūlakalpa* referring to Bindusāra succeeding to the throne as a boy. A verse on poet Subandhu and his composition featuring Bindusāra and Vatsarāja, found in a manuscript of the *Avanti-sundarī* has reference only to this Subandhu whom we may take as the minister under the last Nanda and the first two Mauryan emperors.

The Jain *Bṛhatkathākośa* while mentioning Subandhu along with Chāṇakya (story 143), refers to a third minister Kavi, which too may be a reminiscence of a literary figure of these times. Of the literary activities of Kātyāyana Vararuchi, we can say something definite. Patañjali's *Mahābhāshya* opens our eyes to the rich crop of classical literature produced in these times. Among literary productions mentioned by Patañjali with the author's name is a poem by Vararuchi, *Vārarucham Kāvyam* (IV. iii. 101). In Bhoja's *Śṛṅgāra Prakāśa*, a half verse in the Vasantatilakā metre from a poetic composition of Kātyāyana is quoted[3].

The other Kāvyas presupposed by Patañjali must have all been produced in this period : we have thus a good number of Ākhyānas and Akhyāyikās on the stories of Yayāti, Yavakrīta, Priyaṅgu, Sumanottarā, Bhīmaratha, Vāsavadattā and the

1. See IHQ. XIX, 1943, pp. 69-71.

2. Kauṭilya's *Arthaśāstra* has two references to Udayana's story; one in IX. 7, his return to power after a flight and another in XIII. 2. where the ruse of capturing one fond of hunt with the aid of an alluring elephant in the *nāgavana* reminds us of Udayana's capture by Pradyota.

3. Madras Ms. Vol. I Ch. I p. 45 tathā ca Kātyāyanaḥ : '*uttāraṇāya jagataḥ prapitāmahena tasmāt padāt tvamasi rajjuriva pravrittā*. This is evidently a praise of the Ganges, the celestial river that descended from the heavens, and we know from the Bṛhatkathā versions that Vararuchi was a great devotee of Gaṅgā whom he propitiated and who appeared before Vararuchi every day to make him a present of gold.

Daivāsura and Rākshosura on the wars of the Devas and the Asuras (IV. ii. 60 ; IV. iii. 87-8).

Perhaps more value is to be attached to the many citations of verses and parts of verses embodying a highly evolved poetic expression and metrical finish which Patañjali makes in his *Mahābhāshya*, and which should clearly convince us of the high development of Kāvya in this period. We have specimens here of verses of erotic, lyric, panegyric and gnomic poetry ; of lines belonging to a poem on the Mahābhārata theme and of metrical varieties like Anushṭubh, Upajāti, Praharshiṇī, Pramitāksharā and Vasantatilakā ; the grammatical *kārikās* disclose even greater metrical advancement, these employing even rarer metres, Vaktra, Śālinī, Vamśastha, Samānī, Vidyunmālā, Toṭaka and Dodhaka. This metrical material surely points to the existence of prosodial treatises in these times, and we may not be wrong in assigning Piṅgala's *Chhandas-sūtras* to this period. In a verse in Rājaśekhara's *Kāvyamīmāmsā* enumerating the Śāstrakāras examined at Pāṭaliputra, Piṅgala figures between Pāṇini and Vyāḍi[1], and Haraprasad Śāstri has drawn attention to a tradition recorded in the *Divyāvadāna* that Bindusāra put his son Aśoka to school under Piṅgala Nāga[2]. In the *Abhinavabhāratī* of Abhinavagupta we have quotations from an anushṭubh treatise of Kātyāyana on metres, in which Kātyāyana examines the emotional and thematic appropriateness of particular metres.[3]

Whatever the date of the present text of the *Nāṭya Śāstra* of Bharata, we know that his text incorporates within itself and cites passages and verses handed down to him from the past, *ānuvamśya*. That the histrionic art was not in a crude stage at this time, but was highly developed can be gathered not only from the *Vāsavadattā Nāṭyadhārā* of Subandhu, but also from the sure evidence of Pāṇini's sūtras (IV. iii. 110-1) which say that even so early, the actors' art had been codified into two texts of aphorisms (Naṭasūtras) by two different authors Śilālin and Kṛśāśva. More important than Patañjali's reference to Śobhanikas who show Kamsavadha and Balibandhana is his

1. *Kāvyamīmāmsā*, GOS, p. 55.
2. *Magadhan Literature*, p. 36.
3. *Journal of Oriental Research, Madras vi* pp. 222-3.

reference to the actor who feels the *rasa* which he acts *rasiko naṭaḥ* (V. ii. 59). The repeated mention in the *Arthaśāstra* of accomplished courtezans, *naṭas* and *nartakas*, supports the view that dance and drama prevailed as popular and evolved forms of art at this time. The ancillary art of music too is spoken of by Kauṭilya both in its vocal and instrumental form. *Gīta, vādya, kuśīlava,, śilpakārikāḥ, śilpavatyaḥ striyaḥ* (I. 12), *ātodya* (I. 21), *naṭas, nartakas, gāyanas, vādana* (II. i), *pāṭhya, nṛtta, nāṭya, vīṇā, veṇu, mṛidaṅga, raṅgopajīvinīs* (II. 27) and the specific mention of *prekshā* or dramatic show seen by the king (XIII. 2)—these in Kauṭilya picture a time and society which delighted in the arts of music, dance and drama. The fine art of painting occurs in *chitrālekhya* (I. 16) ; and the numerous references to the images of gods (*devapratimās*) give a glimpse into sculptural art of these times.

The dramatic variety called Vīthī as described by Bharata involves a good deal of verbal ingenuity, wit and foiling of one another in repartees. That such an art of verbal skill was cultivated in these times is shown by the frequent mention by Kauṭilya of a social entertainer called *vāgjīvana* (II. 1 ; II. 27 ; III. 14).

Not only had much poetry been produced by this time, but factors of poetic appeal and appreciation had also come to be analysed ; already in Yāska we find several classes of simile or upamā and several words expressive of similarity (upamāvāchakas) ; in Pāṇini, in addition to several rules involving simile, we have the actual mention of Upamā and Sāmānya-śabda. In the chapter on the writing of Śāsana or a royal document, Kauṭilya enumerates and defines in his *Arthaśāstra* excellences or guṇas pertaining to calligraphy and literary composition ; arthakrama or the proper order of ideas, sambandha or cogent development of the theme, paripūrṇatā or fulness in respect of idea, expression, arguments and illustrations, these being adequate and at the same time not superfluous, mādhurya or sweetness and charm of words and ideas, audārya or dignified utterance and spashṭatva or the use of well-known words ; in the same context, Kauṭilya speaks of doshas or defects of writing and composing, vyāghāta or mutual contradiction, punarukta (redundance) and apaśabda (grammatical flaw).

Religious literature, Purāṇa, Dharma, Śrauta and Gṛhya Sūtras

Kauṭilya defines Veda as Trayī but immediately adds that Atharvan and the Itihāsas also are Vedas (I.3); in the subsequent chapters very large use is made of the Artharvaṇic practices of Śānti, Pushṭi and Ābhichāra; the separate mention and juxtaposition with Itihāsa shows however that the Artharvan had not yet become completely canonised and that this was the time when it was coming into increasing prominence and acceptance. Confirmation of this may be had from the *Āpastamba Dharma Sūtra* which defines Veda primarily as the three Vedas but says at the end that all the popular arts and lores which are current among women and śūdras are to be brought under the Atharvan. (II.11.29.11-12.) The six Vedāṅgas (*Arthaśāstra* I.3., I.9) and Itihāsa-Purāṇa (*ib.*I.5, V.6) are mentioned. That some Purāṇas had already come into being is proved also by the *Āpastamba Dharma Sūtra* which besides referring to Purāṇas quotes verses from Purāṇas (I.6.19.13 and II.9.23.3), the metrical imperfection of a few lines here indicating their antiquity. A *Bhavishyat Purāṇa* is expressly mentioned by Āpastamba II. 9. 24. 6. Kauṭilya refers to Itivṛtta and Purāṇa (I. 5.) and to Dharma Śāstra (I. 5 and III. 1); he speaks of Arthaśāstra (I. 5) and Āśrama-dharma (I. 12). These as well as the numberless references to Yajana, Prāyaścitta, Śānti, Homa etc., in the *Arthaśāstra* show that by this time the Dharma, Śrauta and Gṛhya Sūtras had come into being and were in full force. The Vārttikakāra Kātyāyana also knows Dharmaśāstra (I. 12. 64). According to MM. Kane, to the Nanda-Maurya age could be assigned the Dharma-sūtras of Gautama, Baudhāyana, Āpastamba, Vasishṭha, Vishṇu in part, Hārīta and Śaṅkha-Likhita. Bühler also considers the *Āpastamba Dharma Sūtra* to have been produced in the five centuries before Christ[1], and that both Gautama and Baudhāyana were earlier than Āpastamba. These Dharma sūtras form one part of the Kalpa sūtras and deal with the duties of varṇas and āśramas. The other two parts of the Kalpa sūtras are the Śrauta and Gṛhya sūtras, and we may take it that where we have Śrauta, Gṛhya and Dharma sūtras by the same author, as for instance Āpastamba, they were all of identical authorship and formed part of one integral kalpa or manual of

1. Sacred Books of the East, Vol. 2, Introduction.

ritual and conduct of that school. According to the ideology of these sūtras, life is not something to be lived as the body and mind please, but a disciplined activity towards sublimation through a series of sacramental acts, Vedic and domestic rites, and personal samskāras from the time of conception to death. Human nature is here smelted and purified in these acts of Karman and Dharma, or as Kālidāsa puts it, the raw stone of man is ground, polished, and cut into a gem of a Dvija by these processes (*Raghuvamśa* III. 18).

Philosophy

The Dharma sūtras speak of four stations of life (āśramas), student, householder, ascetic and forest-dwelling hermit. The last two stages were devoted to a life which stood in contrast to that of the first two. While the former emphasised a life of Karma or ordained acts, the latter showed the path of contentment, renunciation and the seeking of the knowledge of the soul or ātman as the means to the supreme welfare. The older Upanishads must have certainly come into being by this time and the path of ātmajñāna declared by them greatly prized. We know from Pāṇini that there were already in his days codified Sūtras bearing on the life and conduct of Bhikshus or mendicants by two different authors Pārāśarya and Karmanda (IV. iii. 110-1). These Bhikshus were also known as Parivrājakas and Maunins as the Dharma Sūtras show (Āpast. II. 9.21; Baudh. II. vi. 14; Gaut. III. 2). Gautama (III. 10. 11) refers to Upanishads and Vedānta and in the Adhyātmapaṭala (I. 8. 22-23) of the *Āpastamba Dharma Sūtra* we have an epitome of the doctrine of Ātmajñāna as taught in the Upanishads. However the general teaching of the Dharma Sūtras was in favour of combining an observance of Dharma with Jñāna as can be seen in Āpastamba (II. 9. 21) who refutes the doctrine of Jñāna as the sole means of welfare. The Vānaprastha of these texts is identical with Strabo's Hylobioi or forest dwellers, a subdivision of the Śramaṇas (Greek sarmanes); their mode of life was regulated by the institutes of their school, and Baudhāyana (II. 6. 14) defines Vānaprastha as one who follows the institutes of the *Vaikhānasa Śāstra* which was thus a text in existence at that time.

These evidences show that when Buddhism arose and even earlier still, Brahmanism had within its fold its own class of mendicants and ascetics, and that the term Śramaṇa need not refer exclusively to the Buddhist ascetics. In Kauṭilya's *Arthaśāstra* too, references are only to these Brahmanical ascetics. Kauṭilya mentions Parivrājaka, Tāpasa, Muṇḍa and Jaṭila (I. 10, 11, 12), Śramaṇas (I. 12), Vānaprastha and Yati (III. 16), Tāpasas, Tapovanas, Tapasvins, and Āśramas (II. 2, II. 35, 36, III. 9 and IV. 3), and Muṇḍas and Jaṭilas with pupils inhabiting mountain caves (XIII. 2). Kauṭilya imposes punishment on those renouncing life without making proper provision for their family (II. 1, 28) which is understandable as a stricture passed on the easy increase in the Buddhistic ascetic fold.

It is remarkable that Kauṭilya refers more than once to female ascetics (I. 12 ; III. 3, 4). That Brahmavādinīs were not taboo within the Brahmanical fold is proved not only by the *Bṛhadāraṇyaka Upanishad* but by an illustration of Patañjali as well. Patañjali speaks of women studying the Mīmāmsā of Kāśakṛtsna (IV. i. 14), and as Kāśakṛtsna is an author cited by Bādarāyaṇa in his *Vedānta Sūtras,* we may take it that the Mīmāmsā of Kāśakṛtsna referred to by Patañjali was an Uttaramīmāmsā text current in that time. But such women ascetics or students of philosophy must have been few.

A certain amount of metaphysical discussion on even such topics as the exact nature and identity of the import of a word (padārtha) is seen from Kātyāyana's reference to Vyāḍi holding vyakti or dravya to be padārtha. Āpastamba twice refers to Vedic interpretation as being decided by principles of Nyāya, and as Bühler has pointed out, we have here nearly the Pūrva Mīmāmsā Śāstra. Upavarsha, whom the legends in the *Bṛhatkathā* assign to Pāṭaliputra of this period and whom Rājaśekhara's verse also connects with Pāṭaliputra, is known from later references as an old author on Pūrva and Uttara Mīmāmsās. More definite is Kauṭilya's reference to philosophical branches of learning and study, Ānvīkshikī (I. 2) which, according to him, comprised Sāṅkhya, Yoga and Lokāyata. The last is a school of material philosophy ; Sāṅkhya is to be taken as knowledge in general, and Yoga as observance of ordained Dharma, or other purificatory practices or Hetuvidyā. In Baudhāyana

(II. vi. 30) there is an interesting discussion on āśramas ; it is said that the fourfold classification of āśramas is not authoritative, that the householder's is the only āśrama and that one Kapila, an Asura, son of Prahlāda, devised this fourfold division. It can be seen that the four āśramas fall into two groups of two, Brahmachārin and Gṛhastha observing the ordained Dharmas ; and the Vānaprastha, who retired from home to forest, and Bhikshu who was not particular about a life of Karma. The Dharmasūtrakāras as believers in Karma are, it is to be expected, always for upholding the Gṛhastha, while the philosopher will denounce the Gṛhastha's futile routine and hold up the latter āśramas as capable of bringing real solace to the soul and reedom from the threefold distress. Now Kapila, author of the Sāṅkhya, is one of our earliest philosophers who belittled Karma and advocated Jñāna or Viveka. As this path of knowledge gained greater popularity, its adherents had to be approved of and assigned a place in the accepted scheme of things, and thus probably did the aśramas amplify themselves.

That philosophical debate and systematic investigation of subjects had advanced in this period is borne out by the thirty-two topics of methodology in the exposition of a system of thought, called Tantrayuktis, which Kauṭilya enumerates, defines and illustrates at the end of his work, and most of which became later part of the Nyāya system of Akshapāda.

Arthaśāstra

The entire Mauryan age is dominated by two remarkable records, one of literature and the other of epigraphy, viz. the *Arthaśāstra* of Kauṭilya and the edicts of Aśoka. It is needless to add anything here on the *Arthaśāstra* which has received full treatment in the historical sections. It is enough to point out that Kauṭilya refers to his own work as a critical compendium based on the Arthaśāstras, prevalent at his time, and that he refers to works of nearly a dozen writers, Bhāradvāja (Kaṇiṅka), Viśālākshā (Śiva), Parāśara, Piśuna (Nārada), Kauṇapadanta (Bhīshma), Vātavyādhi (Uddhava), Bāhudantīputra (Indra), the Mānavas, the Bārhaspatyas, Auśanasas and Āmbhīyas. This active exercise of thought on polity, echoes of which are to be heard in the epic *Mahābhārata*, might well have been occasioned by the intense political activity of the times which were full of Saṅghas of different descriptions and numerous small monarchies. That leaders of thought such as the Brahmans took a leading part in the political life of the country is shown by the evidence of Greek writers like Plutarch who say that the philosophers gave Alexander no less trouble than the mercenaries by reviling the princes who declared for him and encouraged the free states to revolt from his authority. The mercenaries referred to by the Greek writers were the Āyudhajīvi Kshatriya Saṅghas, just as the robbers referred to by them were the Āraṭṭas (Arāshṭras) or republicans. The genius of Chandragupta and Chāṇakya saw the danger of these numerous small free states, communities and kingships, and not only consolidated an empire and a centralised power but also set forth the scheme of the detailed working of such a huge centralised authority in a new *Arthaśāstra*.

Kāma-Śāstra

While the Dharma, Śrauta and Gṛhya Sūtras are concerned with one side of life as a round of sacramental rites, performance of rituals and sacrifices, and observance of social, religious and spiritual codes of conduct, quite another side of it, the gaiety and joy of life, is represented by the numerous references to the courtezan and her *milieu* in the *Arthaśāstra*. The courtezans were so popular that they could be effectively employed in the machinery of state. Śilpakārikās and śilpavatyaḥ striyaḥ (I. 12), veśyās (II. 6), gaṇikas who served the king with their kuśīlavakarman, singing, (II, 27); raṅgopajīvinīs (II. 27), kauśikastriyaḥ, gāyanas, and nartakis (XI. 1)—all formed such a vital part of the polity that a special superintendent was appointed to look after their organized management (Gaṇikādhyaksha). Not only was their life regulated by a government department, but the art of love was also codified by an eminent authority on erotics. The Mauryan capital, Pāṭaliputra, was renowned for its courtezans and Vātsyāyana tells us in his *Kāma Sūtra* (II. i. 11) that at the request of the courtezans of Pāṭaliputra, Dattaka who must have lived at this time codified the courtezan's art, Vaiśika. Kauṭilya also mentions the Vaiśikakalā (II. 27). The gay side of life is to be seen also in the dictum of Kauṭilya that one ought not to deny oneself pleasures (na nissukhaḥ syāt, I. 7) and by his allotment to the king of the sixth part of the day for enjoyment (svaira-vihāra, I. 19). The cities had halls and gardens intended for recreation (vihārārthāḥ śālāḥ ārāmāḥ, II. 1) ; gambling was in vogue especially in the republican communities to a dangerous extent (VIII. 3) ; gambling and drinking halls were provided for (II. 26, 36) ; people went to the festivals and gatherings for entertainment, utsavas, samājas and yātrās (II, 26. XIII. 2. 3), and water-sports and sylvan games were also indulged in (XIII. 2, V. 2).

Popular Worship

There were temples where people worshipped images, and Kauṭilya names a number of popular deities in worship in his time. The temples (koshṭhas) were in the north-west part of the city for gods and goddesses like Aparājita, Apratihata, Jayanta, Vaijayanta, Śiva, Vaiśravaṇa (Kubera), Aśvins and Śrī (Lakshmī) (II.4). Deities of Vāstu (site) and Dik (quarters) were adored (II. 4), and to ward off natural calamities or to invite natural benefits, people made offerings and oblations and incantations of peace, worshipping Fire. Rivers, Indra, Gaṅgā, Seashore, Forests (Vanayāga), Mountains, and Caityas of Rākshasas (IV. 3). People went on pilgrimages to holy places, Puṇyasthānas (II. 35-36, III. 9-10) and Tīrthāyatanas (II. 35). Nāga-pratimās or Snake-images and Dhvaja-pratimās or flag-staffs standing for some deities were objects of worship. Persons who practised inferior magical arts invoked Bali, Śambara, Vairocana, presiding deities of several Narakas, sages like Nārada, Devala, Sāvarṇi and Gālava, Manu, Devas and Devalokas, Vedic scholars, Siddhas, Tāpasas, Brahmā, Brahmāṇī, Paulomī, Tantukaccha a great Asura, and others of his class (XIV. 1).

Popular lores

A notice of works of literature, grammar or philosophy does not exhaust the branches of knowledge and lore which prevailed at this time and played an important part in popular life. Other arts and lores are reflected in the *Arthaśāstra*. Kauṭilya speaks of astrologers and experts in omens, mauhūrtikas and naimittikas (I. 9, 12 ; IV. 4 ; V. 3.), readers of fortune from physical features, Lakshaṇa (I. 12) and Aṅgavidyā (XIII. 1), magicians and sorcerers (Jambhaka-vidyā, Māyā and Māyā-yoga, I. 12 and IV. 3), snake charmers (Jāṅgalīvids), adepts in black magic (kṛtyābhicāraśīlas IV. 4, XIV), minstrels (śūtas and māgadhas), oracles (praśna-vidyā), and readers of dreams and birds' voices (svapna-pakshi-vyāhāra, XXIII. 1). The lore of the serpent, (IV. iii. 13) mentioned even in the Upanishads, is noticed by Arrian too.

Of more important subjects, Kauṭilya speaks of a highly developed art of healing, producing and counteracting diseases poisons, etc. (XII), maternity and care of the child (I. 17, kumārabhṛtyā and garbhabharman) and of the profession of the doctor, cikitsaka (I. 18). He refers to the lapidary art (II. 2), to the science of agriculture (kṛshitantra, II. 25) and the science of plant-life (vṛkshāyurveda) and to the astronomical factors favourable for cultivation. He speaks of reading others' minds, perfumer's art, garlanding and shampoo (II. 27). There was an advanced veterinary science pertaining to the elephant and horse (II. 30, 31). Mineral science, dhātu-śāstra, is also mentioned in Kauṭilya (II. 12).

Architecture

The development of architecture is seen in Kauṭilya's elaborate description of the fort and the palace and their various parts including mechanical manipulations (yantras). Secret passages within walls (gūḍha-bhitti-sañcāra) and underground ways (suraṅgas) were devised (I. 20). In the same place fire-proofing is also mentioned. Śulbaśāstra is referred to expressly (II. 12 and 25). Special buildings with suitable features are described for elephants and horses ; pleasure-halls (vihāraśālās II. 1), drinking halls with rooms, seats, couches, garden etc. (pānāgāra II. 26, III. 8), gambling halls (dyūtāvāsa II. 36) and hospitals (II. 6) are other special types of buildings mentioned by Kauṭilya. The architectural magnificence of the Mauryan capital is borne out by the testimony of the Greek writers and by excavations. It has already been pointed out that the *Artha-śāstra* contains numerous references to temples and images (I. 6. 18, II. 1. 4. II. 6, 33, 36, III. 9, 10, 16, IV. 10, V. 2

XIII. 1, 3.). Idols for worship were highly popular and Deva-dānas and Deva-dravyas were guarded by village elders (I. 18, II. 1), a superintendent looking after all temples (II. 6), and from a reference in Patañjali we know that the Mauryas probably augmented their revenues by a share in the fees forthcoming in the popular worship of images.

Prākṛit, Buddhistic and Jain literature

The earliest literature of Buddhism and Jainism which arose and grew in Kosala and Magadha adopted the Prākṛit as its vehicle of expression. Tradition which is late and which receives support from some citations in works like the gloss of Malayagiri on a Jain work and from a reference in Bhoja's *Śṛṅgāra Prakāśa*, ascribes a Prākṛit grammar to Pāṇini himself, but this is only a late attempt to invest Prākṛit with a status equal to that of Sanskrit. Equally undependable is the ascription of the *Prākṛtaprakāśa* on the Mahārāshṭrī and other dialects to Vararuchi, the Vārttikakāra, for the languages dealt with here are of later form. The early Ardhamāgadhī originals of the Jain canon have not survived, what we now have being later redactions.

The Buddhistic canon was in Pāli which had close affinities with Pāiśācī. Pāli-Paiśācī, and in fact all the later Prākṛits, owe their origin, according to Hoernle[1] to the ways in which the non-Sanskritic populations of the different localities spoke the Sanskrit tongue. Konow[2] draws attention to the fact that according to a Tibetan tradition the Sthaviras or Theras had their books in Paiśācī, and that according to Pischel these Paiśācī books may be the Pāli canon. Pāli-Paiśācī dialects with slight local variations were current in wide parts of India from the north-west to the Deccan, and it is this language which influenced or bore affinities to the Dravidian.[3]

Any considerable or authentic Prākṛit material of this time that we possess is confined to the edicts of Aśoka. The language of these edicts is in three dialects, closely related to one another and exhibiting only slight differences, one of these the eastern, prevalent in Magadha and the language of the capital, gave

1. ZDMG. 64 (1910) pp, 103-4, 118.
2. Ibid. p. 103,
3. Ibid. pp. 107-118.

rise to the later Māgadhī Prākṛit ; the other two were of the west and north-west, the latter being the earliest of the three. That Aśoka adopted this language for the propagation of Dharma proves that it was widely prevalent among the people.

These edicts are valuable in another direction too. For, whether one believes or not in the traditions about the Buddhistic councils and the compilation of the Pāli canon soon after the Nirvāṇa of the Buddha or in the time of Aśoka, we have the irrefutable evidence of these edicts of Aśoka to show that some Buddhistic texts were in existence at this time. The Calcutta-Bairat edict names seven texts which have been traced in the canon. Of equal value are the inscriptions on the Bharhut and Sāñchī stūpas of the second and first centuries B.C. ; while their carvings presuppose Buddhajātaka legends, the inscriptions there mention actually reciter (bhāṇaka), Sūtta reciter (Sūttāntika), one versed in the five Nikāyas (Pañcanekāyika), one versed in the Piṭakas (Peṭakin) and preacher of Dhamma (Dhammakathika). These epigraphical references are some indication that at the time of Aśoka there was a Buddhistic canonical literature to which the available Pāli canon bears general resemblance.

Jainism does not lag behind in recording legends of the constitution of the Ardhamāgadhī canon at Pāṭaliputra in the time of Chandragupta, and of the Jain affiliations of the Nanda and Maurya kings and ministers. To Badrabāhu, whom Jain legend brings to Karṇāṭaka along with king Chandragupta who too became a Jain, are ascribed the ten Niryuktis and the *Kalpasūtra*. While it may be true that the Jain Aṅgas have in them portions going to the Mauryan times in antiquity, it is well understood that their bulk represents very late work.

CHAPTER XI

MAURYAN ART

I

Introduction

It is indeed curious that the first organised art activity in India in large scale and durable material of which datable examples have come down to us in any recognisable number belongs to the period of the Mauryas. The Chalcolithic civilisation of the Indus valley has left behind relics, few in number but varied in subject and treatment, that may safely be said to belong to the domain of high art with a long artistic tradition and experience behind it. Indeed, the art represented by the reliefs on the seals and figure sculptures in the round found at Harappa, Mohen-jo-Daro and other sites in the Punjab, Sind, Baluchistan, and further north and east, is already highly developed, sophisticated and conscious, and expresses most fully and significantly the culture-ideology of a people urban in upbringing, highly sophisticated in the luxury of living, and probably industrial and feudal in socio-economic organisation. Like the civilisation itself its art also had already reached the creative climax of a tradition. Into the relation of this art with the art of the contemporary civilised world it is not the place to enter ; but it must needs be told that this art in spite of its affinities with contemporary Mediterranean art has its own essential qualities and its own character cf form that link it with the art of India of the historical period[1]. Yet the fact remains that the art of the Indus valley is still largely an unknown factor in so far as it remains chronologically unexplained, and we hardly know anything definite of what happened along the arrow of time between the final phase of the Indus valley civilisation and the civilisation that flourished in the Ganges valley more than two thousand years later.

1. St. Kramrisch, *Indian Sculpture*, pp. 3—7.

The earliest that the Ganges valley is alleged to have offered to us in the shape and form of what may be called an art object is a small gold tablet representing a naked woman standing on her legs in symmetrical rigidity, with exaggerated hips and sexual organs, heavy and clumsy ornaments and rigidly angular composition. It was dug out of a tomb near Lauriya, was identified by Bloch, the explorer, as the iconic representation of the Earth goddess, and was ascribed by him to about the eighth and seventh centuries B.C. There can hardly be any doubt that such images in metal as well as in clay served as fetish symbols ; there are passages in the *Rig Veda* and later also in the *Gṛihya sūtras* which can be interpreted to suggest that figures of gods and animals were fashioned in metal and clay for such purposes[1]. A small gold tablet similar to that found at Lauriya and a small gold figure, forming part of the relics from the ruins of the Piprahva stūpa, evidently Buddhistic, and belonging to a period not earlier than that of the Mauryas[2], reveals the same motive and treatment as those of the Lauriya tablet, so that the latter can hardly be ascribed to so early a period as Bloch does. Some of the oldest terracotta pieces recovered by Marshall from the ruins of Bhita seem also to belong more or less to this category[3]; their motive, if not their treatment, is the same, so that all these objects may be taken to be typical representations of a primitive phase of imagination centering round fetishistic beliefs. They are not definitely the products of any organised and conscious art movement in any considerable scale, though primitive faiths and beliefs may have helped and favoured the development of sculptural and architectural art in India at a later stage of history.

That this was indeed the case is fully borne out by early Buddhist and Jaina texts and supported by early Buddhist reliefs that reveal the flourishing existence, particularly in eastern India, of a primitive religion that indulged in the worship of such symbols as the Chaitya which was either a holy tree or

1. Th. Bloch, '*Excavations at Lauriyā*', *A. S. R.*, 1906—7, pp. 122 ff ; A. B. Keith, *C. H. I.* I, p. 97 ; E. W. Hopkins, *C. H. I.* I, p. 232 ; *Sāṅkhyāyana Gṛhya Sūtra*, IV. 19 ; L. Bachhofer, *Early Indian Sculpture*, pp. 2—3, 14—15.

2. W. C. Peppé, The Piprahva Stūpa....... *J. R. A. S.*, 1898, pp. 573 ff. V. A. Smith, note, pp. 579 ff., figs. 11 and 15 ; J. Marshall, *C. H. I.* p. 623.

3. J. Marshall, 'Excavations at Bhitā', *A. S. R.*, 1911—12, p. 4, pl. 23.

groves of trees (*rukkhacetiya*, *vanacetiya*, *arāmacetiya* etc.), and not infrequently these trees were the abodes of gods or spirits known as *Vṛikṣadevatās*, *Yakshas* etc. Another important symbol that received worship was the stūpa, a hemispherical tumulus, either votive or dedicatory or commemorative. All such objects and places of primitive worship were enclosed for protection with railings which must have given the people some scope for the play of their artistic and decorative instincts.[1] A third object that also seems to have been an important element in the primitive religion of middle and eastern India was the animal standard —the *dhvajastambha* of later Indian literature,—i.e. posts or pillars crowned by animals considered sacred and worshipped by primitive peoples. This trait of primitive religion was not particularly characteristic of India, but was equally potent in Babylonia and Assyria as well as in ancient Greece. Later Brahmanical mythology knows of such standards or *stambhas* of at least three different animal gods, namely the Garuḍa, the Vṛisha and the Makara, the *vāhanas* of Vishnu, Śiva and Gaṅgā (also Kandarpa) respectively. Sometimes the animal was replaced by certain trees considered sacred, the *Kalpadruma* or the wishing tree and the palm-tree represented by its crowning cluster of leaves. It was evidently from such early specimens of primitive animal standards made of impermanent materials like wood and bamboo that Aśoka derived the inspiration of erecting monumental pillars crowned by sacred animals[2].

But of such objects of worship before the days of Aśoka-Maurya we have no remains extant, nor of the *Yaksha-devatās* or spirits referred to in a general way or specifically by name in early Buddhist and Jaina texts. Attempts have been made on epigraphic reasons to identify the two round standing male figures from Patna in reddish-grey sandstone of the Chunar region and bearing *chauris* as those of *Yakshas* ; indeed behind the shoulder of one of these statues, on the scarf, is a short inscription paleographically assignable to about the first century A.D.—that may be read as : *Yakh(o) sa* (?) *Vatanaṁdi*. That they are

1. R. P. Chanda, *The beginnings of art in Eastern India*, *M. A. S. I.*, 30, pp. 3—8, 31—33.

2. Ibid ; Mitra, A. K. 'Origin of the bell-capital,' *I. H. Q.* VII, pp. 224—25, 238—44.

monumental sculptural representations of *Yakshas* there can hardly be any doubt, though persistent attempts were once made to identify them as statues of two kings of the Śaiśunāga dynasty of Magadha[1]. This latter theory is no longer seriously pressed ; but it is still generally held that they belong stylistically to the later phase of Mauryan art. I shall try to show later on that the so-called Mauryan polish which is the rock-argument on which the assumption is based can hardly be considered sufficient for their being labelled as Mauryan, and that not only paleographically but stylistically as well, they cannot belong to a period of art earlier than that represented at Sāñchī and in the early primitives of Mathurā.

The fact remains therefore that we have no examples extant of either sculpture or architecture that can definitely be labelled chronologically as pre-Mauryan or perhaps even as pre-Aśokan. Indeed, all evidences suggest that whatever specimens of these two branches of visual art we know cf are directly the products of the Maurya court and the initiative came definitely from the all powerful King himself. Except one or two pillars that stylistically may be ascribed to a date anterior to that of Aśoka, all the rest belong definitely to the latter's reign along with the animal figures that crown them or exist independently. The description of the city of Pāṭaliputra and of the royal palace we read of in the accounts of classical writers like Megasthenes, Arrian, and Strabo, and the excavations at the site of the old city by Waddel and Spooner[2] to which we shall turn at a later stage, may be taken to suggest that Chandragupta, the first Maurya, may have been responsible for the original planning and execution of the building of the city as well as of the royal

1. K. P. Jayaswal, 'Statues of two Saisunāka Emperors', *J. B. O. R. S.*, V. pp. 88—106. The discussion continued through vols. V and VI of the same journal and a number of scholars including R. D. Banerji, V. A. Smith, L. D. Barnett and H. P. Sastri joined. It was further taken up by R. P. Chānda, 'Four ancient Yaksha statues', *J. D. L., Cal. Univ.*, IV, pp. 47—84 ; 'Inscriptions on two Patna Statues in the Indian Museum', *Ind. Ant*, XLVIII, pp. 25—28 ; R. C. Majumdar, 'Alleged Śaiśunāga Statues' Ibid., pp. 419—424 ; O. C. Gangoly, 'A note on Mr. Jayaswal's discovery of two Śaiśunāga statues', *Modern Review*, 1919, October, pp. 419—24 and A. K. Coomaraswamy, *Catalogue of the Indian Collection in the Museum of Fine Arts*, Boston, 1923, Pt. II, p. 4 ; *History of Indian and Indonesian Art*, pp. 16—17.

2. Waddell, *Report on excavations at Pataliputra*, Calcutta, 1903. pp. 22—26; Spooner, *A. S. R.*, 1912—13, pp. 73 ff. *A. S. R, E. C.* 1915—16, pp. 27—28 ; McCrindle, *Ancient India*, 1901, p. 42.

palace ; but there can be little doubt that Bindusāra and Aśoka, particularly the latter, added considerably to the original lay out and the buildings. The Maurya Pillared Hall and the stupendous buildings remains of which were laid bare by Spooner may have been built by Aśoka himself, since their essential ideology and conception agree so remarkably well with all that we already know of the aims, ideals, motives and general ideological mental design of that great benevolent autocrat. Such large designs executed with almost imperial thoroughness can for all that we know only be associated with his name. Of other architectural remains that can definitely be associated with the Maurya dynasty are a few cave-dwellings dedicated by Aśoka and his grandson Daśaratha for the use of the monks of the Ājīvika sect. The sum total of the Mauryan treasury of art may thus on proven grounds, be said to include (1) the remains of the royal palace and city of Pāṭaliputra; (2) a monolithic rail at Sārnāth; (3) the Bodhimaṇḍa or the altar resting on four pilasters at Bodhgayā; (4) the excavated *chaitya*-halls or cave dwellings in the Barābar and Nāgārjunī hills of Gayā including the Sudāmā cave dated in the twelfth year of Aśoka's reign; (5) the non-edict bearing and edict-bearing pillars; (6) the animal sculptures crowning the pillars with animal and vegetal reliefs decorating the abaci of the capitals; and (7) the front half of the representation of an elephant carved out in the round from a live rock at Dhauli in Orissa[1].

1. Other architectural and sculptural remains that are generally ascribed to the Maurya period, on either stylistic or traditional grounds, include (1) A railing (?) pillar with inscription from the Arjunapura site, Mathurā, now lost ; (2) the oldest parts, subsequently enclosed by later additions, of *stūpas* : (3) foundations of chaitya-halls at Sāñchī and Sonārī : (4) two Patna Yaksha statues, now in the Indian museum ; (5) a few fragments of grey polished stone-sculptures from Sārnāth ; (6) a few fragments of sculptures in red spotted sand stone from Mathurā ; (7) a fragmentary relief from Bhitā ; (8) fragments of a ribbed polished stone umbrella from Sāñchī ; (9) two carved perforated circular stone plaques from the Bhīr mound site, Taxila ; (10) a considerable number of terracottas from such widely separated sites as Sārnāth, Basarh, Bulandibagh, Kumrahar and other places round about the old site of Pāṭaliputra, Bhitā, Nagari, Mathurā, Kosam, Sankissa and Taxila ; (11) a chauri-bearing Yaksha statue from Didarganj ; (12) a more than life size Yaksha statue from Parkham ; (13) torso of a Yaksha or king from Baroda, Mathurā ; (14) a seated image now worshipped as Manasā from near Parkham ; (15) two polished stone images with legs and heads broken off of Jaina Tīrthaṅkaras from Lohānīpur, near Patna, and now in the Patna Museum ; and (16) a hooded serpent canopy from Rajgir. About nos. 1, 2 and 3 we are not in a position to make any definite assertion ; the only argument that labels No. 8 as Mauryan is the glossy polish of the stone ; it is difficult to say anything about the date of No. 9 ;

A few characteristics are common to all these sculptural and architectural remains. They are all monumental in conception and design, and inordinately fine, orderly, thorough and precise in execution. Moreover, with the exception of the remains of the royal palace and city-buildings of Pāṭaliputra, all of them were executed in hard grey sandstone of more or less big dimensions, always very finely chiselled and very highly polished to a glossiness that has hardly any parallel in India of later ages and in the world except in ancient Iran. And thirdly, all of them were reared up directly under the shadow of the royal throne of the Mauryas, Aśoka and his grandson fixing their stamp on the majority of them. We are thus confronted with an historical phenomenon that calls for an explanation. Here we are face to face with a period in ancient Indian history when a royal dynasty with imperial ambition and outlook suddenly discards wood and bamboo, perhaps also brick and clay, and takes to the employment of stone as the material *par excellence* for monumental sculpture and architecture, and this new material is handled with such perfect ease and mastery as to suggest that the art of hard and large size stone-cutting was as it were already long in practice. Except those carved out of live rock, all removable pieces were worked out of grey sandstone quarried at Chunar ; the Mauryan columns are all carved out of this material, and it should be remembered that these huge columns are distributed over a very wide area, between Delhi in the west, Basarh in the east and Sāñchī in the south. Most certainly the huge resources of the state made available to the artists rendered possible the conception, planning and execution in such large and gigantic proportions. But royal will and state resources alone cannot explain the sudden transformation from wood, sun-dried brick, clay, ivory and metal to stone or from the fine workmanship and exquisite finish of ivory and metal work to bold and rounded work in stone of huge dimensions. It is possible to postulate that similar bold and large scale work was long in practice in wood in pre-Maurya days,

here too the main argument rests on the glossy polish of the stone. To try to date terracottas on stylistic grounds alone is often dangerous as has so convincingly been shown by Kramrisch and Gordon ; the items under No. 10 and Nos. 4, 5, 6, 7, 11, 12, 13, 14, and 15, I shall have occasion to refer to and discuss at a later stage.

and what the Maurya emperors did was only to initiate the artists and art-guilds into the use of stone and make them translate their traditional skill in terms of a new material. Such an explanation is certainly admissible ; one has only to read through the description of the city and royal palace of Pāṭaliputra left by classical writers[1], and examine the design and execution of many an architectural element of the Maurya, Śuṅga and other early Indian monuments, e.g. the pillars, the railings, the gates, the Chaitya facades, etc. and be convinced of the force of the argument[2]. But the very fact that stone henceforward became the material *par excellence* for Indian plastic art is by itself significant ; equally significant is it that stone sculpture when it first comes to view in India during the Maurya period is already the expression of a civilised and sophisticated and fully developed art that had generations of artistic effort, experience and tradition behind it ; that it is a work in the round, it exists by itself and is borne by its own volume and strength, and that it has an inherent technical and psychological character that the jeweller's or carpenter's art fails to explain and account for. Indeed, past artistic tradition and the art of the wood, clay, ivory, mineral, stone and metal worker in howsoever large a scale and with whatever technical skill and efficiency cannot fully explain the art tradition Mauryan sculptures represent, the technical skill and efficiency of the Mauryan sculptor who worked in stone of huge and heavy proportions, and the atmosphere the sculptures themselves breathe.

II

Socio-historical Background

Any attempt at an explanation of the phenomenon referred to above must take into account the state of artistic effort and activities in India itself during the centuries immediately preceding that of the Mauryas, i.e. during the period of the Haryaṅka, the Śaiśunāga and the Nanda domination. Storeyed buildings presumably of wood and brick, were already widely known, and mention is made of round and square huts perhaps

1. See McCrindle, cited above.
2. Smith, *A history of Fine Art in India & Ceylon*, Chap. III ; Brown, *Indian Architecture : Buddhist & Hindu*, Chaps. II—VI.

of wood and bamboo. An advanced knowledge of the use of metals like tin, lead, silver, copper and iron shaped and formed into objects meant for various domestic and other purposes is already attested by the later Vedic texts; and the *jātakas* reveal that there were eighteen different kinds of *śilpas* or arts and crafts including carpentry, smithery, leather-dressing and painting. Metal workers in general were probably known by the word *kamāra* (*Skt. karmakāra*), and there are definite evidences to suggest that these artists and craftsmen were organised into *seṇis* or guilds. Localisation of certain industrial crafts also took place to the extent that an entire village or a particular locality in the town came to be designated according to the craft practised in the locality. The *jātakas* also afford a more or less vivid picture of contemporary city and village life, villages with scattered huts made of wood and bamboo and reed, cities with roads and lanes lined with buildings of brick and wood, all set off against the background of an agricultural, industrial and commercial life in small scale and within narrow proportions[1]. If we set aside certain stories of the *Mahābhārata*, there is nothing else to suggest that the canvas of contemporary life was large and that it was conceived in any magnificent and monumental scale. Tribal and primitive was indeed the character of the social psychology of Northern India during all these centuries. This tribal and primitive outlook is also fully in evidence in the remains of the old city of Rājagṛiha with its walls and remains of dwellings built of rough cyclopean masonry[2], which is the one definite architectural example that can be said to belong to pre-Mauryan times.

But a slow and steady widening of the tribal and primitive outlook was being effected in the political sphere. Already in the *Aitareya Brāhmaṇa* we hear of such sacrifices as the *Rājasūya* and the *Aindramahābhisheka*, of *sārvabhauma* kings, of paramount rule and of all-encompassing sovereignty. The same political conception of *rājā sārvabhauma* is repeated in *Baudhāyana Śrauta-*

1. *C. H. I.*, I. p. 206.

2. Fergusson, *History of Indian & Eastern Architecture*. 2nd Edn. I. pp. 75—76. For alleged pre-Mauryan antiquities see Coomaraswamy, *History of Indian and Indonesian Art*, p. 10 and notes, Lauriya-Nandangarh gold-plaque of a nude female, fig. 105.

sūtra, and that of *rāja chakkavatti* in early Buddhist and Jaina texts[1]. In reality however the normal political condition of northern India till the fifth and fourth centuries B.C. was not that of an empire of any considerable extent under a *sārvabhauma* monarch but it was that of separate small and independent states and kingdoms each under a king or tribal leader. It was only towards the third quarter of the fourth century B.C. that the ideal was partially achieved in the person of Mahāpadmananda who has been referred to in the Purāṇas as *sarvarājocchettā*, *sarvakshatrāntakanṛpaḥ* and *ekarāṭ*, the supreme monarch, and one of his sons, the last of the dynasty, as the powerful monarch of the Prasioi and the Gangaridai, in the accounts of classical writers.

It is difficult to say whether the evolution of the wider political outlook was the outcome of natural historical process or was directly or indirectly conditioned by India's contact with the contemporary west-Asiatic world. In any case the chronological and historical background is significant and is worth consideration. Already in prehistoric times, the Indus valley civilisation formed a part of the civilisation that extended to ancient Sumer ; much later, the civilisation represented by the *Ṛigveda* was but a cognate of that represented by the *Āvestā*. There is no reason to assume that this intimate relation of India with Iran and the ancient Asiatic west lapsed at any time during the centuries that followed. Indeed, from about 800 B.C. almost continuous contact of Aryanised India with Iran can either be inferred from actual remains of art objects, from lithic records, and from cognate political and cultural ideas and ideologies. In the sixth century B.C. part of northern India went under the political domination of Iran, and gradually the Indus came to form the eastern boundary of the wide Iranian empire of Darius ; indeed this part of India came to be politically organised into the 20th satrapy of that empire[2]. Darius describes himself in his inscriptions as *Kshayathiyanam Kshayathiya*, the King of kings, the great King[3]; he was in reality a *sārvabhauma* monarch of the

1. Keith, *Rigveda Brāhmaṇas*, 1920, p. 331 ; *Sutta-nipāta*, p. 99, Rhys Davids, *Dialogues of the Buddha*, part 2, p. 13 etc ; Chanda cities authorities in *Beginnings of Art in Eastern India*, pp. 13 ff.

2. Ray Chaudhuri, *PHAI* 4th edn. pp. 193-6.

3. A Suez Inscription of Darius in Tolman, *Ancient Persian Lexicon & Texts*, New York, 1908, p. 50.

old Indian conception, an *ekarāṭ* like Mahāpadmananda. Indeed the Achaemenid dynasty was the first to evolve and give reality to the idea of imperial suzerainty which a century later was partially achieved by the Nandas, and fully by the Mauryas[1]. Certainly no contemporary borrowing can at once be postulated but it is likely that both India and Iran participated in a common politico-historical process.

This is more evident in the domain of art and general culture. Indeed early Indian art can be viewed and understood fully only against the background of age-old but very potent and effective Indo-Sumerian and Indo-Iranian contacts maintained through long centuries. In Maurya, Śuṅga, Andhra and Kushāna art, there is a rich treasure of art and decorative *motifs*, ornamentations, devices and patterns that we meet with for the first time and that suggest 'parallels in Sumerian, Hittite, Assyrian, Mycenaean,. Cretan, Trojan, Lycian, Phoenician, Achaemenid and Scythian cultures'. Coomaraswamy gives a long list of such common elements and technical analogies, and finally argues that 'so far as its constituent elements are concerned, and apart from any question of style, there is comparatively little in Indian decorative art that is peculiar to India, and much that India shares with Western Asia.' It is difficult to disagree with Coomaraswamy when further he says :

'All this amounts to proof that the themesand *motifs* of pre-Maurya art cannot have differed very greatly from those of Maurya and Śuṅga ; fantastic animals, palmettes, rosettes, and bell-capitals must have been common elements of the craftsman's repertory under the Nandas as in the time of Aśoka. India, in centuries and perhaps millenniums B.C., was an integral part of an 'Ancient East' that extended from the Mediterranean to the Ganges Valley'[2].

1. In West Asia the idea of the conquest of the 'four regions' or 'four quarters' originated with the Kings of Babylonia and Assyria. But it was actually realised later by the Achaemenian monarchs, notably Cyrus, his son Cambyses, and Darius, son of Hystaspes. In a Suez Incription commemorating the completion of the canal from the Nile to the Red Sea Darius proudly records : 'I (am) Darius, the great King, King of kings, king of countries possessing all people, (king) of this great earth far and wide.' The phrases are almost exactly such as we find in the *Aitareya Brāhmaṇa* and *Baudhāyana Śrauta Sūtra*. Also see Chanda, *Beginnings of Art*......pp. 17—20.

2. Coomāraswamy, *History of Indian and Indonesion Art*, pp. 11-14 where the whole aspect is fully discussed. Also Combaz—*L'Inde et L'orient Classique* (Paris, 1937).

Apart from India forming an integral part of an 'Ancient East' and sharing in a common cultural heritage from very early times, there is more or less definite evidence of intimate cultural contact of India with Iran in particular from about the eighth and seventh centuries B.C. The North-west and the Indus valley forming a part of Darius's empire made contacts with Iran easier still. This intimate contact must have been responsible for certain elements in Buddhist and later Brahmanical mythology, tradition, worship and iconography, especially those connected with the cults of the Sun and Fire[1]. It was also responsible for the origin and evolution of the Kharoshṭhī script in about the fifth or fourth century B.C. An Aramaic inscription belonging to about the fourth century B.C. has actually been found at Taxila[2]. The Haryaṅkas, the Śaiśunāgas and the Nandas must have more or less felt the pressure of this contact, but since their dominions lay far away from the regions where presumably the effects of the impact of the two civilisations were directly felt, Eastern India was perhaps only indirectly touched by Iranian contacts.

With the coming of the Mauryas to power on the throne of Pāṭaliputra, with the building up of an all-India empire by Chandragupta extending up to modern Afghanistan and therefore touching almost what had once been the heart of Achaemenid power and culture, with the establishment of intimate friendly relations with contemporary Hellenistic powers, and friendly contact of Maurya kings and court with Greek political and cultural representatives from Graeco-Bactrian courts and kingdoms, the situation took a new turn. The Achaemenid empire had long gone to dust and India had ceased to form a part of that empire. In 330 B. C. Alexander the Great overthrew the once mighty Persian Empire, but in the process of consolidating his conquest the Greek conqueror came under the overpowering influence of Achaemenian imperialism and Achaemenian art and culture. Plutarch has a long and vivid description of how Alexander behaved himself at Persepolis and how he worked for a fusion of the cultures of Greece and of Iran of the

1. Coomaraswamy, p. 22.
2. Marshall, *A Guide to Taxila*, pp. 9, 77—78.

Achaemenid monarchs. Donned in the robes of Iranian monarchs he used to sit on the throne of Darius under a golden canopy. He himself married Darius's daughter Statira, and married his Greek friends to Iranian ladies ; one of these friends was Seleucus, later known as Seleucus Nicator, who married Apama, the daughter of Spitamenes. Not satisfied with having simply adopted somewhat the Persian mode of dress, Alexander, says Plutarch, 'accommodated himself more than ever to the manner of the Asiatics, and at the same time persuaded them to adopt some of the Macedonian fashions ; for by a mixture of both he thought an union might be promoted much better than by force, and his authority maintained even when he was at a distance. For the same reason he selected thirty thousand (Persian) boys and gave them masters to instruct them in Grecian literature as well as train them to arms in the Macedonian manner'.[1]

The same process seems to have been fully at work in the realm of art. Colonial Hellenistic art was slowly coming under the influence of Persian art, specially of Persian *motifs*, patterns and designs on the one hand, while Persian art itself began to feel the pressure of Ionian and Hellenistic influences onwards from the fifth century B.C.[2] This pressure became active during and after the Achaemenid period, so that when the Mauryas came into intimate contact with the colonial Greeks of Western Asia, both Achaemenid and Hellenistic art-traditions had largely influenced each other.

After the withdrawal of the Macedonian army of Alexander and the establishment of an alliance of Chandragupta Maurya with Seleucus, the Mauryas came into very intimate friendly relations with the Seleucid Greek houses, and this relation continued from generation to generation. Besides contracting a matrimonial alliance Chandragupta repeatedly received Megasthenes as an ambassador from Seleucus, is reported to have sent Seleucus some strange Indian drugs presumably through his own envoy, and is further said to have been used to offer sacrifices in Hellenic manner to Alexander's altars on the Hyphases. The ceremonial at the court of this king described

1. Plutarch quoted by Chanda, *Beginnings*......p. 18.

2. Sarre, *Die Kunst des Alten Persiens*, pp. 20—25 ; Carotti, *A History of Art*, I, pp. 93—794 ; Bell, *Early Architecture in Western Asia*, p. 231.

by classical writers also reveals Achaemenian influence[1]. His son Bindusāra had also in his court a Greek envoy, Deimachus of Plataea, sent by Antiochus I, son of Seleucus. Bindusāra also, like his father seems to have been a Hellenophil ; he wrote back to Antiochus requesting him to buy and send on to him sweet wine, dried figs and a Greek sophist. From Antiochus came the reply : 'We shall send you dried figs and sweet wine, but it is not lawful in Greece to sell a sophist.' Diodorus speaks of a Greek author Iamboulus by name who found his way to the king of Palibothra, and this king of Palibothra, presumably Bindusāra or at least one of the first three Maurya monarchs, 'had a great love for the Grecians.' Aśoka's friendly relations with the *Yavanas* or the Greek states of Western Asia and Egypt are well-known ; the world that he claims to have conquered by his policy of *Dhammavijaya* was preeminently this Hellenistic world ; he arranged for the medical treatment of men and cattle, among others, in the dominions of Antiochus Theos and his neighbours ; and it is not unlikely that his description of himself as *devānampiya Piyadasi* is an echo of the deification of kings current among Alexander's successors in Hellenistic Orient. Both Megasthenes and Kauṭilya refer to a State department run and maintained specifically for the purpose of looking after foreigners[2] who evidently were quite numerous not only in the capital city of Pāṭaliputra but in other provincial capitals and trade centres. There can hardly be any doubt that these foreigners were mostly colonial Greeks and a very large majority of them were merchants and businessmen. Indeed in the third century B.C. a caravan highway ran from Taxila *via* Kandahar, Persepolis and Susa to Seleuceia on the Tigris, while another old main road ran *via* Kandahar, Herat, Hecatompylos, Ecbatana and Seleuceia and was joined by the Taxila-Kabul-Bactria route[3]. Taxila, it is well known, was the seat of an important Maurya province, and from here a great high-

1. Hultzsch, *C.I.I.* I, pp. xxxiv-xxxv, xlii,; *C.H.I.* I, p. 433 ; Bevan, *The House of Seleucus*, Lond., 1902, I, p. 297 ; Smith, *Early History of India*, pp. 128 ff ; 'Persian Influence on Mauryan India', *I. A.* 1905. pp. 201-3.

2. McCrindle, *Ancient India*, p. 54 ; Kauṭilya *Arthaśāstra*, Shamasastry's edn. p. 144 (II 36).

3. Tarn, W. W., *Hellenistic Civilisation*, Chap. VII, pp. 199—214 ; Jouguet, P., *Macedonian Imperialism*, pp. 93—107, 353, 358.

way ran direct to connect Pāṭaliputra with the Hellenic east. Besides, there was also a coastal sea-borne trade route to Seleuceia along the Persian Gulf and up the Tigris, and to Egypt following the coastline. It is this trade route that explains the Aramaic inscription referred to above and datable in the fourth century B. C. It was along this route also that foreigners including envoys, Greek traders, travellers, artists and craftsmen must have flocked to Mauryan India in such numbers as to oblige the State to maintain a department to look after their comfort and well-being. This intimate contact indeed explains such finds as the fragmentary handle of a terracotta vase showing Alexander's head in lion's skin and recovered from Taxila[1], or random finds from Sārnāth, Basarh and the Patna region of terracotta pieces of distinctive Hellenistic appearance or with definite Hellenistic *motifs* and design[2]. That they belong probably to a later date does not minimise the importance of the very intimate relations the Maurya court maintained with the Hellenic east ; rather they point out that even after the decline and downfall of the Mauryas parts of India continued to remain in touch with the Hellenistic world. Within a century after the death of Aśoka a Greek army penetrated as far east as Mādhyamika near Chitor and Sāketa near Ayodhyā.

The Maurya kings and the Maurya court were indeed Hellenophils, but it was evidently their Hellenophilism that also brought them into an indirect contact with the art and culture of the Achaemenids. The grandiose and magnificent monuments of the Achaemenid monarchs were still standing when the Mauryas came to exercise all India suzerainty and Maurya art was making its appearance. Certain Achaemenian forms and *motifs* had presumably already migrated to the Punjab and the Indus valley during the Achaemenian occupation of the region. Exacavations at the Bhir mound at Taxila yielded from the pre-Hellenistic strata a scaraboid of steatite exhibiting a winged

1. *A. S. R.* Pt. I, 1920—21, p. 20, Pl. XVI, Fig. 2.

2. Bachhofer, op. cit. p. 12, Pl. 13 ; *A. S. R.* Pt. I., 1917—18, p. 27 Pl. XVI, Fig. 2 ; ibid, 1913—14, p. 182, No. 791, Pl. xliii, fig. (h). Read with this Nearchus's statement to the effect that 'the Indians quickly learnt to make Greek articles such as the scrapers and oilflasks used by athletes'. *C.H.I.* I, p. 418. For the Hellenophilism of the Mauryas see also Ray Chaudhuri, *P. H. A. I.* 4th edn., p. 245.

stag which is reminiscent of similar objects of Achaemenian origin[1]. 'The Indian punch-marked silver coinage struck on the Persian standard perhaps represented the Achaemenian coinage for India'[2]. But even after the extinction of Achaemenian power importation of Achaemenian art objects to India seems to have continued. Curtius, Diodorus, and Arrian state that Alexander presented to the king of Taxila among other things a large number of gold and silver vessels and an enormous quantity of Babylonian and Persian embroideries from the treasury of old Persian monarchs[3]. It has also been pointed out that a few minor antiquities found in the upper strata of the Bhir mound excavations 'reflect the influence of Achaemenian art.' Among these, four bangles of thin beaten gold terminating in lion's heads, and a fragment of pottery from the side of a vase decorated with the conventional leaf design and reminiscent of the capitals of well-known Aśoka pillars, are particularly noteworthy. Moreover a polished sandstone head from Sārnāth wearing a crenellated crown, the method of wearing the waist cloth without the *Kaccha* as we find in the two Patna Yaksha statues in the Indian Museum, and the coiled armlets decorated spirally and terminating in a Dragon's head, of the same statues, inevitably recall Achaemenian parallels[4]. It is evident that the trade routes referred to above opened up avenues through which Maurya India came to acquire more direct and intimate contact with Medo-Achaemenian art and culture, perhaps through Greek intermediaries.

But more important evidence of Achaemenian cultural influence on the Maurya court and Maurya cultural ideology is afforded by the accounts of the city and royal palace of Pāṭaliputra left by classical authors, evidently following Megasthenes, and by the actual remains of the same city and palace unearthed by Waddell and Spooner[5]. Strabo says that the city of Palibothra was situated at the confluence of the Ganges and the Erannoboas (Hiraṇyavāha, the modern Son) ; it was 80 stadia

1. *A. S. R.* Pt. I, 1919—20, p. 23, Pl. XI. fig. 2.
2. *Camb. Anc. Hist.* VI., p. 402 ; *C. H. I.*, I, pp. 319—44.
3. *C. H. I.* I. p. 359 ; Smith *Early History of India*, 4th edn. pp. 65—66.
4. Mitra, 'Origin of the Bell-Capital', *I. H. Q.* VII, pp. 229—230.
5. McCrindle, Waddell and Spooner, op. cit.

in length and 15 in breadth and was of the shape of a parallelogram. The city was surrounded by a wooden wall pierced with loop-holes for the discharge of arrows, crowned with 560 towers and provided with 60 gates. In sumptuousness and magnificence, according to Strabo, Pāṭaliputra compared very favourably with Susa and Ecbatana. Waddell's excavations actually laid bare the remains of what had been once the city wall, and Spooner later brought to light remains of huge wooden buildings at Bulandibagh and Kumrahar, both near Patna. The remains of one of these buildings are of particular significance—those of a pillared hall in which stone columns were employed to support the roof. Of the eighty pillars that had once stood on a wooden platform and supported a wooden roof Spooner was able to discover the entire lower part of at least one in almost perfect condition—it is more or less like an Aśokan pillar, smooth, highly polished and made of grey Chunar sandstone. Writing about Indian towns Arrian says, 'All their towns which are down beside the rivers or the sea are made of wood ; for towns built of brick would never hold out for any length of time with the rains on the one hand, and on the other, the rivers which rise above their banks and spread a sheet of water over the plains. But the towns which are built on elevated places out of reach, these are built of brick and clay.' The excavations of Waddell and Spooner admirably confirm what we are told by Strabo and Arrian, and constitute one more proof of the fact that before the employment of stone for building purposes, wood was generally the only material for even the most sumptuous and magnificent buildings. Spooner's excavations however revealed for the first time that stone was employed for building purposes in at least one building of the Maurya royal city, and that it was a pillared hall. That the magnificent palaces of Pāṭaliputra reminded Megasthenes of the palaces of Susa and Ecbatana is not without significance when it is remembered that the Maurya Pillared Hall reminded Spooner of the famous Hall of Hundred Columns erected at Persepolis by Darius the Great. 'Whereas no other structure of really early date in ancient India disclosed,' says Spooner, 'an arrangement of pillars in square bays over the whole floor the hall at Kumrahar did show this otherwise unparalleled arrangement, and this was identical with the arrangement of the pillars in the Achaemenian Hall. The columns themselves moreover showed a technique in their polished surface which is not only known to have been un-Indian, and outside the line of Indian architectural development, but which again is identical with Persepolitan workmanship'. Apart from the question of the origin and morphology of the Aśokan pillars to which we shall have occasion to turn later on, there can hardly be any doubt that the Maurya Pillared Hall owed its inspiration and general design to the Hall of Hundred Columns erected by Darius. We have it on the authority of classical writers that Chandragupta's palace at Pāṭaliputra consisted of halls whose gilded pillars were adorned with golden vines and silver birds ; indeed fragments of golden vines have been discovered in the excavations at Kumrahar. We know that the halls of the palaces of Ecbatana had gilded pillars constructed of cedar and cypress and golden vines of the pillars invariably recall the vines hanging over the couch of Darius—a gift of the Lydian Pythias and perhaps of Ionian workmanship. It is difficult to say whether the Maurya Pillared Hall at Pāṭaliputra was the conception of Chandragupta himself or one of his successors—personally I think it was built at the direction of Aśoka —but there can be no doubt that one of the three early Maurya emperors was responsible for it, nor is it unlikely that 'this adoption of the Persepolitan style of building at Pāṭaliputra was not the normal result of the contact of the Achaemenian and Indian sculptures but was due to conscious adoption of the plan of the Achaemenian Hall of Public Audience by the Mauryan emperor (Aśoka) as a part of the paraphernalia of his imperialism....'[1].

It has been argued with some force that Mauryan imperialism as revealed in the inscriptions of Aśoka was largely influenced by the imperial ideology of the Hellenistic and Achaemenian monarchs[2]. This may not be altogether unlikely, but be that as it may, the fact remains that the inscriptions themselves reveal the extent to which Aśoka was indebted to his great Achaemenian predecessor Darius, not only for the idea of making his royal edicts known throughout his empire but also for the form of the

1. Chanda, *Beginnings*......p. 12.
2. Ibid, p. 17—20.

inscriptions themselves[1]. At the end of the Susian version of the Behistun inscription of Darius we have the following :

'(Thus) saith Darius, the king : By the grace of Auramazda I made inscriptions in another fashion....such as was not formerly ....and it was written and I....then I sent the same inscriptions into all lands, and the people....'

The duplicate copies were evidently written on leather or brick as the one discovered by Koldeway suggests. This was also the arrangement made by Aśoka for the circulation of his edicts (R.E. XIV, Kaliṅga Edict I, P. E. VII). The very idea indeed of recording royal orders and directions on such permanent material as rocks (and pillars) seems to have been inspired by Achaemenian practice. In respect of the form of the Aśokan inscriptions Senart long ago pointed out their strong resemblance with that of the inscriptions of the Achaemenian kings. The edicts of Aśoka begin with the usual formula *Devanampiya Piyadasi evamāha* which according to Senart 'is an absolutely isolated example in Indian epigraphy....In the entire series of the inscriptions of the Achaemenides, from Darius to Artaxerxes Ochus, the phrase *thatey Darayavaush Kshayathiya*, "thus saith the king Darius," or its equivalent *thatey Kshayarsha*, etc., inevitably forms the preamble of each of the proclamations. In both cases, this phrase in the third person is immediately succeeded by the use of the first person, and we are still further justified in drawing attention to this curious fact that, again in both cases the same word—*dipi*, *lipi*—is used to designate the inscriptions, and that, as we have seen, we are led to admit, on altogether independent grounds, that the Indian form of the word was originally borrowed from Persia.' Aśoka's peculiar way of exhorting people to follow the laws of Dhamma also seems to have been adopted from Achaemenian practice initiated by Darius in his inscriptions (Behistun and Naksh-i-Rustam inscriptions).[2]

Two important facts emerge. First, that whatever extant remains we can lay our hands on as definitely belonging to the Maurya Period are products of the Maurya Court, i.e. they were worked out by orders of the Maurya monarchs and perhaps also

1. Ibid, pp. 21—26.
2. *Ind. Ant.* XX. pp. 255—56.

under their direct supervision. Secondly, that this court and its presiding lords were all ardent Hellenophils and were largely under the influence of Achaemenian art and culture at the same time. It is to this second factor that we can ascribe the fixation of Indian art in permanent materials during this period for the first time and the handling of stone for sculptural and architectural purposes with perfect ease and efficiency. At the same time it has to be recognised that there existed in India a pre-Mauryan art mainly practised in wood and partly in sun-dried brick, clay, ivory, metal and mineral stone. Admittedly this art could hardly conceive life and things in huge proportions and large dimensions ; tribal and primitive outlook circumsscribed the vision of the artists and craftsmen who must also have been handicapped by the very nature of the materials they used. But this art happened to be the repository of certain patterns, designs, and *motifs* that India shared in common with the rest of the early Asiatic world.

For the rest, we know from Megasthenes, Kauṭilya and the Inscriptions of Aśoka himself that the Maurya administration was a highly centralised bureaucracy ; and the Maurya monarch nothing short of a benevolent autocrat. Aśoka's *dhammavijaya* was more an imperial policy than a religious missionary movement and his moral exhortations to his people had almost the force of law behind them. He had even gone to the length of regulating the social and religious life of his people according to his conception of *Dhamma*. The king and the court were both highly conscious of their power and their imperial glory—Aśoka's inscriptions breathe the very air of this consciousness. And if the *Arthaśāstra* of Kauṭilya is to be believed, law, order and precision were the watchwords of the Mauryan government. This is surprisingly reflected in the writings of the inscriptions themselves ; not only are they beautifully executed, but they are indeed remarkable for their clarity, orderliness and precision ; every single letter is cut into the stone with accuracy and care, lines are more often than not straight and well-ordered, and mistakes, considering the enormous output, few and far between. The socio-economic policy of the Mauryan State was also highly centralised and monopolistic.

Mauryan art has to be viewed and understood against this historical, cultural, and sociological background. This would help us to understand the outlook and ideology of Mauryan art.

III
Columns

The highly polished, tall and well proportioned columns with slightly tapering monolithic shafts, and standing free in space and complete and independent by themselves are admittedly the best representatives of the court art of the Mauryas. The columns that bear the edicts of Aśoka include those of Delhi-Mirath, Allahabad, Lauriya-Araraj, Lauriya-Nandangarh, Rampurva (with lion capital), Delhi-Topra, Sankissa, Sāñchī and Sārnāth ; the non-edict bearing columns known up till now include those of Rampurva (with bull-capital), Basarh-Bakhira (with single lion capital), and Kosam (capital not yet recovered) the third category, that of columns bearing dedicatory inscriptions, includes at least two well-known specimens, those of Rummindei and Nigālī Sāgar. Of these the capitals of Basarh-Bakhira and Lauriya-Nandangarh pillars are in *situ* ; those of Rampurva (both bull and lion crowned), Sankissa, Sārnāth and Sāñchī have been recovered in more or less damaged condition. The Lauriya-Nandangarh and Basarh-Bakhira pillars and one of the two Rampurva columns are crowned by a single lion seated on its haunches ; the Sankissa pillar by a standing elephant ; the second Rampurva column by a standing bull ; and the Sārnāth and Sāñchī columns by four semi-lions addorsed or united back to back. The Lauriya-Araraj column seems once to have been crowned by a Garuḍa capital[1], while the fragment of a capital of Chunar sandstone with Mauryan polish and probably of Mauryan date, (now in the Patna Museum) recovered from the village called Salempur, Muzaffarpur District, shows that it consisted of four semi-bulls seated back to back on a plain square abacus, the animals themselves being superimposed by a square block decorated with honey-suckle

1. Chanda, *Beginnings*, p. 23.

ornaments. Perhaps the Rummindei pillar was once crowned by a horse[1].

It has been suggested on an eighth century Sinhalese parallel that these crowning animals—elephant, horse, bull and lion—should be considered as guardians of the four cardinal points[2] Doubts may be entertained if such an interpretation derivable from an eighth century Sinhalese monument can with equal force be ascribed to the Aśokan animal capitals. Nor can it definitely be said theyare all even exclusively Buddhist Symbols. Except the horse, all the three other animals as well as the Garuḍa that is assumed to have once crowned the Lauriya-Araraj pillar are symbols associated with early Brahmanical tradition and mythology, though the elephant, especially the white elephant, was considered particularly sacred in Buddha-legend as well. (Cf. also the Dhauli elephant and the word, 'seto' or the 'White One' at the end of the sixth edict ; the phrase alluding to the white elephant below the thirteenth Girnār R.E. ; the word '*gajatame*' or 'the best of elephants' and the drawing of an elephant on the north face of the Kālsī rock). Moreover, a close study of the Rupnath and Sahasram Rock Inscriptions, and the Seventh Pillar Edict suggests definitely that some at least of the pillars bearing his edicts must have been in existence before Aśoka chose to have his rescripts on morality engraved on them—they may even be pre-Aśokan, and consequently may have nothing to do with Buddhism—while others were erected by Aśoka himself and were his own *Dharmastambhas*. And lastly, it has been argued with some force that these pillars with animal capitals are but translations in stone of primitive animal standards[3].

The internal evidence of the Inscriptions themselves helps us to arrive at a rough chronological sequence of the columns. The Rummindei pillar was raised in the 20th year of the great monarch's reign while the Rampurva column with the lion capital in the 26th year, followed a year later by the Lauriya-Nandangarh column bearing the six pillar edicts dated in the

1. Smith, *A History of Fine Art in India & Ceylon*, p. 18 ; Hultzsch, *C.I.I.*, I. p. xxii.
2. Smith, 'The Monolithic Pillars of Aśoka,' *Z. D. M. G.*, 1911.
3. Chanda, *Beginnings*......pp. 31—33.

27th year. The Sārnāth pillar could not have been raised before the 28th year ; it bears edicts that do not find place in other columns. In any case, all scholars agree that this column belongs to the last years of Aśoka's reign.

We may add to this the stylistic evidence afforded by the columns and capitals themselves. So far as columns are concerned a definite starting point is furnished by the Basarh-Bakhira column. Compared with the other columns of known Aśokan dates the shaft of this column is heavy and of shorter proportions, its workmanship crude and rough. The plain square abacus which is by itself an almost sure indication of an earlier date has no integral relation with the bell-capital below, and is moreover heavy in proportion. The crowning lion recouchant, though a free and independent figure, is not only rough and crude in execution, but has not yet evolved the form and appearance so as to make of itself an integrated whole together with the shaft, capital and the abacus. The next milestone is furnished by the elephant-crowned Sankissa column. The clumsy and heavy workmanship of the animal, its plump shape, and the sense of form revealed seem to suggest a near parallel with the Dhauli elephant which has to be dated in the twelfth or thirteenth year of the reign of Aśoka. The filling up of the depth between the legs by rock-designs and the decorations of the abacus framed only at the lower border are both primitive in design and workmanship and are presumably translated from wooden designs ; the border decoration is particularly reminiscent of wood. But already the abacus has changed from square to round and has been given a form that keeps rhythmic balance between the animal above and the capital below. The bull-crowned Rampurva pillar seems to form a pair with the one just described so far as stylistic chronology is concerned or comes not very long after. The crowning bull though rendered with energy and evident naturalism indeed fails to keep harmony with the abacus and the capital, and the rosettes and honey-suckle decoration on the abacus itself is a little heavy and rough in execution. But it cannot be far out in date from either the lion-crowned Rampurva column or the similarly crowned Lauriya-Nandangarh column. In both instances the abacus, which is artistically integrated and harmonised with the capital below, is decorated with a row of pecking geese ; but while the Rampurva lion is entirely contained within the abacus, the Nandangarh lion finds it difficult to fit itself to the round abacus ; its rump and part of its hind legs project beyond the abacus in an unbalanced manner. The last stage in the evolution is marked by the Sārnāth and Sāñchī pillars both crowned by four semi-lions joined back to back at the shoulders and carrying the Buddhist symbol of the Wheel, instead of by a single animal (whether lion, bull or elephant) as had hitherto been the practice, and that without any crowning symbol. The Salempur column crowned by four semi-bulls joined back to back must also belong to this stage of evolution.

We shall try to see at a later stage to what extent this chronological sequence is upheld by a stylistic analysis of the animal sculptures themselves.

A clear idea of the whole and of component parts of a Maurya column is afforded by the Lauriya-Nandangarh column which is a perfect specimen of the long series of such columns. All Maurya columns, no matter where they are set up, are chiselled out of grey Chunar sandstone and have a lustrous polish due to the application perhaps of silicious varnish on the stone. This uniform place of origin of the material probably suggests that there was at or near Chunar an art-centre established and patronised directly by the Maurya Court, an assumption supported by the additional fact that all the component parts of the columns including the crowning animal, abacus and the shaft tend increasingly to form one whole so far as form and technique are concerned. At least this was the problem the artists were confronted with and which they tried to solve with increasing success. The component parts that are easily known are (1) the shaft always plain and smooth, circular in section and slightly tapering upwards, without any base whatsoever, and always and invariably chiselled out of one piece of stone ; (2) the capital having the shape and appearance of a gently arched bell formed of lotus petals, the proportionate ratio of breadth and height being variable from capital to capital, and joined with the shaft by a copper-bolt of cylindrical shape bulging in the middle (Cf. the Rampurva lion-capital column and the copper bolt that used once to connect the capital with the shaft) ; (3) the abacus, square and plain in the earlier specimens and circular and decorated in the later ones, and of variable proportions ; (4) and the crowning animal, seated or standing, always and invariably in the round, and always constituting a single piece with the abacus. The constituent elements may now be taken up one by one.

The surface of the shaft as of the other elements is cut and executed with remarkable precision and accuracy, and except in the case of the Basarh-Bakhira pillar which is heavy and massive, the shafts, to judge by the Lauriya-Nandangarh example as well as fragments of the column, seem to have maintained a graceful and elegant proportion throughout. They are maintained in position by simply being buried in the earth and by plain slabs of stone or plain brickwork at the bottom. This gives them an appearance of stability, as if they stand by their own weight. The shaft is superimposed by the bell-shaped capital. In some cases as in the Rummindei column the transition from the shaft to the capital is abrupt, while in other instances it is made easy and gradual by the introduction of intermediate mouldings of variable stages and designs ; in the Basarh-Bakhira column there are three retreating mouldings decorated with rope-bead-reel designs ; similar mouldings are to be seen in the Lauriya-Nandangarh example as well ; elsewhere the mouldings are plain. The surface of the gently arched bell-shaped capital is decorated with highly stylised longitudinal lotus-petals with sharp and thin ridges in the middle, and wide and roundish border mouldings, the spaces between the ends of the petals being filled up with short mouldings. In the earliest Mauryan example, i.e. the Basarh-Bakhira specimen, the transition from the capital to the square abacus is marked by a cable moulding of West-Asiatic twisted rope design which is repeated in later examples also, except in the lion-topped Rampurva and Sārnāth examples. In other Mauryan examples the formal appearance of the capital is the same, but there is a progressive attempt towards a clearer and sharper definition of the middle ridge and border mouldings and increasing stylisation which are all fully in evidence in the Sārnāth specimen. The real aesthetic significance of the beautifully arched and elegantly ribbed floral bell of the Mauryan capital lies in its gentle curve, its chaste and rhythmic proportion and in its very effective contrast with the chaste, elegant, plain, smooth, tall and tapering shaft that it crowns. The capital also, like the abacus and the shaft, shows the different stages of a process of artistic evolution, though the chronological sequence cannot be definitely established ; but the steady growth of the feeling for form and more and more linear rhythm is unmistakable. The abacus is indeed the pedestal for the crowning animal ; in the change of its form from square to round, of its appearance from plain to decorated surface beginning with low and culminating in bold and high relief work in various *motifs* and designs, and in the attempt for increasing harmonisation of the abacus with the bell-shaped capital below and the crowning animal above, a discerning eye can clearly trace the stages of the progressive evolution of an architectonic form existing by itself. This becomes further evident when we compare the entire ensemble formed by the crowning animal, the abacus and the capital as we see it in various stages from the Basarh-Bakhira example through Sankissa and Rampurva to Sārnāth. Beginning from disjoined and ununified parts of unequal proportions and a broken linear rhythm at Basarh-Bakhira, it steadily marches towards integration of the component parts into one whole until it reaches its perfection at Sārnāth where the parts are clear, distinct and well-defined, well-proportioned and singularly evenly balanced and forming one integrated whole and maintaining a linear rhythm throughout, so much so that the crowning elements on the shaft contribute the most positive character that gives the Maurya columns the independent effect of complete monumental works. From primitive animal standards to such monumental works it must have been a long journey, but royal will and state resources, the individual taste and ideology of a benevolent autocrat, and perhaps also foreign hand and inspiration so potently at work at the Maurya court achieved the end of this long and arduous journey within a very short space of time. The total aesthetic effect of Maurya columns has never been surpassed in later Indian art, and in the whole realm of independent monumental columns of the world, Mauryan columns occupy a proud position by reason of their very free and significant artistic form in space, the rhythmic and balanced proportion of their constituent elements, the unitary and integrated effect of the whole, the chaste and elegant shaft and capital, and no less by the conscious, proud and dignified attitude of the crowning ornaments.

There can be no doubt that the impetus came from outside. The very sudden use of stone and that at once for monumental art of large designs and huge proportions, and the quick process of evolution from primitive to conscious, civilised and sophisticated form and appearance, from tribal to imperial outlook that is evident in the total effect of the columns point unmistakably in that direction. It has been repeatedly suggested, not without reason, that this extraneous impetus and inspiration came from Iran of the Achaemenid emperors ; some have even suggested that Mauryan columns are but Indian adaptations of the Achaemenian prototype. As repeatedly attempts have been made to deny the alleged extent of debt, not again without a certain amount of justice ; but few have seriously doubted that West Asiatic art-forms in general and Achaemenian impetus and inspiration directly and in particular were at work at the root. Nor against the background of what we know of Mauryan relations with Hellenic East and the Mauryan court ideology and tradition deeply tinged with Achaemenian ideas were such impetus and inspiration unlikely, especially when we take into account the extent of Achaemenian influence on Aśokan epigraphs, his imperial idea and policy and the conception of the Mauryan Pillared Hall referred to above. But the differences that separate the Mauryan columns from the Achaemenian ones are also considerable and must not be lost sight of.

The stone columns of the Maurya Pillared Hall were evidently without capitals whereas the columns of the pillared halls of Persepolis are provided with more or less elaborate capitals. Achaemenian columns stand either on bell-shaped bases or on plain rectangular blocks or on plain circular mouldings while the independent Mauryan columns have no base at all. The bell form that is used as supporting base in Persian columns serves as capital in Mauryan ones and makes altogether a different aesthetic effect ; and moreover in form, shape and appearance the Mauryan bell, which along with the Achaemenian may have originally been derived from stylised lotus design and which may have been a common art-*motif* in both Indian and Iranian art-heritage, is a long way off from the Achaemenian bell in which a ring of leaves and petals plays an important part in the decoration of the upper end of the *motif* and which has no bulge whatsoever in the middle that makes the Mauryan bell so gainly and conspicuous. The Achaemenian shaft is fluted in all cases 'save in the facades of the necropolis at Persepolis and the single column that still remains of the palace of Cyrus in the upland valley of Polvar. In the latter case the anomaly is to be explained by the fact that the building to which the support belonged dates from a time when Persian art had not constituted itself and was as yet groping to strike out a path of its own. On the contrary, the rockcut tombs are coeval with the palaces of Darius and Xerxes and if in them the shaft is plain, it was because the vaults stood at a considerable height above ground. To have made them fluted therefore would have still further reduced the column and divested it of a frank clear aspect when viewed at that distance. To obviate so untoward a contingency the Persian sculptor modified the forms as the Greeks often did in similar cases[1].' Mauryan columns are all plain and circular, but evidently they did not adopt the type from Achaemenian unfluted ones which had for ordinary purposes been discarded by the Achaemenians themselves. A funeral mound at Lauriya-Nandangarh has yielded to the excavator's spade a plain and circular piece of a column carved out of *sāla* wood ; such columns are in our literature known as *sthūṇa*, and the primitive animal standards were evidently comprised of such *sthūṇa* columns[2]. It is not unlikely that the Mauryan shaft was derived from such wooden originals. The assumption derives further support from the fact that Achaemenian shafts are indeed built of separate pieces or segments of stone and evidently present the essential character of the work of a mason, while the Mauryan shaft is one piece which pertains to the character of the work of a wood-carver or carpenter. The Achaemenian capitals crowned with a cluster of stylised palm-leaves after the old Egyptian manner, and formed of either of

1. Perrot and Chipiez, *History of Art in Persia*, pp. 87—88.

2. *A. S. R.* 1908—09, pp. 123—24, Pl. XL ; also see, Maitra, 'Mauryan Art,' *I. H. Q.* III, pp. 543—45.

two semi-bulls or unicorns or lions seated back to back, or of an upright or inverted cup, and the whole crowned with projecting double volutes have nothing whatsoever in common with the Mauryan capitals which consist, as we have seen, of simply a bell formed of stylised lotus-petals. The crowning abacus and the round and independent animal *motif* of Mauryan columns are also altogether absent from Achaemenian examples.

The result achieved by this almost thorough transformation is altogether different. The Achaemenian column intended invariably as part of a larger architectural conception is composed of much too many component parts presenting harsh contrasts and looking complex and complicated, while the Mauryan column intended to produce the effect of an independent monument at least in its latest and best specimen is simpler, more harmonious in conception and execution, and gives the feeling of greater stability, dignity and strength, born perhaps of other primitive and elemental origins. The indigenous and original contribution to the creation of this item of Mauryan art is therefore undeniable. Equally undeniable is also the fact that in their lustrous varnish, in their adoption and adaptation of the bell-shaped capital, in the higher plane of conception and driving idea and in the general monumental and dignified quality and appearance they exhibit, the Mauryan columns seem to reveal clearly the debt they owe to Achaemenian art, as well as to Hellenistic Art so far as the crowning member of the columns and part of the general effect are concerned. The twisted rope design, the bead-reel-cable design and so on to mark the transitions, the acanthus-leaf and palmette and other designs to decorate the abacus may have however been derived from the older and common West-Asiatic art-heritage.

IV

Animal Figures

The almost colossal animal sculptures that crown the Mauryan columns along with the elephant of Dhauli in Orissa may conveniently be studied separately. Here too as in the case of the column itself a rough chronological sequence of the stages of striving after the desired effect can well be traced. The Basarh-Bakhira lion evidently marks one of the earliest stages ; the next definite stage is reached at Dhauli where the elephant but half emerges from live rock and which is datable as we know in the twelfth or thirteenth year of Aśoka's reign ; to this stage must also be ascribed the elephant of Sankissa. The Rampurva bull marks the next stage in the ascending scaleclosely followed by the Lauriya-Nandangarh lion ; while the Rampurva lion leads us to the final stage represented by the quadripartite semi-lions of Sārnāth and Sāñchī—an unmistakable evidence of clever accumulation that always comes at a later stage of the evolution of form.

The Basarh-Bakhira lion is clumsy in form and appearance and crude in execution. The feeling for linear rhythm is evident in the flowing line gliding downwards from the top of the head but ends abruptly at the hard line of the slab where the tail turns inwards. The manes are already highly stylised and locks are treated in separate volumes clumsily arranged. The facial expression is quaint and primitive and the entire attitude lacks dignity. The volume of the lion's body has undoubtedly been fully visualised and reproduced, but the essential plastic sense has not yet matured. The living body is hardly moved by any energy and vigour that is within ; it exists only by the weight of its volume.

Compared to this the Dhauli elephant shows a much more developed sense of form and is artistically far superior to its Sankissa cousin. Indeed, such plastic presentation of bulky volume, such feeling for living flesh rendered with remarkable realism, such knowledge of the physiognomical form of the subject treated and such sense of dignified movement and linear rhythm have no parallel in Mauryan animal sculptures. Compared to this even the Rampurva lion or the Sārnāth quadripartite with their tight and coagulated treatment of the veins and muscles shown in meaningless tension, in spite of full reproduction of volume and advanced proof of visualisation appear sapless and lifeless. The loud exhibitionism of pomp and power of the Rampurva or Sārnāth specimens has nothing to compare with the quiet dignity of the Dhauli elephant. With its right front leg slightly tilted and the left back straight in short angle exhibiting a slight forward motion, and with its heavy trunk flowing rhythmically in a delightful curve, it walks majestically out of a deep ravine as it were. It indeed symbolises His

Imperial Majesty King Aśoka presenting himself with quiet dignity before the people of Kaliṅga. The Sārnāth quadripartite is on the other hand an exhibition of imperial pomp, power and authority before the Buddhist monks that had chosen the site of the First Turning of the Wheel as their place for the quiet pursuit of the religion of Śākyamuni. Compared to the Dhauli elephant the Sārnāth quadripartite and its Sāñchī counterpart are bombastic in style.

The Sankissa elephant is on a lower level of artistic conception. In spite of an appearance of movement the huge and plumpy animal is plastically speaking comparatively static, though there is some evidence of movement in the modelling of the muscles and of the volume of live flesh of the hind portion and the legs. The front legs are however treated pillar-like though the intended effect was presumably one of tension, since the animal appears to shrink backwards with the body-weight pressed in that direction. This attitude of the body, by the way, fails to harmonise with the abacus and the capital below. From Dhauli to Sankissa there is a steady direction, it seems, towards a stylised treatment of the plastic volume, of muscles and body-flesh. This is evident in the treatment of the upper but more in the lower portion of the chest and abdomen of the Sankissa elephant, but nowhere increasingly more and more than in the lion-figures.

Compared to the Basarh-Bakhira lion, the Lauriya-Nandangarh example is more tense and tight without doubt ; the surface treatment is also more clear and precise. On the whole the stylisation of the treatment of veins, muscles and flesh is on the increase, the form and treatment tends to be more conventional. In visualisation and realistic presentation of volume there is however hardly any advance, nor is there any attempt to harmonise the animal form with the component parts of the columns below.

From the Lauriya-Nandangarh specimen to the Rampurva lion there is a decided advance in the clear and precise cutting of the stone, in general finish, in the feeling for form and in linear rhythm. There is also an evident advance in modelling which is powerful and vigorous, specially in the muscle and thews, but the entire artistic conception is conventional and treatment stylised which is nowhere more evident than in the schematic treatment of the manes and the almost lifeless and conventional presentation of the legs and paws. Yet, compared to the Sārnāth quadripartite the Rampurva lion as a piece of independent sculpture must be considered artistically superior, though the former, architectonically speaking, is more advanced since nowhere else in the Maurya columns has been achieved a better and more efficient harmony with the abacus and the capital.

The Rampurva bull is architectonically less advanced than the lion from the same place since 'it fails to harmonise with the capital on which it stands'[1]. Marshall argues that it is not 'so well-executed as the (Rampurva) lion'. If he means that it is not as tense and tight in formal appearance or does not show as conventionally powerful and modelled treatment or stylisation of form he is undoubtedly correct. But at the same time it has to be recognised that the artist responsible for this piece of sculpture had a remarkable sense of form as well as of plastic volume and of the quality of the flesh. Here is indeed realistic vision and close observation of nature and full understanding of the character of the object ; nothing stylised or conventional or abstract has blurred the mental image of the artist or stood in the way of his execution. The animal is supposed to stand with full weight on earth in quiet and restrained dignity, and the artist has rendered that idea with remarkable clarity and perfect realism. Here too the modelling is vigorous but not conventional, plastic and linear sense fully mature but not schematised ; the energy and vitality that are within express themselves in restrained but powerful dignity ; a dynamic naturalism gives it potency and strength.

A comparison with the vigorously striding bull on the abacus of the Sārnāth column is at once suggested. Here the bull is rendered with all the tension and accentuation of muscles, veins and bones that a vigorous movement brings into play ; the sense of linear rhythm and plasticity of volume are also fully in evidence ; the execution is clear and precise, but it is at the same time hard to deny that the entire treatment is conventional in as much as the muscles are unduly exaggerated, the tension

1. *J. R. A. S.*, 1908, p. 1088.

in movement overemphasised and the modelling coagulated. A different aesthetic vision and tradition are indeed at work here.

The Sārnāth quadripartite is on a most superior level and must be admitted to be a very successful solution of a problem the Maurya artists grappled with from the very beginning. Of all Maurya sculptures it is the best known, most highly spoken of and reproduced on most occasions. Marshall is justified in saying that 'the Sārnāth capital,though by no means a masterpiece, is the product of the most developed art of which the world was cognisant in the third century B.C.—the handiwork of one who had generations of artistic effort and experience behind him. In the masterful strength of the crowning lions, with their swelling veins and tense muscular development, and in the spirited realism of the reliefs below, there is no trace of primitive art. So far as naturalism was his aim, the sculptor modelled his figures direct from nature, and has delineated their forms with bold, faithful touch....Equally mature is the technique of his relief work.'[1] But at the same time it must not be lost sight of that the entire conception and execution is conventional from beginning to end. Compositionally the accumulation of form of the four semi-lions is schematic, though from consideration of technique clever and efficient. The veins and muscles are overemphasised, and with all their seeming tenseness and bold delineation appear lifeless and conventional. The heads with gaping mouths and curved moustaches treated conventionally are more decorative and ornamental than endowed with real life ; the same is true of the manes treated conventionally and arranged schematically. The extravagance of form saps the life out of the object that it represents, though from the point of view of technique the art is fully developed and civilised and its appearance conscious and conventional.

The animal reliefs on the abacus are all worked almost in the round showing deep contrast of light and shade. Technically therefore they are far in advance of the row of pecking geese that decorates the Rampurva lion abacus, though the latter is very realistically treated and imparts a sense of movement that

1. *C. H. I*, I, p. 620.

comes from life itself. One of the four animals of the Sārnāth abacus is a galloping horse very spirited in movement, and the modelling and treatment of its plastic volume partake of the same conventional attitude and execution as those of the lions discussed above. This is equally applicable to the two other animals on the abacus namely the vigorously striding lion and the humped Indian bull, the forms and types in each case having been already fixed by convention, as we shall see later on. The only animal on the abacus that is treated in a different manner and viewed from a different attitude is the elephant slowly striding forward. It is much less conventional and the modelling shows a more realistic feeling for plasticity of volume, though the form has been but inadequately realised. Compared to the Dhauli elephant the elephant of the Sārnāth abacus looks like a wooden toy.

The Sāñchī counterpart of Sārnāth belongs to the same style and is equally conventional and stylised. The manes of the lions are rendered with increasing schematisation which is perhaps an indication of a date later than Sārnāth. Architectonically it conforms to the solution already achieved at the latter place, but the Sāñchī abacus which is decorated like the Rampurva lion capital with a row of pecking geese done in higher and bolder relief, is narrower than the Sārnāth one, and is aesthetically more in harmony with the capital below and the crowning lions above.

It is somewhat curious that the lions in Mauryan art are always and invariably done in a manner that seems already to have been fixed by convention. Their formal pose and appearance, the rendering of their volume, bold and vigorous but stylised, their plastic conception in one word, and the sense of form as revealed in them are on the whole the same and already pre-determined. The trend of the style is already evident in the Basarh-Bakhira lion and it is within the limits of the given trend that the style evolves and advances in treatment and execution. The aesthetic vision and imagination and the attitude and outlook of the artist do not mark any definite change. This is partly true as well of the lion, the horse and the bull on the Sārnāth abacus. It raises the presumption that this style and convention came from outside where they were already fixed and well established. The horse on the Sārnāth abacus in its movement and modelling recalls the two horses in the relief on the Sarcophagus of the Amazons[1] ; the vigorously striding lion and the bull recall well-known Achaemenian prototypes of the same style and convention[2]. Even the elephant on the abacus has a distant kinship with the horned elephants on the early coins of the Seleucids, though the Sārnāth elephant is much less conventional and shows somewhat a different sense of form and treatment.

The aesthetic vision and imagination and the conventional style and fixed expression just spoken of are most evident in the crowning lions. Compared with later figural sculptures in the round of Yakshas and their female counterparts or the reliefs of Bhārhut, Sāñchī and Bodhgayā, the art represented by these crowning lions belongs to an altogether different world of conception and execution, of style and technique, altogether much more complex, urban and civilised. They have nothing archaic or primitive about them, and the presumption is irresistible that the impetus and inspiration of this art must have come from outside. Did it come from the Achaemenian west ? This seems to be very doubtful, for the modelling of these sculptures has nothing in common with Achaemenian sculptures, nor does the powerful feeling for volume and preference for rounded forms have anything in common with Achaemenian Iran. Moreover West-Asiatic art, especially Iranian Art during the Achaemenian period came heavily under the influence of Hellenistic Art ; further, 'the few attempts made in Iran in the domain of free plastic art bear an entirely different stamp in their preference for angular forms'[3]. Marshall therefore argued for Hellenistic plastic tradition as practised by Graeco-Bactrian artists. From what we know of the Hellenistic colonies in West Asia and the part they played in Mauryan India, it is possible, nay highly probable, that Hellenistic art and culture played also a very dominant rôle in Mauryan Art. The Mauryan lions indeed in their aesthetic conception and plastic vision, in their

1. Carotti, *A History of Art*, I, p. 218, fig. 298.
2. Perrot & Chipiez, *History of Art in Persia*, p. 407, fig. 195 ; *C. H. I.*, I, p. 463, Pl. II, figs. 1 and 2.
3. Bachhofer, *Early Indian Sculpture*, I p. 6—7.

conventional modelling, advanced visualisation, feeling for volume and sense of form invariably recall conventional and decadent colonial Greek works of the same art-form and design. It is here that we can trace the source of the impetus and inspiration of the conventional art of the crowning lions of Mauryan columns. Here then, in a tradition familiar with lions and bulls and horses, was the convention fixed and determined.

These remarks are however hardly applicable to the Dhauli elephant or the Rampurva bull which both seem to belong to a somewhat different aesthetic vision and outlook, perhaps to a different art-tradition. True, indeed, so far as feeling for volume and its reproduction are concerned they belong to the same fully developed stage of art as the crowning lions discussed above and there is nothing archaic and primitive about them ; but it is equally true there is nothing conventional about them as well, and the plastic sense and method of treatment is altogether different. The modelling betrays a full knowledge of the softness of the flesh and of the flowing current of life that is within ; it is also restrained and is not contaminated by any conventional exaggeration or localised emphasis. Nor is there any evidence of schematisation of form. Indeed these two examples (with the Sankissa elephant as a close third) represent a different aesthetic outlook, a different art-tradition than those of the crowning lions and the lion, horse and bull reliefs on the Sārnāth abacus. This difference in outlook and tradition is clearly brought to the fore when the Rampurva bull is compared with the relief of the same animal from the Sārnāth column ; the two bulls belong to two different worlds as it were. It is, I think, permissible to assume that it is Indian aesthetic vision and imagination and Indian art-tradition that are here largely at work, so far as art-style at least is concerned. The same plastic conception and quality of modelling constitute the pivot round which early Indian art moves, and the same restraint and quiet dignity are the qualities that Indian art ideal has sought to achieve in higher art from the very beginning. Moreover, if the Dhauli and Sankissa elephants, particularly the former be compared with the figures of elephants in bold and high relief in the frieze of the facade of the Lomaśa Ṛishi cave, it will at once be seen that they belong to the same style and tradition of art. This cave may not be of Mauryan date, but it cannot be very much later also ; all scholars recognise that the entire facade of this cave is the exact and literal translation in stone of a wooden prototype. It may be assumed therefore that figures of elephants in the same style and tradition as we see them on the stone-facade were already being rendered in wood for generations before they came to be transferred on stone. It is not unlikely that in the Dhauli elephant, the Rampurva bull and partly in the Sankissa elephant, all of which are decidedly Indian in feeling, appearance andspirit, we but witness the traditional Indian conception of these objects and the older or contemporary Indian art-style and tradition transferred into stone in terms of the requirements of that particular material and according to the dictates of bolder designs and bigger dimensions. The mastery of the third dimension, in other words the solution of the difficult problem of free figure as revealed in them, is the only lesson the artists seem to have learnt from Graeco-Bactrian art-tradition. But here too it is possible to present the counter-hypothesis that there must have existed in pre-Mauryan India an art of wood-carving and clay-modelling that carved and modelled free and round figures of men and animals out of wood and clay, and perhaps also of big dimensions.

It is difficult to say anything about the nationality of the artists of the Maurya court ; there is no evidence on the point. But from what has been said above, it is permissible to assume that the Dhauli elephant, the Rampurva bull and perhaps also the Sankissa elephant are works of Indian artists working in contemporary Indian style and tradition, and having a thorough mastery of the third dimension and a full consciousness of the Indian outlook. The crowning lions of the early phases, namely the Basarh-Bakhira and Lauriya-Nandangarh examples, are also works of Indian artists but tutored in the style and tradition of contemporary Western art; this is marked in the grappling with the problem of form and its precise execution evident in these sculptures. There is decided advance in the Rampurva, Sārnāth and Sāñchī specimens ; this may have been achieved by the same Indian artists working increasingly in the direction of contemporary Western art, or by colonial artists of the Hellenistic Orient imported by the Maurya Court. In any case, there are in these specimens a strong and undeniable Hellenisticstamp that may not have been imprinted by Indian hands.

V

Alleged Mauryan Sculptures

Besides the animal sculptures described anddiscussed above, quite a considerable number of independent figure sculptures in the round and of various size and proportion and a few fragments of reliefs have been ascribed to the Maurya period[1] mainly on the ground of their having the so-called Mauryan polish on them and their being carved out of grey sandstone from Chunar. These are insufficient grounds indeed. The art of giving a lustrous polish to the stone, the Maurya artists learnt evidently from the Achaemenians and once they practised it in large scale and made it current, it is only in the nature of things that the practice would continue for some time at least, and at least in stray instances even when the power and authority of the Maurya court had vanished and Maurya court art that apparently found in this polish an expression of imperial glory and splendour had become a thing of the past. Nor is the argument of a common place of origin so far as the material is concerned more potent. Stone as the material *par excellence* for sculptural work was a sort of a new learning with the Mauryan court artists, and this material was quarried at Chunar. It was handled for at least a few generations and found to respond very well to the hammer and chisel of the stone-sculptor. It is only likely therefore that later sculptors would continue at least for some time to have their material imported from the same quarry until they struck at other quarries and found their stone good enough to meet their requirements. It is therefore on the arguments of conception and style that we must take our stand to argue whether they can be labelled as Mauryan or not.

The two Patna Yakshas almost identical in form and appearance, conception and treatment, dress and ornament, and now in the Indian Museum come first in the list of alleged Mauryan

1. Marshall, Chanda, Kramrisch, Coomaraswamy, Bachhofer, indeed all authorities have so far ascribed these sculptures to the Maurya period.

sculptures. It deserves consideration that both the statues have on the scarf of their shoulder a line of Brāhmī inscription that has paleographically been dated round about the beginning of the Christian era, and that helps to identify the statues as those of Yakshas. No reason is adduced why the statues should not be considered as belonging to the same period as that of the inscriptions. The so-called Mauryan polish on which the main argument for a Mauryan date rests is conspicuous only on the upper half of the bodies, which may be taken to point to the fact that the practice of Maurya court art was already on the wane. While there is nothing peculiarly Mauryan about this couple there are elements that seem to connect them with some of the sculptures on the eastern gate of the Great Stūpa at Sāñchī on the one hand and the Kushāṇa school of Mathurā on the other. The heaviness, the almost archaic stolidity and weighty volume, the conflict between fully rounded and modelled volume as seen in the arms, breast and abdomen on the one hand and flat surface at the back on the other seem to suggest a close parallel with the huge heavy and 'primitive' Boddhisattvas of the Mathurā school. The treatment of the garment when it does not cling to the body as volumes separate from the body is a particular characteristic of the Kushāṇa school of Mathurā. The same remark applies to the treatment of ornaments. Where the garment clings to the body it is treated as a wet cloth and is almost invisible except for the parallel ridges that indicate the folds. A similar treatment of the garment characterises the Didarganj Yakshī also, to be considered later. On the other hand so far as general shape and appearance of the upper part of the body and the quality and character of the modelling are concerned, a kinship with the art of the bigger reliefs on the eastern gate of the Great Stūpa at Sāñchī seems to be admissible.

Much less known than either the Patna Yakshas or the two other colossal polished sandstone standing statues from Parkham and Didarganj are the two torsos of naked Jaina images, both recovered from Lohanipur near Bankipur, Patna, and now in the Patna Museum. The larger torso, a free and round sculpture carved out of Chunar sandstone, has the high Maurya polish on it ; while the smaller one, identical in appearance and style and of the same material has no polish on it. They have both been found together on the same level underground along with a silver punch-marked coin which Jayaswal says 'precedes Maurya coinage'. He ascribes the larger torso to the Maurya period and the unpolished smaller one to the 'Śuṅgan or later', on what grounds he does not state[1]. If one is to go by style and appearance, both the torsos must belong to the same period which may not be far out of date from the Patna Yakshas on the one hand and the Parkham Yaksha on the other. In their tight and stiff modelling, in their fully rounded arms and thighs and in their general earthy heaviness of form they have a kinship with the Patna statues ; both pairs are characterised by a smooth and lifeless inertia, and by a comparatively flat surface treatment of their backs. The Lohanipur statues, moreover, are more primitive and archaic in outlook and appearance, heavy and a little bit unbalanced in proportion which seem to link them with the Baroda and Parkham Yakshas to be discussed later.

The same conflict in a rather accentuated form of fully rounded volume and flat surface, the same complex relation of ornaments and garments to the body, the same heaviness and archaism, rigidity and lifeless smoothness, characterise what remains of the colossal sandstone statue of a Yaksha[2] recovered from Baroda near Parkham and another slightly smaller but comparatively well-preserved Yaksha statue from Parkham itself (both now in the Mathurā Museum), the latter having the same polish as that on the Mauryan columns. There can be no doubt that in all these statues we have a clear expression of the weighty and imposing earthiness that traditional Indian imagination connects with its Yakshas and Yakshiṇīs, gods and goddesses of material plenty and physical welfare. The lightly bent knees and the comparatively thin legs of the standing Parkham figure have some kinship with those of the Maṇibhadra Yaksha statue from Pawaya near Gwalior[3], while the

1. Jayaswal, 'Jaina Image of the Maurya Period', *J. B. O. R. S.*, XXII, pp. 130—32 and plates.

2. Coomaraswamy, *History of Indian & Indonesian Art*, p. 17, fig. 15 ; Vogel, 'Mathurā School of Sculpture', *A. S. R.*, 1909—10, p. 76, Pl. XXVIII, a.

3. Bachhofer, *Early Indian Sculpture*, I, plate 62.

frank and unconditional frontality of both Baroda and Parkham statues, attaching little or no importance to the back reminds one again of primitive Bodhisattvas of the Mathurā school. Compared to the Patna Yakshas the Parkham specimen is more stiff and archaic in appearance, more rough and crude in execution ; but in the relation of ornament and dress with the body and in the quality of the tight and stiff modelling it betrays the same essential characteristics. In its upper part it shows no doubt a tendency towards flattened surface treatment, but in the lower half fully rounded and powerfully modelled mass is in full evidence giving the legs a lively form and appearance in strong contrast to the torso with a protruding and deformed abdomen that is possibly an individual characteristic. The flowing drapery which is treated as transparent where it clings to the body, and as separate though in thin and flat volumes where it is gathered together, is indicated at the front by incised wave lines as in Bhārhut and at the ends by a single rounded ridge. It seems that such treatment of drapery as we see in the Parkham image can in no way be dated earlier than Bhārhut, and similar shape and modelled form of the legs cannot be earlier than the first century B.C. In any case the Baroda and Parkham statues constitute what we may call the earliest Mathurā primitives and the initial chapter of the Mathurā school of sculpture. They have hardly anything to connect them with Mauryan sculpture of known date and locality, and are perhaps later than even the Patna Yakshas discussed above.

Artistically the Didarganj Yakshiṇī is the best of the series and can in no way be considered as archaic or primitive. In the easy and light stoop and forward movement of the upper part of the body helped by a slight bend of the right knee-joint, the narrow waist and full round breasts with the necklace hanging rhythmically along and between the breast-lines, the broad hips, the shapely legs gradually tapering down to the thin ankles decorated by heavy and fully jewelled ornaments, the style of doing and decorating the hair, and not the least in the sensitiveness of flesh as revealed in what remains of the modelling of the abdomen, the chin and the region round the eyes, but more fully and clearly of the back—one witnesses here perhaps an earliest urban, conscious and sophisticated female type and form immortalised in later Indian art and literature. The fact that the treatment of its ornaments and drapery, especially of the latter, is the same as that of the Patna Yakshas is no reason why it should be labelled as primitive or considered as belonging to the same period or phase of early Indian art. The statue, plastically fully round, is bound by no 'law of frontality' and is meant to be seen from all sides—it has no primitivity whatsoever about it. Its heavy but loose mass of hair, its full soft bosoms and the firmness of the flesh at the back, and its attenuated waist with soft abdominal muscles and the broad hips at once recall the still daintier and more lively Yakshiṇīs of the Mathurā reliefs of the second century A.D. which are characterised by fully round and lively modelling of their limbs, scarfs and anklets. Indeed the Didarganj Yakshiṇī cannot be very much earlier than the latter, in spite of so-called Mauryan polish or its material which is Chunar sandstone.

These life size, plastically round statues belong thus to different aspects and phases of Indian art. They are all Indian in form and appearance ; and in style and treatment they have hardly any relation with the court art of the Mauryas. The third dimension was already mastered by the courtly Indian tradition, in the Dhauli elephant and the Rampurva bull for example, so that the conception and execution of either the Didarganj Yakshiṇī or perhaps the Patna Yakshas presented them with no new problem. Indeed they belong to the same line of evolution, but at later stages, reflecting on themselves the currents of the flowing tradition and fashions of contemporary practice. The Baroda and Parkham statues along with a seated Yakshiṇī (now in worship as Manasādevī) from Mathurā[1] on the other hand belong perhaps to a different conception and tradition altogether, a primitive folk tradition much older and more rooted to the soil, that was current and co-existent with the Maurya court art but of which the latter knew nothing. The fixation of that art in permanent materials is first to be

1. Chanda, 'Mathura School of Sculpture,' *A. S. R.* 1922—23, p. 164 ; *A. S. R.* 1920—21, Pl. XVIII.

seen at Bhārhut and later in various other places where it slowly and steadily grappled stage by stage and with varying measure of success with the problem of the third dimension. The Baroda and Parkham statues along with others of still later date represent the different stages in that direction.

Two male heads and three small fragments of head, of the same material and similarly polished, all from Sārnāth, have usually been assigned to the Maurya period for no other reason than that they are carved out of Chunar sandstone and have the so-called Mauryan polish on them. It is very likely as Coomaraswamy surmises on the ground of their 'extraordinary actuality' and 'marked individuality' that these are 'parts of portrait-figures, and presumably portraits of donors'. Their head-dress consisting of either a fillet with a laurel wreath or a mural crown is certainly reminiscent of Hellenistic *motifs*. Similar fragments of stone heads with identical head-dresses hail also from Bhita and Mathurā which along with the Sārnāth examples constitute a 'well-marked stylistic group', but there is nothing to connect them definitely with Mauryan art. All that they—together with some terracotta heads and figures from Mathurā, Sārnāth, Basarh, Bulandibagh, Kumrahar, and other places with Greek *motifs* on their head-dress and sometimes even foreign facial types—prove is that Greek *motifs* and types along with Hellenistic provincial art had migrated as far east as the Ganges valley[1]. Since Hellenistic contacts were potent and effective even after the fall of the Mauryas, migration and adoption of Hellenistic art forms and *motifs* at later periods of history cannot be ruled altogether out of consideration.

A few other fragmentary reliefs have also been assigned to the Mauryan period, again without sufficient reason. Intensely lyrical and qualitatively of a very subtle significance is the figure worked in high relief out of the fragment of an arch, of a young sorrowing lady[2]. The soft and delicate modelling of the nude upper body nowhere so sensitively rendered as in the back and the fresh young breasts, the soft linear rhythm and the composi-

1. Bachhofer, *Early Indian Sculpture*, I, pp. 12—14, plates 12 and 13 ; Coomaraswamy, *History of Indian & Indonesian Art*, pp. 19—20, figs 18, 19, 20, 22, 23. Fig. 21 of Coomaraswamy is much later still.

2. Kramrisch, *Grunduzuge der Indischen Kunst*, *Indian Sculpture*, p. 12, fig. 11.

tional unity has no parallel in early Indian art. Indeed its plastic and linear expressiveness does not fit in against the background of either Maurya or Śuṅga art. The style and treatment of the hair, ornaments and garment have indeed a primitive heaviness of form but the modelling and linear composition are very much in advance. Another relief from Bhita[1] also shows decided advance in general appearance, pose and movement, and from the character of relief composition, facial type and surface treatment it cannot be dated earlier than the reliefs of Bodhgayā and Sāñchī.

A considerable number of terracottas said to have been recovered from 'the lowest, or nearly the lowest, levels at several widely separated sites, extending from Pāṭaliputra to Taxila'[2] have sometimes been assigned to the Maurya period, mainly on grounds of style and appearance. Kramrisch and Gordon have drawn pointed attention to the hazards of trying to date terracottas—moulded or modelled—on ground of style or that of appearance[3]. Moreover, excavation methods pursued in India till very lately were not such as to make level or stratification a dependable argument for determining chronological sequence, so far as terractottas at least are concerned. Most terracotta pieces, except perhaps a few from the ancient site of Pāṭaliputra, that had originally been labelled Mauryan, are now being ascribed to the Śuṅga, Kushāṇa or early Gupta periods[4].

VI

Cave Architecture

Of the architectural remains usually ascribed to the Maurya period very few are artistically significant. Tradition ascribes a large number of *stūpas* and *chaitya*-halls to the building activities of Aśoka, but none of them exists today in their original form and plan except the excavated *chaitya*-halls, bearing inscriptions of Aśoka and Daśaratha, in the Barābar caves. The monolithic rail at Sārnāth in grey and polished Chunar sandstone may have been erected under the direction and patronage

1. Coomaraswamy, op. cit., p. 20, fig. 13.
2. Coomaraswamy. op. cit., pp. 20—21, figs, 16, 23, 57, 60,
3. Kramrisch, *J. I. S. O. A.*, VII pp. 89-110. Gordon, *J. I. S. O. A.* XI pp. 136-95.
4. Ibid, Kramrisch.

of Aśoka himself. Its architectural form is exactly that of the rails of Bhārhut, and must have been literally transferred into stone from contemporary wooden originals without possibly any understanding of its constructional characteristics. The plinth or the *ālambana*, the uprights or the *stambhas*, the horizontal bars or the *sūchis* and the coping or the *ushṇīsha* have all been just carved out of what must have been a huge slab of stone ; an understanding of the constructional characteristics would have certainly made the task easier by piecing together the constituent parts of smaller slabs of stone exactly in the same way as we see them done at Bhārhut or Sāñchī or Bodhgayā. The altar or the *bodhimaṇḍa* at Bodhygayā is also traditionally associated with Aśoka. It is permissible to assume that it was perhaps much like the *bodhimaṇḍa* as we see it on one of the Bhārhut reliefs[1] bearing the inscription in Brāhmī characters 'Bhagavato Sakya Munino Bodho.' The point of architectural interest is that the Bhārhut altar consists of four pilasters the forms of which were evidently derived from wooden prototypes and had nothing to do with the monumental Aśoka columns.

The Barābar and Nāgārjuni caves of which the Sudāma seems to be the earliest are lineal descendants of similar rock-hewn caves that must have been in use by peoples of rude primitive tribes and recluses. They are the earliest examples of the rock-cut method, and are exact translations in stone of existing wood and thatch structures. The exterior walls and roofs of these simple cells, including that of the Lomaśa Ṛishi cave of the same Barābar-Nāgārjuni series have all received the high polish so typical of Mauryan art. The earliest of these caves is presumably the one bearing an inscription dated in the twelfth year of Aśoka's reign—the Sudāmā—and saying that it was dedicated to the monks of the Ājīvika sect. This rock-hewn cave consists of two chambers ; a rectangular antechamber with barrel-vaulted roof and a doorway with sloping jambs—an indication of adoption of wooden prototypes—in the long side of the chamber at the end of which there is a separate circular cell with a hemispherically domed roof. The two chambers

1. Coomaraswamy, op. cit., fig. 41

are connected by a central interior doorway. At the outer side the circular cell has overhanging eaves which are but transference in wood of thatch construction ; moreover the live rock walls are marked by irregular perpendicular grooves which are but translation on live rock of upright wooden or bambco planking[1].

Furgusson states that a second of this series of caves 'called the Karṇa Chaupār, bears an inscription which records the excavation of the cave in the nineteenth year after the coronation of Aśoka. It is simply a rectangular hall....and except in an arched roof....has no architectural feature of importance. At the right, or west end is a low platform as if for an image.....'[2]

In the granite Nāgārjuni hill are three more caves, each bearing an inscription of the Maurya king Daśaratha that purports to dedicate them to the same Ājīvika sect. Two of these are very small, consisting of a simple rectangular cell each, each entered from the end, and having a barrel-vaulted roof. The largest is the one known locally as Gopī or Milkmaid's cave which is a long rectangular hall with a barrel-vaulted roof and with circular ends. It is entered through a doorway in the centre of the south side[3].

Chronologically the latest and architecturally the best of the series is undoubtedly the Lomaśa Ṛishi[4] which though bearing no inscription may be taken to belong to the Maurya period. In ground plan and general design it is much like the Sudāmā, and consists similarly of a rectangular antechamber with barrel-vaulted roof entered by the long side through a doorway with sloping jambs ; this antechamber is connected at the end through a central doorway with a separate cell which is oval and not round as in the Sudāmā. But the most interesting architectural element in the Lomaśa Ṛishi is its facade which is frankly an exact translation of the gable end of a wooden structure in the language of stone. The carpenter's handiwork has been copied in stone in every little detail. From this facade can easily be

1. Fergusson, *History of Indian & Eastern Architecture*, I. pp. 130—31 ; Brown, *Indian Architecture : Buddhist & Hindu*, pp. 12—13.

2. Fergusson, op. cit. p. 130.

3. Ibid, p. 132 ; Brown, op. cit. p. 13.

4. Fergusson, op. cit. p. 131—32 ; Brown, op. cit. p. 13.

reconstructed the wood-built structural *chaityas* of this period[1]. The finial that surmounts the gable of the facade also seems to be translated from either terracotta originals or from wooden copies of them.

These caves or rock-cut *chaityas* represent about half-a-century of building activity, but unlike Mauryan sculpture these almost primitive architectural essays show no process of evolution. From the Sudāmā to the Lomaśa Ṛishi there is no doubt an elaboration, but the three caves of Daśaratha do not fit in along the line of any supposed or actual evolution. Indeed these caves do not represent, except in their high polish, any conscious attempts towards architectural achievement. The architects of the Maurya court, so far as these caves are concerned, merely copied in stone what they saw before them constructed of wood and bamboo and clay. But the facade of the Lomaśa Ṛishi proves once for all that even here in these primitive caves there was no slipshod work permitted in the actual cutting of the stone; every little detail is sharply and precisely chiselled. Whatever their architectural quality these rock-cut chaitya halls represent the earliest extant remains of and perhaps the second stage in the evolution of this type of Indian monuments. The history of later chaitya architecture is roughly the history of the evolution of the ground plan and elevation of the Sudāmā and the Lomaśa Ṛishi.

VII

Concluding Remarks

With all its urban, conscious and civilised quality, its advanced power of visualisation and full knowledge and comprehension of the third dimension, Maurya court art constitutes only an interlude, in the history of Indian art. Kramrisch rightly hits the point when she says, 'in the organism of Indian art Mauryan sculpture has only marginal importance'[2]. It was indeed a hot-house plant reared up by the will, care and patronage of a court heavily under the influence of foreign culture and ideology. In course of time the glass walls fell to pieces

1. Ibid.
2. Kramrisch, *Indian Sculpture*, p. 11—12.

and the plant withered. Maurya court art failed to make any notable permanent contribution to the growth of Indian art except that it directly helped the fixation of the latter in permanent material. A most important exponent of Maurya court ideology in sculpture are the crowning lion figures which, we have seen, were conditioned by a plastic vision and artistic convention already fixed and determined within a foreign art tradition. They raise the presumption that they for the first time introduced into the realm of Indian Art a highly advanced power of visualisation and a fuller comprehension of the problem of the third dimension. But here a counter-hypothesis, I have already pointed out, presents itself. It is quite permissible to assume that these two essential qualities of high art were not unknown to Indian artists who used to work in wood and clay and shape images in fully rounded form. This assumption seems to find strong support not only from the spirit and appearance but also from the general conception, treatment and execution of the Dhauli elephant and the Rampurva bull which undoubtedly belong to a different art tradition. I have tried also to point out that the Patna Yakshas, the Didarganj Yakshiṇī, and the Lohānīpur Jaina images to an extent belong to the line of evolution of this tradition, though it must be admitted that the Maurya elephant and the bull belong qualitatively to a higher aesthetic level. This court art does not seem to have taken cognisance of another tradition of art, a more primitive, perhaps folk tradition of presumably some significance, that was hardly conscious of the third dimension and fully rounded form. This tradition came to be fixed in permanent material for the first time in Bhārhut where already the conflict between round volume and flat surface makes its appearance and gradually shows itself not only in the Baroda and Parkham Yakshas and the so-called Manasādevī of Parkham still in worship but also in the Patna Yakshas, the Lohānīp r images and some of the huge primitives of the early Mathurā school.

No less important an exponent of Maurya court art is the independent column standing free in space. The idea and impetus persisted even after the Mauryas, but the form underwent considerable change. It was never adopted as part of any larger architectural entity in which case pillars and pilasters invariably show and evolve other forms directly derivable from wooden prototypes. Already in the first century B.C. the Garuḍa column from Besnagar[1] raised by the direction and patronage of a colonial Greek converted to Bhāgavata Vaishṇavism, shows form and features that are different from those of Aśokan columns. The lowest third of the shaft is octagonal terminated by eight half-lotus designs; the middle third is sextagonal which is terminated by an octagonal band, each side of the band being decorated by a stylised full and round lotus design ; the upper third is round and is super-imposed by a bell-shaped capital that in its shape, form and appearance is related not so much with the Aśokan capitals as with the typical Persepolitan ones with a ring of pointed lotus petals at the upper end of the base. The crowning adornment is not that of an animal but consists of a high cube supporting a stylised cluster of palmyra branches which again recall similar *motifs* in West Asiatic art. The fact that this column was raised by a colonial Greek probably explains this emphasis on Achaemenian and west Asiatic *motifs*, but the fact remains that post-Maurya art and architecture discarded the type and form of columns made current by the Maurya monarchs. This is further supported by the shape and form of pilasters met with at Bhārhut and derivable from wooden prototypes.

In the realm of architecture also Maurya court art failed to make any impress. The Mauryan palaces and the Pillared Hall brought into existence directly by the impetus and inspiration of Achaemenian architectural form and ideal do not seem to have captured the imagination of Indian builders and architects, and there is no evidence in later Indian art to show that such plans and designs were ever adopted. On the other hand the few rock-hewn chaitya-cells patronised by the Maurya monarchs reveal that they were exactly and literally translated from wooden prototypes. The evidence of civil and religious architecture furnished by the early Indian reliefs of Bhārhut, Sāñchī, Amarāvatī and other places also points to that conclusion[2].

1. Bachhofer, op. cit. plate, 14.

2. Fergusson, op. cit. chaps. IV—VI. Brown, op. cit. chaps. II and III ; Smith, *History of Fine Art in India & Ceylon*, pp. 21—28.

Here also the Indian style, form and tradition made themselves felt.

It is true, that early Indian art knowsof certain *motifs*, patterns and designs made current and popular by Maurya court art—this without any reference to the question of art-style, and that quite a large portion of this repertory of *motifs* and designs belongs to the art of Asiatic west which was for a time dominated by Achaemenian and later by colonial Greek imperialism ; but it would be short-sightedness to assume that 'the whole group of *motifs* of western Asiatic aspect was introduced by Aśoka's Persian craftsmen *en bloc*'. There can hardly be any doubt that quite a few of such *motifs* were made current even before the Mauryas, while those that are definitely Hellenistic came in during and after the Maurya period.

The imperialism of the Maurya monarchs, especially of Aśoka, was a synthesis of Indian, Achaemenian and Hellenistic ideals. It was the expression of an individualistic taste and ideology, not of collective social will. Aśoka's personal religion, his conception of Dhamma and his policy of *Dhammavijaya* also reflect the individual ideology and preference of a resolute but intelligent and benevolent autocrat who dominated the Maurya court and administration. Maurya court art also was no exception to this basic and fundamental factor. Nanda-Maurya, particularly Maurya imperialism and Aśokan policy of *Dhammavijaya* drew India out of her primitive local tribal outlook. Aśokan policy in the realm of religion raised Buddhism to the status of an international religion right from the position of a tribal and regional cult. So in the realm of art as well. Individual taste and preference of Maurya monarchs like Chandragupta, Bindusāra and Aśoka for ideas and objects from Achaemenian and Hellenistic Orient furnished the impetus and inspiration, and Indian art not only came to be fixed in permanent material but it was raised from the position of handicraft and primitive art to the dignity and status of higher art. The main lines of this art, just as the main lines of Aśoka's policy of *Dhammavijaya* were chiefly determined by individual will, taste and preference. Both lacked deeper roots in the collective social will, taste and preference, and were therefore destined to have isolated and short lives coeval and coexistent with and within the four limits of the powerful Maurya court. This explains why Maurya court art with all its dignified bearing, monumental appearance and civilised quality forms but a short and isolated chapter of the history of Indian art. Like the columns and the animal figures themselves Maurya Art stands aloof and apart.

GENERAL BIBLIOGRAPHY

Barnett, L.D. : Antiquities of India, (London, 1913).

Cambridge History of India, Vol. I, (Cambridge 1922).

Lassen, Christian : Indische Alterthumskunde Vol. II 2nd Edn. (Leipzig, 1874).

Masson-Oursel and others : Ancient India and Indian Civilization, (London, 1934).

Rapson, E. J. : Ancient India from the earliest times to the first century A.D., (Cambridge, 1914).

Raychauhuri, H. C. : Political History of Ancient India, 4th Edn., (Calcutta, 1938).

Vallée-Poussin, Louis de la : L'Inde aux Temps des Mauryas (Paris, 1930).

Chapters I (India in the age of the Nandas) and IV Chandra-Gupta and Bindusāra.

SOURCES :—

Arrian : Anabasis of Alexander and Indica (English Tr.) E. J. Chinnock, (London, 1893).

The Invasion of India by Alexander the Great as described by Q. Curtius, Diodorus, Plutarch and Justin, translation by J. W. McCrindle, Westminster, 1896).

Hāthīgumphā Inscription of Khāravela—Ep. Indica, X., App. No. 1345 ; J.B.O.R.S., Dec. 1917 ; J.R.A.S., 1910 (Fleet), 1918 (Smith), 1919 (Chanda) ; IA. 1919 (Majumdar, R. C.), 1920 (Sankara Aiyer), Ep. Indica, XX, pp. 71-89.

Kalpasūtra of Bhadrabāhu, Ed. H. Jacobi, (Leipzig 1877) Trans. by H. Jacobi S.B.E. XXII.

Kalpasūtra of Bhadrabāhu, Trans. by H. Jacobi, S. B. E. XXII.

McCrindle : Ancient India as described in classical literature (Westminster, 1901)

Mudrārākshasa of Viśākhadatta, (Bombay, 1928).

Pargiter : Purāṇa Texts of the Kali Age, (Oxford, 1913)

Rigveda Brahmanas—A. B. Keith (Harvard, 1920).

Shama Sastri, R. : Arthaśāstra of Kauṭilya, (Mysore 1909).

Strabo—Geography, Eng. Tr. Hamilton and Falconer (London, 1854—7).

Sthavirāvaḷicarita of Hemachandra, ed. H. Jacobi, (Calcutta 1891, 2nd Edn. 1932).

MODERN WORKS :—

Archaeological Survey of India, Annual Reports.

Rhys Davids : Buddhist India (London 1903).

Spooner, D. B. : The Zoroastrian period of Indian History, J. R. A. S., (1915, pp. 63-89, 405-55). Further discussion by (1) V. A. Smith *ib.* pp. 800-2 (2) A. B. Keith *ib.* 1916, pp. 138-43 and (3) F. W. Thomas *ib.* pp. 362-6. See Modern Review, 1916 (XIX).

Tarn, W. W. : The Greeks in Bactria and India (Cambridge, 1938).

Waddell, L.A. : Report on the excavations at Pāṭaliputra, (Calcutta, 1903).

Chapter II—Alexander's Campaigns in India

Breloer, B. : Alexander's Kampf Gegen Poros (Stuttgart, 1932-3).

Cambridge History of India : I, (1922) chapters XV and XVII beginning.

Cambridge Ancient History, VI, ch. XIII, esp. iv-vii. In his account of the battle of Jhelam, Tarn, following Baer, says that Alexander divided his cavalry force in order to draw the Indian cavalry, a weaker force than his own, to charge him and thus draw them away from the elephants (1928).

Cavaignac, E. : A propos de la bataille d'Alexandre contre Porus (JA.1923 ii 332-4), points out that Alexander crossed the river above his camp as Curtius (viii. 13) says that Ptolemy's troops watched by Porus occupied the bank of the river lower down. (Contra. C.H.I. i, p. 361 *n.* 2 and p. 365).

Holdich : The gates of India (London, 1910)—'Aornos appears to have been a kind of generic name with the Greeks, applied to mountain positions of a certain class' (109). 'We shall never recognise Aornos by its superficial features' (118).

Lassen : Indische Alterthumskunde[2] ii pp. 124—205 (Leipzig 1874).

McCrindle, J.W. : The Invasion of India by Alexander the Great as described by Arrian, Curtius, Diodorus, Plutarch and Justin (Westminster, 1896)

McCrindle, J. W. : Strabo and the Itinerary of Alexander the Great (pp. 6-101, and 150-155 of Ancient India as described in Classical literature).

(I have followed Arrian's narrative in the main ; where I have preferred Curtius or Diodorus, this is indicated in the text. For the references, very few, to occurrences after Alexander's death I have depended on citations in standard modern works).

Smith, V. A. : Early History of India[4]—chapters III and IV, (Oxford, 1924).

Stein : Alexander's campaign on the Indian N. W. Frontier, Geographical Journal, 1927.

Stein : On Alexander's track to the Indus (London. 1929).

Stein : An Archaeological Tour in Upper Swat and adjacent Hills Tracts (A.S.I. Memoir, No. 42 ; 1930).

Stein : Serindia, Vol. i. pp. 1-5 (London, 1921).

Thirlwall : History of Greece Vol. vii (pp. 1-75), (London, 1852).

Chapter III—India in early Greek and Latin Literature

Breloer, B. : Kauṭilya—Studien

(i) Die Grundeigentum in Indien (Bonn, 1927).

(ii) Altindisches Privatrecht bei Megasthenes und Kautalya (Bonn, 1928).

" Megasthenes (etwa 300 v. chr.) uber die indische Gesellschaft, ZDMG, 1934, pp. 130-164.

" Megasthenes uber die indische Stadtverwaltung, ZDMG, 1935, pp. 40-67.

[Breloer has sought to offer very plausible interpretations of Megasthenes' statements on Indian society and polity and to explain them in the light of the mental equipment of a Hellenistic Greek administrator who was fully acquainted with all that had been written before him by his countrymen about India. Unlike Otto Stein, he discovers fundamental agreement between Megasthenes and Kauṭilya.]

Cambridge History of India, Vol. I (1922), Ch. XVI.

Falconer, W. (and H. C. Hamilton) : The Geography of Strabo, 3 vols. (Bohn's Classical Library). (London 1854-7).

Godley, A. D. : Herodotus, with an English translation, 4 vols. (Loeb Classical Library).

Lassen : Indische Alterthumskunde[2] (1874), II, pp. 626-751.

McCrindle : Ancient India as Described by Megasthenes and Arrian (Calcutta, 1877).

" : Ancient India as described by Ktesias the Knidian (Calcutta 1882).

" : The Invasion of India by Alexander the Great[2] (Westminster, 1896).

" : Ancient India as described in Classical Literature (Westminster, 1901).

Monahan, F. J. : The Early History of Bengal (Oxford University Press, 1925).

Rawlinson, George : The History of Herodotus (Everyman's Library) 2 Vols.

Stein, O : Megasthenes und Kautilya (Wien, 1921).

(Stein's method of a mechanical confrontation of data from Megasthenes with those from *Arthaśāstra* is of questionable value as Breloer has demonstrated ; but his discussions contain much that is useful).

Chapter V—Mauryan Polity

Arthaśāstra of Kauṭilya ed. Shama Sastri (Mysore, 1909 2nd. edn. 1919).

„ „ „ Gaṇapati Śāstri (Trivandram, 1924-25).

„ „ „ Jolly (Lahore, 1923—4).

Modern Works :

Bandyopadhyaya, N. C. : Kauṭilya (Calcutta, 1927).

Barnett. : Antiquities of India (London, 1913).

Breloer : Kauṭilya Studien I—III (Bonn, 1927-34).

Cambridge History of India I, Ch. XIX (Cambridge, 1922).

Gopal, M. H. : Mauryan Public Finance (London, 1935).

Gowen, H. H. : 'The Indian Machiavelli or Political Theory in India Two Thousand years ago'. Political Science quarterly Vol. 44, 1929, pp. 173—92.

Hillebrandt, Alfred. : Altindische Politik. (Jena 1923).

Jayaswal : Hindu Polity (Calcutta 1924).

Law, N. N. : Studies in Ancient Hindu Polity (Calcutta, 1914).

Monahan : The Early History of Bengal, (Oxford University, Press, 1925).

Inscriptions

Barua, B. M. : The old Brahmi inscription of Mahasthan (Indian Historical Quarterly, Vol. X (1934) pp. 57-66.

Bhandarkar, D. R. : Maurya Brahmi inscription of Mahasthan (Epigraphia Indica, Vol. XXI (1931—32) pp. 83—91.

Bühler George : The Sohgaura Copper plate (Indian Antiquary, Vol. XXV, (1896) pp. 261—66; also JRAS, 1907, pp. 501 ff ; E.I., XXII pp. 1-3 (K. P. Jayaswal) and ABORI. XI pp. 32 ff.

Chapter VI—Aśoka and his successors

Inscriptions of Aśoka :

Henning, W. B : The Aramaic Inscriptions of Aśoka found in Lampaka, Bulletin of the School of Oriental and African Studies, XIII, pt. 1, pp 80.—88.

Hultzsch : Inscriptions of Aśoka (Oxford, 1925).

Sahni, Dayaram : The Yeṛṛaguḍi Rock edicts of Aśoka ASI. Annual Report, 1928-29 pp. 161-7.

Senart E., : The Inscriptions of Piyadasi, Eng. Tr. by G. A. Grierson, IA. 1890-92.

The Gāvīmaṭh and Pālkiguṇḍu inscriptions of Aśoka (Hyderabad Archaeological Series, No. 10, 1932).

Literary Sources :

Divyāvadāna, Ed. E. B. Cowell and R. A. Neil (Cambridge, 1886).

Dipavamsa Ed. and Tr. H. Oldenberg, (London, 1879).

Hiuen-Tsang—Beal, Buddhist records of the Western World, (London, 1884).

Watters—On Yuan Chwang's Travels in India, (London 1904—5).

Mahāvamsa Ed. Geiger (London, 1908), Tr. by same (London, 1912)

Mahābhāshya ed. Kielhorn, (Bombay, 1880-5)

Rājataranginī Ed. Stein, (Bombay 1892), Trans. by same (Westminster 1900).

Tāranātha : German Trans. by Schiefner—Geschichte des Buddhismus in Indien (St. Petersburg, 1869).

Modern Works :

Burnouf E., : Introduction a L'histoire du Buddhisme Indien (Paris, 1876).

Davids, T. W. Rhyes : Buddhist India, (London, 1903).

Dikshitar, V. R. R. : The Mauryan Polity, (Madras, 1932)

Franke : Pali und Sanskrit (Strassburg, 1902).

Hardy Edmund : Konig Asoka, (Mainz, 1913).

Lassen Christian, Indische Alterthumskunde (pp. 224-88) II (Leipzig, 1874).

Levi, Sylvain : Le Nepal—3 vols. (Paris, 1905-8).

Macphail, J. M., Asoka, (Heritage of India Series, Calcutta, n.d.)

Marshall and Foucher : Monuments of Sanchi 3 vols. (Calcutta, 1941).

Mookerji, R. K. : Asoka, (London, 1928).

Monahan : The early history of Bengal (Oxford, 1925)

Pr̀zyluski, J : La Legende de L'empereur Acoka (Paris 1923).

Smith V. A. : Aśoka (Oxford, 1920).

Vallée Poussin, L. de : L'Inde aux temps des Mauryas (Paris, 1930)

Asoka and Khotan

Beal: Buddhist Records of the Western World (above).

Beal : Life of Hiuen-Tsang, p. 203. (London, 1914)

Konow Sten : Khotan Studies, JRAS, 1914, pp. 344 ff.

Rockhill : Life of the Buddha—Ch. VIII (Trubner's Oriental Series.)

Stein, Sir Aurel : Ancient Khotan i. pp. 156-166; 368 (Oxford, 1907).

Chapter VII—South India & Ceylon

Sources : Śaṅga Ilakkiyam (Madras, 1940).

Modern Works :

Aiyangar S. K. : Beginnings of South Indian History (Madras 1918).

Geiger W. : The Mahāvamsa (Eng. Tr.) (London, 1912).

Kanakasabhai : Tamils 1800 years ago (Madras 1904).

Parker : Ancient Ceylon. (London 1909).

Sastri, K. A. N. : The Pāṇḍyan Kingdom Chh. II and III (London, 1929).

" The Colas I Ch. III-IV (Madras, 1935).

Sesha Aiyar, K. G. : Cera kings of the Sangam Period, (London, 1937).

Chapter VIII—Industry, Trade and Currency

I. *Sanskrit and Pali Works* :

The Arthaśāstra of Kauṭilya (or Kauṭalya) Ed. R. Shama Sastry, 2nd Ed. (Mysore, 1919).
Ed. J. Jolly and R. Schmidt, Vol. I, (Lahore, 1929).
Ed. (with original Sanskrit commentary) T. Ganapati Sastri, Parts I-III, Trivandrum Sanskrit Series. (Trivandrum 1921, 1924, 1925).
Trans. R. Shamasastry, 2nd Ed. (Mysore).
Trans. (Das Altindische Buch Von. Welt—und Staatsleben) von Johann Jakob Meyer, (Leipzig, 1926).

Jātaka. Ed. V. Fausböll. (London 1877-97).
Trans. by various hands under the editorship of E. B. Cowell. (Cambridge 1895-1913).

(None of the above works can be definitely stated to refer to the economic conditions of the Nanda-Maurya times. But they may at least be taken to reflect the general or traditional environment).

II. *Greek and Latin authors* :

Arrian (Flavius Arrianus) : Indica. Trans. J. W. McCrindle in Ancient India as described by Megasthenes and Arrian, (London, 1877. Reprinted, Calcutta, 1926).
Anabasis of Alexander and Indica. Trans. E. J. Chinnock, (London, 1893).

Diodorus : Bibliotheke. Book II. Chs. 35-42, giving epitome of Megasthenes. Trans. J. W. McCrindle in Ancient India as described by Megasthenes and Arrian.

Pliny the Elder (Gaius Plinius Secundus) : The Naturalis Historia. The portions relating to India trans. J. W. McCrindle in Ancient India as described in Classical Literature. (London, 1901).
Trans. in the Loeb Classical Library, ten volumes.

Quintus Curtius Rufus : Historiae Alexandri Magni. The part relating to India trans. J. W. McCrindle in

The Invasion of India by Alexander the Great. (London, 1896).

Strabo. Geography. Book XV, Ch. 1—gives connected account of India. Incidental notices of India in other books. Trans. J. W. McCrindle in Ancient India a sdescribed in Classical Literature, (London, 1901).
Trans. Horace Leonard Jones in the Loeb Classical Library. Eight volumes, (1917-32).

III. *Inscriptions* :

Bhandarkar, D. R. : Maurya Brahmi Inscription of Mahasthan. EI., xxi, pp. 83-91.

Hultzsch, E. : Corpus Inscriptionum Indicarum, Vol. I The Inscriptions of Aśoka New and revised ed. (Oxford, 1925).

IV. *Coins* :

(Only the recent and more important publications are noticed)

Allan, John : A Catalogue of the Indian Coins in the British Museum, (London 1936).

Bhandarkar, D. R. : Lectures on Ancient Indian Numismatics, (Calcutta, 1921).

Bhattacharya, P. N. : A Hoard of Silver Punch-marked Coins from Purneah. Memoir No. 62 of Archaeological Survey of India. (Delhi 1940).

Chakravortty, Surendra Kisore : A Study of Ancient Indian Numismatics, 1931.

Chatterji, Charan Das : Numismatic Data in Pali Literature (in Buddhistic Studies, ed. B.C. Law, Calcutta, 1931).

Hemmy, A. S. : The Weight Standards of Ancient Indian Coins (JRAS, 1937).

Jayaswal, K. P. : Early Signed Coins of India, JBORS, xx. September-December 1934. (Other papers in JBORS, 1935, 1936, xxiii, Part i, 1937).

Kosambi, D. D. : On the Study and Metrology of Silver Punch-marked Coins (NIA. iv. pp. 1-35, 49-76).

Prasad, Durga : The Classification and Significance of Symbols on the Silver Punch-marked Coins of Ancient

India. JASB. xxx, 1934, No. 3 (Num. Supp. No. xlv 1934).

Observations on the Different types of Silver Punch-marked coins, their periods and *locale.* JASB, 1937, No. 2, (Num. Supp. xlvii for 1937).

Rapson, E. J. : A Catalogue of the Indian Coins in the British Museum. (London, 1908).

Indian Coins, (Strassburg, 1897).

Sreenivas, T. : Annual Report of the Archaeological Department of H. E. H. the Nizam's Dominions (1928-29). 1931. Appendix O—'Punch-marked coins in the cabinet of the Hyderabad Museum'.

Walsh, E. H. C. : An examination of a find of punch-marked coins in Patna City with reference to the subject of punch-marked coins generally. (JBORS. v, 1919).

An examination of fifty-eight silver punch-marked coins found at Gorho Ghat, (JBORS. v, 1919).

Punch-marked Silver coins, their standard of weight, age and minting. (JRAS, 1937).

Notes on two hoards of silver punch-marked coins, one found at Ramna and one at Machhuatoli (JBORS. 1939).

Punch-marked coins from Taxila. Memoir No. 59 of ASI. (Delhi, 1939).

Paila Hoard of Punch-marked Coins, JNSI. No. ii, 1940.

An Examination of a Hoard of 105 Silver Punch-marked coins found in the United Provinces in 1916. (JNSI, No. ii, Part i, June 1941).

A Comparative study of the Patraha (Purnea) hoard of silver punch-marked coins. (JNSI, No. iv, Part II, December 1942).

V. *General works* :

Breloer, Bernhard. : Kauṭaliya-Studien. (Bonn, 1927 etc.).

Ghoshal, U. N. : Contributions to the History of the Hindu Revenue System, (Calcutta, 1930).

Majumdar, R. C. : Corporate Life in Ancient India. 2nd ed. (Calcutta, 1922).

Mehta, Ratilal N.: Pre-Buddhist India. (Bombay, 1939).

Neogi, Panchanan.: Iron in Ancient India. (Calcutta, 1914).
Copper in Ancient India. (Calcutta, 1918).

Puri, K. N.: Excavations at Rairh during Samvat years 1995 and 1996 (A. D. 1938-39 and 1939-40) Department of Archaeological and Historical Research, Jaipur State.

Rhys Davids, Mrs. C. A. F.: Economic Conditions according to Early Buddhist Literature in Cambridge History of India, Vol. i, (Cambridge, 1922).

„ T. W. Buddhist India. (London, 1902).

Rostovtzeff, M.: The Social and Economic History of the Hellenistic World. Three Vols. (Oxford, 1941).

Sahni, Daya Ram.: Archaeological Remains and Excavations at Bairat. Department of Archaeological and Historical Research, Jaipur State. (Not dated).

Spooner, D. B.: Exacavations at Paṭāliputra. Annual Rep. of ASI., 1912-13.

Subba Rao, N. S.: Economic and Political Conditions in Ancient India. (Mysore, 1911).

Chapter IX—Religion.

Banerjea J. N. : The Development of Hindu Iconography. (Calcutta, 1941).

Barua, B. M. : The Pre-Buddhistic Indian Philosophy The Ajivikas.

Bhandarkar, R. G. : Vaiṣṇavism, Śaivism and Minor Religious Systems, (Strassburg, 1913).

Bhandarkar, D. R. : Asoka (2nd edition). (Calcutta).

Bühler, G. : The Indian Sect of the Jainas (translation by J. Burgess).

Chanda, Ramprasad : Archaeology and Vaishnava tradition. (Calcutta, 1920).

De la Vallée Poussin : L'Inde Jusque Vers 300 av. J.C. (Paris, 1931).

Dutt N. : Early Monastic Buddhism, Vol. I. (Calcutta, 1941).

Geiger : The Mahāvaṁsa. (Eng. Tr. 1912).

Guerinot : La Religion Djaina. (Paris, 1926).

Hopkins, W. E. : The Great Epic of India, (Yale, 1920).

Jacobi : Jaina Sutras (S. B. E., 2 Vols.)

Keith : The Religion and Philosophy of the Veda. (Harvard, 1925).

Kern : Manual of Indian Buddhism, (Strassburg, 1896).

Lévi Sylvain : Le Nepal 3rds (Paris 1905-8).

Une langue pre-canonique du Bouddhisme J. As.

Le Laghulovado et l'edit de Bhabra, J. As. 1896.

McCrindle : Ancient India as described by Megasthenes and Arrian. (Calcutta, 1877).

Minayeff : Recherches sur le Bouddhisme (French translation).

Oldenberg : Buddha, (London, 1882).

Pali Texts : (editions of the P. T. S.).

Ray Chaudhuri, H. : The early history of the Vaiṣṇava sect.

The Political History of Ancient India, (Calcutta University, 1932).

Rhys Davids : Buddhist India, (London, 1911).

Stevenson : The Heart of Jainism, (Oxford, 1915).

Chapter X—Language and Literature

Āpastamba Dharma Sūtra, Ed. Bühler, III Edn. (Bombay 1932).

Āryamañjuśrīmūlakalpa Text as edited by Rāhula Sānkrityāyana in K. P. Jayaswal's An Imperial History of India, (Lahore, 1934).

Bhartṛihari's Vākyapadīya, Benares Sanskrit Series, Kāṇḍas 1 and 2 (1887).

Bharata's Nāṭyaśāstra with Abhinavagupta's Abhinavabhāratī, Gaekwad Oriental Series, Baroda Pt. 1, 1926, Pt. 2, 1934 Manuscript in the Madras Govt. Oriental Mss. Library.

Bhoja's Śringāra Prakāśa, V. Raghavan, (Karnatak Publishing House, Bombay. Ms. in the Madras Govt. Oriental Mss. Library).

Bōdhāyana's Dharma Sutra (Government Oriental Library Series, Mysore, 1907).

Bṛhatkathākośa of Harisena Ed. by Dr. A. N. Upadhye, (Bhāratīya Vidyā Bhavan, 1943).

Bṛhatkathāmañjarīof Kṣemendra, (Kāvyamālā 69, Nirṇayasāga Press, Bombay, 1901).

Commemorative Essays presented to Sir R. G. Bhandarkar, (Bhandarkar Oriental Research Institute, Poona, 1917).

Gṛhya Sūtras Pts. 1 Oxford, (1886) and 2. (1892).

Haraprasad Shastri, Magadhan Literature (Calcutta, 1923).

Hultzsch, E. Inscriptions of Aśoka Corpus Inscriptionum Indicarum, Vol. I (Oxford 1925).

Kāmasūtras of Vātsyāyana, (Chowkhamba Sanskrit Series, Benares).

Kane, Mm. P.V. History of Dharma Śāstra Vol. I, (Bhandarkar Oriental Research Institute, Poona, 1930).

Kāvyalaṅkāra Sūtra and Vṛtti of Vāmana, (Vānīvilas Press, (Srirangam, 1909).

Kathāsaritsāgara of Somadeva, (Nirṇayasāgar Press, Bombay, 1903).

Kāvyamīmāmsā of Rājaśekhara, (Gaekwad Oriental Series, Baroda, 1934).

Kauṭilya's Arthaśāstra, Ed. by Mm. R. Shama Sastri, (Mysore, 1924).

A. B. Keith : History of Sanskrit Literature, (Oxford 1928).

McCrindle : Ancient India as described in Classical literature (Westminster, 1901).

MaxMüller : History of Ancient Sanskrit Literature, (London, 1892).

Pāṇini's Aṣṭādhyāyī with Kātyāyana's Vārttikas, (Madras, 1917).

Pāṇini, His place in Sanskrit literature by Th. Goldstucker, (London, MDCCCLXI).

Patañjali's Mahābhashya. Ed. Kielhorn, (Bombay, 1892, 1906, 1909).

Prabhatchandra Chakravarti : Patañjali as he reveals himself in his Mahabhaṣya (IHQ. Vol. 2).

Sacred Books of the East, Vols. II, XXIX, XXX.

Sthavirāvalī Caritra or Pariśiṣṭaparvam of Hemchandra Ed. by H. Jacobi, (Asiatic Society of Bengal, Calcutta 1932).

M. Winternitz, History of Indian Literature, English translation Vols. I and II, (Calcutta University, 1927, 1933).

Wilson Philology Lectures on Sanskrit and Derived languages (1887) by R. G. Bhandarkar Collected Works of R. G. Bhandarkar, Vol. IV, Bhandarkar Oriental Research Institute, (Poona, 1929).

Yāska's Nirukta.

Sten Konow, The Home of Pairśāchi Z. D. M. G. 64. (1910).

Chapter XI—Mauryan Art.

Bachhofer, L. : Early Indian Sculpture. (Paris, 1929). Vol. I, Chap. I. pp. 1 ff.

Brown, Percy : Indian Architecture : Buddhist and Hindu, (Bombay), Chaps. II and III. pp. 5 ff.

Carotti, G. : A History of Art, I (Ancient Art). (London, 1908).

Chanda, R. P. : Four ancient Yaksha Statues, (J. D. L., C. U., IV, 1921).

do The beginnings of Art in Eastern India with special reference to sculptures in the Indian Museum, Calcutta, M. A. S. I., No. 30. (1927).

Codrington, K. de B. : Ancient India from the earliest time to the Guptas....(London, 1926).

Combaz, Gisbert : L'Inde et L'Orient, Classique, (Paris 1937).

Coomaraswamy, A. K. : History of Indian and Indonesian Art, (London, 1927) Parts I and II, pp. 3 ff.

do Origin of the Lotus (so-called Bell) Capital. (Ind. Hist. Q. VI, pp. 373-375).

Cotterill : History of Art. I.

Dalton, O.M. : The Treasure of the Oxus, 2nd edn.

Delaporte, L. : La Mesopotamie, (Paris 1923).

Fergusson, J. : A History of Indian and Eastern Architecture, 2nd Edn. (London, 1910). Chap. V. pp. 125 ff.

Hultzsch : Inscriptions of Asoka (C. I. I., I Vol. I, 1925).

Jastrow, M. : The Civilisation of Babylonia & Assyria, 2nd Edn. (Boston, 1898).

Jayaswal, K. P. : Statues of two Śaiśunāka Emperors, (J. B. O. R. S. V. 1919).

do. Another Śaiśunāka Statue, (J.B.O.R. S., V. 1919).

do. Jaina image of the Maurya period. (JBORS., XXII. 1937).

King and Thompson : The sculptures and inscriptions of Bahistun. (London, 1907).

Kramrisch, Stella—Grundzüge der indischen Kunst. (Hellerau, 1924).

do. Contact of Indian Art with the Art of other countries, (J.D.L., C.U., X. 1923).

do. Indian Sculpture. (Calcutta, 1933). Chap. I. Sec. 2. pp. 9 ff.

Lawrence, A. W. : Later Greek sculpture and its influence on East and West.

Mitra, A. K. : Mauryan Art, (Ind. Hist. Q. III. pp. 541 ff.)

do. Origin of the Bell-capital, (Ind. Hist. Q. VII. pp. 213 ff.).

Marshall, John : Monuments of Ancient India, in C. H. I., I.

McCrindle : Ancient India as described in classical literature.

Perrot, George and Chipiez, Charles : History of Art in Persia. (London, 1892).

Sarre, Friedrich : Die Kiunst des alten Persien, (Berlin, 1923).

Smith, V. A. : History of Fine Art in India and Ceylon 2nd edn. (Oxford, 1930), Chaps. II and III. pp. 15 ff.

do. The monolithic pillars or columns of Asoka, (Z.D. M.G., LXV. 1911).

do. Persian influence on Mauryan India, (I.A. 1905 pp. 201 ff.).

Spooner, D. B. : Didarganj image now in the Patna Museum. (J.B.O.R.S. V. 1919).

do. Mr. Ratan Tata's excavations at Pataliputra, (A. S. R. 1912-13).

do. The Zoroastrian period of Indian history (J.R.A.S. 1915).

Tarn, W. W. : Hellenistic Civilisation. (London, 1927).

Tolman : Ancient Persian Lexican and Texts. Vanderbilt Oriental Series, VI. (New York, 1908).

Waddell, L.A. : Report on excavations at Paṭaliputra, (Calcutta, 1903).

INDEX

B

D

L

N

O

T

Plate I

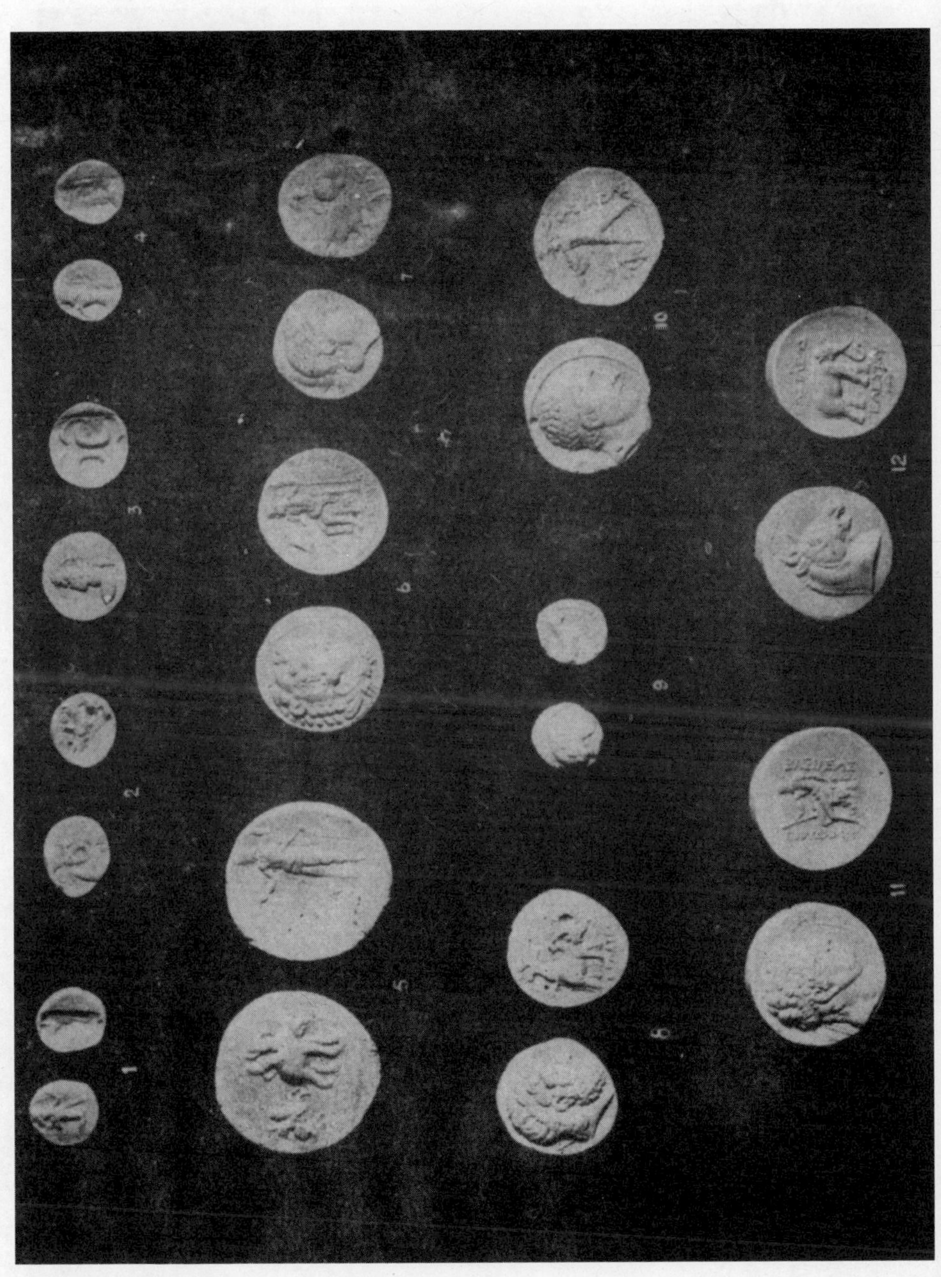

Foreign Coins (British Museum)

Plate II

The Lion-Crowned Column of Basarh.

The Lion-Crowned Column of Lauriya-Nandangarh.

Plate IV

Elephant Capital Sanskissa.

Plate V

Bull Capital, Rampurva.

Plate VI

Lion Capital, Rampurva.

Plate VII

Sarnath Lion Capital.

Plate VIII

Lion Capital, Sanchi.

Plate IX

Rock Cut Elephant, Dhauli

Plate X

Elephant from the abacus of the Sarnath Capital.

Plate XI

Horse from the abacus of Sarnath Capital

Plate XII

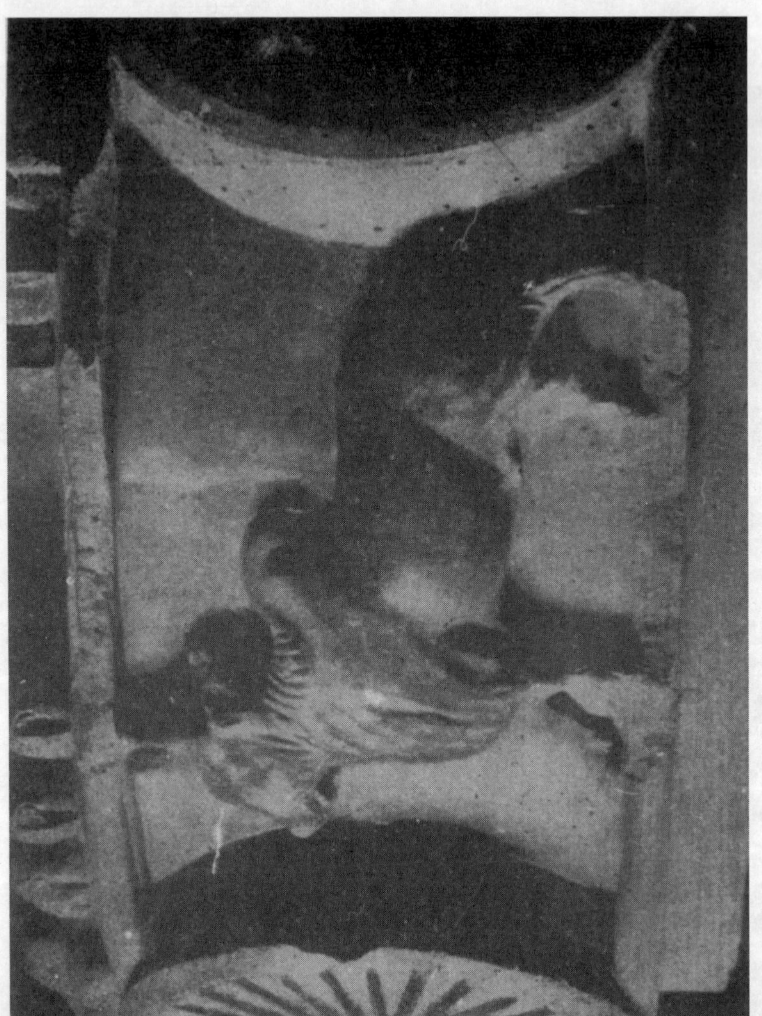

Bull faom the abacus of Sarnath

Plate XIII

Lion from the abacus of Sarnath Capital.

Plate XIV

Yaksha from Patna, front view.

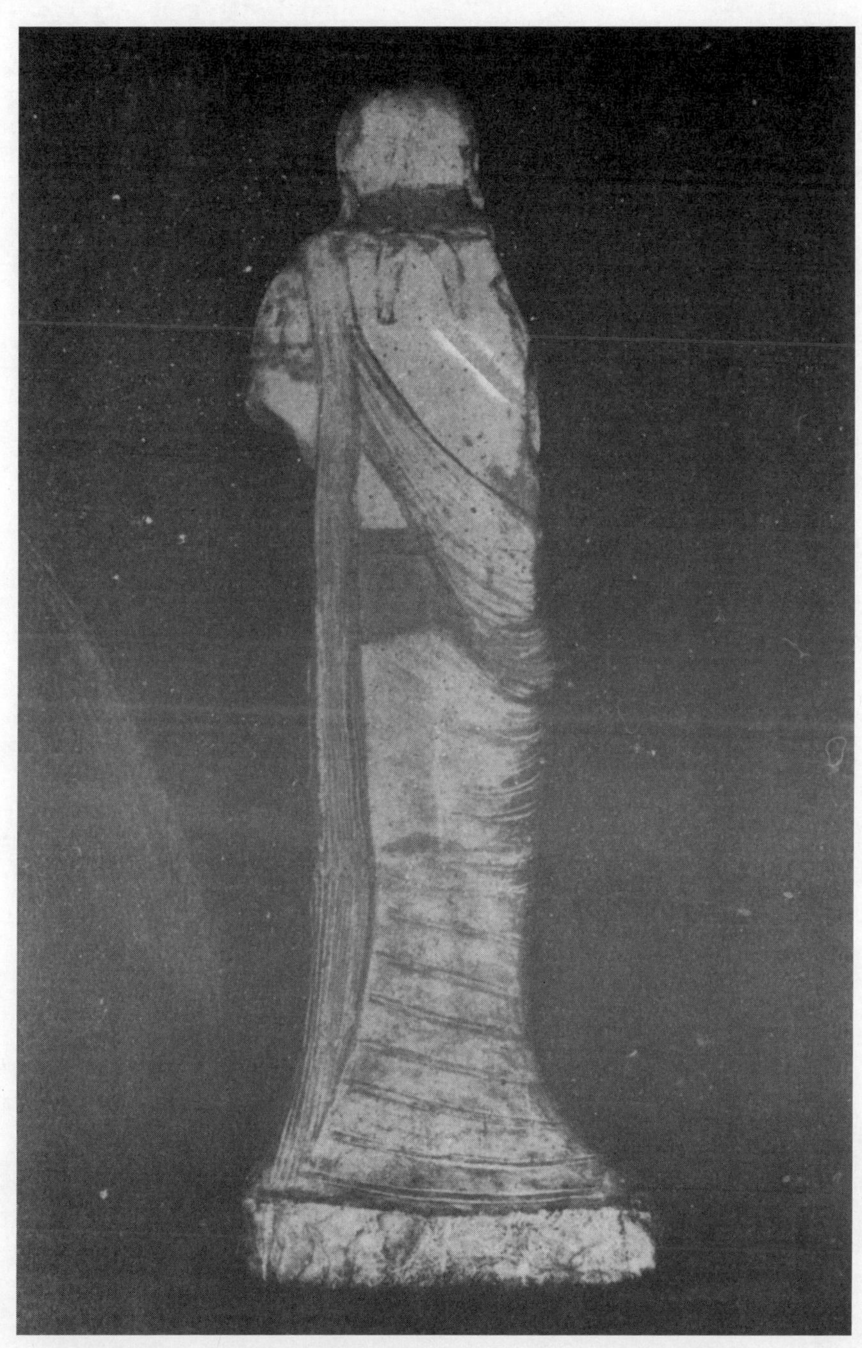

Yaksha from Patna, back view.

Plate XVI

Yaksha from Patna, back view

Yaksha from Patna, front view

Platc XVIII

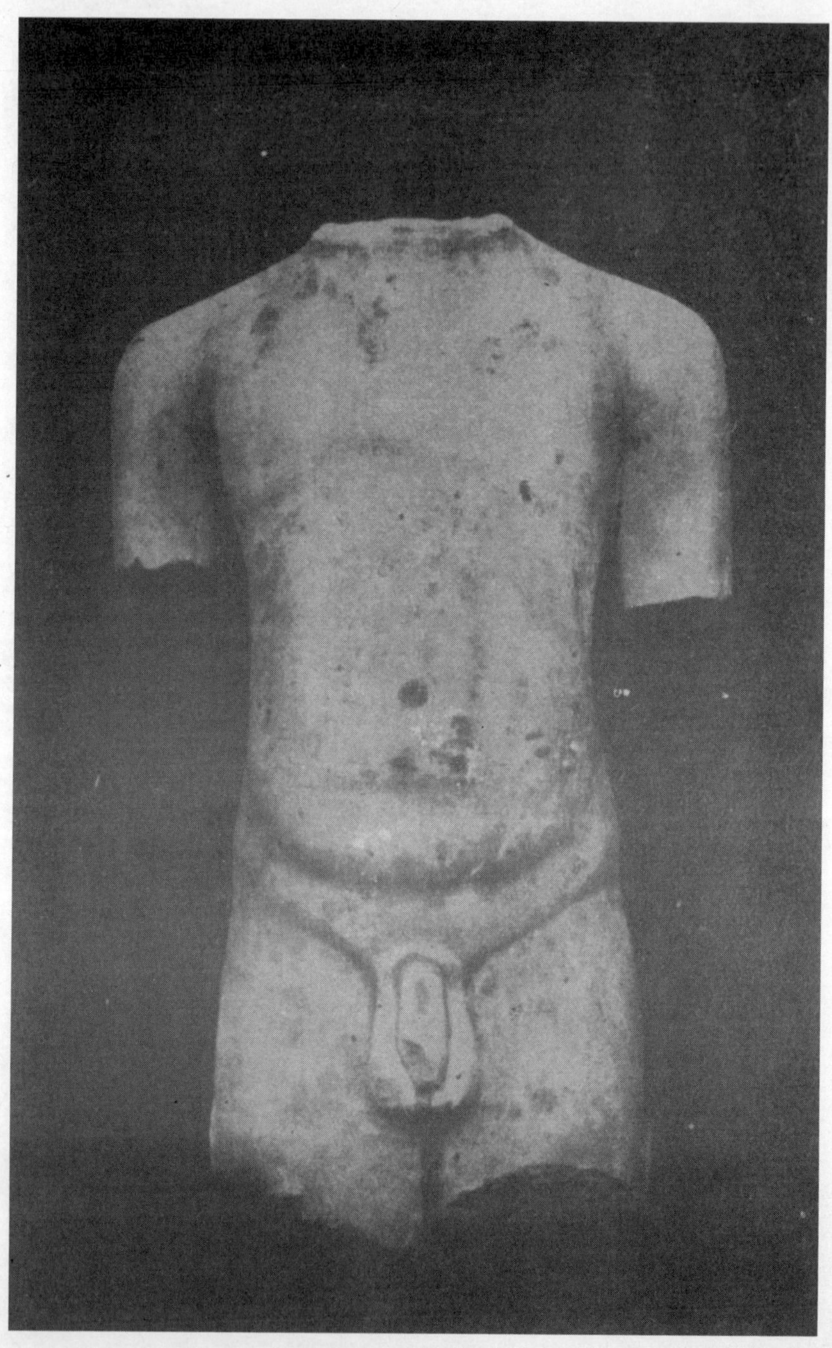

Stone torso of a Jaina image, Lohanipur.

Plate XIX

Baroda Yaksha, back view.

Plate XX

Parkham Yaksha.

Didarganj Yaksha, front view

Plate XXII

Didarganj Yaksha, back view

Besnagar Yakshi.

Plate XXIV

Terracotta from Pāṭaliputra.

Terracotta from Pāṭaliputra.

Plate XXVI

Terracotta from Pāṭaliputra.

Terracotta from Pāṭaliputra.

Plate XXVIII

Terracotta from Pāṭaliputra.

Plate XXIX

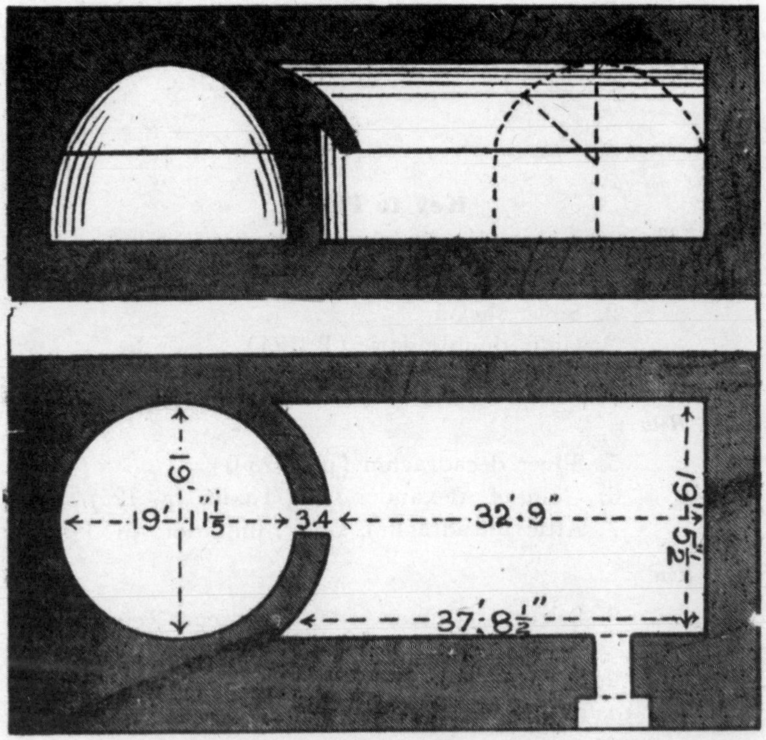

Sudama Cave

Plate XXX

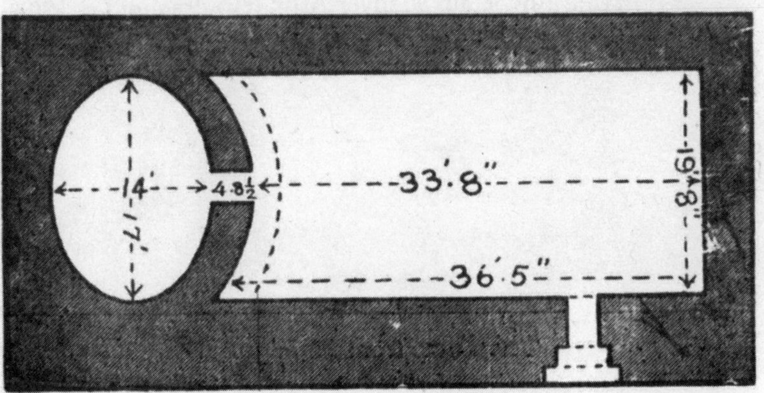

Lomas Rishi Cave

Key to Plate I

First Row :

1. Gold daric
2. Silver shekel
3. Gold double daric (P. 124)
4. Coin of Philip Arideaus from Taxila (p. 125)

Second Row :

5. Silver decadrachm (pp. 125-6)
6. Coin of Alexander from Taxila (p. 125)
7. Attic tetradrachm, silver, imitation (p. 128)

Third Row :

8. Seleucus I, silver Attic tetradrachm Zeus/Athene (p. 129)
9. Sophytes, silver, (p. 126-7)
10. Diodotus II, silver, Attic tetradrachm (p. 130)

Fourth Row :

11. Euthydemus I, silver Attic tetradrachm (p. 130)
12. Seleucus I, silver, Horse/Elephant (p. 129)